HISTORY OF WOMEN IN THE UNITED STATES

HISTORY OF WOMEN IN THE UNITED STATES
Historical Articles on Women's Lives and Activities

Edited by Nancy F. Cott

Series ISBN 3-598-41454-4

1. Theory and Method in Women's History
ISBN 3-598-41455-2 Part 1
ISBN 3-598-41477-3 Part 2

2. Household Constitution and Family Relationships
ISBN 3-598-41456-0

3. Domestic Relations and Law
ISBN 3-598-41457-9

4. Domestic Ideology and Domestic Work
ISBN 3-598-41458-7 Part 1
ISBN 3-598-41475-7 Part 2

5. The Intersection of Work and Family Life
ISBN 3-598-41459-5 Part 1
ISBN 3-598-41476-5 Part 2

6. Working on the Land
ISBN 3-598-41460-9

7. Industrial Wage Work
ISBN 3-598-41461-7 Part 1
ISBN 3-598-41693-8 Part 2

8. Professional and White-Collar Employments
ISBN 3-598-41462-5 Part 1
ISBN 3-598-41694-6 Part 2

9. Prostitution
ISBN 3-598-41463-3

10. Sexuality and Sexual Behavior
ISBN 3-598-41464-1

11. Women's Bodies: Health and Childbirth
ISBN 3-598-41465-X

12. Education
ISBN 3-598-41466-8

13. Religion
ISBN 3-598-41467-6

14. Intercultural and Interracial Relations
ISBN 3-598-41468-4

15. Women and War
ISBN 3-598-41469-2

16. Women Together: Organizational Life
ISBN 3-598-41470-6

17. Social and Moral Reform
ISBN 3-598-41471-4 Part 1
ISBN 3-598-41695-4 Part 2

18. Women and Politics
ISBN 3-598-41472-2 Part 1
ISBN 3-598-41697-0 Part 2

19. Woman Suffrage
ISBN 3-598-41473-0 Part 1
ISBN 3-598-41696-2 Part 2

20. Feminist Struggles for Sex Equality
ISBN 3-598-41474-9

HISTORY OF WOMEN IN THE UNITED STATES

Historical Articles on Women's Lives and Activities

11. Women's Bodies: Health and Childbirth

Edited with an Introduction by

Nancy F. Cott
Yale University

K · G · Saur
Munich · New Providence · London · Paris · 1993

Publisher's Note

The articles and chapters which comprise this collection originally appeared in a wide variety of publications and are reproduced here in facsimile from the highest quality offprints and photocopies available. The reader will notice some occasional marginal shading and text-curl common to photocopying from tightly bound volumes. Every attempt has been made to either correct or minimize this effect.

Copyright information for articles reproduced in this collection appears at the end of this volume.

Library of Congress Cataloging-in-Publication Data

History of women in the United States : historical articles on
women's lives and activities / edited with
an introduction by Nancy F. Cott.
p. cm.
Includes bibliographical references and indexes.
Contents: 1. Theory and method in women's history -- 2. Household constitution and family relationships -- 3. Domestic relations and law -- 4. Domestic ideology and domestic work -- 5. The intersection of work and family life -- 6. Working on the land -- 7. Industrial wage work -- 8. Professional and white-collar employments -- 9. Prostitution -- 10. Sexuality and sexual behavior -- 11. Women's bodies -- 12. Education -- 13. Religion -- 14. Intercultural and interracial relations -- 15. Women and war -- 16. Women together -- 17. Social and moral reform -- 18. Women and politics -- 19. Woman suffrage -- 20. Feminist struggles for sex equality.
ISBN 3-598-41454-4 (set)
1. Women--United States--History. 2. Women--United States--Social conditions. I. Cott, Nancy F.
HQ1410.H57 1992
305.4'0973--dc20 92-16765
CIP

Die Deutsche Bibliothek - CIP - Einheitsaufnahme

History of Women in the United States: historical articles
on women's lives and activities / ed. with an introd. by Nancy F. Cott.
- Munich ; New Providence ; London ; Paris : Saur.
ISBN 3-598-41454-4
NE: Cott, Nancy F. (Hrsg.)
Vol. 11. women's bodies: health and childbirth - (1993)
ISBN 3-598-41465-X

∞
Printed on acid-free paper/Gedruckt auf säurefreiem Papier

A Reed Reference Publishing Company

Printed in the United States of America
Printed/Bound by Edwards Brothers Incorporated, Ann Arbor

ISBN 3-598-41465-X (vol. 11)
ISBN 3-598-41454-4 (series)

Contents

CONTENTS

CONTENTS

Series Preface

In the space of one generation, women's history has become the fastest-growing area of scholarship in U.S. history. Since the resurgence of feminism in the late 1960s and 1970s, insistent questions about the historical meanings of "woman's place" have sowed and reaped a garden of scholarship. Where scholarly works used to be bare of mention of women, academic enterprise has now produced a vigorous growth of books and articles, bringing to light diverse women of every region, race, class and age. This research is marked by a renovating intent that refuses to accept as "human" history a history of men. Interest is lively and debate is stimulating and sought after: attendance at the Berkshire Conference on the History of Women rivals the size of the annual convention of the American Historical Association.

While books in women's history are daily increasing in numbers and strength, as in any fast-developing field the scholarly literature in the form of articles is most expansive and up-to-the-minute. All the history journals now publish articles on women's work, domestic settings, family relations, household matters, female politics and organizations and so forth, and new journals have sprung into being to concentrate on such topics. Women's historians publish in numerous regional and thematic history journals as well as in feminist outlets and in journals of other social science disciplines. This series brings together a collection of outstanding articles from the field, almost all written in the past twenty years and more than half published during the 1980s. It brings together, in volumes organized by topic, essays otherwise widely dispersed. These volumes reprint only articles that originally appeared in journals, not chapters of books; review articles are not included. Articles have been chosen for overall quality and for range. Each one was chosen for one or more of the following reasons: because it is the standard authority on its subject matter; represents an important statement on a topic by a recognized scholar; presages an important book to come; provides a first look at new evidence or new methods; or opens an untapped area or new controversy. Older articles have been reprinted if their data or interpretation have not been surpassed or if they marked an important stage in the historiography, even if since superseded.

The historical coverage of the series extends from the Revolutionary era to the 1960s. The articles themselves are dated from the 1940s through 1988. Volumes are organized by topic rather than time period. Within each volume, the articles are ordered chronologically (with respect to substance), so that the whole can be read as an historical overview. The only exception to this ordering principle is Volume One, on Theory and Method, in which the contents are arranged in order of publication. Within each volume there is an attempt to include articles on as diverse kinds of women as possible. None of the volume topics is regionally or racially defined; rather, all volumes are topically designed so as to afford views of women's work, family lives, and public activities which cut across races and regions. Any volume in the series stands on its own, supplying as full a treatment of a designated subject matter as the scholarly literature will provide. Several groupings of volumes also make sense; that is, volumes two through five all center around domestic and family matters; volumes five through nine consider other varieties of women's work; volumes nine through eleven concern uses and abuses of women's bodies; volumes twelve through fourteen look at major aspects of socialization; and volumes fifteen through twenty include organizational and political efforts of many sorts.

As a whole, the series displays in all its range the vitality of the field of women's history. Aside from imbuing U.S. history with new vision, scholarship in this area has informed, and should continue to inform, current public debate on issues from parental leave to the nuclear freeze. By bringing historical articles together under topical headings, these volumes both represent accurately the shape of historical controversy (or consensus) on given issues and make historians' findings most conveniently available for current reference.

Introduction

To bring the history of women's health and childbearing, or what might be called the "somatic" history of women, into conjunction with economic and social factors, was one of the earliest and most distinctive features of the new women's history. Contemporary concern with issues of birth control and abortion and women's sexuality formed part of the reason for this, but so did the fact that through history women's reproductive capacities and therefore their bodily conditions have constituted a more recognized aspect of their purpose and being than has been the case for men. To a much greater extent than it need be today, biology was destiny for women in past centuries. Without means of contraception beyond abstinence or the "withdrawal" method (coitus interruptus), a married woman in the seventeenth or eighteenth century would likely be pregnant, or nursing an infant, for the better part of her adult life. (Average life expectancy did not extend more than a decade beyond the age of menopause.) Since medical understanding of the female reproductive organs and their disruptions was still quite primitive, most women saw "female problems" as their lot. If pregnancies were complicated, or childbearing resulted in injuries, women usually suffered and endured.

Well into the nineteenth century, medical science had got little beyond the catch-all designation "prolapsus uteri," or fallen womb, to diagnose most problems resulting from repeated childbearing. But some observers had grown extremely agitated about what they saw as the general ill health of American women. Catharine Beecher, a noted writer on domestic topics and educator of girls (herself daughter of the evangelical preacher Lyman Beecher and sister of Harriet Beecher Stowe), traveled around the country in the 1850s and gathered statistics about women's health from two hundred sites. She found "delicate," "sickly" and "feeble" women all over, and rarely anyone in complete buoyant health. "I am not able to recall, in my immense circle of friends and acquaintances all over the Union, so many as ten married ladies born in this century and country, who are perfectly sound, healthy and vigorous," she recounted.[1] Remaining unmarried and thus not subject to the difficulties of "married ladies," Beecher had plenty of recommedations regarding dress, behavior, nutrition, and education, to address these worrisome circumstances. So did other health reformers, doctors, and advisors.

During this same era in which women's reproductive and general health emerged as an object of social commentary, reformers and practitioners of many stripes and both sexes voiced many alternative remedies. The regular medical establishment, such as it was, employed "heroic" treatments such as bleeding, or the use of powerful emetics and drugs; health reformers instead relied on less harsh or invasive approaches, from "water-cure," or hydropathic treatment, to regimented diet, to fresh air and exercise. A struggle to define the principles and approaches of the modern profession of medicine was under way in the mid-nineteenth century. The presence of many antagonists in this multi-directional struggle—licensed doctors against "irregulars," European-trained physicians against homegrown surgeons, practitioners of heroic versus homeopathic medicine, forceps-wielding doctors versus traditional midwives—all gave witness to a new anti-fatalistic emphasis on the possibility of *control* of human sickness or health, death or life.

A striking drop in marital fertility also manifested the burgeoning assumption that humans might dare to control their bodily fates. During the course of the nineteenth century, the fertility rate, or number of children per woman of childbearing age among the white population in the U.S., was cut in half: from seven children per woman in 1800, to 3.5 children per woman in 1900. Demographers can now trace that the drop in fertility was accomplished in part by postponing marriage (thus avoiding a few childbearing years), by wider spacing of births, and by women's ending childbearing at younger ages than ever before. What were the means to wider-spaced, overall fewer pregnancies? No major advances in birth control *technology* were widely circulated before 1900. The diaphragm, and condoms, were available by the end of the century; the vaginal sponge and vaginal douche had been around for a longer time—but use of all these was so low that they could not have accounted for so prolonged and large a demographic change. Although medical science had arrived at some understanding of the female menstrual cycle by the latter part of the century, the timing of ovulation in relation to menstruation was generally misunderstood, so that recommended "rhythm method" approaches to avoiding pregnancy also must have backfired.

The means to fewer pregnancies were principally abstinence, or lowered frequency of sexual intercourse, the withdrawal method, and abortion. Recent research has shown that resort to abortionists by married women became much more frequent in the middle forty years of the nineteenth century. Historian James Mohr estimated that the ratio went up from about one abortion to every 25 live births before 1820, to one for every five or six live births by 1860. The use of abortion as a remedy for marital fertility created fierce splits of opinion among medical practitioners; trained male physicians who were increasingly defining themselves as professionals staunchly opposed abortion, and lobbied successfully to make the practice of abortion a crime.[2] Thus once the possibility of exercising some control over women's reproductive capacities emerged, the question of who would exercise that control became contested. The ways in which "regular" and "irregular" doctors, midwives and other female practitioners and ordinary women themselves attempted to define, address and cure "female" problems—and came into conflict doing so—have occupied many historians' interests. The double-edged quality of medical science wielded by male physicians toward female patients has been a matter of particular attention. This volume brings together historians' most important investigations into women's experience of illness, hygiene, pregnancy, and childbirth, and analyses of how these conditions have been viewed and treated.

Notes

[1] Catharine Beecher, *Letters to the People on Health and Happiness* (N.Y., Harper and Bros., 1855), 129-130.

[2] James C. Mohr, *Abortion in America: The Origins and Evolution of National Policy 1800-1900* (N.Y., Oxford University Press, 1978); Carl Degler, *At Odds: Women and the Family in America from the Revolution to the Present* (N.Y., Oxford, 1980), chapters VIII, IX, X.

Women's Bodies:
Health and Childbirth

"On the Importance of the Obstetrick Art": Changing Customs of Childbirth in America, 1760 to 1825

Catherine M. Scholten

In October 1799, as Sally Downing of Philadelphia labored to give birth to her sixth child, her mother, Elizabeth Drinker, watched her suffer "in great distress." Finally, on the third day of fruitless labor, Sally's physician, William Shippen, Jr., announced that "the child must be brought forward." Elizabeth Drinker wrote in her diary that, happily, Sally delivered naturally, although Dr. Shippen had said that "he thought he should have had occasion for instruments" and clapped his hand on his side, so that the forceps rattled in his pocket.[1]

Elizabeth Drinker's account of her daughter's delivery is one of the few descriptions by an eighteenth-century American woman of a commonplace aspect of women's lives—childbirth.[2] It is of special interest to social historians because it records the participation of a man in the capacity of physician. Shippen was a prominent member of the first generation of American doctors trained in obstetrics and, commencing in 1763, the first to maintain a regular practice attending women in childbirth.[3] Until that time

Catherine M. Scholten is a doctoral candidate in history at the University of California, Berkeley, where she is writing her dissertation on childbearing in America. She read an earlier version of this article at the St. Louis meeting of the Organization of American Historians, April 1976, and she wishes to thank Gunther Barth, J. William T. Youngs, Jr., Regina Morantz, and Linda Auwers for comments on that draft.

[1] Cecil K. Drinker, *Not So Long Ago: A Chronicle of Medicine and Doctors in Colonial Philadelphia* (New York, 1937), 59-61.

[2] Although births are noted frequently in diaries and letters of the 17th, 18th, and early 19th centuries, the event itself is rarely described. For the most part, information on the medical procedures and social customs of birth analyzed in this article is derived from midwives' manuals, medical textbooks, and lecture notes of medical students. This literature mingles plain observation with partisan advocacy of medical reform. It seems reasonable to accept the physician's evaluations of midwifery as evidence of their desire for change, and their case histories as documents of the actual circumstances of birth. Despite ambiguities, the material provides a glimpse of social change not directly reflected in many conventional sources.

[3] Betsy Copping Corner, *William Shippen, Jr.: Pioneer in American Medical Education* (Philadelphia, 1951), 103; Irving S. Cutter and Henry R. Viets, *A Short History of Midwifery* (Philadelphia, 1964), 150.

midwives managed almost all deliveries, but with Shippen male physicians began to supplant the midwives.

The changing social customs and medical management of childbirth from 1760 to 1825 are the subjects of this article. By analyzing the rituals of childbirth it will describe the emergence of new patterns in private and professional life. It shows that, beginning among well-to-do women in Philadelphia, New York, and Boston, childbirth became less a communal experience and more a private event confined within the intimate family. In consequence of new perceptions of urban life and of women, as well as of the development of medical science, birth became increasingly regarded as a medical problem to be managed by physicians. For when Shippen, fresh from medical studies in London, announced his intention to practice midwifery in Philadelphia in 1763, he was proposing to enter a field considered the legitimate province of women.[4] Childbearing had been viewed as the inevitable, even the divinely ordained, occasion of suffering for women; childbirth was an event shared by the female community; and delivery was supervised by a midwife.

During the colonial period childbearing occupied a central portion of the lives of women between their twentieth and fortieth years. Six to eight pregnancies were typical, and pregnant women were commonly described as "breeding" and "teeming."[5] Such was women's natural lot; though theologians attributed dignity to carrying the "living soul" of a child and saluted mothers in their congregations with "Blessed are you among women," they

[4] Cutter and Viets, *Short History*, 148-149.

[5] For a discussion of childbearing patterns see Wilson H. Grabill, Clyde V. Kiser, and Pascal K. Whelpton, "A Long View," in Michael Gordon, ed., *The American Family in Social-Historical Perspective* (New York, 1973), 392; J. Potter, "The Growth of Population in America, 1700-1860," in D. V. Glass and D. E. C. Eversley, eds., *Population in History: Essays in Historical Demography* (Chicago, 1965), 644, 647, 663, 679; Robert V. Wells, "Demographic Change and the Life Cycle of American Families," in Theodore K. Rabb and Robert I. Rotberg, eds., *The Family in History: Interdisciplinary Essays* (New York, 1971), 85, 88.

When William Byrd II wrote in his diary in 1712, "my wife was often indisposed with breeding and very cross," he used a term common until the 19th century. Louis B. Wright and Marion Tinling, eds., *The Secret Diary of William Byrd of Westover, 1709-1712* (Richmond, Va., 1941), 548. "Breeding" was used colloquially and in popular medical literature. The use of the term to describe the hatching or birth of animals parallels its application to humans. The word lingered longest in speech in the American South, where fertile or pregnant black slaves were called "breeding women," an indication of the animality implied in the word. *The Oxford English Dictionary*, s.v. "breeding"; Mitford M. Mathews, ed., *A Dictionary of Americanisms on Historical Principles* (Chicago, 1951), s.v. "breeding." "Teeming," also considered archaic dialect by the *OED*, applied to women from the 16th through 18th centuries.

also depicted the pains of childbirth as the appropriate special curse of "the Travailing Daughters of Eve."[6] Two American tracts written specifically for lying-in women dwelt on the divinely ordained hazards of childbirth and advised a hearty course of meditation on death, "such as their pregnant condition must reasonably awaken them to."[7]

Cotton Mather's pamphlet, *Elizabeth in Her Holy Retirement*, which he distributed to midwives to give to the women they cared for, described pregnancy as a virtually lethal condition. "For ought you know," it warned, "your Death has entered into you, you may have conceived that which determines but about Nine Months more at the most, for you to live in the World." Pregnancy was thus intended to inspire piety.[8] John Oliver, author of *A Present for Teeming American Women*, similarly reminded expectant mothers that prayer was necessary because their dangers were many. He noted that women preparing for lying-in "get linnen and other necessaries for the child, a nurse, a midwife, entertainment for the women that are called to the labour, a warm convenient chamber, and etc." However, "all these may be miserable comforters," argued Oliver, for "they may perchance need no other linnen shortly than a Winding Sheet, and have no other chamber but a grave, no neighbors but worms."[9] Oliver counseled women to "arm themselves with patience" as well as prayer, and "abate somewhat those dreadful groans and cries which do so much to discourage their friends and relatives who hear them."[10]

Surely women did not need to be reminded of the risks of childbirth. The fears of Mary Clap, wife of Thomas Clap, president of Yale College, surface even through the ritual phrases of the elegy written by her husband after her death in childbirth at the age of twenty-four. Thomas remembered that before each of her six lyings-in his wife had asked him to pray with her that God would continue their lives together.[11] Elizabeth Drinker probably

[6] Benjamin Colman, *Some of the Honours that Religion Does unto the Fruitful Mothers in Israel* . . . (Boston, 1715), 8; Cotton Mather, *Elizabeth in Her Holy Retirement. An Essay to Prepare a Pious Woman for her Lying-in. Or Maxims and Methods of Piety, to Direct and Support an Hand Maid of the Lord, Who Expects a Time of Travail* (Boston, 1710), 3; Cotton Mather, *Ornaments for the Daughters of Zion, or the Character and Happiness of a Woman: in a Discourse*, 3d ed. (Boston, 1741), 2-3. Even a secular medical manual affirmed the curse of Eve: American edition of *Aristotle's Master Piece*, 1766, discussed in Otho T. Beall, Jr., "*Aristotle's Master Piece* in America: A Landmark in the Folklore of Medicine," *William and Mary Quarterly*, 3d Ser., XX (1963), 216.

[7] Mather, *Elizabeth in Her Retirement*, 1.

[8] *The Diary of Cotton Mather* (Massachusetts Historical Society, *Collections*, 7th Ser., Pt. II [1912]), VIII, 618, 700; Mather, *Elizabeth in Her Retirement*, 2, 6, 7.

[9] John Oliver, *A Present for Teeming American Women* (Boston, 1694), 3.

[10] *Ibid.*, 118.

[11] [Thomas Clap], "Memoirs of a College President: Womanhood in Early America," ed. Edwin Stanley Wells, *The Connecticut Magazine*, XII (1908), 233-239, esp. 235.

echoed the sentiments of most women when she reflected, "I have often thought that women who live to get over the time of Child-bareing, if other things are favourable to them, experience more comfort and satisfaction than at any other period of their lives."[12]

Facing the hazards of childbirth, women depended on the community of their sex for companionship and medical assistance. Women who had moved away at marriage frequently returned to their parents' home for the delivery, either because they had no neighbors or because they preferred the care of their mothers to that of their in-laws. Other women summoned mothers, aunts, and sisters on both sides of the family, as well as female friends, when birth was imminent.[13] Above all, they relied on the experience of midwives to guide them through labor.

Women monopolized the practice of midwifery in America, as in Europe, through the middle of the eighteenth century. As the recognized experts in the conduct of childbirth, they advised the mother-to-be if troubles arose during pregnancy, supervised the activities of lying-in, and used their skills to assure safe delivery. Until educated male physicians began to practice obstetrics, midwives enjoyed some status in the medical profession, enhanced by their legal responsibilities in the communities they served.

English civil authorities required midwives to take oaths in order to be licensed but imposed no official test of their skills. The oaths indicate that midwives had responsibilities which were serious enough to warrant supervision. They swore not to allow any infant to be baptized outside the Church of England, and promised to help both rich and poor, to report the true parentage of a child, and to abstain from performing abortions. Oath-breaking midwives could be excommunicated or fined.[14]

Some American midwives learned their art in Europe, where midwifery was almost exclusively the professional province of women. Though barber surgeons and physicians increasingly asserted their interest in midwifery

[12] Drinker, *Not So Long Ago*, 48.

[13] Stewart Mitchell, ed., *New Letters of Abigail Adams, 1788-1801* (Boston, 1947), 3-5, 56; Clayton Harding Chapman, "Benjamin Colman's Daughters," *New England Quarterly*, XXVI (1953), 182; Malcolm R. Lovell, ed., *Two Quaker Sisters, from the Original Diaries of Elizabeth Buffam Chace and Lucy Buffam Lovell* (New York, 1937), 1, 12; Drinker, *Not So Long Ago*, 51-60; Mary Vial Holyoke's diary, in George Francis Dow, ed., *The Holyoke Diaries, 1709-1856* (Salem, Mass., 1911), 70, 73, 75, 83, 95, 100, 101, 107; *Diary of Samuel Sewall* (Mass. Hist. Soc., *Colls.*, 5th Ser., V-VII [1878-1882]), I, 11, 40, 110, 166, 222-223, 351, 394, 426, II, 49, hereafter cited as *Diary of Sewall:* Ethel Armes, ed., *Nancy Shippen: Her Journal Book* (Philadelphia, 1935), 122-124.

[14] James Hobson Aveling, *English Midwives: Their History and Prospects* (London, 1967 [orig. publ. 1872]), 3-4, 7, 10; E. H. Carter, *The Norwich Subscription Books: A Study of the Subscription Books of the Diocese of Norwich, 1637-1800* (London, 1937), 17-18, 134; facsimile oath of 1661, in Thomas Forbes, *The Midwife and the Witch* (New Haven, Conn., 1966), 145.

during the seventeenth century, midwives and patients resisted the intruders.[15] The midwives' levels of skill varied. Some acquired their medical education in the same way as many surgeons and physicians, by apprenticeship; some read manuals by more learned midwives and physicians; and after 1739, when the first British lying-in hospital was founded, a few were taught by the physicians who directed such hospitals.[16] But more often than not, women undertook midwifery equipped only with folk knowledge and the experience of their own pregnancies.[17]

Disparity of skills also existed among American midwives. Experienced midwives practiced alongside women who were, one physician observed, "as ignorant of their business as the women they deliver."[18] By the end of the eighteenth century physicians thought that the "greater part" of the midwives in America took up the occupation by accident, "having first been *catched*, as they express it, with a woman in labour."[19] The more diligent

[15] Cutter and Viets, *Short History*, 5-55; Isaac Flack, *Eternal Eve* (London, 1950), 218-219; Alfred McClintock, ed., *Smellie's Treatise on the Theory and Practice of Midwifery* (London, 1876-1878), II, 248-250, III, 26-27, 298, 317-319; Percival Willughby, *Observations in Midwifery*, ed. Henry Blenkinsop (Wakefield, Eng., 1972 [orig. publ. 1803]), 37, 155.

Save for midwifery, medical practice in England was divided among three guilds of physicians, surgeons, and apothecaries. Physicians, titled "doctor" and usually possessing university degrees, theoretically as gentlemen did not work with their hands. Surgeons, trained by apprenticeship and rarely holding degrees, dealt with structural emergencies. Apothecaries, also apprenticed, sold drugs. These distinctions disappeared in the rural areas and small towns of England, as well as in colonial America, where medical men, usually without formal training and indiscriminately called doctor, engaged in general practice. Even after 1765, the American men who were by strict definition physicians practiced general medicine. Richard Harrison Shryock, *Medicine and Society in America, 1660-1860* (Ithaca, N.Y., 1960), 2-3, 7, 10.

[16] Aveling, *English Midwives*, 138-144; Alice Clark, *Working Life of Women in the Seventeenth Century* (London, 1919), 265, 269, 270-275; *The Compleat Midwifes Practice, in the Most Weighty and High Concernments of the Birth of Man* ... (London, 1656), 119-124; John Memis, *The Midwive's Pocket Companion: or a Practical Treatise on Midwifery* (London, 1765), v-vii; Jane Sharp, *The Compleat Midwife's Companion: or, the art of midwifery improved* ..., 4th ed. (London, 1725), x-xii; Willughby, *Observations in Midwifery*, ed. Blenkinsop, 73.

[17] John Kobler, *The Reluctant Surgeon: A Biography of John Hunter* (New York, 1960), 31; Sharp, *Compleat Midwife's Companion*, introduction; Willughby, *Observations in Midwifery*, ed. Blenkinsop, 102.

[18] Valentine Seaman, *The Midwives Monitor, and Mothers Mirror: Being Three Concluding Lectures of a Course of Instruction of Midwifery* (New York, 1800), viii.

[19] *Ibid.* See also Joseph Brevitt, *The Female Medical Repository* ... (Baltimore, 1810), 6.

sought help from books, probably popular medical manuals such as *Aristotle's Master Piece.*[20]

American midwives conducted their practice free, on the whole, from governmental supervision and control. Only two colonies appear to have enacted regulatory statutes, and it does not seem that these were rigorously enforced. In the seventeenth century Massachusetts and New York required midwives, together with surgeons and physicians, not to act contrary to the accepted rules of their art. More specifically, in 1716 the common council of New York City prescribed a licensing oath for midwives, which was similar to the oaths of England, though without the provision on baptism. The oath included an injunction—significant for the theme of this article—that midwives not "open any matter Appertaining to your Office in the presence of any Man unless Nessessity or Great Urgent Cause do Constrain you to do so."[21] This oath, which was regularly re-enacted until 1763, suggests the common restriction of midwifery to women, excluding male physicians or barber surgeons, who, in any case, were few and usually ill trained. There are records of male midwives in New York, Philadelphia, Charleston, and Annapolis after 1740, but only one, a Dr. Spencer of Philadelphia, had London training in midwifery, and it was said of another that "he attended very few natural labors."[22]

Though their duties were not as well defined by law, American midwives served the community in ways similar to those of their British counterparts. In addition to assisting at childbed, they testified in court in cases of bastardy, verified birthdates, and examined female prisoners who pleaded pregnancy to

[20] Beall, "*Aristotle's Master Piece,*" *WMQ*, 3d Ser., XX (1963), 209-210; Seaman, *Midwives Monitor,* ix. Beall's article is the best study of the popular manuals of "Aristotle." The *Master Piece,* which was the creation of an English physician, "W. S.," and a succession of hack writers, first appeared in England in 1684. The numerous later editions were the only works on sex and gynecology widely available to 18th-century Americans.

[21] Jane B. Donegan, "Midwifery in America, 1760-1860: A Study in Medicine and Morality" (Ph.D. diss., Syracuse University, 1972), 9-10, 12; "A Law for Regulating Mid Wives Within the City of New York," Minutes of the Common Council of New York, 1716, Appendix I, in Claire E. Fox, "Pregnancy, Childbirth and Early Infancy in Anglo-American Culture, 1675-1830" (Ph.D. diss., University of Pennsylvania, 1966), 442-445; Richard Harrison Shryock, *Medical Licensing in America, 1650-1965* (Baltimore, 1967), 3, 16; James J. Walsh, *History of Medicine in New York: Three Centuries of Medical Progress,* II (New York, 1919), 22, 25.

[22] Cutter and Viets, *Short History,* 145, 150; *Maryland Gazette* (Annapolis), Sept. 30, 1747; Francis R. Packard, *History of Medicine in the United States,* I (New York, 1931), 52-53; Shryock, *Medicine and Society,* 11-12; J. Whitridge Williams, *A Sketch of the History of Obstetrics in the United States up to 1860* (Baltimore, 1903), 1.

escape punishment.[23] Some colonials also observed the English custom of having the midwife attend the baptism and burial of infants. Samuel Sewall reported that Elizabeth Weeden brough his son John to church for christening in 1677, and at the funeral of little Henry in 1685 "Midwife Weeden and Nurse Hill carried the Corps by turns."[24]

The inclusion of the midwife in these ceremonies of birth and death shows how women's relationships with their midwives went beyond mere respect for the latters' skill. Women with gynecologic problems would freely tell a midwife things "that they had rather die than discover to the Doctor."[25] Grateful patients eulogized midwives.[26] The acknowledgment of the services of one Boston midwife, recorded on her tombstone, has inspired comment since 1761. The stone informs the curious that Mrs. Phillips was "born in Westminister in Great Britain, and Commission'd by John Laud, Bishop of London in ye Year 1718 to ye Office of a Midwife," came to "this Country" in 1719, and "by ye Blessing of God has brought into this world above 3000 Children."[27]

We may picture Mrs. Phillips's professional milieu as a small room, lit and warmed by a large fire, and crowded by a gathering of family and friends. In daytime, during the early stages of labor, children might be present, and while labor proceeded female friends dropped in to offer encouragement and help; securing refreshments for such visitors was a part of the preparation for childbirth, especially among the well-to-do families with which we are concerned. Men did not usually remain at the bedside. They might be summoned in to pray, but as delivery approached they waited elsewhere with the children and with women who were "not able to endure" the tension in the room.[28]

During the final stages of labor the midwife took full charge, assisted by

[23] Wyndham B. Blanton, *Medicine in Virginia in the Seventeenth Century* (Richmond, 1930), 166; Packard, *History of Medicine*, I, 52; Julia C. Spruill, *Women's Life and Work in the Southern Colonies* (Chapel Hill, N.C., 1938), 272; Herbert Thoms, *Chapters in American Obstetrics* (Springfield, Ill., 1961), 10.

[24] *Diary of Sewall*, I, 40, 114; Sharp, *Compleat Midwife's Companion*, frontispiece of midwife at christening.

[25] Aristotle (pseud.), *Aristotle's Compleat and Experienc'd Midwife, in two Parts. I. Guide for Childbearing Women. II. Proper and Safe Remedies for the Curing of all those Distempers that are incident to the Female Sex . . .*, 9th ed. (London, [1700?]), iii.

[26] Broadside of elegy to Mary Broadwell, in Francisco Guerra, *American Medical Bibliography, 1639-1783* (New York, 1962), 69.

[27] Packard, *History of Medicine*, I, 49.

[28] Drinker, *Not So Long Ago*, 51, 52, 54, 59; Dow, ed., *Holyoke Diaries*, 70, 73, 75, 81, 83, 95, 101, 107; *Diary of Sewall*, V, 40, 222-223, 394, VI, 49; Charles White, *A Treatise on the Management of Pregnant and Lying-in Women* (Worcester, Mass., 1793), 19-20.

other women. As much as possible, midwives managed deliveries by letting nature do the work; they caught the child, tied the umbilical cord, and if necessary fetched the afterbirth. In complicated cases they might turn the child and deliver it feet first, but if this failed, the fetus had to be destroyed. In all circumstances the midwife's chief duty was to comfort the woman in labor while they both waited on nature, and this task she could, as a woman, fulfill with social ease. Under the midwife's direction the woman in labor was liberally fortified with hard liquor or mulled wine. From time to time the midwife examined her cervix to gauge the progress of labor and encouraged her to walk about until the pains became too strong. There was no standard posture for giving birth, but apparently few women lay flat in bed. Some squatted on a midwive's stool, a low chair with an open seat. Others knelt on a pallet, sat on another woman's lap, or stood supported by two friends.[29]

Friends were "welcome companions," according to one manual for midwives, because they enabled the woman in labor "to bear her pains to more advantage," and "their cheerful conversation supports her spirits and inspires her with confidence."[30] Elizabeth Drinker endeavored to talk her daughter into better spirits by telling her that as she was thirty-nine "this might possibly be the last trial of this sort."[31] Some women attempted to cheer the mother-to-be by assuring her that her labor was easy compared to others they had seen, or provoked laughter by making bawdy jokes.[32]

For some attendants, a delivery could be a wrenching experience. Elizabeth Drinker relived her own difficult deliveries when her daughters suffered their labors, and on one such occasion she noted with irony, "This day is 38 years since I was in agonies bringing her into this world of troubles: she told me with tears that this was her birthday."[33] For others the experience of assisting the labors of friends was a reminder of their sex. Sarah Eve, an unmarried twenty-two-year-old, attended the labor of a friend in 1772 and carried the tidings of birth to the waiting father. "None but those that were like anxious could be sensible of a joy like theirs," she wrote in her journal

[29] Aristotle (pseud.), *Compleat and Experienc'd Midwife*, 50-51, 56, 57; Nicholas Culpeper, *A Directory for Midwives: or, a Guide for Women in Their Conception, Bearing, and Suckling their Children* (London, 1651), 167; Drinker, *Not So Long Ago*, 60; *Diary of Sewall*, V, 40; Sharp, *Compleat Midwife's Companion*, 81, 82, 124, 125, 128; White, *Treatise on Pregnant Women*, 20, 74; Willughby, *Observations in Midwifery*, ed. Blenkinsop, 4, 11, 13, 19.

[30] Seaman, *Midwives Monitor*, 90-91.

[31] Drinker, *Not So Long Ago*, 59.

[32] William Buchan, *Advice to Mothers on the Subject of Their Own Health* (Charleston, S.C., 1807), 28; *The London Practice of Midwifery by an American Practitioner* (Concord, N.H., 1826), 129; Thomas Chalkey James, "Notes from Drs. Osborne's and Clark's Lectures on Midwifery taken by T. C. James, London, 1790-1791," MS, Historical Collections, College of Physicians of Philadelphia.

[33] Drinker, *Not So Long Ago*, 53, 59.

that night. "Oh! Eve! Adam's wife I mean—who could forget her to-day?"[34]

After delivery, the mother was covered up snugly and confined to her bed, ideally for three to four weeks. For fear of catching cold she was not allowed to put her feet on the floor and was constantly supplied with hot drinks. Family members relieved her of household duties. Restless women, and those who could not afford weeks of idleness, got up in a week or less, but not without occasioning censure.[35]

The social and medical hold of midwives on childbirth loosened during the half century after 1770, as male physicians assumed the practice of midwifery among urban women of social rank. Initially, physicians entered the field as trained practitioners who could help women in difficult labors through the use of instruments, but ultimately they presided over normal deliveries as well. The presence of male physicians in the lying-in chamber signaled a general change in attitudes toward childbirth, including a modification of the dictum that women had to suffer. At the same time, because medical training was restricted to men, women lost their position as assistants at childbirth, and an event traditionally managed by a community of women became an experience shared primarily by a woman and her doctor.

William Shippen, the first American physician to establish a steady practice of midwifery, quietly overcame resistance to the presence of a man in the lying-in room. Casper Wistar's *Eulogies on Dr. Shippen*, published in 1809, states that when Shippen began in 1763, male practitioners were resorted to only in a crisis. "This was altogether the effect of prejudice," Wistar remarked, adding that "by Shippen this prejudice was so done away, that in the course of ten years he became very fully employed."[36] A few figures testify to the trend. The Philadelphia city directory in 1815 listed twenty-one women as midwives, and twenty-three men as practitioners of midwifery. In 1819 it listed only thirteen female midwives, while the number of men had risen to forty-two; and by 1824 only six female midwives remained in the directory.[37] "Prejudice" similarly dissolved in Boston, where

[34] Mrs. Eva Eve Jones, ed., "Extracts from the Journal of Miss Sarah Eve," *Pennsylvania Magazine of History and Biography*, V (1881), 195.

[35] Mitchell, ed., *New Letters of Adams*, 4-5; Jack P. Greene, ed., *The Diary of Colonel Landon Carter of Sabine Hall, 1752-1788*, II (Charlottesville, Va., 1965), 86; Dow, ed., *Holyoke Diaries*, 49, 56, 58, 62, 63, 65, 67, 73, 77, 78, 82, 95, 100, 107; *Diary of Sewall*, II, 51; Sharp, *Compleat Midwife's Companion*, frontispiece drawing of lying-in; McClintock, ed., *Smellie's Treatise*, I, 380.

[36] Corner, *William Shippen*, 124; Cutter and Viets, *Short History*, 150.

[37] *Kite's Philadelphia Directory for 1815* (Philadelphia, 1815), xi-xii; John Paxton, *The Philadelphia Directory and Register for 1819* (Philadelphia, 1819), n.p.; Robert Desilver, *The Philadelphia Directory and Register for 1824* (Philadelphia, 1824), n.p.

in 1781 the physicians advertised that they expected immediate payment for their services in midwifery; by 1820 midwifery in Boston was almost "entirely confined" to physicians.[38] By 1826 Dr. William Dewees, professor of midwifery at the University of Pennsylvania and the outstanding American obstetrician of the early nineteenth century, could preface his textbook on midwifery with an injunction to every American medical student to study the subject because "everyone almost" must practice it. He wrote that "a change of manners within a few years" had "resulted in almost exclusive employment of the male practitioner."[39]

Dewees's statement must be qualified because the "almost exclusive" use of men actually meant almost exclusive use among upper- and middle-class urban women. Female midwives continued throughout the nineteenth century to serve both the mass of women in cities and women in the country who were "without advantage of regular practitioners."[40] During the initial years of their practice physicians shared obstetrical cases with midwives. On occasion Philadelphia women summoned Shippen together with their midwives, and Dewees reports that when he began to practice in the 1790s he depended on midwives to call him when instruments were needed.[41] It is clear, however, that by the 1820s Dewees and his colleagues had established their own practice independent of midwives.

On one level the change was a direct consequence of the fact that after 1750 growing numbers of American men traveled to Europe for medical education. Young men with paternal means, like Shippen, spent three to four years studying medicine, including midwifery, with leading physicians in the hospitals of London and the classrooms of Edinburgh. When they returned to the colonies they brought back not only a superior set of skills but also British ideas about hospitals, medical schools, and professional standards.[42]

[38] Walter Channing (John Ware?), *Remarks on the Employment of Females as Practitioners in Midwifery* (Boston, 1820), 1; *Independent Chronicle and the Universal Advertiser* (Boston), Nov. 8, 1781.

[39] William Potts Dewees, *A Compendious System of Midwifery, Chiefly Designed to Facilitate the Inquiries of Those Who may be Pursuing This Branch of Study* (Philadelphia, 1826), xiv.

[40] William Buchan, *A Compend of Domestic Midwifery for the Use of Female Practitioners, Being an Appendix to Buchan's Domestic Medicine* (Charleston, S.C., 1815), 3; Frances E. Kobrin, "The American Midwife Controversy: A Crisis of Professionalization," *Bulletin of the History of Medicine*, XL (1966), 350; M. D. Learned and C. F. Brede, "An Old German Midwife's Record, Kept by Susanna Muller, of Providence Township, Lancaster County, Pennsylvania, during the years 1791-1815" (n.d.), Hist. Colls., College of Physicians of Philadelphia; Mrs. Joseph Sarber, Memorandum Kept by Mrs. Joseph Sarber, Midwife at the Falls of the Schuykill from 1814 to 1831, MS, Historical Society of Pennsylvania, Philadelphia.

[41] Drinker, *Not So Long Ago*, 51-52; Dewees, *Compendious System of Midwifery*, 303.

[42] Charles M. Andrews, *Colonial Folkways: A Chronicle of American Life in the Reign of the Georges* (New Haven, Conn., 1919), 147; Maurice Bear Gordon,

In the latter part of the eighteenth century advanced medical training became available in North America. At the time of Shippen's return in 1762 there was only one hospital in the colonies, the Pennsylvania Hospital, built ten years earlier to care for the sick poor. Shippen and his London-educated colleagues saw that the hospital could be used for the clinical training of physicians, as in Europe. Within three years the Philadelphia doctors, led by John Morgan, established formal, systematic instruction at a school of medicine, supplemented by clinical work in the hospital.[43] Morgan maintained that the growth of the colonies "called aloud" for a medical school "to increase the number of those who exercise the profession of medicine and surgery."[44] Dr. Samuel Bard successfully addressed the same argument to the citizens of New York in 1768.[45]

In addition to promoting medical schools, Morgan and Bard defined the proper practitioner of medicine as a man learned in a science. To languages and liberal arts their ideal physician added anatomy, material medicine, botany, chemistry, and clinical experience. He was highly conscious not only of his duty to preserve "the life and health of mankind,"[46] but also of his professional status, and this new emphasis on professionalism extended to midwifery.

The trustees of the first American medical schools recognized midwifery as a branch of medical science. From its founding in 1768, Kings College in New York devoted one professorship solely to midwifery, and the University of Pennsylvania elected Shippen professor of anatomy, surgery, and midwifery in 1791. By 1807 five reputable American medical schools provided courses in midwifery.[47] In the early years of the nineteenth century some professors of midwifery began to call themselves obstetricians or professors of obstetrics, a scientific-sounding title free of the feminine connotations of the word midwife.[48] Though not compulsory for all medical students, the new

---

Aesculapius Comes to the Colonies: The Story of the Early Days of Medicine in the Thirteen Original Colonies (Ventnor, N.J., 1949), 156-157, 460-465; Francis Packard, "How London and Edinburgh Influenced Medicine in Philadelphia in the Eighteenth Century," College of Physicians of Philadelphia, *Transactions*, 3d Ser., LIII (1931), 167.

[43] Gordon, *Aesculapius*, 465; Packard, *History of Medicine*, I, 181-230; Packard, "How London and Edinburgh Influenced Medicine," College of Physicians of Philadelphia, *Trans.*, 3d Ser., LIII (1931), 163, 166.

[44] John Morgan, *A Discourse Upon the Institution of Medical Schools in America* (Baltimore, 1937 [orig. publ. 1765]), 33.

[45] Samuel Bard, *Two Discourses Dealing with Medical Education in Early New York* (New York, 1921), 1.

[46] *Ibid.*, 10, 16, 19; Morgan, *Discourse Upon the Institution of Medical Schools*, 14-17.

[47] Packard, *History of Medicine*, II, 1125-1127; Williams, *Sketch of the History of Obstetrics*, 5-7.

[48] *OED*, s.v. "obstetrics"; Packard, *History of Medicine*, II, 1125-1126.

field was considered worthy of detailed study along the paths pioneered by English physicians.

Dr. William Smellie contributed more to the development of obstetrics than any other eighteenth-century physician. His influence was established by his teaching career in London from 1741 to 1758, and by his treatise on midwifery, first published in 1752.[49] Through precise measurement and observation Smellie discovered the mechanics of parturition. He found that the child's head turned throughout delivery, adapting the widest part to the widest diameter of the pelvic canal. Accordingly, he defined maneuvers for manipulating an improperly presented child. He also recognized that obstetrical forceps, generally known for only twenty years when he wrote in 1754, should be used to rectify the position of an infant wedged in the mouth of the cervix, in preference to the "common method" of simply jerking the child out. He perfected the design of the forceps and taught its proper use, so that physicians could save both mother and child in difficult deliveries, instead of being forced to dismember the infant with hooks.[50]

To Smellie and the men who learned from him, the time seemed ripe to apply science to a field hitherto built on ignorance and supported by prejudice. Smellie commented on the novelty of scientific interest in midwifery. "We ought to be ashamed of ourselves," he admonished the readers of his *Treatise*, "for the little improvement we have made in so many centuries." Only recently have "we established a better method of delivering in laborious and preternatural cases."[51] Smellie's countryman Dr. Charles White reflected in his text on midwifery in 1793 that "the bringing of the art of midwifery to perfection upon scientific and medical principles seems to have been reserved for the present generation."[52]

Some American physicians shared this sense of the new "Importance of the Obstetrick Art." Midwifery was not a "trifling" matter to be left to the uneducated, Thomas Jones of the College of Medicine of Maryland wrote in 1812. Broadly defined as the care of "all the indispositions incident to women from the commencement of pregnancy to the termination of lactation," it ranked among the most important branches of medicine. "With the cultivation of this branch of science," women could now "reasonably look to men for safety in the perilous conditions" of childbirth.[53]

[49] Cutter and Viets, *Short History*, 26-28.

[50] *Ibid.*, 44-59; John Glaister, *Dr. William Smellie and His Contemporaries* (Glasgow, 1894), 170, 174, 178-179, 187; McClintock, ed., *Smellie's Treatise*, II, 250-251, 339.

[51] McClintock, ed., *Smellie's Treatise*, II, 339.

[52] White, *Treatise on Pregnant Women*, viii, 70-71.

[53] Thomas Dashiell Jones, *An Essay on the Importance of the Obstetrick Art: Submitted to the Examination of Charles Alexander Warfield, M.D., President of the Medical Faculty of the College of Medicine of Maryland* . . . (Baltimore, 1812), 5, 11, 21, 23.

Jones maintained, as did other physicians, that the conditions of modern urban life produced a special need for scientific aid in childbirth. Both rich and poor women in large cities presented troublesome cases to the physician. Pelvic deformities, abortions, and tedious labors Jones considered common among wealthy urban women because of their indolent habits and confining fashionable dress, and among the poor because of inadequate diet and long hours of work indoors. There was, he believed, a greater need for "well informed obstetrick practitioners in large cities than in country places."[54]

Although it cannot be established that there was an increase in difficult parturitions among urban women, social as well as medical reasons account for the innovations in the practice of midwifery in such cities as Boston, Philadelphia, and New York. Physicians received their medical education in cities, and cities offered the best opportunities to acquire patients and live comfortably. Urban families of some means could afford the $12 to $15 minimum fee which Boston physicians demanded for midwife services in 1806.[55] Obstetrics was found to be a good way to establish a successful general practice. The man who conducted himself well in the lying-in room won the gratitude and confidence of his patient and her family, and they naturally called him to serve in other medical emergencies. It was midwifery, concluded Dr. Walter Channing of Boston, that ensured doctors "the permanency and security of all their other business."[56]

The possibility of summoning a physician, who could perhaps insure a safer and faster delivery, opened first to urban women. The dramatic rescue of one mother and child given up by a midwife could be enough to convince a neighborhood of women of a physician's value and secure him their practice.[57] Doctors asserted that women increasingly hired physicians because they became convinced "that the well instructed physician is best calculated to avert danger and surmount difficulties."[58] Certainly by 1795 the women of the Drinker family believed that none but a physician should order medicine for a woman in childbed, and had no doubts that Dr. Shippen or his colleague Dr. Nicholas Way was the best help that they could summon.[59]

[54] Thomas Denman, *An Introduction to the Practice of Midwifery*, I (New York, 1802), 47; Jones, *Essay on Obstetrick Art*, 8, 17-19; Seaman, *Midwives Monitor*, x; White, *Treatise on Pregnant Women*, 79.

[55] Boston Medical Association, *Rules and Regulations of the Boston Medical Association* (Boston, 1806), 4-5. The minimum fee escalated to $15/day case, $20/night by 1819. Boston Med. Assoc., *Rules and Regulations* (1819 ed.).

[56] Channing, *Remarks on Employment of Females*, 19; Edward Warren, *The Life of John Collins Warren, M.D., Compiled Chiefly from his Autobiography and Journals*, I (Boston, 1860), 219.

[57] Dewees, *Compendious System of Midwifery* (Philadelphia, 1824), 307.

[58] *Ibid.* (1826), xiv.

[59] Drinker, *Not So Long Ago*, 51, 54-56, 59.

Although she accepted a male physician as midwife, Elizabeth Drinker still had reservations about the use of instruments to facilitate childbirth and was relieved when Shippen did not have to use forceps on her daughter. Other women feared to call a physician because they assumed that any instruments he used would destroy the child.[60] However, once the capabilities of obstetrical forceps became known, some women may have turned to them by choice in hope of faster deliveries. Such hope stimulated a medical fashion. By about 1820 Dewees and Bard felt it necessary to condemn nervous young doctors for resorting unnecessarily to forceps.[61]

The formal education of American physicians and the development of midwifery as a science, the desire of women for the best help in childbirth, the utility of midwifery as a means of building a physician's practice, and, ultimately, the gigantic social changes labeled urbanization explain why physicians assumed the ordinary practice of midwifery among well-to-do urban women in the late eighteenth and early nineteenth centuries. This development provides insight into the changing condition of women in American society.

The development of obstetrics signified a partial rejection of the assumption that women had to suffer in childbirth and implied a new social appreciation of women, as admonitions to women for forbearance under the pain of labor turned to the desire to relieve their pain. Thus did Dr. Thomas Denman explain his life's work: "The law of a religion founded on principles of active benevolence, feelings of humanity, common interests of society, and special tenderness for women" demanded that men search for a method by which women might be conducted safely through childbirth.[62] In his doctoral dissertation in 1812 one American medical student drew a distinction between childbirth in primitive societies and his own. In the former, "women are generally looked on by their rugged lords as unworthy of any particular attention," and death or injury in childbirth is "not deemed a matter of any importance." Well-instructed assistants to women in childbirth were one sign of the value placed on women in civilized societies.[63]

The desire to relieve women in childbirth also signified a more liberal interpretation of scripture. At the University of Pennsylvania in 1804, Peter Miller, a medical student, modified the theological dictum that women must bear in sorrow. The anxieties of pregnancy and the anguish caused by the

[60] Dewees, *Compendious System of Midwifery* (1824), 307; Drinker, *Not So Long Ago*, 60.

[61] Samuel Bard, *A Compendium of the Theory and Practice of Midwifery*, 5th ed. (New York, 1819), v, 176, 289; Dewees, *Compendious System of Midwifery* (1826) xv.

[62] Denman, *Introduction to Midwifery*, 235.

[63] Jones, *Essay on Obstetrick Art*, 8.

death of so many infants constituted sorrow enough for women, argued Miller. They did not need to be subjected to bodily pain as well.[64] Reiterating this argument, Dewees bluntly asked, "Why should the female alone incur the penalty of God?"[65] To relieve the pain of labor Dewees and his fellows analyzed the anatomy and physiology of childbirth and defined techniques for the use of instruments.

If the development of obstetrics suggests the rise of a "special tenderness for women" on the part of men, it also meant that women's participation in medical practice was diminished and disparaged. A few American physicians instructed midwives or wrote manuals for them, but these efforts were private and sporadic, and had ceased by 1820. The increasing professionalization of medicine, in the minds of the physicians who formed medical associations that set the standards of the field, left little room for female midwives, who lacked the prescribed measure of scientific training and professional identity.[66]

William Shippen initially invited midwives as well as medical students to attend his private courses in midwifery. His advertisement in the *Pennsylvania Gazette* in January 1765 related his experience assisting women in the country in difficult labors, "most of which was made so by the unskillful old women about them," and announced that he "thought it his duty to immediately begin" courses in midwifery "in order to instruct those women who have virtue enough to own their ignorance and apply for instructions, as well as those young gentlemen now engaged in the study of that useful and necessary branch of surgery." Shippen taught these private lessons until after the Revolution, when he lectured only to the students at the University of Pennsylvania, who, of course, were male.[67]

At the turn of the century Dr. Valentine Seaman conducted the only other known formal instruction of midwives. He was distressed by the ignorance of many midwives, yet convinced that midwives ought to manage childbirth because, unlike physicians, they had time to wait out lingering labors, and, as women, they could deal easily with female patients. Seaman offered his private lectures and demonstrations at the New York Almshouse lying-in ward, and in 1800 published them as the *Midwives Monitor and Mothers Mirror.*[68] A handful of other men wrote texts at least nominally

[64] Peter Miller, *An Essay on the Means of Lessening the Pains of Parturition* (Philadelphia, 1804), 340.

[65] William Potts Dewees, *Essays on Various Subjects Connected with Midwifery* (Philadelphia, 1823), 24.

[66] Channing, *Remarks on Employment of Females,* 6-12; Jones, *Essay on Obstetrick Art,* 20; Joseph F. Kett, *The Formation of the American Medical Profession: The Role of Institutions, 1780-1860* (New Haven, Conn., 1968), 10-30.

[67] *Pennsylvania Gazette* (Philadelphia), Jan. 31, 1765.

[68] Williams, *Sketch of the History of Obstetrics,* 13; Seaman, *Midwives Monitor,* iii-vii.

directed to midwives between 1800 and 1810; some of these, like Seaman's, discussed the use of instruments.[69] In 1817 Dr. Thomas Ewell proposed that midwives be trained at a national school of midwifery in Washington, D.C., to be supported by a collection taken up by ministers. There is no evidence that Ewell's scheme, presented in his medical manual, *Letters to Ladies*, ever gained a hearing.[70]

Seaman and Ewell, and other authors of midwives' manuals, presumed that if women mastered some of the fundamentals of obstetrics they would be desirable assistants in ordinary midwifery cases. In 1820 Dr. Channing of Boston went further in his pamphlet, *Remarks on the Employment of Females as Practitioners of Midwifery*, in which he maintained that no one could thoroughly understand the management of labor who did not understand "thoroughly the profession of medicine as a whole." Channing's principle would have totally excluded women from midwifery, because no one favored professional medical education for women. It was generally assumed that they could not easily master the necessary languages, mathematics, and chemistry, or withstand the trials of dissecting room and hospital. Channing added that women's moral character disqualified them for medical practice: "Their feelings of sympathy are too powerful for the cool exercise of judgement" in medical emergencies, he wrote; "they do not have the power of action, nor the active power of mind which is essential to the practice of the surgeon."[71]

Denied formal medical training, midwives of the early nineteenth century could not claim any other professional or legal status. Unlike Great Britain, the United States had no extensive record of licensing laws or oaths defining the practice of midwifery. Nor were there any vocal groups of midwives who, conscious of their tradition of practice or associated with lying-in hospitals, were able to defend themselves against competition from physicians.[72] American midwives ceased practice among women of social rank with few words uttered in their defense.

The victory of the physicians produced its own problems. The doctor's sex affected the relationships between women and their attendants in childbirth, and transformed the atmosphere of the lying-in room. In his advice to

[69] Bard, *Compendium of Theory and Practice of Midwifery*, iv, 289; Brevitt, *Female Medical Repository*, 149-155; Buchan, *Compend of Domestic Midwifery*; Samuel Jennings, *Married Lady's Companion, or Poor Man's Friend* . . . (New York, 1808), 135; Seaman, *Midwives Monitor*, 31-32. All of these works were directed entirely or in part to midwives.

[70] Thomas Ewell, *Letters to Ladies, Detailing Important Information Concerning Themselves and Infants* (Philadelphia, 1817), vii-viii.

[71] Channing, *Remarks on Employment of Females*, 4-7.

[72] Aveling, *English Midwives*, 138-144, 153-159; Cutter and Viets, *Short History*, 43; Glaister, *William Smellie*, 32-36.

his male students Dewees acknowledged that summoning a man to assist at childbed "cost females a severe struggle."[73] Other doctors knew that even the ordinary gynecologic services of a physician occasioned embarrassment and violated woman's "natural delicacy of feeling," and that every sensitive woman felt "deeply humilated" at the least bodily exposure.[74] Doctors recognized an almost universal repugnance on the part of women to male assistance in time of labor.[75] Because of "whim or false delicacy" women often refused to call a man until their condition had become critical.[76] It is unlikely that physicians exaggerated these observations, although there is little testimony from women themselves about their child-bed experience in the early nineteenth century.

The uneasiness of women who were treated by men was sometimes shared by their husbands. In 1772 the *Virginia Gazette* printed a denunciation of male midwifery as immoral. The author, probably an Englishman, attributed many cases of adultery in England to the custom of employing men at deliveries. Even in labor a woman had intervals of ease, and these, he thought, were the moments when the doctor infringed on the privileges of the husband. It would be a matter of utmost indifference to him "whether my wife had spent the night in a bagnio, or an hour of the forenoon locked up with a man midwife in her dressing room."[77] Such arguments were frequently and seriously raised in England during the eighteenth century.[78] They may seem ludicrous, but at least one American man of Dr. Ewell's acquaintance suffered emotional conflict over hiring a male midwife. He sent for a physician to help his wife in her labor, yet "very solemnly he declared to the doctor, he would demolish him if he touched or looked at his wife."[79]

Physicians dealt with the embarrassment of patients and the suspicion of husbands by observing the drawing-room behavior of "well-bred gentlemen." Dewees told his students to "endeavor, by well chosen conversation, to divert your patient's mind from the purpose of your visit."[80] All questions of

[73] Dewees, *Compendious System of Midwifery* (1826), xv.

[74] Channing, *Remarks on Employment of Females*, 16, 17; Ewell, *Letters to Ladies*, 27.

[75] Jones, *Essay on Obstetrick Art*, 11.

[76] Seaman, *Midwives Monitor*, iv.

[77] *Virginia Gazette* (Purdie and Dixon), Oct. 1, 1772; reprinted in *New-London Gazette* (Conn.), Jan. 29, 1773.

[78] Elizabeth Nihill, *A Treatise on the Art of Midwifery, Setting Forth Various Abuses Therein, Especially as to the Practice With Instruments* (London, 1760), and S. W. Fores, *Man-Midwifery Dissected* (London, 1793), are outstanding examples of arguments made about the supposed immorality of man midwives. Glaister, *William Smellie*, discusses other examples of such literature.

[79] Ewell, *Letters to Ladies*, 27.

[80] Dewees, *Compendious System of Midwifery* (1826), 189; Daniel B. Smith, "Notes on lectures of Thomas Chalkey James and William Potts Dewees, University of Pennsylvania, 1826," MS. Hist. Colls., College of Physicians of Philadelphia.

a delicate nature were to be communicated through a third party, perhaps the only other person in the room, either a nurse or an elderly friend or relative. The professional man was advised "never to seem to know anything about the parts of generation, further than that there is an orifice near the rectum leading to an os."[81]

Physicians did not perform vaginal examinations unless it was absolutely important to do so, and they often had to cajole women into permitting an examination at all. Nothing could be more shocking to a woman, Shippen lectured his students, "than for a young man the moment he enters the Chamber to ask for Pomatum and proceed to examine the uterus."[82] Doctors waited until a labor pain clutched their patients and then suggested an examination by calling it "taking a pain." During examination and delivery the patient lay completely covered in her bed, a posture more modest, if less comfortable, than squatting on a pallet or a birth stool. The light in the room was dimmed by closing the shutters during the day and covering the lamps at night. If a physician used forceps, he had to manipulate them under the covers, using his free hand as a guide.[83] On this point doctors who read Thomas Denman's *Obstetrical Remembrancer* were reminded that "Degorges, one of the best obstetricians of his time, was blind."[84]

The crowd of supportive friends and family disappeared with the arrival of the doctor. The physician guarded against "too many attendants; where there are women, they must talk."[85] The presence of other women might increase the doctor's nervousness, and they certainly did not help the woman in labor. Medical men interpreted women's talk of other experiences with childbirth as mere gossip "of all the dangerous and difficult labours they ever heard any story about in their lives," which ought to be stopped lest it disturb the patient.[86] Especially distracting were the bawdy stories visitors told, expecting the physician to laugh, too. Medical professors recommended "grave deportment," warning that levity would "hurt your patient or yourself in her esteem."[87] Far from providing the consolation of a friend, the physician was often a stranger who needed to "get a little acquainted" with

[81] *London Practice of Midwifery*, 109.

[82] Bard, *Compendium of Theory and Practice of Midwifery*, 181; lecture notes from lectures of William Shippen, Jr., University of Pennsylvania, n.d., MS, Hist. Colls., College of Physicians of Philadelphia.

[83] Bard, *Compendium of Theory and Practice of Midwifery*, 181; Dewees, *Compendious System of Midwifery* (1826), 189-190; *London Practice of Midwifery*, 108-109.

[84] Thomas Denman, *The Obstetrical Remembrancer, or Denman's Aphorisms on Natural and Difficult Parturition* (New York, 1848 [orig. U.S. publ. 1803]), 46.

[85] *London Practice of Midwifery*, 129.

[86] *Ibid.*, 129-130.

[87] James, "Notes from Osborne's and Clark's Lectures," Hist. Colls., College of Physicians of Philadelphia; notes on Shippen lectures, *ibid.*

his patient. One medical text went so far as to coach him in a series of conversational ice breakers about children and the weather.[88]

Etiquette and prudery in the lying-in chamber affected medical care. Physicians were frustrated by their inability to examine their patients thoroughly, for they knew full well that learning midwifery from a book was "like learning shipbuilding without touching timber."[89] Examinations were inadequate, and the dangers of manipulating instruments without benefit of sight were tremendous. Dewees cautioned his students to take great care before pulling the forceps that "no part of the mother is included in the locking of the blades. This accident is frequent."[90] Accidental mutilation of infants was also reported, as the navel string had to be cut under the covers. Lecturers passed on the story of the incautious doctor who included the penis of an infant within the blades of his scissors.[91]

In view of such dangers, the conflict between social values and medical practice is striking. The expansion of medical knowledge brought men and women face to face with social taboos in family life. They had to ask themselves the question, Who should watch a woman give birth? For centuries the answer had unhesitatingly been female relatives and friends, and the midwife. The science of obstetrics, developing in the eighteenth century, changed the answer. Though women might socially be the most acceptable assistants at a delivery, men were potentially more useful.

In consequence of the attendance of male physicians, by 1825, for some American women, childbirth was ceasing to be an open ceremony. Though birth still took place at home, and though friends and relatives still lent a helping hand, visiting women no longer dominated the activities in the lying-in room. Birth became increasingly a private affair conducted in a quiet, darkened room. The physician limited visitors because they hindered proper medical care, but the process of birth was also concealed because it embarrassed both patient and physician.

Between 1760 and 1825 childbirth was thus transformed from an open affair to a restricted one. As one consequence of the development of obstetrics as a legitimate branch of medicine, male physicians began replacing midwives. They began to reduce childbirth to a scientifically managed event and deprived it of its folk aspects. Strengthened by the professionalization of their field, these physicians also responded to the hopes of women in Philadelphia,

[88] Notes on Shippen lectures, *ibid.*; *London Practice of Midwifery*, 127.

[89] Bard, *Compendium of Theory and Practice of Midwifery*, 220; Seaman, *Midwives Monitor*, ix.

[90] Dewees, *Compendious System of Midwifery* (1826), 313.

[91] Kobler, *Reluctant Surgeon*, 32; *London Practice of Midwifery*, 132-133.

New York, and Boston for safe delivery. Although they helped some pregnant women, they hurt midwives, who were shut out of an area of medicine that had been traditionally their domain. All these innovations took place in the large urban centers in response to distinctly urban phenomena. They reflected the increasing privatization of family life, and they foreshadowed mid-nineteenth-century attitudes toward childbirth, mother, and woman.

WOMEN, MENSTRUATION, AND NINETEENTH-CENTURY MEDICINE *

VERN BULLOUGH AND MARTHA VOGHT

One of the recurrent themes in medical history is the reluctance of physicians to accept new scientific findings. This may well be due to the innate conservatism of medical practitioners and their unwillingness to use patients as guinea pigs for treatment about which they are unsure. Sometimes, too, the reluctance comes because new findings demonstrate that previous practices might have been harmful to the patient; this turn of events is difficult to accept. Often, however, the reluctance is not attributable to any medical reason but results when new findings upset the emotional attachments, some would say political prejudices, that most physicians hold and which have little to do with medicine itself. This paper is concerned with this kind of opposition.

When the belief structure of the physician is threatened, even in fields outside of medicine, he often uses his medical expertise to justify his prejudices and in the process strikes back with value laden responses which have nothing to do with scientific medicine. Unfortunately, since he is assumed to speak with authority, his response, perhaps as he intended, has influence far beyond that of the ordinary men. One of the best examples of this is the controversy over the physical disabilities of women which took place in the last part of the nineteenth century as women began to demand more education, greater political equality, and to challenge many of the male stereotypes about woman's place. Since medical pratitioners were almost all men, and many of them were hostile to any change in the status quo in male-female relationships, they inevitably entered the struggle with what today appears not only as ludicrous arguments, but which even in the period they were writing were not based upon any scientific findings and in fact went contrary to those findings. This is particularly true in their understanding of the consequences of menstruation.

During the last part of the nineteenth century American physicians toyed with several theories of menstruation. In general they were aware of the

* Presented at the 45th annual meeting of the American Association for the History of Medicine, Montreal, Canada, May 4, 1972. Research sponsored by the Erickson Educational Foundation, Baton Rouge, La.

theories of John Power of London who postulated that ovulation and menstruation were connected. American medical journals also made an attempt to keep their readers current on the English researches which tended to support his theories.[1] At the same time, however, many physicians seriously discussed various folk theories about menstruation, retaining with little change in content ideas which appear in the Hippocratic *corpus* or in Aristotle. Many still held that it was the effect of the moon upon women that caused them to menstruate, others held that the fetus was formed from the menstrual flow. The popular underground pseudonymous marriage manual, *Aristotle's Masterpiece* held that menstruation was due to the casting out of the excess blood which would have nourished the embryo if pregnancy had occurred.[2] Even as late as the 1890s when the first experimental work leading to the understanding of human hormones was taking place, American physicians were still discussing the question of whether the ovaries triggered menstruation, whether the uterus was an independent organ and performed the menstrual function without external aid, or whether the Fallopian tubes were responsible for the monthly flow.[3] A few, however, perhaps influenced by the Victorian disgust at the sexual and reproductive processes, considered menstruation a pathological condition. These physicians believed that in Paradise humans had reproduced asexually and it was only when man had fallen that perfection had been replaced by the evil of sex. An article in the *American Journal of Obstetrics* in 1875, for example, argued that menstruation was pathological, proof of the inactivity and threatened atrophy of the uterus. As evidence of its unnaturalness the author claimed that conception was most likely when intercourse occurred during the monthly flow, but intercourse at such times was dangerous and forbidden because the menstrual blood was the source of male gonorrhea. Since menstruation therefore stood in the way of fruitful coitus it obviously had not been ordained by nature.[4]

[1] John Power, *Essays on the Female Economy* (London: Burgess and Hill, 1831); G. F. Girdwood, "Theory of menstruation," *Lancet*, 1842-3, i: 825-30; J. Bennet, "On healthy and morbid menstruation, *Lancet*, 1852, i: 35, 65, 215, 328, 353.

[2] Aristotle (pseud.), *The Works of Aristotle in Four Parts*, containing *I. His complete Master-piece;... II. His Experienced Midwife;... III. His Book of Problems;... IV. His Last Legacy...* (London: published for the bookseller, 1808), p. 126.

[3] See M. M. Smith, "Menstruation and some or its effects upon the normal mentalization of woman," *Memphis Med. Monthly*, 1896, *16*: 393-399; C. Frederick Fluhmann, *Menstrual Disorders, Diagnosis and Treatment* (Philadelphia: W. B. Saunders, 1939), pp. 17-26.

[4] A. F. A. King, "A new basis for uterine pathology," *Am. J. Obst.*, 1875-76, *8*: 242-43.

In 1861 E. F. W. Pflüger demonstrated that menstruation did not take place in women whose ovaries had been removed, a finding which reinforced the ovarian theory but did not end the debate since Pflüger himself in 1863 hypothesized that there was a mechanical stimulus of nerves by the growing follicle which was responsible for congestion and menstrual bleeding. This led him to believe that menstruation and ovulation occurred simultaneously.[5] It was not until the twentieth century and a better understanding of the hormonal process that the timing of ovulation was fully understood. In the meantime, many American physicians accepted Pflüger's theory that nervous stimulation triggered menstruation and it was this belief which led large numbers of physicians to express opposition to any emancipation of women.

This paper is not the place to discuss the movement for female emancipation but even a brief synopsis must point out that women were much more assertive of their rights in the last part of the nineteenth century than earlier. Though traditionally women in the United States had received some sort of primary education, if only to learn to read the *Bible*, they had been denied entrance to any of the grammar schools or colleges. In 1783, for example, twelve-year-old Lucinda Foote was examined for admission to Yale and found capable of giving the "true meaning of passages in the *Aeneid* of Virgil, the *Select Orations* of Cicero and the Greek *Testament*." She was, however, declared unqualified to enter the college because of her sex[6] Physicians of the time were generally more inclined to favor female education than oppose it. Perhaps the best example is Benjamin Rush. He urged female education on the grounds that it would allow women to better fulfill their familial responsibilities, be less prone to superstition, have talent in managing their family's affairs, and be better teachers for their sons. Rush also pointed out to his fellow males who might be somewhat hesitant to accept his ideas that the ignorant were the most difficult to govern and an educated wife could, by virtue of her education, be more easily shown the wisdom of her husband's orders and decisions.[7] It was only later that a significant portion of the medical community appear in opposition to female education.

During the first part of the nineteenth century the female academies

[5] E. F. W. Pflüger, *Ueber die Eierstöcke der Säugethiere und des Menschen* (Leipzig: Engelmann, 1863).

[6] Thomas Woody, *A History of Women's Education in the United States*, 2 vols. (New York: The Science Press, 1929), II, p. 137.

[7] Benjamin Rush, *Essays, Literary, Moral and Philosophical* (Philadelphia: Thomas & Samuel Bradford, 1798), pp. 75-92.

and seminaries began to multiply and in the 1830s full-fledged colleges were proposed for women, and Oberlin College opened its doors to both sexes.[8] Soon medical schools also found themselves under attack for failure to admit women, and a few women such as Elizabeth Blackwell managed to receive medical training. Most women, however, turned to nursing as an alternative to challenging the male bastion of medicine,[9] but it is perhaps no accident that medical opposition to feminine emancipation began to increase as the physician himself felt threatened by the few women attempting to enter medical school. About 1870 several medical writers began proclaiming that education for women was a disastrous error since girls between twelve and twenty could not stand the strain of higher education, in large part because of the physiological strains which puberty and ovulation put upon them.

One of the first and by far the most influential theorist of menstrual disability was Edward H. Clarke, a professor of materia medica at Harvard and a fellow of the American Academy of Arts and Sciences. In 1873 he wrote that though women undoubtedly have the right to do anything of which they are physically capable, one of the things they could not do and still retain their good health was to be educated on the pattern and model of men. He held that while the male developed steadily and gradually from birth to manhood, the female, at puberty, had a sudden and unique period of growth when the development of the reproductive system took place.[10] If this did not take place at puberty, it would never occur, and since the system can never do " two things well at the same time, " the female between 12 and 20 must concentrate on developing her reproductive system. To digest one's dinner, he held it was necessary to temper exercise and brain work; likewise, during the growth of the female reproductive system, brain work must be avoided. The overuse of the central nervous system would overload the switchboard, so to speak, and signals from the developing organs of reproduction would be ignored in favor of those coming from the overactive brain. Even after puberty females were not to exercise their minds without restriction because of their monthly cycles. The menstrual period was vital, Clarke held, and any mental activity during the " catamenial week " would inter-

[8] Woody, *History of Women's Education*, II, p. 231.

[9] See Vern and Bonnie Bullough, *Emergence of Modern Nursing* (New York: Macmillan, 1969), *passim*.

[10] Edward H. Clarke, *Sex in Education; or a Fair Chance for Girls* (Boston: James R. Osgood & Co., 1874), pp. 37-8.

fere with ovulation and menstruation,[11] the necessary physiological processes of being female.

He then proceeded to demonstrate, at least to his own satisfaction, that higher education left a great number of its female adherents in poor health for life. He was alarmed that the increase in the number of young women being educated would so deplete the population that within fifty years " the wives who are to be mothers in our republic must be drawn from trans-Atlantic homes. "[12] For proof of his assertion he offered as evidence the cases of young women he had as patients whose ill health he ascribed to hard study. One had entered a female seminary at 15 in good health but after a year of application to her studies and following the routine of the school, which included standing to recite, she was pale and tired " every fourth week. " A summer's rest restored her but by the end of the second year she was not only pale but suffering from an " uncontrolable twitching of a rhythmical sort " in the muscles of her face. On the advice of the family physician she was taken for a year of travel in Europe and returned cured. Unfortunately she then returned to school where she studied without regard to her menstrual periods and, though she graduated at nineteen as valedictorian, she was an invalid and it took two years in Europe for her to recover. Her illness, according to Dr. Clarke's diagnosis, resulted from making her body do two things at once. He reported the case of another young woman, a student at Vassar, who began to have fainting spells and suffer painful and sparse menses. Inevitably she graduated at nineteen as an invalid, suffering from constant headaches. Dr. Clarke believed this was because she suffered from the arrested development of her reproductive system due to her education. As evidence he claimed she not only had menstrual troubles but was rather flat chested. Another young college woman came to him with a history of diminishing menstrual flow, constant headaches, mental depression, acne, and rough skin. Eventually Dr. Clarke committed her to an asylum.[13] It was also of some concern to Dr. Clarke that young women of the lower classes were expected, during puberty, to take jobs in domestic service or in factories. In his practice he had seen evidences of ill health among such women which he blamed upon their work. Yet, he concluded that labor in factory at a loom was far less damaging than study to a woman, because it worked the body, not the

[11] *Ibid.*, pp. 40-1.
[12] *Ibid.*, p. 63.
[13] *Ibid.*, pp. 65-72.

brain. It was primarily brain work which destroyed feminine capabilities.[14]

Women who concentrated upon education rather than the development of their reproductive system also underwent mental changes, according to Clarke. Not possessing the physical attributes of a man, they also tended to lose the "maternal instincts" of a woman to become coarse and forceful. By educating women, said Dr. Clarke, we were creating a class of sexless humans analogous to eunuchs. To solve this alarming problem, he recommended strict separation of the sexes during education, particularly after elementary school. He urged that female schools provide periodic rest periods for students during their menstrual periods. The young women would also have shorter study periods since they were by nature weak and less able to cope with long hours.

> A girl cannot spend more than four, or, in occasional instances, five hours of force daily upon her studies, and leave sufficient margin for the general physical growth that she must make.... If she puts as much force into her brain education as a boy, the brain or the special apparatus (i. e., the reproductive system) will suffer.[15]

He held up as models some reports on German education, showing that menstrual rest for female students was practiced.[16]

Though there was immediate unfavorable reaction to Clarke's thesis, it still became widely accepted. His critics pointed out, for example, that Clarke had done no scientific study on the matter, that he generalized from a few clinical cases in his own practice, and that his description of periodic rests in European education were totally untrue. One critic commented that "Dr. Clarke has thrown out to a popular audience a hypothesis of his own, which has no place in physiological or medical science. . . . His whole reasoning is singularly unsound." [17] There was some suspicion that Clarke's argument was designed to end speculation at Harvard about admitting female students.[18] Nevertheless, the popularity of his message is indicated by the fact that within thirteen years, *Sex in Education* went through seventeen editions.

[14] *Ibid.*, p. 133.
[15] *Ibid.*, pp. 156-57.
[16] *Ibid.*, pp. 162-81.
[17] George F. and Anna Manning Comfort, *Woman's Education and Woman's Health* (Syracuse: Thomas W. Durston & Co., 1874), p. 154.
[18] G. Stanley Hall, *Adolescence, Its Psychology and Its Relations to Physiology, Anthropology, Sociology, Sex, Crime, Religions and Education*, 2 vols. (New York: D. Appleton and Co., 1904), II, p. 569.

Those physicians who followed Clarke tended to exaggerate his position and to ascribe far more harm to the education of women than even he had dared. T. S. Clouston, a physician of Edinburgh, Scotland, wrote a lengthy series for the *Popular Science Monthly* to demonstrate to the public the dangers of the education of females. He pointed out that it was medically accepted that the "female organism is far more delicate than that of men; . . . it is not fitted for the regular grind that the man can keep up." Overstimulation of the female brain causes stunted growth, nervousness, headaches and neuralgias, difficult childbirth, hysteria, inflammation of the brain, and insanity. The female character is likewise altered by education; the educated woman becomes cultured, but "is unsympathetic; learned, but not self denying." Clouston admitted the weak point of his argument, "that it is not founded on any basis of collated statistical facts," only based upon observations of physicians of their own patients. Nonetheless, he expressed the hope that research to gather the facts would be carried on in the future.[19]

This, in fact, began to happen but the results were not what Clouston anticipated. The Massachusetts Labor Bureau made the first report on the health of American college women based upon statistical evidence and not the "haphazard estimate of physicians and college instructors."[20] The results indicated that of 705 college women, 78% were in good or excellent health, 5% were classed as in fair health, and 17% were in poor health. When these women had started college, 20% were in poor health. The report concluded that there were no marked differences in health between college women and the national average.[21] John Dewey, in his analysis of the report, decided that worry over personal matters was more harmful to health than overstudy.[22]

In spite of the publicity given the study, there was little change in attitudes among those who believed women and education made a dangerous mixture. In the same year that it appeared, Henry Maudsley wrote in *Sex in Mind and in Education* that the concurrence of puberty and higher education meant that mental development was accomplished at the expense of physical. While acknowledging that there were no

[19] T. S. Clouston. "Female education from a medical point of view," *Popular Science Monthly*, (Dec., 1883; Jan., 1884), *24*: 322-33.

[20] John Dewey, "Health and sex in higher education," *Popular Science Monthly*, March, 1886, *28*: 606.

[21] Annie G. Howes, et al, *Health Statistics of Women College Graduates: Report of a Special Committee of the Association of Collegiate Alumnae* (Boston: Wright & Potter, 1885), p. 9.

[22] Dewey, "Health and sex in higher education," 611.

facts to provide an answer to the question—what are the effects of coeducation?—he nonetheless answered the question by citing Clarke and declaring that girls educated in the traditional ways were loosing "their strength and health." The imperfect development of the reproductive system interfered with the development of the feminine character, leaving the educated woman without a sufficiently feminine frame of mind. The education of women must be designed to prepare them for their proper sphere.

> It will have to be considered whether women can scorn delights and live laborious days of intellectual exercise and production, without injury to their functions as the conceivers, mothers, and nurses of children. For, it would be an ill thing, if it should so happen that we got the advantage of a quantity of female intellectual work at the price of a puny, enfeebled, and sickly race.[23]

Clarke and most of his imitators ascribed to the Pflüger theory of menstruation, but it was not a necessary preliminary to the belief in the physical disability of women. John Goodman, a Louisville physician, believed that the ovular theory of menstruation was untenable. Instead menstruation was "presided over by a law of monthly periodicity," a "menstrual wave" which affected the entire female being and from whose dictates women could not escape.[24] This theory, although in conflict with that of Pflüger, was appropriated to the cause of those who opposed female education. A good example is George J. Engelmann who, in his presidential address before the American Gynecological Society in 1900, expressed the opinion that female schools should heed the "instability and susceptibility of the girl during the functional waves which permeate her entire being," and provide rest during the menstrual periods. At the same time he said that menstruation was controlled by "physical conditions and nerve influences," and that the first menses were accelerated by mental stimulation. His observations contradicted those of Clarke, since while Clarke found educated women ceasing menstruation, Engelmann found that mental work increased the frequency of menstrual flow.[25] Nevertheless he would agree with Clarke that women could not endure the rigors of higher education.

[23] Henry Maudsley, *Sex in Mind and in Education* (Syracuse: C. W. Bardeen, 1884), p. 14.

[24] John Goodman, "The menstrual cycle," *Transactions*, American Gynecological Society, 1877, *2*: 650-62; "The cyclical theory of menstruation," *Am. J. Obst.*, 1878, *11*: 673-94.

[25] George J. Engelmann. "The American girl of to-day. The influence of modern education on functional deveplopment," *Transactions*, American Gynecological Society, 1900, *25*: 8-45.

J. H. Kellogg, whose *Plain Facts for Old and Young* was responsible for inculcating vast numbers of Americans with the idea that masturbation led to insanity, added also to the public misinformation about menstruation. Part of Kellogg's success was due to the fact that he appeared to be so scientific:

There has been a great amount of speculation concerning the cause and nature of the menstrual process. No entirely satisfactory conclusions have been reached, however, except that it is usually accompanied by the maturation and expulsion from the ovary of an ovum, which is termed ovulation. But menstruation may occur without ovulation, and vice versa.[26]

He then stated that the first occurence of menstruation is a very critical period in the life of a female and each recurrence renders her specially susceptible to morbid influences and liable to serious derangements and a female must carefully watch out during these periods.

There is no doubt that many young women have permanently injured their constitutions while at school by excessive mental taxation during catamenial period, to which they were prompted by ambition to excel, or were compelled by the "cramming" system too generally pursued in our schools, and particularly in young ladies' seminaries.

He adds, however, that a moderate amount of study would not be injurious and he had no doubt that a large share of the injury which has been attributed to overstudy during the catamenia was caused by improper dress, exposure to taking cold, keeping late hours, and improper diet. Kellogg also wondered about women workers and felt that female workers should be protected during their periods. He felt it was wrong that women in order to keep their situations were required to be on hand daily and allowed no opportunity for rest at the menstrual period.

In many cases, too, they are compelled to remain upon their feet all day behind a counter, or at a work table, even at periods when a recumbent position is actually demanded by nature. There should be less delicacy in relation to this subject on the part of young women, and more consideration on the part of employers.[27]

As the movement for female emancipation grew, the physicians who discussed the frailties of the female did so with increasing emotional fervor. The president of the Oregon State Medical Society, F. W. Van Dyke, in 1905, claimed that hard study killed sexual desire in women,

[26] J. H. Kellogg, *Plain Facts for Old and Young* (Burlington, Iowa: I. F. Segner, 1882), p. 83.
[27] *Ibid.*, p. 86.

took away their beauty, brought on hysteria, neurasthenia, dyspepsia, astigmatism, and dysmenorrhea. Educated women, he added, could not bear children with ease because study arrested the development of the pelvis at the same time it increased the size of the child's brain, and therefore its head. The result was extensive suffering in childbirth by educated women. Van Dyke concluded by declaring that the women who were remembered in history were faithful wives and good mothers such as Penelope, Cornelia, St. Elizabeth; and these would still be remembered when "the name of the last graduate of the woman's college shall have faded from the recollection of men forever."[28]

Dr. Ralph W. Parsons in the *New York Medical Journal* in 1907 cited many of the above authorities to show that the results of higher education for women could only lead to ill health. He claimed college women suffered from digestive disorders as well as nervous and mental diseases.

> The nervous system has been developed at the expense of other bodily organs and structures. The delicate organism and sensitive and highly developed nervous system of our girls was never intended by the Creator to undergo the stress and strain of the modern system of higher education, and the baneful results are becoming more and more apparent as the years go by.[29]

He offered as proof the fact that in 1902, 42% of the women admitted to New York insane asylums were well educated, while only 16% of the men admitted had gone beyond grade school. He concluded that women "who have undergone the strain of the modern system of education, are much more liable to become victims of insanity than men of the same class."

One of the mental diseases to which college women were prone was the modification of feminine traits of mind. These women developed distaste for the duties of home life, were egotistical, assumed independence of speech and manner, and were not attentive to the advice of their parents. Educated women neglected to cultivate refined speech, had loud voices, laughed with gusto, and sometimes even used slang and profanity. "They do not exhibit," said Dr. Parsons, "the modesty of demeanor which we have been taught to believe is one of the most admirable traits of the feminine character." Colleges encouraged unwomanly behavior. At one school girls publicly appeared on stage in knee breeches, and in the

[28] F. W. Van Dyke, "Higher education a cause of physical decay in women," *Med. Records*, 1905, *67*: 296-98.

[29] Ralph Wait Parsons. "The American girl *versus* higher education, considered from a medical point of view," *New York Med. J.*, 1907, *85*: 116.

performance used such words as "devilish" and "damned." Such women as these would never be able to fulfill their female functions, for not only was their reproductive apparatus stunted by education, but no man would ever love them. This was because men had deep sentiment for women with "feminine traits of character with which God intended they should be endowed."

Parsons' solution went far beyond anything proposed in the nineteenth century by medical men. Girls, he decided, should not learn Latin, Greek, civics, political economy, or higher math, for these subjects could be of no use to them in their proper sphere. They should have shorter school hours than boys, and spend most of their time in home economics classes.[30]

All of these twentieth-century physicians had available to them a careful study on the health of college and non-college women, printed in the *Publications* of the American Statistical Association, 1900-1901. This study, carried out during the 1890s compared college women, not to the "average" woman of the census, as past projects had done, but to a control group of non-college women composed of their own relatives and friends of their own social class. The study found that though college women married two years later than non-college women there was a growing tendency to marry later among both groups. Non-college women had "a slightly larger number of children," but college women had more children per years of married life. There were no differences in problems of pregnancy and mortality of children. The health of the children was roughly equal; although among college educated mothers the researchers felt they detected slightly fewer delicate children and slightly more robust children. The study found no significant difference between the health of the two groups of women before or after college age. Seventy-five percent of the college women had been employed before marriage, while only 34% of the non-college women had had outside employment. The college women chose different kinds of husbands than the control group. Seventy-five percent of them married college men, while their non-educated cousins married a college educated husband in only half the cases. Sixty-five percent of college women married professional men, while only 37% of the non-college women had husbands in the professions.[31]

The physicians who persisted in accepting the theories of Clarke *et al.*

[30] *Ibid.*, p. 119.

[31] Mary Roberts Smith, "Statistics of college and non-college women" *Publications*, American Statistical Association, 1900-01, *7*: nos. 49-56, 1-26.

simply ignored such studies. G. Stanley Hall who, though one of the outstanding psychologists of the early twentieth century, strongly believed that woman's place was in the home, simply dismissed the statistical studies as inaccurate. Instead, he felt, physicians who treated over-educated women were more likely to see the true circumstances. Inevitably Hall's classic on *Adolescence* repeated all the fears and superstitions concerning female education. For example, he connected menstruation to mental exercise. As proof he offered the fact that American girls had their first menses at an average of 14 years of age, while European girls were, on the average, 15.5 years of age before menstruation started. This precocity of American girls was " due chiefly to mentality and nerve stimulation," in other words, education. " Education," theorized Hall, " in a temperate or subartic zone is more productive of precocity than in the south, and if general nervous stimulus is the cause, the same schooling is more dangerous in the city than in the country."[82] Hall was heavily influenced by Clarke's concept of rest during the menstrual periods, and suggested that the female, rather than observing the weekly Sabbath, should have rest periods of four successive days per month. These days would be devoted to leisure and religion, since during menstruation the female was inclined " to a natural piety and sense of dependence," which accounted for the fact that women were more religious than men.[83] Women were by nature intuitive, Hall claimed, not mental. By being " bookish " woman lapsed into male manners and fashions, declined from "her orbit," and obscured her " original divinity." [84]

He believed with Goodman that the ruling factor of female life was periodicity. For most of her life a women had no alternative but to give way to its dictates, and for this reason special schools should be established for girls. Under no circumstances should coeducation exist, for putting adolescents into the intimacy of the classroom destroyed " the bloom and delicacy " of the girls. Female schools should be in the country, with plenty of places for exercise and privacy. All students should observe the " monthly Sabbath during their menstrual periods, during which time

the paradise of stated rest should be revisited, idleness be actively cultivated; reverie, in which the soul, which needs these seasons of withdrawal for its own development, expatiates over the whole life of the race, should be provided for and encouraged in every legitimate way, for in rest the whole momentum of heredity is felt in ways most favorable to full and complete development. Then woman

[82] Hall, *Adolescence*, I, p. 478.
[83] *Ibid.*, I, p. 511.
[84] *Ibid.*, II, p. 646.

should realize that *to be* is greater than *to do;* should step reverently aside from her daily routine and let Lord Nature work.[35]

Such opinions as this were unlikely, in 1905, to go unchallenged by the feminists. Martha Carey Thomas, president of Bryn Mawr College, attacked this lyrical report on periodicity as "sickening sentimentality" and "pseudo-scientific." She held that the seventh and seventeenth chapters of Hall's work were more degrading to womanhood than anything written since Michelet's *La Femme*. She recalled her student days, when she was "terror-struck lest I, and every other woman with me, were doomed to live as pathological invalids in a universe merciless to woman as a sex." Now "we know" that it is not "we," but the "man who believes such things about us, who is himself pathological, blinded by neurotic mists of sex, unable to see that women form one-half of the kindly race of normal, healthy human creatures in the world."[36]

Serious research also questioned the point of view Hall represented. One such study hypothesized that if the menstrual cycle had such influence on women, it ought to show up on tests comparing motor and mental abilities of both men and women. When the results were analyzed it was found that none of the efficiency curves correlated with the menstrual cycles and that the males in the tests had varying efficiencies similar to the females rather than being stable and unvarying as had been thought. In fact, the curves produced by the two sexes were indistinguishable when the notations of the menstrual periods were removed. How, asked the researcher, Leta Stetter Hollingworth, were such results to be accounted for when they had such a striking disparity from what had been the accepted scientific position. Two possible explanations were offered. First the scientific and medically accepted facts were not facts at all but traditions carried on by mystic and romantic writers that "woman is a mysterious being, half hysteric, half angel," and this attitude had somehow found its way into the scientific writing. Scientists seeking to justify this had "seized" upon the menstrual cycle as the probable source of the alleged "mystery" and "caprice of womankind." Once formulated, then, the dogma became cited as authority from author to author until the present day. A second possible explanation of the error was that physicians had not based their conclusions upon accurate evidence.

[35] *Ibid.*, II, p. 639.
[36] M. Carey Thomas, "Present tendencies in women's college and university education," Feb., 1908, in William O'Neill, ed., *The Woman Movement: Feminism in the United States and England* (Chicago: Quadrangle Books, 1969), p. 168.

She postulated that normal women did not come under the care and observations of physicians but rather only those with mental and physical diseases. Physicians generalized from these patients, and determined that women were chronically ill. Moreover, once these observations were accepted, experiments to disprove them were difficult since, until the end of the nineteenth century, all investigators were men and the taboo upon mention of the menstrual function made such research next to impossible.[37]

In actuality the explanation is probably far more complex than this. It is quite possible that physicians were simply blind to what was going on and were so prejudiced that they refused to see reality. There is also the possibility that during the nineteenth century young women did have more than their share of menstrual difficulties. One source of such problems was undoubtedly diet. It was generally believed a century ago that certain foods, especially highly flavored dishes and meats, aroused the sexual appetites. It was, accordingly, desirable to regulate the diets of young girls so as to protect them from unhealthy desires, and physicians found that protein deprivation was a successful cure for female masturbation.[38] Female boarding schools, to minimize sexual interest among their charges, were likely to follow such a prescribed vegetable diet. A study of female higher education in the 1890s deplored the low state of boarding school health, due, it was believed, to diet and lack of exercise, as well as the pressures of the curriculum.[39]

Clelia Mosher, whose research into menstruation among college women spanned several generations between 1890 and 1920, found that girls in the earlier period probably did have greater menstrual difficulties than those in the 1920s. She at first concluded that the reason for this was that during the nineteenth century girls were taught that they were going to be sick during menstruation and the result was a self fulfilling prophecy. She also found, however, that there was a correlation between dress and menstrual difficulties. During the 1890s and the early years of the twentieth century most young women were put into tight corsets, banded

[37] Leta Stetter Hollingworth, *Functional Periodicity: An Experimental Study of the Mental and Motor Abilities of Women During Menstruation*, Teachers College, Columbia University Contributions to Education, No. 69 (New York: Columbia University Press, 1914), pp. 44, 66, 93, 95.

[38] John Tompkins Walton, "Case of nymphomania successfully treated," *Am. J. Med. Sci.* 1857, *33*: 47-50.

[39] Anna C. Brackett, ed., *Women and the Higher Education* (New York: Harper., 1893), p. 90.

clothing, and unsupported heavy skirts. This clothing interfered with the respiration, made the abdominal muscles flabby, restricted physical activity, and deformed the body on the same principle that the binding of feet in China did. The result was, Mosher held, chronic disturbances of the organs and prolonged menstrual flow.[40] She prepared tables correlating menstrual pain among college women with the width and weight of their skirts and the measurements of their waists. Her figures showed that as the skirt grew shorter and skimpier, and the waist larger, the functional health of women improved. In 1894, 19% of the college women were free from menstrual difficulties; in 1915-16, 68% considered their periods no problem. In the earlier period the average skirt was 13.5 feet around the hem, the average waist measurement was twenty inches, and the woman also wore several petticoats, some fifteen pounds of clothing hanging from a constricted waist. By the beginning of World War I women wore their skirts above the ankle, skirts were narrowed, petticoats fewer, and waist measurements had increased by 40%.[41]

Such studies did much to ease the traumas inflicted by some of the male medical writers of the last part of the nineteenth century. Increasing reassurance came from the growth in numbers of college educated and career women who seemed none the worse for their years of hard study or work. While the generation of Martha Thomas had been haunted by the "clanging chains of that gloomy little spector," Dr. Edward H. Clarke's *Sex in Education,* several generations of educated women tended to prove that "college women were not only not invalids, but that they (were) better physically than other women in their own class of life."[42] In part too, the development of the sanitary pad in the aftermath of World War I also freed women from some of the more confining aspects of menstruation. Not all physicians, however, adjusted their thinking to correspond with the latest scientific findings. At the beginning of the twentieth century most sex manuals warned against exciting lives and mental stimulation for pubertal girls.[43] Perhaps this was to be expected but, when the same sort of material was still being published thirty years later, it is possible to wonder what motivated the physicians who

[40] Clelia Duel Mosher, "Normal menstruation and some of the factors modifying it," *Johns Hopkins Hosp. Bull.,* 1901, *12*: 178-79.

[41] Clelia Duel Mosher, *Woman's Physical Freedom* (New York: The Woman's Press, 1923), pp. 1, 29.

[42] Thomas, "Present tendencies in women's college and university education," p. 169.

[43] See, for example, William H. Walling, *Sexology* (Philadelphia: Puritan Publishing Co., 1904), p. 207.

wrote it. William J. Robinson's book, for example, in 1931 in its twenty-second edition, still warned that only a minority of women were free from illness during their menstrual periods, and that most should rest at least two days, avoid dancing, cycling, riding, rowing, or any other athletic exercises, and probably postpone travel by auto, train, or carriage.[44]

That some of the medical hesitation to change seems political, a hesitation to accept women as equals, is evident even in the 1970s. After all it was in 1970 that Edgar Berman, previously best known as the friend and physician of Hubert Humphrey, remarked that women could not fill leadership roles because of the influences of their periodicity, that is their menstrual cycles and menopause.[45] This statement cost him his position in the Democratic Party and made not only him but Humphrey an object of attack by the militant members of women's lib. That the belief still has currency is also indicated by the fact that the first issue of the new woman's magazine *Ms.* found it relevant enough to counter the theory of female periodicity with an article on male cycles and gave hints to women on how to discover whether the men in their life were ebbing or flowing.[46]

This is not the place to argue the existence of male cycles, however, but only to indicate that it is very possible for medical concepts to get mixed up with political and social beliefs. Perhaps this is inevitable since we are human, but it ought to make the physician a little more cautious in distinguishing his biases from his objective findings. In retrospect it does seem that the nineteenth-century physician grew somewhat more shrill in his emphasis on the instability of the female at the very time that women and their male allies were challenging the old stereotypes. A few physicians jumped into the controversy citing their own clinical observations as evidence in ways that today we can only regard as ludicrous. This in fact happened with a whole series of physiological functions and human activities but were particularly harmful when they dealt with such sexual topics as menstruation, masturbation, or birth control. Obviously women are anatomically different from men, and they do have monthly periods, but to generalize from this and a few isolated patients a whole theory of female inferiority seems to be an example of poor med-

[44] William J. Robinson, *Woman: Her Sex and Love Life*, 22nd ed. (New York: Eugenics Publishing Co., 1931), pp. 80-1.

[45] *New York Times*, July 26, 1970; *Los Angeles Times*, Feb. 21, 1972.

[46] Estelle Ramey, "Men's Cycles," *Ms.*, Spring, 1972, 8-15.

ical theorizing. The difficulty with past medical theory, whether good or bad, however, is that it often remains a part of the popular ideology of a later generation. One of the things that women of today have to overcome is some of the mistaken concepts about menstruation and its effect.[47]

[47] For a survey of some recent research on the topic see Mary E. Luschen and David M. Pierce, "Menstrual cycle, mood and arousability," *Sex Research*, February, 1972, 8: 41-47.

The Female Animal: Medical and Biological Views of Woman and Her Role in Nineteenth-Century America

CARROLL SMITH-ROSENBERG
AND
CHARLES ROSENBERG

SINCE at least the time of Hippocrates and Aristotle, the roles assigned women have attracted an elaborate body of medical and biological justification. This was especially true in the nineteenth century as the intellectual and emotional centrality of science increased steadily. Would-be scientific arguments were used in the rationalization and legitimization of almost every aspect of Victorian life, and with particular vehemence in those areas in which social change implied stress in existing social arrangements.

This essay is an attempt to outline some of the shapes assumed by the nineteenth-century debate over the ultimate bases for woman's domestic and child-bearing role.[1] In form it resembles an exercise in the history

Carroll Smith-Rosenberg is assistant professor of history and psychiatry in the University of Pennsylvania. Charles Rosenberg is professor of history in the University of Pennsylvania.

[1] For historical studies of women's role and ideological responses to it in nineteenth-century America, see William L. O'Neill, *Everyone was Brave: A History of Feminism in America* (Chicago, 1969); William Wasserstrom, *Heiress of all the Ages: Sex and Sentiment in the Victorian Tradition* (Minneapolis, 1959); Eleanor Flexner, *Century of Struggle: The Woman's Rights Movement in the United States* (New York, 1968); Aileen S. Kraditor, *The Ideas of the Woman Suffrage Movement, 1890-1920* (New York, 1965). For studies emphasizing the interaction between social change and sex role conflict see, Carroll Smith Rosenberg, "Beauty, the Beast and the Militant Woman: A Case Study in Sex Roles and Social Stress in Jacksonian America," *American Quarterly*, XXIII (Oct. 1971), 562-84; Carroll Smith Rosenberg, "The Hysterical Woman: Sex Roles and Role Conflict in 19th-Century America," *Social Research*, XXXIX (Winter, 1972), 652-78. The problem of sexuality in the English-speaking world has been a particular subject of historical concern. Among the more important, if diverse, attempts to deal with this problem are Peter T. Cominos, "Late-Victorian Sexual Respectability and the Social System," *Internation Review of Social History*, VIII (1963), 18-48, 216-50; Stephen Nissenbaum, "Careful Love: Sylvester Graham and the Emergence of Victorian Sexual Theory in America, 1830-1840" (doctoral dissertation, University of Wisconsin, 1968); Graham Barker-Benfield, "The

of ideas; in intent it represents a hybrid with social and psychological history. Biological and medical views serve as a sampling device suggesting and illuminating patterns of social continuity, change, and tension.

The relationships between social change and social stress are dismayingly complex and recalcitrant to both psychological theorists and to the historian's normal modes of analysis. In an attempt to gain insight into these relationships the authors have chosen an analytic approach based on the study of normative descriptions of the female role at a time of widespread social change; not surprisingly emotion-laden attempts to reassert and redefine this role constitute one response to the stress induced by such social change.

This approach was selected for a variety of reasons. Role definitions exist on a level of prescription beyond their embodiment in the individuality and behavior of particular historical persons. They exist rather as a formally agreed upon set of characteristics understood by and acceptable to a significant proportion of the population. As formally agreed upon social values they are, moreover, retrievable from historical materials and thus subject to analysis. Such social role definitions, however, have a more than platonic reality; for they exist as parameters with which and against which individuals must either conform or define their deviance. When inappropriate to social, psychological, or biological reality such definitions can themselves engender anxiety, conflict, and demands for change.

During the nineteenth century, economic and social forces at work within Western Europe and the United States began to compromise traditional social roles. Some women at least began to question—and a few to challenge overtly—their constricted place in society. Naturally enough, men hopeful of preserving existing social relationships, and in some cases threatened themselves both as individuals and as members of particular social groups, employed medical and biological arguments to rationalize traditional sex roles as rooted inevitably and irreversibly in the prescriptions of anatomy and physiology. This essay examines the ideological attack mounted by prestigious and traditionally minded men against two of the ways in which women expressed their dissatisfaction and desire for change:

Horrors of the Half Known Life: Aspects of the Exploitation of Women by Men" (doctoral dissertation, University of California, Los Angeles, 1968); Nathan G. Hale, Jr., *Freud and the Americans: The Beginnings of Psychoanalysis in the United States, 1876-1917* (New York, 1971), 24-46; David M. Kennedy, *Birth Control in America: The Career of Margaret Sanger* (New Haven, 1970), 36-71; Steven Marcus, *The Other Victorians: A Study of Sexuality and Pornography in Mid-Nineteenth-Century England* (New York, 1966). See also Charles E. Rosenberg, "Sexuality, Class and Role in 19th-Century America," *American Quarterly*, XXV (May 1973), 131-54.

women's demands for improved educational opportunities and their decision to resort to birth control and abortion. That much of this often emotionally charged debate was oblique and couched in would-be scientific and medical language and metaphor makes it even more significant; for few spokesmen could explicitly and consciously confront those changes which impinged upon the bases of their particular emotional adjustment.

The Victorian woman's ideal social characteristics—nurturance, intuitive morality, domesticity, passivity, and affection—were all assumed to have a deeply rooted biological basis. These medical and scientific arguments formed an ideological system rigid in its support of tradition, yet infinitely flexible in the particular mechanisms which could be made to explain and legitimate woman's role.

Woman, nineteenth-century medical orthodoxy insisted, was starkly different from the male of the species. Physically, she was frailer, her skull smaller, her muscles more delicate. Even more striking was the difference between the nervous system of the two sexes. The female nervous system was finer, "more irritable," prone to overstimulation and resulting exhaustion. "The female sex," as one physician explained in 1827,

> is far more sensitive and susceptible than the male, and extremely liable to those distressing affections which for want of some better term, have been denominated nervous, and which consist chiefly in painful affections of the head, heart, side, and indeed, of almost every part of the system.[2]

"The nerves themselves," another physician concurred a generation later, "are smaller, and of a more delicate structure. They are endowed with greater sensibility, and, of course, are liable to more frequent and stronger impressions from external agents or mental influences."[3] Few if any questioned the assumption that in males the intellectual propensities of the brain dominated, while the female's nervous system and emotions prevailed over her conscious and rational faculties. Thus it was only natural, indeed

[2] Marshall Hall, *Commentaries on some of the more important of the Diseases of Females, in three parts* (London, 1827), 2. Although this discussion centers on the nineteenth century, it must be understood that these formulations had a far longer pedigree.

[3] Stephen Tracy, *The Mother and her Offspring* (New York, 1860), xv; William Goodell, *Lessons in Gynecology* (Philadelphia, 1879), 332; William B. Carpenter, *Principles of Human Physiology: With Their Chief Applications to Pathology, Hygiène, and Forensic Medicine* (4th ed., Philadelphia, 1850), 727. In mid-nineteenth century many of these traditional views of woman's peculiar physiological characteristics were restated in terms of the currently fashionable phrenology. For example, see Thomas L. Nichols, *Woman, in All Ages and Nations: A Complete and Authentic History of the Manners and Customs, Character and Condition of the Female Sex in Civilized and Savage Countries, from the Earliest Ages to the Present Time* (New York, *ca.* 1849), xi.

inevitable, that women should be expected and permitted to display more affect than men; it was inherent in their very being.

Physicians saw woman as the product and prisoner of her reproductive system. It was the ineluctable basis of her social role and behavioral characteristics, the cause of her most common ailments; woman's uterus and ovaries controlled her body and behavior from puberty through menopause. The male reproductive system, male physicians assured, exerted no parallel degree of control over man's body. Charles D. Meigs, a prominent Philadelphia gynecologist, stated with assurance in 1847 that a woman is "a moral, a sexual, a germiferous, gestative and parturient creature."[4] It was, another physician explained in 1870, "as if the Almighty, in creating the female sex, had taken the uterus and built up a woman around it."[5] A wise deity had designed woman as keeper of the hearth, as breeder and rearer of children.

Medical wisdom easily supplied hypothetical mechanisms to explain the interconnection between the female's organs of generation and the functioning of her other organs. The uterus, it was assumed, was connected to the central nervous system; shocks to the nervous system might alter the reproductive cycle—might even mark the gestating fetus—while changes in the reproductive cycle shaped emotional states. This intimate and hypothetical link between ovaries, uterus, and nervous system was the logical basis for the "reflex irritation" model of disease causation so popular in middle and late nineteenth-century medical texts and monographs on psychiatry and gynecology. Any imbalance, exhaustion, infection, or other disorders of the reproductive organs could cause pathological reactions in parts of the body seemingly remote.[6] Doctors connected not only the paralyses and headaches of the hysteric to uterine disease but also ailments in virtually every part of the body. "These diseases," one physician explained,

[4] Charles D. Meigs, *Lecture on Some of the Distinctive Characteristics of the Female. Delivered before the Class of the Jefferson Medical College, January 5, 1847* (Philadelphia, 1847), 5.

[5] M. L. Holbrook, *Parturition without Pain: A Code of Directions for Escaping from the Primal Curse* (New York, 1882), 14-15. See also Edward H. Dixon, *Woman, and her Diseases, from the Cradle to the Grave: Adapted Exclusively to her Instruction in the Physiology of her System, and all the Diseases of her Critical Periods* (New York, 1846), 17; M. K. Hard, *Woman's Medical Guide: Being a Complete Review of the Peculiarities of the Female Constitution and the Derangements to which it is Subject. With a Description of Simple yet Certain Means for their Cure* (Mt. Vernon, Ohio, 1848), 11.

[6] In the hypothetical pathologies of these generations, the blood was often made to serve the same function as that of the nerves; it could cause general ills to have local manifestations and effect systemic changes based on local lesions. By mid-century, moreover, physicians had come to understand that only the blood supply connected the gestating mother to her child.

"will be found, on due investigation, to be in reality, no disease at all, but merely the sympathetic reaction or the symptoms of one disease, namely, a disease of the womb."[7]

Yet despite the commonsensical view that many such ailments resulted from childbearing, physicians often contended that far greater difficulties could be expected in childless women. Motherhood was woman's normal destiny, and those females who thwarted the promise immanent in their body's design must expect to suffer. The maiden lady, many physicians argued, was fated to a greater incidence of both physical and emotional disease than her married sisters and to a shorter life-span.[8] Her nervous system was placed under constant pressure, and her unfulfilled reproductive organs —especially at menopause—were prone to cancer and other degenerative ills.

Woman was thus peculiarly the creature of her internal organs, of tidal forces she could not consciously control. Ovulation, the physical and emotional changes of pregnancy, even sexual desire itself were determined by internal physiological processes beyond the control or even the awareness of her conscious volition.[9] All women were prisoners of the cyclical aspects of their bodies, of the great reproductive cycle bounded by puberty and menopause, and by the shorter but recurrent cycles of childbearing and menstruation. All shaped her personality, her social role, her intellectual abilities and limitations; all presented as well possibly "critical" moments in her development, possible turning points in the establishment—or deterioration—of future physical and mental health. As the president of the American Gynecological Society stated in 1900: "Many a young life is battered and forever crippled in the breakers of puberty; if it crosses these unharmed and is not dashed to pieces on the rock of childbirth, it may still ground on the ever-recurring shallows of menstruation, and lastly, upon the

[7] M. E. Dirix, *Woman's Complete Guide to Health* (New York, 1869), 24. So fashionable were such models in the late-nineteenth century that America's leading gynecologist in the opening years of the present century despaired of trying to dispel such exaggerated notions from his patients' minds. "It is difficult," he explained, "even for a healthy girl to rid her mind of constant impending evil from the uterus and ovaries, so prevalent is the idea that woman's ills are mainly 'reflexes' from the pelvic organs." Gynecological therapy was the treatment of choice for a myriad of symptoms. Howard A. Kelly, *Medical Gynecology* (New York, 1908), 73.

[8] [Dr. Porter,] *Book of Men, Women, and Babies. The Laws of God applied to Obtaining, Rearing, and Developing the Natural, Healthful, and Beautiful in Humanity* (New York, 1855), 56; Tracy, *Mother and Offspring*, xxiii; H. S. Pomeroy, *The Ethics of Marriage* (New York, 1888), 78.

[9] On the involuntary quality of female sexuality, see Alexander J. C. Skene, *Education and Culture as Related to the Health and Diseases of Women* (Detroit, 1889), 22.

final bar of the menopause ere protection is found in the unruffled waters of the harbor beyond the reach of sexual storms."[10]

Woman's physiology and anatomy, physicians habitually argued, oriented her toward an "inner" view of herself and her worldly sphere. (Logically enough, nineteenth-century views of heredity often assumed that the father was responsible for a child's external musculature and skeletal development, the mother for the internal viscera, the father for analytical abilities, the mother for emotions and piety.[11]) Their secret internal organs, women were told, determined their behavior; their concerns lay inevitably within the home.[12] In a passage strikingly reminiscent of some mid-twentieth-century writings, a physician in 1869 depicted an idealized female world, rooted in the female reproductive system, sharply limited socially and intellectually, yet offering women covert and manipulative modes of exercising power:

> Mentally, socially, spiritually, she is more interior than man. She herself is an interior part of man, and her love and life are always something interior and incomprehensible to him. . . . Woman is to deal with domestic affections and uses, not with philosophies and sciences. . . . She is priest, not king. The house, the chamber, the closet, are the centres of her social life and power, as surely as the sun is the centre of the solar system. . . . Another proof of the interiority of woman, is the wonderful secretiveness and power of dissimulation which she possesses. . . . Woman's secrecy is not cunning; her dissimulation is not fraud. They are intuitions or spiritual perceptions, full of tact and wisdom, leading her to conceal or reveal, to speak or be silent, to do or not to do, exactly at the right time and in the right place.[13]

The image granted women in these hypothetical designs was remarkably consistent with the social role traditionally allotted them. The instincts connected with ovulation made her by nature gentle, affectionate, and nurtu-

[10] George Engelmann, *The American Girl of To-Day: Modern Education and Functional Health* (Washington, 1900), 9-10.

[11] Alexander Harvey, "On the Relative Influence of the Male and Female Parents in the Reproduction of the Animal Species," *Monthly Journal of Medical Science*, XIX (Aug. 1854), 108-18; M. A. Pallen, "Heritage, or Hereditary Transmission," *St. Louis Medical & Surgical Journal*, XIV (Nov. 1856), 495. William Warren Potter, *How Should Girls be Educated? A Public Health Problem for Mothers, Educators, and Physicians* (Philadelphia, 1891), 9.

[12] As one clerical analyst explained, "All the spare force of nature is concerned in this interior nutritive system, unfitting and disinclining the woman for strenuous muscular and mental enterprise, while providing for the shelter and nourishment of offspring throughout protracted periods of embryo and infancy." William C. Conant, "Sex in Nature and Society," *Baptist Quarterly*, IV (April 1870), 183.

[13] William H. Holcombe, *The Sexes here and hereafter* (Philadelphia, 1869), 201-02. William Holcombe was a Swedenborgian, and these contrasting views of the masculine and feminine also reflect New Church doctrines.

rant. Weaker in body, confined by menstruation and pregnancy, she was both physically and economically dependent upon the stronger, more forceful male, to whom she necessarily looked up to with admiration and devotion.

Such stylized formulae embodied, however, a characteristic yet entirely functional ambiguity. The Victorian woman was more spiritual than man, yet less intellectual, closer to the divine, yet prisoner of her most animal characteristics, more moral than man, yet less in control of her very morality. While the sentimental poets placed woman among the angels and doctors praised the transcendent calling of her reproductive system, social taboos made woman ashamed of menstruation, embarrassed and withdrawn during pregnancy, self-conscious and purposeless during and after menopause. Her body, which so inexorably defined her personality and limited her role, appeared to woman often degrading and confining.[14] The very romantic rhetoric which tended to suffocate nineteenth-century discussions of femininity only underlined with irony the distance between behavioral reality and the forms of conventional ideology.

The nature of the formalistic scheme implied as well a relationship between the fulfilling of its true calling and ultimate social health. A woman who lived "unphysiologically"—and she could do so by reading or studying in excess, by wearing improper clothing, by long hours of factory work, or by a sedentary, luxurious life—could produce only weak and degenerate offspring. Until the twentieth century, it was almost universally assumed that acquired characteristics in the form of damage from disease and improper life-styles in parents would be transmitted through heredity; a nervous and debilitated mother could have only nervous, dyspeptic, and undersized children.[15] Thus appropriate female behavior was sanctioned not only by traditional injunctions against the avoidance of individual sin in the form of inappropriate and thus unnatural modes of life but also by the higher duty of protecting the transcendent good of social health, which could be maintained only through the continued production of healthy children. Such arguments were to be invoked with increasing frequency as the nineteenth century progressed.

In mid-nineteenth-century America it was apparent that women—or at

[14] In regard to pregnancy many middle-class women "sought to hide their imagined shame as long as possible," by tightening corsets and then remaining indoors, shunning even the best of friends—certainly never discussing the impending event. Henry B. Hemenway, *Healthful Womanhood and Childhood: Plain Talks to Non-Professional Readers* (Evanston, Ill., 1894); Elizabeth Evans, *The Abuse of Maternity* (Philadelphia, 1875), 28-29.

[15] For a brief summary of late nineteenth-century assumptions in regard to human genetics, see Charles E. Rosenberg, "Factors in the Development of Genetics in the United States: Some Suggestions," *Journal of the History of Medicine*, XXII (Jan. 1967), 31-33.

least some of them—were growing dissatisfied with traditional roles. American society in mid-nineteenth century was committed—at least formally—to egalitarian democracy and evangelical piety. It was thus a society which presumably valued individualism, social and economic mobility, and free will. At the same time it was a society experiencing rapid economic growth, one in which an increasing number of families could think of themselves as middle class and could seek a life-style appropriate to that station. At least some middle-class women, freed economically from the day-to-day struggle for subsistence, found in these values a motivation and rationale for expanding their roles into areas outside the home. In the Jacksonian crusades for piety, for temperance, for abolition, and in pioneering efforts to aid the urban poor, women played a prominent role, a role clearly outside the confines of the home. Women began as well to demand improved educational opportunities—even admission to colleges and medical schools. A far greater number began, though more covertly, to see family limitation as a necessity if they would preserve health, status, economic security, and individual autonomy.

Only a handful of nineteenth-century American women made a commitment to overt feminism and to the insecurity and hostility such a commitment implied. But humanitarian reform, education, and birth control were all issues which presented themselves as real alternatives to every respectable churchgoing American woman.[16] Contemporary medical and biological arguments identified, reflected, and helped to eliminate two of these threats to traditional role definitions: demands by women for higher education and family limitation.

Since the beginnings of the nineteenth century, American physicians and social commentators generally had feared that American women were physically inferior to their English and Continental sisters. The young women of the urban middle and upper classes seemed in particular less vigorous, more nervous than either their own grandmothers or European contemporaries. Concern among physicians, educators, and publicists over the physical deterioration of American womanhood grew steadily during the nineteenth century and reached a high point in its last third.

[16] Since both male and female were ordinarily involved in decisions to practice birth control, the cases are not strictly analogous. Both, however, illustrate areas of social conflict organized about stress on traditional role characteristics. This discussion emphasizes only those aspects of the birth control debate which placed responsibility on the woman. Commentators did indeed differ in such emphases; in regard to abortion, however, writers of every religious and ideological persuasion agreed in seeing the matter as woman's responsibility.

Many physicians were convinced that education was a major factor in bringing about this deterioration, especially education during puberty and adolescence. It was during these years that the female reproductive system matured, and it was this process of maturation that determined the quality of the children which American women would ultimately bear. During puberty, orthodox medical doctrine insisted, a girl's vital energies must be devoted to development of the reproductive organs. Physicians saw the body as a closed system possessing only a limited amount of vital force; energy expended in one area was necessarily removed from another. The girl who curtailed brain work during puberty could devote her body's full energy to the optimum development of its reproductive capacities. A young woman, however, who consumed her vital force in intellectual activities was necessarily diverting these energies from the achievement of true womanhood. She would become weak and nervous, perhaps sterile, or more commonly, and in a sense more dangerously for society, capable of bearing only sickly and neurotic children—children able to produce only feebler and more degenerate versions of themselves.[17] The brain and ovary could not develop at the same time. Society, mid-century physicians warned, must protect the higher good of racial health by avoiding situations in which adolescent girls taxed their intellectual faculties in academic competition. "Why," as one physician pointedly asked, "spoil a good mother by making an ordinary grammarian?"[18]

Yet where did America's daughters spend these years of puberty and adolescence, doctors asked, especially the daughters of the nation's most virtuous and successful middle-class families? They spent these years in schools; they sat for long hours each day bending over desks, reading thick books, competing with boys for honors. Their health and that of their future children would be inevitably marked by the consequences of such unnatural modes of life.[19] If such evils resulted from secondary education, even more

[17] "The results," as Edward H. Clarke put it in his widely discussed polemic on the subject, "are monstrous brains and puny bodies; abnormally active cerebration, and abnormally weak digestion; flowing thought and constipated bowels; lofty aspirations and neuralgic sensations. . . ." Edward H. Clarke, *Sex in Education: Or, a Fair Chance for Girls* (Boston, 1873), 41. Thomas A. Emmett, in his widely used textbook of gynecology, warned in 1879 that girls of the better classes should spend the year before and two years after puberty at rest. "Each menstrual period should be passed in the recumbent position until her system becomes accustomed to the new order of life." Thomas Addis Emmett, *The Principles and Practice of Gynecology* (Philadelphia, 1879), 21.

[18] T. S. Clouston, *Female Education from a Medical Point of View* (Edinburgh, 1882), 20; Potter, *How Should Girls be Educated?* 9.

[19] The baleful hereditary effects of woman's secondary education served as a frequent sanction against this unnatural activity. Lawrence Irwell, "The Competition of the Sexes and its

dramatically unwholesome was the influence of higher education upon the health of those few women intrepid enough to undertake it. Yet their numbers increased steadily, especially after a few women's colleges were established in the East and state universities in the Midwest and Pacific Coast began cautiously to accept coeducation. Women could now, critics agonized, spend the entire period between the beginning of menstruation and the maturation of their ovarian systems in nerve-draining study. Their adolescence, as one doctor pointed out, contrasted sadly with those experienced by healthier, more fruitful forebears: "Our great-grandmothers got their schooling during the winter months and let their brains lie fallow for the rest of the year. They knew less about Euclid and the classics than they did about housekeeping and housework. But they made good wives and mothers, and bore and nursed sturdy sons and buxom daughters and plenty of them at that."[20]

Constant competition among themselves and with the physically stronger males disarranged the coed's nervous system, leaving her anxious, prey to hysteria and neurasthenia. One gynecologist complained as late as 1901:

> the nervous force, so necessary at puberty for the establishment of the menstrual function, is wasted on what may be compared as trifles to perfect health, for what use are they without health? The poor sufferer only adds another to the great army of neurasthenia and sexual incompetents, which furnish neurologists and gynecologists with so much of their material . . . bright eyes have been dulled by the brain-fag and sweet temper transformed into irritability, crossness and hysteria, while the womanhood of the land is deteriorating physically.
>
> She may be highly cultured and accomplished and shine in society, but her future husband will discover too late that he has married a large outfit of headaches, backaches and spine aches, instead of a woman fitted to take up the duties of life.[21]

Such speculations exerted a strong influence upon educators, even those connected with institutions which admitted women. The state universities, for example, often prescribed a lighter course load for females or refused to permit women admission to regular degree programs. "Every physiologist is well aware," the Regents of the University of Wisconsin explained

Results," *American Medico-Surgical Bulletin*, X (Sept. 19, 1896), 319-20. All the doyens of American gynecology in the late-nineteenth century—Emmett, J. Marion Sims, T. Gaillard Thomas, Charles D. Meigs, William Goodell, and Mitchell—shared the conviction that higher education and excessive development of the nervous system might interfere with woman's proper performance of her maternal functions.

[20] William Goodell, *Lessons in Gynecology* (Philadelphia, 1879), 353.

[21] William Edgar Darnall, "The Pubescent Schoolgirl," *American Gynecological & Obstetrical Journal*, XVIII (June 1901), 490.

in 1877, "that at stated times, nature makes a great demand upon the energies of early womanhood and that at these times great caution must be exercised lest injury be done. . . . Education is greatly to be desired," the Regents concluded:

> but it is better that the future matrons of the state should be without a University training than that it should be produced at the fearful expense of ruined health; better that the future mothers of the state should be robust, hearty, healthy women, than that, by over study, they entail upon their descendants the germs of disease.[22]

This fear for succeeding generations born of educated women was widespread. "We want to have body as well as mind," one commentator noted, "otherwise the degeneration of the race is inevitable."[23] Such transcendent responsibilities made the individual woman's personal ambitions seem trivial indeed.

One of the remedies suggested by both educators and physicians lay in tempering the intensely intellectualistic quality of American education with a restorative emphasis on physical education. Significantly, health reformers' demands for women's physical education were ordinarily justified not in terms of freeing the middle-class woman from traditional restrictions on bodily movement, but rather as upgrading her ultimate maternal capacities. Several would-be physiological reformers called indeed for active participation in house-cleaning as an ideal mode of physical culture for the servant-coddled American girl. Bedmaking, clothes scrubbing, sweeping, and scouring provided a varied and highly appropriate regimen.[24]

Late nineteenth-century women physicians, as might have been expected, failed ordinarily to share the alarm of their male colleagues when contemplating the dangers of coeducation. No one, a female physician commented sardonically, worked harder or in unhealthier conditions than the washerwoman; yet, would-be saviors of American womanhood did not inveigh against this abuse—washing, after all, was appropriate work for women.

[22] Board of Regents, University of Wisconsin, *Annual Report, for the Year Ending, September 30, 1877* (Madison, 1877), 45.

[23] Clouston, *Female Education*, 19.

[24] James E. Reeves, *The Physical and Moral Causes of Bad Health in American Women* (Wheeling, W.Va., 1875), 28; John Ellis, *Deterioration of the Puritan Stock and its Causes* (New York, 1884), 7; George Everett, *Health Fragments or, Steps Toward a True Life: Embracing Health, Digestion, Disease, and the Science of the Reproductive Organs* (New York, 1874), 37; Nathan Allen, "The Law of Human Increase; Or Population based on Physiology and Psychology," *Quarterly Journal of Psychological Medicine*, II (April 1868), 231; Nathan Allen, "The New England Family," *New Englander* (March 1882), 9-10; Pye Henry Chavasse, *Advice to a Wife on the Management of her Own Health. And on the Treatment of Some of the Complaints Incidental to Pregnancy, Labour and Suckling with an Introductory Chapter especially Addressed to a Young Wife* (New York, 1886), 73-75.

Women doctors often did agree with the general observation that their sisters were too frequently weak and unhealthy; however, they blamed not education or social activism but artificialities of dress and slavery to fashion, aspects of the middle-class woman's life-style which they found particularly demeaning. "The fact is that girls and women can bear study," Alice Stockham explained, "but they cannot bear compressed viscera, tortured stomachs and displaced uterus," the results of fashionable clothing and an equally fashionable sedentary life. Another woman physician, Sarah Stevenson, wrote in a similar vein: " 'How do I look?' is the everlasting story from the beginning to the end of woman's life. Looks, not books, are the murderers of American women."[25]

Even more significant than this controversy over woman's education was a parallel debate focusing on the questions of birth control and abortion. These issues affected not simply a small percentage of middle- and upper-middle-class women, but all men and women. It is one of the great and still largely unstudied realities of nineteenth-century social history. Every married woman was immediately affected by the realities of childbearing and child rearing. Though birth control and abortion had been practiced, discussed—and reprobated—for centuries, the mid-nineteenth century saw a dramatic increase in concern among spokesmen for the ministry and medical profession.[26]

Particularly alarming was the casualness, doctors charged, with which seemingly respectable wives and mothers contemplated and undertook abortions, and how routinely they practiced birth control. One prominent

[25] Sarah H. Stevenson, *The Physiology of Woman, Embracing Girlhood, Maternity and Mature Age* (2nd ed., Chicago, 1881), 68, 77; Alice Stockham, *Tokology: A Book for Every Woman* (rev. ed., Chicago, 1887), 257. Sarah H. Stevenson noted acidly that "the unerring instincts of woman have been an eloquent theme for those who do not know what they are talking about." Stevenson, *Physiology of Woman*, 79. The dress reform movement held, of course, far more significant implications than one would gather from the usually whimsical attitude with which it is normally approached; clothes were very much a part of woman's role. Health reformers, often critical as well of the medical establishment whose arguments we have—essentially—been describing, were often sympathetic to women's claims that not too much, but too little, mental stimulation was the cause of their ills, especially psychological ones. M. L. Holbrook, *Hygiene of the Brain and Nerves and the Cure of Nervousness* (New York, 1878), 63-64, 122-23; James C. Jackson, *American Womanhood: Its Peculiarities and Necessities* (Dansville, N.Y., 1870), 127-31.

[26] For documentation of the progressive drop in the white American birth rate during the nineteenth century, and some possible reasons for this phenomenon, see Yasukichi Yasuba, *Birth Rates of the White Population in the United States, 1800-1860: An Economic Study* (Baltimore, 1962); J. Potter, "American Population in the Early National Period," Paul Deprez, ed., *Proceedings of Section V of the Fourth Congress of the International Economic History Association* (Winnipeg, Canada, 1970), 55-69. For a more general background to this trend, see A. M. Carr-Saunders, *World Population: Past Growth and Present Trends* (London, 1936).

New York gynecologist complained in 1874 that well-dressed women walked into his consultation room and asked for abortions as casually as they would for a cut of beefsteak at their butcher.[27] In 1857, the American Medical Association nominated a special committee to report on the problem; then appointed another in the 1870s; between these dates and especially in the late 1860s, medical societies throughout the country passed resolutions attacking the prevalence of abortion and birth control and condemning physicians who performed and condoned such illicit practices. Nevertheless, abortions could in the 1870s be obtained in Boston and New York for as little as ten dollars, while abortifacients could be purchased more cheaply or through the mail. Even the smallest villages and rural areas provided a market for the abortionist's services; women often aborted any pregnancy which occurred in the first few years of marriage. The Michigan Board of Health estimated in 1898 that one third of all the state's pregnancies ended in abortion. From 70 to 80 percent of these were secured, the board contended, by prosperous and otherwise respectable married women who could not offer even the unmarried mother's "excuse of shame."[28] By the 1880s, English medical moralists could refer to birth control as the "American sin" and warn against England's women following in the path of America's faithless wives.[29]

[27] A. K. Gardner, *Conjugal Sins against the Laws of Life and Health* (New York, 1874), 131. H. R. Storer of Boston was probably the most prominent and widely read critic of such "conjugal sins." Abortion had in particular been discussed and attacked since early in the century, though it was not until the postbellum years that it became a widespread concern of moral reformers. Alexander Draper, *Observations on Abortion. With an Account of the Means both Medicinal and Mechanical, Employed to Produce that Effect* . . . (Philadelphia, 1839); Hugh L. Hodge, *On Criminal Abortion; A Lecture* (Philadelphia, 1854). Advocates of birth control routinely used the dangers and prevalence of abortion as one argument justifying their cause.

[28] *Report of the Suffolk District Medical Society On Criminal Abortion and Ordered Printed . . . May 9, [1857]* (Boston, 1857), 2. The report was almost certainly written by Storer. The Michigan report is summarized in William D. Haggard, *Abortion: Accidental, Essential, Criminal.* Address before the Nashville Academy of Medicine, Aug. 4, 1898 (Nashville, Tenn., 1898), 10. For samples of contemporary descriptions of prevalence, cheapness, and other aspects of abortion and birth control in the period, see Ely Van De Warker, *The Detection of Criminal Abortion, and a Study of Foeticidal Drugs* (Boston, 1872); Evans, *Abuse of Maternity*; Horatio R. Storer, *Why Not? A Book for Every Woman* (2nd ed., Boston, 1868); [N. F. Cook,] *Satan in Society: By A Physician* (Cincinnati, 1876); Discussion, *Transactions of the Homeopathic Medical Society of New York*, IV (1866), 9-10; H. R. Storer and F. F. Heard, *Criminal Abortion* (Boston, 1868); H. C. Ghent, "Criminal Abortion, or Foeticide," *Transactions of the Texas State Medical Association at the Annual Session 1888-89* (1888-1889), 119-46; Hugh Hodge, *Foeticide, or Criminal Abortion: A Lecture Introductory to the Course on Obstetrics, and Diseases of Women and Children. University of Pennsylvania* (Philadelphia, 1869), 3-10. Much of the medical discussion centered about the need to convince women that the traditional view that abortion was no crime if performed before quickening was false and immoral and to pass and enforce laws and medical society proscriptions against abortionists.

[29] Compare the warning of Pomeroy, *Ethics of Marriage*, v, 56, with the editorial, "A Con-

So general a phenomenon demands explanation. The only serious attempts to explain the prevalence of birth control in this period have emphasized the economic motivations of those practicing it—the need in an increasingly urban, industrial, and bureaucratized society to limit numbers of children so as to provide security, education, and inheritance for those already brought into the world. As the nineteenth century progressed, it has been argued, definitions of appropriate middle-class life-styles dictated a more and more expansive pattern of consumption, a pattern—especially in an era of recurring economic instability—particularly threatening to those large numbers of Americans only precariously members of the secure economic classes. The need to limit offspring was a necessity if family status was to be maintained.[30]

Other aspects of nineteenth-century birth control have received much less historical attention. One of these needs only to be mentioned for it poses no interpretative complexities; this was the frequency with which childbirth meant for women pain and often lingering incapacity. Death from childbirth, torn cervixes, fistulae, prolapsed uteri were widespread "female complaints" in a period when gynecological practice was still relatively primitive and pregnancy every few years common indeed. John Humphrey Noyes, perhaps the best-known advocate of family planning in nineteenth-century America, explained poignantly why he and his wife had decided to practice birth control in the 1840s:

> The [decision] was occasioned and even forced upon me by very sorrowful experiences. In the course of six years my wife went through the agonies of five births. Four of them were premature. Only one child lived. . . . After our last disappointment, I pledged my word to my wife that I would never again expose her to such fruitless suffering. . . .[31]

viction for Criminal Abortion," *Boston Medical & Surgical Journal*, CVI (Jan. 5, 1882), 18-19. It is significant that discussions of birth control in the United States always emphasized the role and motivations of middle-class women and men; in England, following the canon of the traditional Malthusian debate, the working class and its needs played a far more prominent role. Not until late in the century did American birth control advocates tend to concern themselves with the needs and welfare of the working population. It is significant as well that English birth control advocates often used the prevalence of infanticide as an argument for birth control; in America this was rarely discussed. And one doubts if the actual incidence of infanticide was substantially greater in London than New York.

[30] For a guide to literature on birth control in nineteenth-century America, see Norman Himes, *Medical History of Contraception* (Baltimore, 1936). See also J. A. Banks, *Prosperity and Parenthood: A Study of Family Planning among the Victorian Middle Classes* (London, 1954), and J. A. and Olive Banks, *Feminism and Family Planning in Victorian England* (Liverpool, 1964); Margaret Hewitt, *Wives and Mothers in Victorian Industry* (London, *ca.* 1958). For the twentieth century, see David M. Kennedy, *Birth Control in America.*

[31] John Humphrey Noyes, *Male Continence* (Oneida, N.Y., 1872), 10-11.

The Noyeses' experience was duplicated in many homes. Young women were simply terrified of having children.[32]

Such fears, of course, were not peculiar to nineteenth-century America. The dangers of disability and death consequent upon childbirth extended back to the beginning of time, as did the anxiety and depression so frequently associated with pregnancy. What might be suggested, however, was that economic and technological changes in society added new parameters to the age-old experience. Family limitation for economic and social reasons now appeared more desirable to a growing number of husbands; it was, perhaps, also, more technically feasible. Consequently married women could begin to consider, probably for the first time, alternative life-styles to that of multiple pregnancies extending over a third of their lives. Women could begin to view the pain and bodily injury which resulted from such pregnancies not simply as a condition to be borne with fatalism and passivity, but as a situation that could be avoided. It is quite probable, therefore, that, in this new social context, increased anxiety and depression would result once a woman, in part at least voluntarily, became pregnant. Certainly, it could be argued, such fears must have altered women's attitudes toward sexual relations generally. Indeed the decision to practice birth control must necessarily have held more than economic and status implications for the family; it must have become an element in the fabric of every marriage's particular psycho-sexual reality.[33]

A third and even more ambiguous aspect of the birth control controversy in nineteenth-century America relates to the way in which attitudes toward contraception and abortion reflected role conflict within the family. Again and again, from the 1840s on, defenders of family planning—including

[32] It is not surprising that the design for a proto-diaphragm patented as early as 1846 should have been called "The Wife's Protector." J. B. Beers, "Instrument to Prevent Conception, Patented Aug. 28th, 1846," design and drawings (Historical Collections, Library of the College of Physicians of Philadelphia).

[33] In some marriages, for example, even if the male had consciously chosen, indeed urged, the practice of birth control, he was effectively deprived of a dimension of sexual pleasure and of the numerous children which served as tangible and traditional symbols of masculinity as well as the control over his wife which the existence of such children implied. In some marriages, however, birth control might well have brought greater sexual fulfillment because it reduced the anxiety of the female partner. Throughout the nineteenth century withdrawal was almost certainly the most common form of birth control. One author described it as "a practice so universal that it may well be termed a national vice, so common that it is unblushingly acknowledged by its perpetrators, for the commission of which the husband is even eulogized by his wife." [Cook,] *Satan in Society*, 152. One English advocate of birth control was candid enough to argue that "the real objection underlying the opposition, though it is not openly expressed, is the idea of the deprivation of pleasure supposed to be involved." Austin Holyyoake, *Large or Small Families* (London, 1892), 11.

individuals as varied and idealistic as Noyes and Stockham, on the one hand, and assorted quack doctors and peddlers of abortifacients, on the other—justified their activities not in economic terms, but under the rubric of providing women with liberty and autonomy. Woman, they argued with remarkable unanimity, must control her own body; without this she was a slave not only to the sexual impulses of her husband but also to endless childbearing and rearing. "Woman's equality in all the relations of life," a New York physician wrote in 1866, "implies her absolute supremacy in the sexual relation. . . . it is her absolute and indefeasible right to determine when she will and when she will not be exposed to pregnancy." "God and Nature," another physician urged, "have given to the female the complete control of her own person, so far as sexual congress and reproduction are concerned."[34] The assumption of all these writers was clear and unqualified: women, if free to do so, would choose to have sexual relations less frequently, and to have far fewer pregnancies.

Implied in these arguments as well were differences as to the nature and function of sexual intercourse. Was its principal and exclusively justifiable function, as conservative physicians and clergymen argued, the procreation

[34] R. T. Trall, *Sexual Physiology: A Scientific and Popular Exposition of the Fundamental Problems in Sociology* (New York, 1866), xi, 202. As women awoke to a realization of their own "individuality," as a birth control advocate explained it in the 1880s, they would rebel against such "enforced maternity." E. B. Foote, Jr., *The Radical Remedy in Social Science: Or, Borning Better Babies* (New York, 1886), 132. See also Stevenson, *Physiology of Women*, 91; T. L. Nichols, *Esoteric Anthropology* (New York, 1824); E. H. Heywood, *Cupid's Yokes: Or, the Binding Force of Conjugal Life* (Princeton, Mass., 1877); Stockham, *Tokology*, 250; Alice Stockholm, *Karezza: Ethics of Marriage* (Chicago, 1896); E. B. Foote, *Medical Commonsense Applied to the Causes, Prevention and Cure of Chronic Diseases and Unhappiness in Marriage* (New York, 1864), 365; J. Soule, *Science of Reproduction and Reproductive Control. The Necessity of Some Abstaining from Having Children. The Duty of all to Limit their Families According to their Circumstances Demonstrated. Effects of Continence Effects of Self-Pollution—Abusive Practices. Seminal Secretion—Its Connection with Life. With all the Different Modes of Preventing Conception, and the Philosophy of Each* (n.p., 1856), 37; L. B. Chandler, *The Divineness of Marriage* (New York, 1872). To radical feminist Tennie C. Claflin, man's right to impose his sexual desires upon woman was the issue underlying all opposition to woman suffrage and the expansion of woman's role. Tennie C. Claflin, *Constitutional Equality: A Right of Woman: Or a Consideration of the Various Relations Which She Sustains as a Necessary Part of the Body of Society and Humanity; With Her Duties to Herself—together with a Review of the Constitution of the United States, Showing that the Right to Vote Is Guaranteed to All Citizens. Also a Review of the Rights of Children* (New York, 1871), 63. Particularly striking are the letters from women desiring birth control information. Margaret Sanger, *Motherhood in Bondage* (New York, 1928); E. B. Foote, Jr., *Radical Remedy*, 114-20; Henry C. Wright, *The Unwelcome Child; or, the Crime of an Undesigned and Undesired Maternity* (Boston, 1858). This distinction between economic, "physical," and role consideration, is, quite obviously, justifiable only for the sake of analysis; these considerations must have coexisted within each family in particular configuration.

of children, or could it be justified as an act of love, of tenderness between individuals? Noyes argued that the sexual organs had a social, amative function separable from their reproductive function. Sex was justifiable as an essential and irreplaceable form of human affection; no man could demand this act unless it was freely given.[35] Nor could it be freely given in many cases unless effective modes of birth control were available to assuage the woman's anxieties. A man's wife was not his chattel, her individuality to be violated at will, and forced—ultimately—to bear unwanted and thus almost certainly unhealthy children.

Significantly, defenders of women's right to limit childbearing employed many of the same arguments used by conservatives to attack women's activities outside the home; all those baleful hereditary consequences threatened by over-education were seen by birth control advocates as resulting from the bearing of children by women unwilling and unfit for the task, their vital energies depleted by excessive childbearing. A child, they argued, carried to term by a woman who desired only its death could not develop normally; such children proved inevitably a source of physical and emotional degeneracy. Were women relieved from such accustomed pressures, they could produce fewer but better offspring.[36]

Many concerned mid-nineteenth-century physicians, clergymen, and journalists failed to accept such arguments. They emphasized instead the unnatural and thus necessarily deleterious character of any and all methods of birth control and abortion. Even coitus interruptus, obviously the most common mode of birth control in this period, was attacked routinely as a source of mental illness, nervous tension, and even cancer. This was easily demonstrated. Sex, like all aspects of human bodily activity, involved an exchange of nervous energy; without the discharge of such accumulated energies in the male orgasm and the soothing presence of the male semen "bathing the female reproductive organs," the female partner could never, the reassuring logic ran, find true fulfillment. The nervous force accumulated and concentrated in sexual excitement would build up dangerous levels of undischarged energy, leading ultimately to a progressive decay in the unfortunate

[35] Noyes, *Male Continence*, 16; Frederick Hollick, *The Marriage Guide, Or Natural History of Generation; A Private Instructor for Married Persons and Those About to Marry, Both Male and Female* (New York, *ca.* 1860), 348; Trall, *Sexual Physiology*, 205-06.

[36] Indeed, in these post-Darwinian years it was possible for at least one health reformer to argue that smaller families were a sign of that higher nervous evolution which accompanied civilization. [M. L. Holbrook,] *Marriage and Parentage* (New York, 1882). For the eugenic virtues of fewer but better children, see E. R. Shepherd, *For Girls: A Special Physiology: Being a Supplement to the Study of General Physiology. Twentieth Edition* (Chicago, 1887), 213; M. L. Griffith, *Ante-Natal Infanticide* (n.p. [1889]), 8.

woman's physical and mental health. Physicians warned repeatedly that condoms and diaphragms—when the latter became available after mid-century—could cause an even more startlingly varied assortment of ills. In addition to the mechanical irritation they promoted, artificial methods of birth control increased the lustful impulse in both partners, leading inevitably to sexual excess. The resultant nervous exhaustion induced gynecological lesions, and then through "reflex irritation" caused such ills as loss of memory, insanity, heart disease, and even "the most repulsive nymphomania."[37]

Conservative physicians similarly denounced the widespread practice of inserting sponges impregnated with supposedly spermicidal chemicals into the vagina immediately before or after intercourse. Such practices, they warned, guaranteed pelvic injury, perhaps sterility. Even if a woman seemed in good health despite a history of practicing birth control, a Delaware physician explained in 1873 that ". . . as soon as this vigor commences to decline . . . about the fortieth year, the disease [cancer] grows as the energies fail—the cancerous fangs penetrating deeper and deeper until, after excruciating suffering, the writhing victim is yielded up to its terrible embrace."[38] Most importantly, this argument followed, habitual attempts at contraception meant—even if successful—a mother permanently injured and unable to bear healthy children. If unsuccessful, the children resulting from such unnatural matings would be inevitably weakened. And if such grave ills resulted from the practice of birth control, the physical consequences of abortion were even more dramatic and immediate.[39]

Physicians often felt little hesitation in expressing what seems to the his-

[37] See Louis François Étienne Bergeret, *The Preventive Obstacle: Or Conjugal Onanism*, P. de Marmon, trans. (New York, 1870); C. H. F. Routh, *Moral and Physical Evils Likely to Follow if Practices Intended to Act as Checks to Population be not Strongly Discouraged and Condemned* (2nd ed., London, 1879), 13; Goodell, *Lessons in Gynecology*, 371, 374; Thomas Hersey, *The Midwife's Practical Directory; Or Woman's Confidential Friend: Comprising, Extensive Remarks on the Various Casualties and Forms of Diseases Preceding, Attending and Following the Period of Gestation, with appendix* (2nd ed., Baltimore, 1836), 80; William H. Walling, *Sexology* (Philadelphia, 1902), 79.

[38] J. R. Black, *The Ten Laws of Health; Or, How Disease Is Produced and Can Be Prevented* (Philadelphia, 1873), 251. See also C. A. Greene, *Build Well. The Basis of Individual, Home, and National Elevation. Plain Truths Relating to the Obligations of Marriage and Parentage* (Boston, *ca.* 1885), 99; E. P. LeProhon, *Voluntary Abortion, or Fashionable Prostitution, with Some Remarks upon the Operation of Craniotomy* (Portland, Me., 1867), 15; M. Solis-Cohen, *Girl, Wife, and Mother* (Philadelphia, 1911), 213.

[39] There is an instructive analogy between these ponderously mechanistic sanctions against birth control and abortion and the psychodynamic arguments against abortion used so frequently in the twentieth century; both served precisely the same social function. In both cases, the assumption of woman's childbearing destiny provided the logical basis against which a denial of this calling produced sickness, in the nineteenth century through physiological, and ultimately, pathological processes—in the twentieth century through guilt and psychological but again, ultimately, pathological processes.

torian a suspiciously disproportionate resentment toward such unnatural females. Unnatural was of course the operational word; for woman's presumed maternal instinct made her primarily responsible for decisions in regard to childbearing.[40] So frequent was this habitual accusation that some medical authors had to caution against placing the entire weight of blame for birth control and abortion upon the woman; men, they reminded, played an important role in most such decisions.[41] In 1871, for example, the American Medical Association Committee on Criminal Abortion described women who patronized abortionists in terms which conjured up fantasies of violence and punishment:

> She becomes unmindful of the course marked out for her by Providence, she overlooks the duties imposed on her by the marriage contract. She yields to the pleasures—but shrinks from the pains and responsibilities of maternity; and, destitute of all delicacy and refinement, resigns herself, body and soul, into the hands of unscrupulous and wicked men. Let not the husband of such a wife flatter himself that he possesses her affection. Nor can she in turn ever merit even the respect of a virtuous husband. She sinks into old age like a withered tree, stripped of its foliage; with the stain of blood upon her soul, she dies without the hand of affection to smooth her pillow.[42]

The frequency with which attacks on family limitation in mid-nineteenth-century America were accompanied by polemics against expanded roles for the middle-class woman indicates with unmistakable clarity something of one of the motives structuring such jeremiads. Family limitation necessarily added a significant variable within conjugal relationships generally; its successful practice implied potential access for women to new roles and a new autonomy.

Nowhere is this hostility toward women and the desire to inculcate guilt over women's desire to avoid pregnancy more strikingly illustrated than in

[40] A. K. Gardner, for example, confessed sympathy for the seduced and abandoned patron of the abortionist, "but for the married shirk, who disregards her divinely-ordained duty, we have nothing but contempt. . . ." Gardner, *Conjugal Sins*, 112. See also E. Frank Howe, *Sermon on Ante-Natal Infanticide delivered at the Congregational Church in Terre Haute, on Sunday Morning, March 28, 1869* (Terre Haute, Ind., 1869); J. H. Tilden, *Cursed before Birth* (Denver, *ca.* 1895); J. M. Toner, *Maternal Instinct, or Love* (Baltimore, 1864), 91.

[41] It must be emphasized that this is but one theme in a complex debate surrounding the issue of birth control and sexuality. A group of more evangelically oriented health reformers tended to emphasize instead the responsibility of the "overgrown, abnormally developed and wrongly directed amativeness of the man" and to see the woman as victim. John Cowan, Henry C. Wright, and Dio Lewis were widely read exemplars of this point of view. This group shared a number of assumptions and presumably psychological needs, and represents a somewhat distinct interpretive task. John Cowan, *The Science of A New Life* (New York, 1874), 275.

[42] W. L. Atlee and D. A. O'Donnell, "Report of the Committee on Criminal Abortion," *Transactions of the American Medical Association*, XXII (1871), 241.

the warnings of "race suicide" so increasingly fashionable in the late-nineteenth century. A woman's willingness and capacity to bear children was a duty she owed not only to God and husband but to her "race" as well.[43] In the second half of the nineteenth century, articulate Americans forced to evaluate and come to emotional terms with social change became, like many of their European contemporaries, attracted to a world view which saw racial identity and racial conflict as fundamental. And within these categories, birthrates became all-important indices to national vigor and thus social health.

In 1860 and again in 1870, Massachusetts census returns began to indicate that the foreign born had a considerably higher birthrate than that of native Americans. Indeed, the more affluent and educated a family, the fewer children it seemed to produce. Such statistics indicated that native Americans in the Bay State were not even reproducing themselves. The social consequences seemed ominous indeed.

The Irish, though barely one quarter of the Massachusetts population, produced more than half of the state's children. "It is perfectly clear," a Boston clergyman contended in 1884, "that without a radical change in the religious ideas, education, habits, and customs of the natives, the present population and their descendants will not rule that state a single generation."[44] A few years earlier a well-known New England physician, pointing to America's still largely unsettled western territories, had asked: "Shall they be filled by our own children or by those of aliens? This is a question that our own women must answer; upon their loins depends the future destiny of the nation." Native-born American women had failed themselves as individuals and society as mothers of the Anglo-Saxon race. If matters continued for another half century in the same manner, "the wives who are to be mothers in our republic must be drawn from trans-Atlantic homes. The Sons of the New World will have to re-act, on a magnificent scale, the old story of unwived Rome and the Sabines."[45]

[43] The most tireless advocate of these views was Nathan Allen, a Lowell, Massachusetts, physician and health reformer. Nathan Allen, "The Law of Human Increase; Or Population based on Physiology and Psychology," *Quarterly Journal Psychological Medicine*, II (April 1868), 209-66; Nathan Allen, *Changes in New England Population. Read at the Meeting of the American Social Science Association, Saratoga, September 6, 1877* (Lowell, Mass., 1877); Nathan Allen, "The Physiological Laws of Human Increase," *Transactions of the American Medical Association*, XXI (1870), 381-407; Nathan Allen, "Physical Degeneracy," *Journal of Psychological Medicine*, IV (Oct. 1870), 725-64; Nathan Allen, "The Normal Standard of Woman for Propagation," *American Journal of Obstetrics*, IX (April 1876), 1-39.

[44] Ellis, *Deterioration of Puritan Stock*, 3; Storer, *Why Not?* 85.

[45] Clarke, *Sex in Education*, 63. For similar warnings, see Henry Gibbons, *On Feticide* (San Francisco, 1878), 4; Charles Buckingham, *The Proper Treatment of Children, Medical*

Such arguments have received a goodly amount of historical attention, especially as they figured in the late-nineteenth and early twentieth centuries as part of the contemporary rationale for immigration restriction.[46] Historians have interpreted the race suicide argument in several fashions. As an incident in a general Western acceptance of racism, it has been seen as product of a growing alienation of the older middle and upper classes in the face of industrialization, urbanization, and bureaucratization of society. More specifically, some American historians have seen these race suicide arguments as rooted in the fears and insecurities of a traditionally dominant middle class as it perceived new and threatening social realities.

Whether or not historians care to accept some version of this interpretation—and certainly such motivational elements seem to be suggested in the rhetorical formulae employed by many of those bemoaning the failure of American Protestants to reproduce in adequate numbers—it ignores another element crucial to the logical and emotional fabric of these arguments. This is the explicit charge of female sexual failure. To a significant extent, contemporaries saw the problem as in large measure woman's responsibility; it was America's potential mothers, not its fathers, who were primarily responsible for the impending social cataclysm. Race suicide seemed a problem in social gynecology.

Though fathers played a necessary role in procreation, medical opinion emphasized that it was the mother's constitution and reproductive capacity which most directly shaped her offspring's physical, mental, and emotional attributes. And any unhealthy mode of life—anything in short which seemed undesirable to contemporary medical moralists, including both education and birth control—might result in a woman becoming sterile or capable of bearing only stunted offspring. Men, it was conceded, were subject to vices even more debilitating, but the effects of male sin and imprudence were, physicians felt, "to a greater extent confined to adult life; and consequently do not, to the same extent, impair the vitality of our race or

or Medicinal (Boston, 1873), 15; Edward Jenks, "The Education of Girls from a Medical Stand-Point," *Transactions of the Michigan State Medical Society*, XIII (1889), 52-62; Paul Paquin, *The Supreme Passions of Man* (Battle Creek, Mich., 1891), 76.

[46] These arguments, first formulated in the 1860s, had become clichés in medical and reformist circles by the 1880s. See Barbara Miller Solomon, *Ancestors and Immigrants: A Changing New England Tradition* (Cambridge, Mass., 1956); John Higham, *Strangers in the Land: Patterns of American Nativism, 1860-1925* (New Brunswick, N.J., 1955). Such arguments exhibited a growing consciousness of class as well as of ethnic sensitivity; it was the better-educated and more sensitive members of society, anti-Malthusians began to argue, who would curtail their progeny, while the uneducated and coarse would hardly change their habits. H. S. Pomeroy, *Is Man Too Prolific? The So-Called Malthusian Idea* (London, 1891), 57-58.

threaten its physical destruction." Women's violation of physiological laws implied disaster to "the unborn of both sexes."[47]

Though such social critics tended to agree that woman was at fault, they expressed some difference of opinion as to the nature of her guilt. A few felt that lower birthrates could be attributed simply to the conscious and culpable decision of American women to curtail family size. Other physicians and social commentators, while admitting that many women felt little desire for children, saw the roots of the problem in somewhat different—and perhaps even more apocalyptic—terms. It was not, they feared, simply the conscious practice of family limitation which resulted in small families; rather the increasingly unnatural life-style of the "modern American woman" had undermined her reproductive capacities so that even when she would, she could not bear adequate numbers of healthy children. Only if American women returned to the simpler life-styles of the eighteenth and early nineteenth centuries could the race hope to regain its former vitality; women must from childhood see their role as that of robust and self-sacrificing mothers. If not, their own degeneration and that of the race was inevitable.

Why the persistence and intensity of this masculine hostility, of its recurring echoes of conflict, rancor, and moral outrage? There are at least several possible, though by no means exclusive, explanations. One centers on the hostility implied and engendered by the sexual deprivation—especially for the male—implicit in many of the modes of birth control employed at this time. One might, for example, speculate—as Oscar Handlin did some years ago—that such repressed middle-class sexual energies were channeled into a xenophobic hostility toward the immigrant and the black and projected into fantasies incorporating the enviable and fully expressed sexuality of these alien groups.[48] A similar model could be applied to men's attitudes toward women as well; social, economic, and sexual tensions which beset late nineteenth-century American men might well have caused them to express their anxieties and frustrations in terms of hostility toward the middle-class female.[49]

[47] Ellis, *Deterioration of Puritan Stock*, 10.

[48] Oscar Handlin, *Race and Nationality in American Life* (5th ed., Boston, 1957), 139-66.

[49] One might postulate a more traditionally psychodynamic explanatory model, one which would see the arguments described as a male defense against their own consciousness of sexual inadequacy or ambivalence or of their own unconscious fears of female sexual powers. These emphases are quite distinct. The first—though it also assumes the reality of individual psychic mechanisms such as repression and projection—is tied very much to the circumstances of a particular generation, to social location, and to social perception. The second kind of explanation is more general, time-free, and based on a presumably ever-recurring

Such interpretations are, however, as treacherous as they are inviting. Obviously, the would-be scientific formulations outlined here mirror something of post-bellum social and psychic reality. Certainly some middle-class men in the late-nineteenth century had personality needs—sexual inadequacies or problems of status identification—which made traditional definitions of gender roles functional to them. The hostility, even the violent imagery expressed toward women who chose to limit the number of children they bore indicates a significant personal and emotional involvement on the part of the male author. Some women, moreover, obviously used the mechanisms of birth control and, not infrequently sexual rejection, as role-sanctioned building blocks in the fashioning of their particular adjustment. Their real and psychic gains were numerous: surcease from fear and pain, greater leisure, a socially acceptable way of expressing hostility, and a means of maintaining some autonomy and privacy in a life which society demanded be devoted wholeheartedly to the care and nurturance of husband and children. Beyond such statements, however, matters become quite conjectural. At this moment in the development of both historical methodology and psychological theory great caution must be exercised in the development of such hypotheses—especially since the historians of gender and sexual behavior have at their disposal data which from a psychodynamic point of view is at best fragmentary and suggestive.[50]

What the nineteenth-century social historian can hope to study with a greater degree of certainty, however, is the way in which social change both caused and reflected tensions surrounding formal definitions of gender roles. Obviously, individuals as individuals at all times and in all cultures have experienced varying degrees of difficulty in assimilating the prescriptions of expected role behavior. When such discontinuities begin to affect comparatively large numbers and become sufficiently overt as to evoke a marked ideological response one can then speak with assurance of having located fundamental cultural tension.[51]

male fear of female sexuality and its challenge to the capacity of particular individuals to act and live an appropriately male role. For the literature on this problem, see Wolfgang Lederer, *The Fear of Women* (New York, 1968).

[50] At this time, moreover, most psychiatric clinicians and theoreticians would agree that no model exists to extend the insights gained from individual psychodynamics to the behavior of larger social groups such as national populations or social classes.

[51] Most societies provide alternative roles to accommodate the needs of personality variants—as, for example, the shaman role in certain Siberian tribes or the accepted man-woman homosexual of certain American Indian tribes. In the nineteenth-century English-speaking world such roles as that of the religious enthusiast and the chronic female invalid or hysteric may well have provided such modalities. But a period of peculiarly rapid or widespread social change can make even such available role alternatives inadequate mechanisms

Students of nineteenth-century American and Western European society have long been aware of the desire of a growing number of women for a choice among roles different from the traditional one of mother and housekeeper. It was a theme of Henry James, Henrik Ibsen, and a host of other, perhaps more representative if less talented, writers. Women's demands ranged from that of equal pay for equal work and equal education for equal intelligence to more covert demands for abortion, birth control information, and sexual autonomy within the marriage relationship. Their demands paralleled and were in large part dependent upon fundamental social and economic developments. Technological innovation and economic growth, changed patterns of income distribution, population concentrations, demographic changes in terms of life expectancy and fertility all affected woman's behavior and needs. Fewer women married; many were numbered among the urban poor. Such women had to become self-supporting and at the same time deal with the changed self-image that self-support necessitated. Those women who married generally did so later, had fewer children, and lived far beyond the birth of their youngest child. At the same time ideological developments began to encourage both men and women to aspire to increased independence and self-fulfillment. All these factors interacted to create new ambitions and new options for American women. In a universe of varying personalities and changing economic realities, it was inevitable that some women at least would—overtly or covertly—be attracted by such options and that a goodly number of men would find such

of adjustment for many individuals. Others in the same society may respond to the same pressures of change by demanding an undeviating acceptance of traditional role prescriptions and refusing to accept the legitimacy of such cultural variants. The role of the hysterical woman in late nineteenth-century America suggests many of the problems inherent in creating such alternative social roles. While offering both an escape from the everyday duties of wife and mother, and an opportunity for the display of covert hostility and aggression, this role inflicted great bodily (though non-organic) pain, provided no really new role or interest, and perpetuated—even increased—the patient's dependence on traditional role characteristics, especially that of passivity. The reaction of society, as suggested by the writings of most male physicians, can be described as at best an unstable compromise between patronizing tolerance and violent anger. See Carroll Smith Rosenberg, "The Hysterical Woman: Sex Roles and Role Conflict in 19th-Century America," 652-78. For useful discussions of hysteria and neurasthenia, see Ilza Veith, *Hysteria: The History of a Disease* (Chicago, 1965); Henri F. Ellenberger, *The Discovery of the Unconscious: The History and Evolution of Dynamic Psychiatry* (New York, 1970); Charles E. Rosenberg, "The Place of George M. Beard in Nineteenth-Century Psychiatry," *Bulletin of the History of Medicine*, XXXVI (May-June 1962), 245-59; John S. Haller, Jr., "Neurasthenia: The Medical Profession and the 'New Woman' of Late Nineteenth-Century," *New York State Journal of Medicine*, LXXI (Feb. 15, 1971), 473-82. Esther Fischer-Homberger has recently argued that these diagnostic categories masked an endemic male-female conflict: "Hysterie und Mysogynie—ein Aspekt der Hysteriegeschichte," *Gesnerus*, XXVI (1969), 117-27.

choices unacceptable. Certainly for the women who did so the normative role of home-bound nurturant and passive woman was no longer appropriate or functional, but became a source of conflict and anxiety.

It was inevitable as well that many men, similarly faced with a rapidly changing society, would seek in domestic peace and constancy a sense of the continuity and security so difficult to find elsewhere in their society. They would—at the very least—expect their wives, their daughters, and their family relationships generally to remain unaltered. When their female dependents seemed ill-disposed to do so, such men responded with a harshness sanctioned increasingly by the new gods of science.

Ann Douglas Wood

"The Fashionable Diseases": Women's Complaints and Their Treatment in Nineteenth-Century America

Historians of nineteenth-century American culture and society have become increasingly aware that many of the medical theories and practices of the period fall within their province rather than within that of the scientist. Furthermore, the consensus of historical opinion seems to be that nineteenth-century treatments of mental illness, "nervous" conditions, and sexual difficulties, although telling little about scientific advancement, are particularly sensitive indicators of cultural attitudes. Historians Huber and Meyer, for example, have considered the "mind cure" movement of the late nineteenth and early twentieth centuries not as incipient psychoanalysis, but as an expression of contemporary conflict-laden ideas of success and achievement. Rothman has based his recent study of development of the asylum in the Jacksonian period on the stated assumption that "the march of science cannot by itself explain the transformation in the American treatment of the insane." He proceeds to analyze the asylum and the methods it adopted as the result of the tensions and ideas of Jacksonian society.[1]

Such an approach is clearly dictated in the consideration of nineteenth-century diagnosis and treatment of American women's nervous and sexual diseases.[2] The historian reading through the health books and medical manuals of the day dealing with the topic is

Ann Douglas Wood is Assistant Professor of English at Princeton University. She is the author of various articles on the history of women in nineteenth-century America and is presently writing a book on feminism and social change.

1 See Richard Huber, *The American Idea of Success* (New York, 1971), 124–186; Donald Meyer, *The Positive Thinkers: A Study of the American Quest for Health, Wealth, and Personal Power* (New York, 1965); David Rothman, *The Discovery of the Asylum: Social Order and Disorder in the New Republic* (Boston, 1971), xvi. For another treatment of insanity in the same period, see Norman Dain, *Concepts of Insanity in the United States 1789–1865* (New Brunswick, N.J., 1964).

2 G. J. Barker-Benfield has given consideration to these medical practices from a cultural point of view in an unpublished paper entitled "The Spermatic Economy: A Nineteenth Century View of Sexuality" delivered at the Organization of American Historians meeting, April 15, 1971, at New Orleans. His primary focus is on masculine sexuality, however, while mine is on feminine sexuality. For a more general, and somewhat superficial survey of American sex mores and roles in the nineteenth century, see Milton Rugoff, *Prudery and Passion* (New York, 1971).

confronted at once with a combination of scientific imprecision and emotionally charged conviction which demands interpretation.

Books written in the period between 1840 and 1900 consistently, if questionably, assert that a large number, even the majority of middle-class American women, were in some sense ill. Catharine Esther Beecher, daughter of the famous minister Lyman Beecher and a pioneer in women's education and hygiene, took as her chief concern in later life "the *health of women and children*" which, she wrote in 1866, had become "a matter of alarming interest" to all. In *Physiology and Calisthenics* she had already warned her readers that "there is a delicacy of constitution and an increase of disease, both among mature women and young girls, that is most alarming, and such as was never known in any former period." In *Letters to the People on Health and Happiness* she attempted to back up her apocalyptic rumblings with statistics. She had asked all of the numerous women she knew in cities and towns across the United States to make a list of the ten women each knew best, and rate their health as "perfectly healthy," "well," "delicate," "sick," "invalid," and so on. Her report, which covered hundreds of middle-class women, was as "alarming" as Beecher could have desired. Milwaukee, Wisconsin, provides a typical example:

> Milwaukee, Wisc. Mrs. A. frequent sick headaches. Mrs. B. very feeble. Mrs. S. well, except chills. Mrs. L. poor health constantly. Mrs. D. subject to frequent headaches. Mrs. B. very poor health. Mrs. C. consumption. Mrs. A. pelvic displacements and weakness. Mrs. H. pelvic disorders and a cough. Mrs. B. always sick. Do not know one healthy woman in the place.[3]

The accuracy of Beecher's findings is clearly open to question. How representative of other American women were her friends? How bad did a headache have to be to qualify a woman for ill health? And what woman in 1855 wanted to admit to so crude a state as robust vitality? Heroines of the sentimental fiction so popular with the women in the middle ranks of society whose health concerned Beecher were more often than not bearing up under a burden of sickness that would have incapacitated any less noble being. Indeed, as commentators

3 Catharine E. Beecher, "The American People Starved and Poisoned," *Harper's New Monthly Magazine*, XXXII (1866), 771; *Physiology and Calisthenics for Schools and Families* (New York, 1856), 164; *Letters to the People on Health and Happiness* (New York, 1855), 124. Her findings were still being referred to in 1870. See the popular manual, Edward B. Foote, *Plain Home Talk* (New York, 1880), 451.

on American society at the time emphasized, ill health in women had become positively fashionable and was exploited by its victims and practitioners as an advertisement of genteel sensibility and an escape from the too pressing demands of bedroom and kitchen.[4]

If the reliability of Beecher's statistics is shaky, their significance, on which this essay will focus, is not. Although American women of the eighteenth century may have been more sickly than their supposedly frail nineteenth-century descendants, they did not talk of themselves as sick; they did not define themselves through sickness, and their society apparently minimized rather than maximized their ill health, whatever its actual extent. As Meyer has argued, "attention" to a problem in a given period is as telling to the cultural historian as its actual "incidence," which may be almost impossible to determine.[5] Beecher's statistics at least reveal that a sizable number of American women wanted or needed to consider themselves ill.

Equally important, the self-diagnosis of these women was confirmed, even encouraged, by their society. Literary observers of the American scene like Cooper and Hawthorne were appalled at the delicate health of American women.[6] The doctors who specialized in women's diseases were equally gloomy and a good deal more verbose on the subject. Alcott, a noted Boston physician and author of several books on women's health, had estimated that one half of American women suffered from the "real disease" of nervousness. When Clarke of the Harvard Medical School published his controversial *Sex in Education*, he saw the ill health of middle- and upper-class American women as so pervasive that he pessimistically concluded they would soon be unable to reproduce at all. "It requires no prophet to foretell

4 For a popular satire on the subject, see Augustus Hopper, *A Fashionable Sufferer: or Chapters from Life's Comedy* (Boston, 1883). There is an interesting chapter on the subject in Page Smith, *Daughters of the Promised Land: Women in American History* (Boston, 1970), 131–140. Wendell Phillips' wife was a typical example of a long-suffering but equally long-lived victim of nervous complaints. See Irving H. Bartlett, *Wendell Phillips: Brahmin Radical* (Boston, 1961), 79. One could multiply examples almost endlessly of women of this period who never expected to live through the next year and survived into their eighties and nineties. Still this evidence, like all the evidence in this area, is ambiguous. There are many diseases and ailments which, in the absence of sufficient medical know-how, can become chronic and make their victim's life a torment without ending it.

5 Meyer, *The Positive Thinkers*, 30.

6 See James Fenimore Cooper (ed. Robert E. Spiller), *Gleanings in Europe* (New York, 1930), II, 92–97; Nathaniel Hawthorne, *Our Old Home*, in *The Complete Works of Nathaniel Hawthorne* (Boston, 1898), VII, 66–68, 390–391.

that the wives who are to be mothers in our republic must be drawn from trans-atlantic homes," he announced.[7]

Beecher not only emphasized that many American women in the middle and upper ranks of society were sick, but she also implied that they were ill precisely *because they were women*. Most of the ailments that she records—pelvic disorders, sick headaches, general nervousness—were regarded as symptoms of "female complaints," nervous disorders thought to be linked with the malfunctioning of the feminine sexual organs.

This is not to imply that men could not and did not display similar symptoms. Napheys, for example, in 1878, noted peevishness, listlessness, pallor, and headaches in men and boys who practiced the "secret vice" of masturbation. Beard found men and women suffering from what he termed "American nervousness."[8] No doctor implied that signs of nervous disorder were apparent only in women in nineteenth-century America, and the historian should not overlook this evidence. The fact remains, nonetheless, that to some extent the *diagnosis*, and to a greater extent the *treatment* by doctors of these symptoms in women, was different from their interpretation of the same signs in men. This difference was inevitable, because medical analysis of a woman began and ended with consideration of an organ unique to her, namely her uterus. Here, supposedly, lay the cause and the cure of many of her physical ailments. As a result of this special focus, medical reactions to female nervous complaints are indicative of nineteenth-century American attitudes not only toward disease and sexuality in general but, more significantly, toward feminine sexual identity in particular.

Doctors in America throughout the nineteenth century directed their attention to the womb in a way that seems decidedly unscientific and even obsessive to a modern observer. Popular manuals on women's

7 William A. Alcott, *The Young Woman's Book of Health* (Boston, 1950), 17; Edward H. Clarke, *Sex in Education: or a Fair Chance for Girls* (Boston, 1878), 63. For the history of similar arguments, see Willystine Goodsell, *The Education of Women: Its Social Background and Problems* (New York, 1923). In 1868, Dr. F. Saunders wrote a book quite frankly pleading with middle-class American women to have more children. See *About Women, Love, and Marriage* (New York, 1868).

8 See George H. Napheys, *The Transmission of Life: Counsels on the Nature and Hygiene of the Masculine Function* (Philadelphia, 1889), 71 ff. This was a standard analysis and countless supporting sources could be cited. One of particular interest is *Satan and Society By a Physician* (Cincinnati, 1872). See also George Beard, *American Nervousness* (New York, 1881).

health neglected discussion of widespread and fatal diseases like breast cancer and consumption and concentrated on every type of menstrual and uterine disorder conceivable.[9] Hubbard, a professor from New Haven, addressing a medical society in 1870, explained that it seemed "as if the Almighty, in creating the female sex, *had taken the uterus and built up a woman around it.*"[10] And the uterus, so essential to womankind, was apparently a highly perilous possession. Dewees, professor of midwifery at the University of Pennsylvania in the early part of the nineteenth century, stated in his standard work on the diseases of females that woman was subject to twice the sicknesses that affected man just because she has a womb. Her uterus exercises a "paramount power" over her physical and moral system, and its sway is "no less whimsical than potent." Furthermore, "she is constantly liable to irregularities in her menstrua, and menaced severely by their consequences."[11] It was these highly contagious irregularities in her womb's workings which were thought to produce the headaches, nervousness, and feebleness detailed by Beecher. Byford, professor of gynecology in the 1860s at The University of Chicago, was moved to exclaim in his monograph on the uterus, "It is almost a pity that a woman has a womb."

Rather complacently viewing the havoc that their natural biological disadvantages wreaked on women, these doctors detailed the symptoms of a typical case of (uterine-caused) nervous prostration. Its victims, like the women on whose health Beecher reported, according to Byford, would usually lose weight: They would frequently show a peevish irritability and suffer every kind of nervous disorder ranging from hysterical fits of crying and insomnia to constipation, indigestion, headaches, and backaches.[12] Since many of the practitioners of the first half of the nineteenth century traced all of these problems to disorders of the uterus, they consequently tried to cure them through

9 See, for example, Alcott, *The Young Woman's Book of Health*; Frederick Hollick, *The Marriage Guide or Natural History of Generation* (New York, 1860); George H. Napheys, *The Physical Life of Woman: Advice to the Maiden, Wife and Mother* (Philadelphia, 1880).
10 Quoted in M. L. Holbrook, *Parturition Without Pain: A Code of Directions for Escaping from the Primal Curse* (New York, 1875), 15.
11 William P. Dewees, *A Treatise on the Diseases of Females* (Philadelphia, 1843), 17, 14. For a discussion of attitudes toward menstruation in the period, see Elaine and English Showalter, "Victorian Women and Menstruation," *Victorian Studies*, XIV (1970), 83–89.
12 William H. Byford, *A Treatise on the Chronic Inflammation and Displacements of the Unimpregnated Uterus* (Philadelphia, 1864), 22–41. For a similar discussion of symptoms, see S. Weir Mitchell, *Doctor and Patient* (Philadelphia, 1888), 25–27, and *Fat and Blood and How to Make Them* (Philadelphia, 1877), 35.

what came to be called "local treatment," remedies specifically directed at the womb. This meant that not only the woman suffering from *prolapsus uteri* as the result of childbearing or the lady with cancer of the uterus or any menstrual difficulty, but also the girl suffering from backache and an irritable disposition with no discernible problem in her uterus might well be subjected to local treatment in the period 1830–1860.

"Local treatment" could mean manual adjustment by a doctor of a slipped uterus, a problem all too current in an age of poor midwifery, and the insertion of various pessaries for its support. It was more frequently used to designate a course of local medication for everything from cancer to cantankerousness. This treatment had four stages, although not every case went through all four: a manual investigation, "leeching," "injections," and "cauterization." Dewees and Bennet, a famous English gynecologist widely read in America, both advocated placing the leeches right on the vulva or the neck of the uterus, although Bennet cautioned the doctor to count them as they dropped off when satiated, lest he "lose" some. Bennet had known adventurous leeches to advance into the cervical cavity of the uterus itself, and he noted: "I think I have scarcely ever seen more acute pain than that experienced by several of my patients under these circumstances."[13] Less distressing to a twentieth-century mind, but perhaps even more senseless, were the "injections" into the uterus advocated by these doctors. The uterus became a kind of catch-all, or what one exasperated doctor referred to as a "Chinese toy shop": Water, milk and water, linseed tea, and "decoction of marshmellow . . . tepid or cold" found their way inside nervous women patients.[14] The final step, performed at this time, one must remember, with no anesthetic but a little opium or alcohol, was cauterization, either through the application of nitrate of silver, or, in cases of more severe infection, through the use of the much stronger hydrate of potassa, or even the "actual cautery," a "white-hot iron" instrument.[15] The principle here is medically understandable and even sound: to drive out one infection by creating a greater inflammation, and thus provoking the blood cells to activity great enough to heal both irritations. But the treatment was used, it must be remembered, even when there was no uterine infection, and it was subject to great

13 James Henry Bennet, *A Practical Treatise on Inflammation of the Uterus, Its Cervix and Appendages and on Its Connection with Other Uterine Diseases* (Philadelphia, 1864), 237.
14 *Ibid.*, 224.
15 *Ibid.*, 255; Byford, *A Treatise on the Chronic Inflammation*, 152.

abuses in itself as its best practitioners realized. "It is an easy matter," Byford noted, "to do violence to the mucous membrane by a very little rudeness of management." In a successful case, the uterus was left "raw and bleeding" and the patient in severe pain for several days; in an unsuccessful one, severe hemorrhage and terrible pain might result.[16] It should be noted that the cauterization process, whether by chemicals or by the iron, had to be repeated several times at intervals of a few days.[17]

In the 1870s and 1880s, this form of treatment was largely dropped. Austin, in his book *Perils of American Women*, came out against local treatment and dismissed cauterization as a relic of the barbaric past of a decade ago:

> Thus it happened that thousands of women have been doomed to undergo the nitrate-of-silver treatment—their mental agony and physical torture were accounted nothing—in cases where soap and water and a gentle placebo would have been amply sufficient.[18]

Austin had his own panacea for women's nervous diseases, however. He was a devoted believer in the Philadelphia doctor S. Weir Mitchell and his famous "rest cure."

Firmly opposed to the cauterization school, Mitchell evolved a method of his own, which, in his own words, was "a combination of entire rest and of excessive feeding, made possible by passive exercise obtained through steady use of massage and electricity."[19] When he said "entire rest," he meant it. For some six weeks, the patient was removed from her home, and allowed to see no one except the doctor and a hired nurse. Confined to her bed flat on her back, she was permitted neither to read, nor, in some cases, even to rise to urinate. The massage treatment which covered the whole body lasted an hour daily. Becoming progressively more vigorous, it was designed to counteract the debilitating effects of such a prolonged stay in bed. Meanwhile the patient was expected to eat steadily, and gain weight

16 *Ibid.*, 103, 117, 158, 164.
17 Bennet, *A Practical Treatise on Inflammation of the Uterus*, 244.
18 G. L. Austin, *Perils of American Women: or, A Doctor's Talk with Maiden, Wife, and Mother* (Boston, 1883), 198, 158–160. See also Monfort B. Allen and Amelia C. McGregor, *The Glory of Woman, or Love, Marriage, and Maternity* (Philadelphia, 1896), 241.
19 Mitchell, *Fat and Blood*, 7. This cure, since it did not focus directly on the uterus, could be used on men as well as women, but rarely was. Significantly, in twenty-four case histories described by Mitchell in an account of his method, only one involved was a male. Furthermore, this man was suffering from consumption rather than a nervous complaint. See *Fat and Blood*, 93.

daily. Mitchell's claims to have cured menstrual disorders and every kind of "nervous" ailment met with widespread acceptance. He was the best known and most successful woman's doctor of his generation.

Both the local treatment and the rest cure look to a modern viewer at best like very imperfect forms of medical treatment for complex problems. The first was always painful and often fruitless; the second was frequently tedious and occasionally irrelevant. Both, as we will see, could exacerbate rather than diminish the nervous state they were designed to cure. One's first temptation is to dismiss them as the products of an unscientific age, and there is ample evidence to support such an attitude.

Before the Civil War the American doctor was quite simply ignorant, and even his post-Civil War successor did not receive the training expected of a doctor today. Few medical schools before 1860 required more than two years of attendance; almost none provided clinical experience for their fledgling physicians.[20] Furthermore, gynecology at this period was perhaps the weakest link in the already weak armor of the nineteenth-century doctor's medical knowledge. Lectures on "midwifery" and the sexual organs, as Elizabeth Blackwell was to learn, usually provided a professor more opportunity for dirty jokes than for the dissemination of knowledge.[21] J. Marion Sims, a pioneer in gynecological surgery, frequently lamented the frightening ignorance which seemed especially to attend doctors on the subject of women's ailments. He wrote feelingly about one lady who had long suffered from internal problems and from the cures designed to relieve them:

> The leeching, the physicking, the blistering, the anodynes, the baths, the mountain excursions, the sea-bathing and sea voyages that this poor patient suffered and endured for years are almost incredible![22]

He restored her to health by a simple operation.

Doctors had some excuse for their ignorance of woman's internal organs, although little for their pretended knowledge. Ladies were expected, even by their doctors, to object to "local examination,"

20 See J. Marion Sims, *The Story of My Life* (New York, 1884).

21 Elizabeth Blackwell, *Pioneer Work in Opening the Medical Profession to Women* (New York, 1895), 257–259.

22 Quoted in Seale Harris, *Woman's Surgeon: The Life Story of J. Marion Sims* (New York, 1950), 181.

to prefer modesty to health, and many of them did.[23] The French physician, Médéric Louis Elie Moreau de St. Méry, had commented on the unwillingness of Philadelphia women in the late eighteenth century to undergo even crucially necessary medical scrutiny, and Dewees, in the same city at the start of the next century, recounted several tales of women who put themselves in the hands of quacks rather than endure this ordeal. Bennet, the London authority, crusaded against the "absolutely criminal" delicacy of doctors who respected such fears in female patients.[24] He rightly attributed the birth of gynecology as a science to the increased possibility of uterine examination because of the use of the speculum and gradually changing attitudes.

Yet the ignorance of American doctors and the difficulties in the way of overcoming it certainly cannot explain the *forms* of the treatments they devised for nervous women. To understand these, one must cease to regard these fledgling gynecological techniques as part of a developing science and scrutinize them as part and parcel of a fully formed culture, and, as such, sharing in all the biases and assumptions about women which that culture possessed. This in no way suggests a failure of concern or good will on the part of nineteenth-century American doctors. Undeniably, the majority of these physicians were anxious to aid their female patients. J. Marion Sims, who devoted his life to the intelligent relief of woman's diseases is only an illustrious example of what was surely a numerous class. Yet it seems equally undeniable that a complicated if unacknowledged psychological warfare was being waged between the doctors and their patients. Even the best-intentioned practitioner was forced into a role in part hostile to his woman patients simply by the misconceptions he was trained to hold. Until well after the Civil War, for example, physicians in America, as in Europe, arguing by analogy with the animal world, maintained that woman's fertile period was right before and after

23 Charles D. Meigs, a conservative gynecologist of Philadelphia, wrote in 1848 that he "rejoiced" at the difficulty of making local examinations since it was "an evidence of a high and worthy grade of moral feeling" in American women (quoted in Harvey Graham, *Eternal Eve: The History of Gynecology and Obstetrics* [New York, 1951], 495).

24 Dewees, *A Treatise on the Diseases of Females*, 224–225, 242–243; Bennet, *A Practical Treatise on Inflammation of the Uterus*, 19. Another widely used foreign authority made the same point. J. W. von Scanzoni (trans. Augustus K. Gardner), *A Practical Treatise on the Diseases of the Sexual Organs of Women* (New York, 1861), 37–38. See also Byford, *A Treatise on the Chronic Inflammation*, 98.

menstruation.[25] Hence the nineteenth-century American woman, perhaps in ill health and eager to practice a semi-respectable form of birth control, conscientiously slept with her spouse squarely in the middle of her menstrual cycle.

Given the presumably disastrous results action on this belief must have produced, one must turn from the world of science to the realm of culture to explain its surprising tenacity, and the equal persistence with which treatments like cauterization and the rest cure kept their hold in the medical world. Physicians both of the cauterist school and of the rest-cure school brought certain unexplored but pervasive presuppositions to their work. They assumed, as already mentioned, that women were physically dominated by their wombs. They held, moreover, even less carefully scrutinized beliefs about the social and psychological nature of femininity and its role and responsibilities in their society, beliefs which colored their attitude toward the illness of their female patients.

The first point to be noted is the element of distrust, even of condemnation lurking behind their diagnoses. Physicians tended to stress a certain moral depravity inherent in feminine nervous disorders and to waver significantly between labeling it a result and analyzing it as the cause of the physical symptoms involved. The patient, according to Byford's experience, may become "a changed woman"—irritable, indecisive, lacking in will power, morose, jealous. She is likely to show "a guarded cunning, a deceitful and perverted consciousness"; indeed, she may commit "acts of a depraved and indecent nature," and neglect her "duty in all the relations of life."[26]

In part, Byford was indirectly expressing his doubts as to whether or not his patients were truly sick. Such doubts were widely shared. Dixon, in *Woman and Her Diseases*, cautioned the physician always to pay "profound attention" to what he delicately called "moral circum-

25 Graham, *Eternal Eve*, 451. For an example, see Napheys, *The Transmission of Life*, 190–191.

26 Byford, *A Treatise on the Chronic Inflammation*, 22–41. Mitchell also testified to this pattern of moral degradation, *Fat and Blood*, 27, 28. One should add here that condemnation disguised as diagnosis and punishment offered as cure were hardly unique to medical treatment of women in this period. Napheys hints at "surgical operations" to curb masturbation in men and advocates blisterings and "infibulation" (*Transmission of Life*, 80–83). Rugoff discusses various painful contraptions used to prevent nocturnal emission (*Prudery and Passion*, 53). I am simply trying to show how two particular courses of punitive medicine reflected and supported culturally induced ideas about female sexual identity.

stances." These moral causes were often, he warned, not of a nature "calculated to move our sympathy," and he was all too aware that women were cunning enough to "pretend hysteric attacks, in order to excite sympathy and obtain some desired end."[27] Even more important, of course, was the doctor's unspoken guess at the *reason* behind this calculated exploitation of illness. Who can doubt that, in an age when sex and childbirth involved very real threats to the health and life of women, some women would use the pretext of being "delicate" as a way not only of escaping household labor but also of closing the bedroom door while avoiding the guilt consequent upon a more flagrant defiance of their "duties"? Harriet Beecher Stowe understood the process and dramatized it at its worst in her portrait of Mrs. St. Clair (in *Uncle Tom's Cabin*) lying on her sofa, shirking responsibility and demanding attention. And Stowe herself, who suffered the burden of relative poverty and of a weak and dependent but potent husband, took periodic refuge from him and their numerous offspring in those havens of escape, the health establishments.[28]

Clearly, in the case of a woman like Stowe, however, we do not have the simple problem of a woman failing to live up to her sexual and domestic responsibilities as we do in the case of her own fictional creation, Mrs. St. Clair. It is rather that her responsibilities, despite all her histrionic and martyred posturings about them, were genuinely more than she could handle: They were almost killing her. Doctors of the period were intermittently and partially aware of the frustrations inherent in the middle-class woman's lot. Alexander Combe, the Scottish phrenologist so influential in America, attributed the high level of insanity in women of this class to the monotony of their lives.[29] In 1834, Dr. Alcott of Boston advocated that ladies be trained as nurses because "these are individuals who need some employment, for the sake even of the emolument; but more especially to save them from ennui, and disgust, and misery—sometimes from speedy or more protracted sui-

27 Edward H. Dixon, *Woman and Her Diseases from the Cradle to the Grave* (New York, 1857), 134, 140.

28 For a discussion of Stowe's marital problems and responsibilities, see the following biographies: Joanna Johnston, *Runaway to Heaven: The Story of Harriet Beecher Stowe* (New York, 1963) and Forrest Wilson, *Crusader in Crinoline: The Life of Harriet Beecher Stowe* (Philadelphia, 1941). Also of value is Edmund Wilson, *Patriotic Gore: Studies in the Literature of the American Civil War* (New York, 1966), 3–58.

29 "Insanity: From Combe's Work on Mental Derangement," *Ladies' Magazine*, VIII (1835), 461–463.

cide."[30] Professional work, however, was hardly a socially acceptable escape from a lady's situation, but sickness, that very nervous condition brought on by the frustrations of her life, was.

Yet, many doctors, despite the apparent conscious understanding shown in the analysis of Combe and Alcott, in practice tended unconsciously to see the neuralgic ailments of their female patients as a threatening and culpable shirking of their duties as wives and mothers, and to look upon those duties as the cure, not the cause, of the illness. Self-sacrifice and altruism on a spiritual level, and childbearing and housework on a more practical one, constituted healthy femininity in the eyes of most nineteenth-century Americans. Dr. Clarke of Harvard, who believed that girls of the 1870s were ill because they were quite literally destroying their wombs and their childbearing potential by presuming to pursue a course of higher education intended by nature only for the male sex, was very much a spokesman for the doctors of his generation.

One finds an underlying logic running through popular books by physicians on women's diseases to the effect that ladies get sick *because* they are unfeminine—in other words, sexually aggressive, intellectually ambitious, and defective in proper womanly submission and selflessness. Bad health habits were often put forth by doctors and others as causes of nervous complaints. But these, consisting as they did of improper diet, light reading, late hours, tight lacing, and inadequate clothing, were in themselves a badge of the "fashionable" and flirtatious female, only a step removed in popular imagination from the infamous one. Byford believed that "the influence of lascivious books" and frequent "indulgence" in intercourse would precipitate neuralgia.[31] Significantly, in Mitchell's fiction, the sick woman is almost invariably the closest thing he has to a villainess and she is often intelligent and usually predatory to an extreme. In *Roland Blake*, published in 1886, Octapia Darnell, an invalid, is branded by her name. Octapuslike, she uses her sickness like tentacles to try to squeeze the life out of her innocent young cousin, Olivia Wynne. Although we see her in genuine nervous spasms, Mitchell never shows her seized by a convulsion where it would be inconvenient to her purposes, nor does he let us forget that when she needs physical strength to accomplish her will, she always summons it. Again, the heroine of *Constance Trescott* (1905), his last and best novel, is driven by a demonic will to possess utterly where she loves and to

30 W. A. Alcott, "Female Attendance on the Sick," *Ladies' Magazine*, VII (1834), 302.
31 Byford, *A Treatise on the Chronic Inflammation*, 15.

revenge totally where she hates. Rather predictably she turns to invalidism at the book's close to gain her ends.

It is not that Mitchell totally condemns these women. Instead, he understands them, and adopts a tone of pitying patronage toward them. He thinks they are genuinely sick, but he believes, as did Clarke, that the root of their sickness was their failure to be women, to sacrifice themselves for others, and to perform their feminine duties. Typically, Octapia Darnell has a brief period of improvement when a "recent need to think of others had beneficently taken her outside of the slowly narrowing circle of self-care and self-contemplation, and, by relieving her of some of the morbid habits of disease, had greatly bettered her physical condition."[32] The truth is that Mitchell does not even need to blame or punish her: In his view, nature has conveniently done that job for him.

Mitchell's analysis, then, one standard with doctors in the nineteenth century, served an important psychological purpose, whatever its medical validity. The doctor, on some unacknowledged level, feared his female patient. Could he so emphasize the diseased potency of woman's unique and mysterious organ, the womb, if he did not worry that his sex, the constant companion of hers, was in some way menaced? How comfortable Mitchell must have felt, when, addressing a graduating Radcliffe class, he expressed his clearly faint hope "that no wreck from these shores will be drifted into my dockyard."[33] They might begin as his competitors, but, despite it—in fact, because of it—they would end as his patients.

Mitchell and his peers could indeed afford to pity the fair sex, even perhaps to "cure" them. Yet the consequent "cures" bore unmistakable signs of their culturally determined origin, for they made a woman's womb very much a liability. Since her disease was unconsciously viewed as a symptom of a failure in femininity, its remedy was designed both as a punishment and an agent of regeneration, for it forced her to acknowledge her womanhood and made her totally dependent on the professional prowess of her male doctor. The cauterizer, with his injections, leeches, and hot irons seems suggestive of a veiled but aggressively hostile male sexuality and superiority, and the rest-cure expert carried this spirit to a sophisticated culmination.

32 S. Weir Mitchell, *Roland Blake* (Boston, 1886), 254.

33 Anna Robeson Burr (ed.), *Weir Mitchell: His Life and Letters* (New York, 1929), 374. Mitchell makes the same point in *Doctor and Patient*, 13.

Mitchell's treatment depended in actuality not so much on the techniques of rest and overfeeding, as on the commanding personality and charismatic will of the physician. "A slight, pale lad of no physical strength" by his own description, he moved as a young man in the shadow of his dominating, joyous, strong doctor-father.[34] To be the strong, healing male in a world of ailing, dependent women had obvious charms for him. "Electric with fascination" for women as his granddaughter saw him, he acknowledged that he played the "despot" in the sickroom, and boasted of reducing patients to the docility of children.[35] Doctors had always preferred to keep women in ignorance, and Mitchell was no exception. In a characteristically urbane and aphoristic remark, he said, "Wise women choose their doctors and trust them. The wisest ask the fewest questions."[36] But he wanted to be more than trusted: He wished to be revered, even adored, and he succeeded. The totality of the power he could acquire is revealed in a letter he received from a sick woman who positively grovels before him as she rhapsodizes on his potency:

> Whilst laid by the heels in a country-house with an attack of grippe, also an invalid from gastric affection, the weary eyes of a sick woman fall upon your face in the *Century* of this month—a thrill passed through me—at last I saw the true physician![37]

It is clear, moreover, that Mitchell encouraged this worshiping attitude as an important element in his "cure." A doctor, in his view, if he had the proper mesmeric powers of will, could become almost god-like.[38] Women doctors would always be inferior to male physicians, he believed, precisely because they could not exercise such tyranny: They were unable to "obtain the needed control over those of their own sex."[39] Mitchell here skated on the edge of a theory of primitive healing through mesmeric sexual powers.[40] Furthermore, his treatment was designed to make his female patients take his view of the

34 Burr, *Weir Mitchell*, 37. The best recent biography is Ernest Earnest, *S. Weir Mitchell: Novelist and Physician* (Philadelphia, 1950).

35 Mitchell, *Fat and Blood*, 48.

36 Mitchell, *Doctor and Patient*, 48.

37 Quoted in Burr, *Weir Mitchell*, 290.

38 There are striking similarities between Mitchell's conception of his role, and that of Freudian psychiatrists. See Earnest, *Weir Mitchell*, 250.

39 Mitchell, *Fat and Blood*, 39.

40 He tried hypnosis in his practice, though with little success. See Earnest, *Weir Mitchell*, 229. Robert Herrick was to dramatize this aspect of the physician's role in *The Healer* (New York, 1911) and in *Together* (New York, 1909).

doctor's role. They were allowed to see no one but him, and to talk of their ills and problems to no one else. As doctor he became the only spot of energy, the only source of *life*, during the enforced repose of a cure process.

Undoubtedly, if Mitchell were aware of what he was doing, he would have felt it justifiable and even merciful. He was curing his patients—by restoring them to their femininity or, in other words, by subordinating them to an enlightened but dictatorial male will. His admirers delighted to tell how, when a strangely recalcitrant patient refused to rise from bed after Mitchell had decreed that her rest cure was over, Mitchell threatened to move into bed with her if she did not get up, and even started to undress. When he got to his pants, she got up. Although the story may well be apocryphal, its spirit is not. Not surprisingly, the lady in question was fleeing the fact where she embraced the shadow, for symbolically, Mitchell, like his cauterizing predecessor, played the role of possessor, even impregnator, in the cure process. Dominated, overfed often to the point of obesity, caressed and (quite literally) vibrating, were not his patients being returned to health—to womanhood?[41] The only other time that the Victorian lady took to her bed and got fat was, in fact, before delivery. J. Marion Sims had noted that his colleagues were erroneously wont to lament about a sick woman: "If she could only have a child, it would cure her."[42] Although he was a generation later, Mitchell was not so different from the doctors Sims opposed who looked to pregnancy for the cure of all feminine ills.

Here one senses a clue to the pertinacity with which doctors told women anxious to avoid pregnancy that they should sleep with their husbands only during what we now know as their most fertile period. In a sense, the practices and writings of the medical profession provide the other half of the picture of ideal womanhood presented in the sentimental literature of the day. Woman was at her holiest, according to the genteel novels and poetry of Victorian America, as a mother. Pregnancy itself, however, was avoided by the authors of such works as completely as the act of impregnation. The medical manual took on the role of frankness disowned by its more discreet companion. All the logic of contemporary medical lore adds up to the lesson that women were at their most feminine when they were pregnant. Pregnant, they were visible emblems of masculine potency.

41 For examples of these weight gains, see Mitchell, *Fat and Blood*, 80–94. One 5′ 8″ woman went from 118 lbs. to 169 lbs.

42 Quoted in Harris, *Woman's Surgeon*, 181.

It is impossible to determine how many nineteenth-century middle-class American women went to doctors, just as it is difficult to tell how real their much-advertised ailments were. Reluctant as American women apparently were to undergo local examination, many of them presumably stayed home and suffered with no medical aid except that provided by earlier versions of Lydia Pinkham's patent medicine. Others trusted to the hydropathic remedies provided at numerous water-cures or used homeopathic drugs, both of which represented forms of protest against current medical practices.[43] Furthermore, the majority of women suffering from uterine and/or nervous disorders who underwent a form of local treatment or, later, the rest cure, were presumably in real distress and glad of whatever help their physician could offer.[44] Some, however, were undoubtedly using prescribed treatments for their own purposes. According to numerous masculine and feminine observers, many women grew positively addicted to local treatment as others did later to the rest cure, but, not surprisingly, these women have not left any direct confessions to posterity.[45]

What we do have record of is a masked but almost hysterical paranoia among a small group of feminist hygiene experts and lady doctors, a paranoia stemming from their exaggerated but astute perception of the unconscious purposes underlying the attitudes and practices of doctors with women patients. In their excited view, current medical treatment was patently not science, for which they professed respect, but a part of their male-dominated culture, for which they had both fear and contempt. They saw it as a form of rape, designed to keep woman prostrate, a perpetual patient dependent on a doctor's supposed professional expertise.

43 Both the homeopathic school, with its distrust of drugs and violent remedies, and the hydropathic school with its reliance on the efficacy of water, advocated relatively mild treatments for women's ailments. For examples, see John A. Tarbell, *Homeopathy Simplified: or Domestic Practice Made Easy* (Boston, 1859), 214–218; R. T. Trall, *The Hydropathic Encyclopedia: A System of Hydropathy and Hygiene* (New York, 1852), II, 285–296. It must also be added, however, that such doctors were outside the higher echelons of American medicine. Furthermore, it is striking how many women turned to such doctors as a result of bad experiences at the hands of more orthodox doctors. In other words, it seems likely that the lady at the water-cure had also sampled other forms of treatment.

44 Angelina Grimké, for instance, a famous abolitionist and speaker for women's rights, suffered terribly from *prolapsus uteri*. See Gerda Lerner, *The Grimké Sisters from South Carolina* (Boston, 1967), 288–292.

45 See Austin, *Perils of American Women*, 94–95.

No one expressed this attitude better than did two Beecher women, Catharine Esther Beecher, who crusaded against local treatment, and her grandniece Charlotte Perkins Gilman, who protested against Mitchell's rest cure a generation later. Each of them wrote a work dedicated to exposing what they felt were the unstated motives of physicians treating women patients. In *Letters to the People on Health and Happiness*, Beecher described with heavy-handed irony the ineffectuality of the string of "talented, highly-educated and celebrated" doctors who had tried to cure her own severe nervous ailments (115).[46] She consumed sulphur and iron, she let one doctor sever the "wounded nerves from their centres," she let another cover her spine with "tartar emetic pustules," she subjected herself to "animal magnetism" and the water cure, but all to no purpose.

Beecher does not admit to having personally undergone local treatment, but when she discusses it, her tone changes from the condescending playfulness she uses to devastate such methods as the "tartar emetic pustules" to one of outraged horror. Doctors playing professional games with pustules had kept her sick perhaps, but they had left her with her honor. Local treatment, roughly equivalent to rape according to Beecher, seldom allowed a lady to retain that valuable possession. It is "performed," she explains, "with bolted doors and curtained windows, and with no one present but patient and operator," by doctors who have all too often "freely advocated the doctrine that there was no true marriage but the union of persons who were in love." Predictably, these immoral practitioners were said to have "lost all reverence for the Bible." With his "interesting" female patients, such a physician "naturally," in Beecher's gloomy view, tries "to lead them to adopt *his views of truth and right*" on moral matters. "Then he daily has all the opportunities indicated [through local examination]. Does anyone need more than to hear these facts to know what the not unfrequent results must be?" she ominously concludes (136). By the time she is through with this subject, she is calling the female patients "victims" and lamenting their "entire helplessness" (137). She refers the reader to an appended letter from a woman doctor, Mrs. R. B. Gleason of the Elmira Water Cure in New York, who solemnly testifies that manual replacement for *prolapsus uteri* was "in most cases totally needless, and in many decidedly injurious" (6*). After such evidence, Beecher can hardly avoid "the painful inquiry": "how can a woman

46 All page references will be to the edition already cited.

ever know to whom she may safely entrust herself . . . in such painful and peculiar circumstances?" (138).

Gilman, a brilliant theorist and critic on women's role in American society, went through periods of nervous prostration strikingly similar to those of her aged relative's.[47] She sampled the fruits of medical wisdom a few decades later, undergoing Mitchell's rest cure. She expressed the result in a story entitled "The Yellow Wall Paper," published in 1890, and designed to convince Mitchell "of the error of his ways."[48]

The story concerns a married woman, the mother of a young child, suffering from "nervous" disorders, and clearly laboring under disguised but immense (and justifiable) hostility for both her spouse and her offspring. Her husband, John, who is a doctor, is ostensibly overseeing her cure, but is in reality intent with sadistic ignorance on destroying her body and soul. John, apparently modeled on Mitchell himself, confines his wife to a country house, which to her seems "haunted," remote from friends or neighbors. Presumably hoping to force her back to her feminine and maternal functions, he symbolically makes her sleep in an old nursery. With its barred windows, rings attached to the wall, bed nailed to the floor, and disturbing and torn yellow wallpaper, this nursery all too significantly and frighteningly resembles a cell for the insane. Treating her like a pet, the doctor alternates condescending tenderness ("Then he took me in his arms and called me a blessed little goose" [323]) with threats of punishment ("John says if I don't pick up faster he shall send me to Weir Mitchell in the fall" [326]). Since John "never was nervous in his life" (323), and is a doctor "of high standing" (320) to boot, he can "laugh" at her fears because he "knows there is no *reason* to suffer, and that satisfies him" (323). Complacently smug in his masculine insensitivity and his professional superiority, he is totally obtuse about the nature of her suffering and its possible cure. An early-day "mad housewife," she has been so browbeaten by his calm assumption of superiority that she can only timidly air the frightening truth:

> John is a physician, and *perhaps*—(I would not say it to a living soul, of course, but this is dead paper and a great relief to my mind)—*perhaps* that is one reason I do not get well faster [320].

47 See her own account in her autobiography, *The Living of Charlotte Perkins Gilman* (New York, 1935), 90 ff. She may have felt her similarities to Beecher since she named her daughter after her.

48 All page references will be to Charlotte Perkins Gilman, "The Yellow Wall Paper," in William Dean Howells (ed.), *The Great Modern American Short Stories* (New York, 1920), 320–337; Gilman, *Living of Charlotte Perkins Gilman*, 121.

He has left her with only one recourse, and she takes it. Slowly but steadily, she goes mad, thus dramatically pointing up the results of his "cure." At the story's close, she is creeping on hands and knees with insane persistence around the walls of her chamber. In a symbolic moment, her husband, suspicious about her behavior, breaks down the door she has finally locked against him. His act is the essence of his "cure" and her "problem"; like Catharine Beecher, Gilman sees the doctor "treating" his patient as violating her. But this patient is finally beyond feeling. When John faints away in shock at her state, their roles have been reversed: *He* has become the woman, the nervous, susceptible, sickly patient, and she wonders with a kind of calm, self-centered vindictiveness fully equal to his former arrogance: "Now why should that man have fainted? But he did, and right across my path by the wall, so that I had to creep over him every time!" (337). She has won, because she can ignore him now as completely as he ignored her, but she has won at the cost of becoming what he subconsciously sought to make her—a creeping creature, an animal and an automaton.

Beecher's *Letters* and Gilman's story are both intended to convey a nightmare vision of sick women dependent on male doctors who use their professional superiority as a method to prolong their patients' sickness and, consequently, the supremacy of their own sex. Both writers also hint, however, at a possible escape for such feminine victims. Beecher, according to her account, was finally cured by a timely tip from a *woman* physician, Dr. Elizabeth Blackwell. Gilman's heroine knows what her cure should be—work and intellectual stimulation—although she is too cowed and powerless to insist on it. Both Gilman and Beecher simply in writing their works, are implying that the untutored common sense of two women can outdo the professionally trained brains of those male doctors who labored in vain to cure them. Both are thus in essence urging that a woman should be independent, that *she be her own physician*, so that the real business of healing can get under way.[49]

After all, Beecher and Gilman realized, there might be two possible ways of looking at the much-advertised problem of the increasingly bad health of middle-class American women. Doctors like Clarke and Mitchell liked to think that the fault lay with the women themselves, who were neglecting their homes and pursuing such an unfeminine goal as higher education. Women like Beecher and Gilman, shrewdly re-

49 The demand for women doctors could be quite explicit. See Julia Ward Howe (ed.), *A Reply to Dr. E. H. Clarke's 'Sex in Education'* (Boston, 1874), 158.

versing the charge, queried whether the blame might not belong to the men who were supposed to cure them and to the professional training which was supposed to enable them to do it. Harriot Hunt, one of the most impressive of the early women doctors in America, put the challenge succinctly: "Man, man alone has had the care of *us* [women], and I would ask how *our health stands now*. Does it do credit to *his* skill?"[50] Hunt is clearly aware that what had been a condemnation of women (the charge of ill health) could be used as a powerful weapon in their defense. The women doctors who began to appear on the American scene in the 1850s saw women's diseases as a *result* of submission, and promoted independence from masculine domination, whether professional or sexual, as their cure for feminine ailments.[51]

In dealing with these pioneer women doctors and their theories, one is at once aware that here, too, the issues are inevitably cultural rather than scientific. Their primary aim, often an unconscious one, was to free ailing women from male control. On the one hand, this desire could and did further scientific advancement, for their distrust of the male doctor made them eager to reject aspects of medical practice that were in fact unscientific, if not harmful. Their paranoid fear that the male doctor was degrading his female patient paradoxically led them to some sound conclusions about the worthlessness of many drugs and the necessity of sanitation and preventive medicine. On the other hand, the same fear also made them, on occasion, throw out the baby with the bath water. Their hostility to the male doctor too often became a hostility to any scientific practice which appeared to their oversensitive consciousness as an invasion of the patient's privacy. Gynecological surgery, for example, which, despite undoubted abuse, represented a significant step in medical treatment of women, was often rejected by these early pioneers. Yet one must keep in mind that what is unwitting stupidity from a scientific point of view can be (albeit equally unwitting) shrewdness from a social or political point of view. These women bypassed science in large part because they had a goal quite distinct from its advancement: namely, the advancement of their sex.

Nowhere is this aim clearer than in the work of Hunt, a well-known, if home-trained, Boston practitioner and the most outspoken

50 Harriot K. Hunt, *Glances and Glimpses: or Fifty Years Social, Including Twenty Years Professional Life* (Boston, 1856), 414.

51 For the history of women doctors in America, see Kate Campbell-Hurd, *Medical Women in America: A Short History of the Pioneer Medical Women of America and of a Few of Their Colleagues in England* (Fort Pierce Beach, Fla., 1933); Esther Pohl Lovejoy, *Women Doctors of the World* (New York, 1957).

of the first generation of women doctors. Her autobiography, *Glances and Glimpses* (1856), published when she was forty-one, is clearly oversimplified, one-sided, and sentimentalized, but one must keep in mind that she was writing not a scientific report, nor even a history, but rather a special kind of mythologized propaganda, a scenario for a sexual revolution.

The ritualized drama begins with Hunt's explanation of why she chose medicine for a career—her stunned realization of the profound ignorance of the male doctors treating feminine diseases (81).[52] Her ailing sister was put through a course of remedies somewhat similar to the one Beecher tried, and she, and Harriot, came away having "lost all confidence in medicine" (85). The male practitioner here emerges as one of the villains of Hunt's piece. According to her testimony, he usually made his living by creating false dependencies in his female patients, by keeping them ignorant and totally reliant on his shortsighted or even harmful remedies (32, 89). Indeed, Hunt insinuates, his professional training led him actually to want his patients to be sick so that he would have something to do with all the games he had learned.

Professional exploitation by the doctor of his female patient was a mask, in Hunt's opinion, for a deeper and more humiliating sexual exploitation. Like Catharine Beecher, Hunt was publically and loudly aghast at local examinations. They were "*too often unnecessary*" (271) and their moral effects were terrible. Many medical men, in her view, were skeptics, who lived "sensually" (177), and contaminated their patients. At this point, Hunt's scenario grows both alarmist and lurid. A woman once forced to submit to local examination, Hunt reveals, was well on the road to ruin: She felt "disgraced, and a don't careativeness [*sic*] and sort of sullen desperation" settled on her (184). Yet this fantasized sexual violation was dreadful, according to Hunt, not so much because of the moral degradation involved as because of the patient's loss of control and her consequent dependence on the doctor's will. In describing a physician who took advantage of a patient and left her with an illegitimate child, she explains significantly: His "will overmastered the weaker will of his patient" (376).

The doctor's was not the only malevolent will pitted against his woman patient's will in Hunt's story. The villainous physicians who kept women sick were only collaborating with the villainous husbands

52 All page references will be to Hunt, *Glances and Glimpses*. For similar motivation in another woman doctor see Helen MacKnight Doyle, *A Child Went Forth* (New York, 1934), 15–18.

who had caused their illnesses in the first place. In her favorite role as minister-doctor, she collected many of what she called the "heart-histories" of her women patients, and publicized them as evidence that women's "physical maladies" stemmed from "concealed sorrows" (139), often at the "sins" of their spouses (159).[53] Hunt never married, but she was always ready with sympathy for those who had. One married patient after another apparently confided to her: "I thank heaven, my dear doctor, that you are a woman; for now I can tell you the truth about my health. It is not my body that is sick but my heart" (120).

Hunt's vision, so filled with villains and victims, has a savior to offer as well. This heroine is of course Hunt herself, as a woman doctor and simply as a woman. As a doctor, she dramatically renounced "medical science" as "full of unnecessary details," but without "a soul . . . a huge, unwieldy body—distorted, deformed, inconsistent and complicated" (121). Medicine was generally "worse than useless" (371), she remarked; moreover, it did not meet her "perception of the dignity of the human body." She did not enter "the medical life through physics, but through metaphysics" (127). She was only too eager to announce her disavowal of "science," because she considered her disrespect precisely her strongest claim to respect. Flaunting her anti-professionalism like a medal of honor, she loved to proclaim herself an eclectic, as indeed she was, the "disciple of no medical sect" (171), but the sworn servant of her sex.[54]

Hunt's treatment consisted of telling her patients to throw away

53 There was some medical truth underlying this apparently sentimental declaration. Aside from subjecting women to the perils of childbirth, men not infrequently unwittingly gave them syphilis. See Elizabeth Blackwell, *Essays in Medical Sociology* (London, 1902), I, 90–91.

54 Anti-professionalism in women doctors had another complex side which mainly lies outside the scope of this article. Women had been active medical practitioners in America as midwives until the time of the Revolution. Then licenses, obtainable only in the newly opened medical schools, which did not take women, began to be required. So, in effect, professional requirements had spelled the demise of the woman physician in the late eighteenth century. Hence, the mistrust felt for such training by her nineteenth-century feminine successor was not surprising. Unquestionably, late eighteenth-century and early nineteenth-century American doctors had welcomed and even pushed for this change (see Victor Robinson, *White-Caps: The Story of Nursing* [Philadelphia, 1946], 137), although a few regretted it (see A. Curtis, *Lectures on Midwifery and the Forms of Disease Peculiar to Women and Children* [Columbus, Ohio, 1841], 9). On the whole question of women and the professions in this period, see Gerda Lerner, "The Lady and the Mill-Girl: Changes in the Status of Women in the Age of Jackson," *Mid-Continent American Studies Journal*, X (1969), 5–15.

their medicines, begin a diary, and think of their mothers (401). The last item of this prescription is not simply the pure sentimentalism that it might appear. Hunt was symbolically turning her patients' thoughts to an acceptable but potent emblem of *female strength*.[55] It was from this source that she expected her patients to find their cure—not in the arms of their husbands, nor under the hands of the male doctor. The medicine that she gave her patients as a sure antidote to the wares peddled by her masculine colleagues was the example of her own ample and self-sufficient womanhood. Could they forget their mothers with Hunt before them?

Hunt was an ardent and proclaimed feminist and suffragist, but other women pioneers in medicine who did not share, or did not avow such sympathies, were almost without exception part of her crusade.[56] The most famous of these was Elizabeth Blackwell, usually considered the first woman doctor in America. In her girlhood an avowed admirer

55 American society throughout this period agreed on the importance and potency of motherhood. In part this was a simple rationale of the fact that, since the American father was at work, the American mother was raising the children. See Anne L. Kuhn, *The Mother's Role in Childhood Education* (New Haven, 1947); Bernard Wishy, *The Child and the Republic: The Dawn of Modern American Child Nurture* (Philadelphia, 1968), 24–29. Contemporary paeans to motherhood are legion, but see Jabez Burns, *Mothers of the Wise and Good* (Boston, 1950); Margaret C. Conklin, *Memoirs of the Mother and Wife of Washington* (Auburn, N. Y., 1851).

56 I have picked the two most famous of the early women doctors in America, but most of the others fall into similar patterns. All of them devoted themselves professionally almost exclusively to women, few of them married, and most met determined opposition from the majority of their male colleagues, in some cases amounting to what Elizabeth Blackwell called "medical starvation" (unpublished letter of Jan. 23, 1855, to Emily Blackwell in Blackwell Collection, Radcliffe Archives, Cambridge, Mass.). For works on and by the other three most famous women doctors of the period, Emily Blackwell, Mary Putnam Jacobi, and Maria Zakrewska, see the Blackwell Collection; Ruth Putnam (ed.), *Life and Letters of Mary Putnam Jacobi* (New York, 1925); *Mary Putnam Jacobi, M.D.: A Pathfinder in Medicine: With Selections from Her Writings* (New York, 1925); Rhoda Truax, *The Doctors Jacobi* (Boston, 1952); and the Jacobi papers, also at Radcliffe.

Jacobi was one of the most brilliant doctors of her day, and her monograph, *The Question of Rest for Women During Menstruation* (New York, 1877), an answer to Clarke, won the Harvard Boylston Medical Prize. For Zakrewska's autobiography, see Caroline H. Dall (ed.), *A Practical Illustration of Woman's Right to Labor: or A Letter from Marie E. Zakrewska, M.D.* (Boston, 1860); Agnes C. Victor (ed.), *A Woman's Quest: The Life of Marie E. Zakrewska, M.D.* (New York, 1924). Also of great interest, although falling outside of official professional ranks, were Lydia Folger Fowler and Mary Gove Nichols. See Frederick C. Waite, "Dr. Lydia Folger Fowler: The Second Woman to Receive the Degree of Doctor in the United States," *Annals of Medical History*, IV (1932), 290–297; T. L. Nichols and Mary S. Gove Nichols, *Marriage: Its History, Character and Results* (New York, 1854); Mary S. Gove Nichols, *Mary Lyndon, or Revelations of a Life: An Autobiography* (New York, 1855); Helen Beal Woodward, *The Bold Women* (New York, 1953), 149–180.

of the fiercely virginal goddess Diana, Blackwell always loved to project an almost monstrous force as woman's natural dowry.[57] Yet she was clearly drawn to such fantasies precisely because of her deep-seated perception and fear of the dependent role women usually played. With paradoxical logic, she explained that precisely *because* she was very "susceptible" to men and perpetually in love, she had determined never to marry. Not initially attracted to medicine, she deliberately chose it as a potentially "strong barrier between me and all ordinary marriage. I must have something to engross my thoughts, some object in life which will fulfill this vacuum and prevent this sad wearing away of the heart."[58]

Professionally, despite her soft-spoken, conciliating manner, she fought the code of the male medical establishment which in her view victimized women as surely as did matrimony. During medical school, she was shocked at the "horrible exposure" of women to male physicians, finding it "indecent for any poor woman to be subjected to such a torture."[59] In her later years, when local treatment was less common, Blackwell crusaded against its medical descendant, ovariotomy, or as she called it with characteristic dramatic flair, "the castration of women." Estimating that 1 of every 250 women in Europe had been "castrated," she collected newspaper clippings which supported her belief that young doctors were performing this operation needlessly on unsuspecting women just to obtain professional practice.[60]

The validity of Blackwell's fears is hard to estimate. Many reputable people shared them. Yet Dr. Maria Zakrewska lamented the fact that women had come to her Boston hospital insisting that their ovaries be removed as a birth control device.[61] Nonetheless, in Blackwell's eyes, male doctors were performing a kind of "vivisection"—a practice that she violently opposed in any form—on their female patients.[62] Ovariotomies for her simply dramatized the anti-woman

57 Ishbel Ross, *Child of Destiny: The First Life Story of the First Woman Doctor* (New York, 1949), 43.

58 Blackwell, *Pioneer Work*, 28, 32. She consistently opposed the marriages of the male members of her large family; the women all stayed single. See Elinor Rice Hays, *Those Extraordinary Blackwells: The Story of a Journey to a Better World* (New York, 1967), 155. Zakrewska felt the same way. See *A Woman's Quest*, 193.

59 Blackwell, *Pioneer Work*, 72.

60 "Increase of Operations," undated paper in the Blackwell Collection. See also Elizabeth Blackwell, *Essays in Medical Sociology* (London, 1902), II, 120.

61 Letter of March 21, 1891, in the Blackwell Collection.

62 See Blackwell, *Essays*, II, 119 ff. Anti-vivisection had many passionate feminine adherents, medical and lay. Elizabeth Stuart Phelps, a popular writer and feminist of

bias of much of modern science. If man were going to dedicate himself to cold-blooded experimentation, would not woman be his ultimate subject? Consequently, despite her fine mind and excellent training, Blackwell, an incipient Christian Scientist, obstinately opposed not just the usual run of drugs and medication, but vaccination and "all medical methods which introduce any degree of morbid matter into the blood of the human system."[63] All such practices were "especially antagonistic to women."[64] Blackwell's medical shortsightedness seems ludicrous, perhaps culpable, but it furthered her underlying and non-medical goals.

To distrust science was to distrust masculinity, and to create an apparent immediate and desperate need for women doctors. She saw these projected new physicians, moreover, as undercover agents in enemy territory. Her advice to them reads a bit like a lesson in subversion. Proud that she had determined early in her career to "*commit heresy* with intelligence" to escape the perils of professionalized medicine, she declared that women doctors should not countenance practices like ovariotomies, vaccination, and vivisection.[65] In a crucial essay entitled "The Influence of Women in the Profession of Medicine" (1889), she urged women medical students, unfortunately, like all of their sex, trained to "accept the government and instruction of men as final" (20), to exercise a "mild skepticism" (21).[66] Their task was quite simply to revamp the whole medical profession, for, as she explained, "methods and conclusions formed by one half the race only must necessarily require revision as the other half of humanity rises into conscious responsibility" (20). They had a sure guide in this apparently momentous undertaking: Nothing that revolted their "moral sense as earnest women" could be scientifically true, and no "logical sophistry" (30) could make it so. In a letter to a medical colleague, she echoes Emerson as she anticipates a day when women will plant themselves firmly "on the God-given force of their maternal nature" and oppose the male intellect in its too restless search for scientific truth.[67]

Blackwell's era, devoted much of her later work to the cause. See especially *Though Life Do Us Part* (Boston, 1908), 54–55, where she explicitly links male cruelty in vivisection with male cruelty in marriage, and *Trixy* (Boston, 1904) in which a girl refuses to marry a vivisectionist.

63 See Blackwell, *Pioneer Work*, 178, 157, 240. See also Blackwell, *Essays*, II, 69 ff.

64 Blackwell, *Essays*, II, 26. Jacobi seems to be making a similar point about the male intellect in "The Mad Scientist," in *Stories and Sketches* (New York, 1907).

65 Blackwell, *Pioneer Work*, 173.

66 All page references for this essay are to Blackwell, *Essays*, II.

67 Undated letter to Dr. McNutt in the Blackwell Collection.

Blackwell was very clever. Male doctors had indirectly told their women patients that their procreative femininity was their dearest treasure. Coining that treasure into current cash, Blackwell pointed to her sacred maternal nature as justification for a revolt against the ways of the male doctor. For the woman physician of Blackwell's vision, womanhood was hardly a liability, and very much a weapon. She was no subordinate, but an aggressive censor of the masculine world.[68] Blackwell herself was only too ready. Calling herself a "Christian physiologist," she fought prostitution, masturbation, and obscene literature in addition to various medical abuses. It was in these crusades that her underlying anti-male bias most dramatically expressed itself. With so many of her feminine peers, she liked to see male sexuality, like male science, as one more method used by men to debase women to their own level by seducing them, and to keep them dependent by forcing them into parasitism. Blackwell's target in the anti-prostitution campaign organized by the Purity Alliance was not the prostitute, but her exploiter.[69] "Male lust must be restrained in order to check female obscenity"[70] was the telling slogan Blackwell issued in one of her many essays on the subject. It is not too much to say that the paid whore whom Blackwell wished to regenerate was simply another version of the female patient corrupted by immoral medical practices whom Beecher and Hunt had sought to redeem.

It is telling that Blackwell, like most of the first generation of women doctors, chose hygiene, or preventive medicine, as her chosen field, and she made great contributions there, despite her distrust of vaccination. There can be no doubt, furthermore, that she and her feminine colleagues contributed significantly to improve treatment of women's and children's diseases.[71] But they also answered a different and more subtle need strongly felt by some members of their sex. If the woman patient dependent on the male doctor had seemed to feminists like Beecher and Gilman emblematic of the most degrading elements in woman's relation to man in nineteenth-century America, the woman

68 Blackwell nowhere makes this more clear than in *The Human Element in Sex: Being a Medical Enquiry Into the Relation of Sexual Physiology to Christian Morality* (London, 1884).

69 A good introduction to the spirit and work of the Purity Alliance is Aaron M. Powell (ed.), *The National Purity Congress: Its Papers, Addresses, Portraits* (New York, 1896).

70 *Wrong and Right Methods of Dealing with Social Evil as Shown by English Parliamentary Evidence* (New York, n.d.), 41. See also "The Purchase of Women: The Great Economic Blunder" in Blackwell, *Essays*, I, 133–174.

71 See Campbell-Hurd, *Medical Women in America*, and Robinson, *White-Caps*.

doctor, able to take care of herself and cure the world's ills, appeared to them not only as a beacon of hope but as an avenger of the wrongs of all those prostrate women, whether victimized in an office or in their own homes.

Elizabeth Stuart Phelps, an immensely popular post-Civil War authoress who knew personally every variety of nervous disorder in its most acute form, celebrated this revengeful angel in *Dr. Zay* (1882), a novel about a woman doctor.[72] Dr. Zay's first name rather appropriately is Atalanta. Totally self-confident, direct, brilliant, and rather unpoetic although womanly, she exudes the independence and the self-sufficiency that Elizabeth Blackwell and Harriot Hunt had so longed to see in their sex. Like them, she has devoted herself to relieving the sufferings of women and, a Christian physiologist of the first order, she even brings off shotgun weddings as part of her healing mission. The novel centers around her relationship with her only male patient—a young man named Waldo Yorke, poetic and unmotivated, although attractive and personally charming. He falls deeply in love with her, and Phelps devotes most of the plot to the resulting role-reversal which apparently fascinates her. Convalescent and ironically suffering from "nervous strain" (69), Yorke needs Dr. Zay, but she, in splendid health, "leaned against her own physical strength, as another woman might lean upon a man's" (110).[73]

By a further twist of irony, a twist clearly delightful to Phelps herself, Dr. Zay, out of her superfluous strength and in her off-hours, can provide salvation for man in the shape of Yorke, but he has nothing to offer her except the so-called feminine gifts of devotion and sexual attractiveness. The circle of revenge is complete, for Phelps is implying through Atalanta that the truly diseased sex is not woman, woman with her radiant maternal strength, but man, man with his barren professional pretenses and sexual excess. And so the last act of mercy Phelps' rather sadistic angel performs is to consent to enter the marriage relation with a sex she has demonstrated so clearly to be the inferior of her own.

72 For her own account see *Chapters from a Life* (Boston, 1897), 228–242. Her most important fictional accounts of illness are "Shut In" in *Fourteen to One* (Boston, 1891), 66–99, about an invalid's recovery, and *Walled In* (New York, 1907), about the relationship between a nurse and a male patient.

73 All page references are to Elizabeth Stuart Phelps, *Dr. Zay* (Boston, 1886). I owe much of my thinking on Phelps to Christine Stansell's "Elizabeth Stuart Phelps: A Study in Female Rebellion," *Massachusetts Review*, XIII (1972), 239–256. For other contemporary fictional works on women doctors, see William Dean Howells, *Dr. Breen's Practice* (Boston, 1881), and Sarah Orne Jewett, *A Country Doctor* (Boston, c. 1884).

Phelps' superwoman Dr. Zay is clearly the exaggerated product of wish-fulfillment fantasies on the part of a lifelong invalid and feminist, but she forcefully symbolizes what some women wanted women doctors to prove to them. With this novel, the drama of women and medicine in nineteenth-century America has in a sense reached its extreme dénouement. Unlike the male and female physicians who preceded (and succeeded) her, Phelps makes no pretense of interest in medicine as science. Her only concern is with medicine as a weapon in a social and political struggle for power between the sexes. In *Dr. Zay*, Phelps has seized upon the cultural assumptions underlying contemporary male doctors' treatments of women's diseases in order triumphantly to reverse them. Dr. Zay's example is meant to testify that, far from being the constitutionally diseased and dependent creature that Dewees and Byford saw, woman could be self-reliant. In Phelps' vision, woman need not be a prisoner in her own sick body, awaiting the coming of her deliverer, man, but a healer herself, the support of her sex, and by caring for its members, the donor to them of a new kind of self-esteem.

WOMEN AS VICTIMS OF MEDICAL EXPERIMENTATION
J. Marion Sims' Surgery on Slave Women, 1845-1850

Diana E. Axelsen

During the Reagan administration, we have seen cuts in federal funding for many programs which directly affect the health of Black women. Unfortunately, lack of concern for the health of poor and minority women is not simply a result of a transitory political climate. From the time that Europeans arrived in America, the health and indeed the lives of minority women have been devalued by the dominant white male culture. Though perhaps this fact is clearest when we look at the provision of health care (or its absence), it is also important to be aware of how minority women have been exploited in the development of medical treatments and technologies. The abuse of poor and minority women in the U.S. and of Third World women generally, is notable today especially in the testing of contraceptives. However, the development of obstetrics and gynecology in the U.S. in the 19th century is another example of how Black women have been exploited as experimental subjects.

In this essay, I shall examine the abuse of slave women in experimental gynecological surgery performed by J. Marion Sims in Montgomery, Alabama, between 1845 and 1849. Since the development of federal guidelines for the use of human subjects, hopefully, we have become more sensitive to the importance of justifying and monitoring all medical experimentation. Yet women, especially poor and non-white women, continue to be victims of ethically unjustifiable medical research. An understanding of how individual values and cultural norms worked together in the Sims' case many help us to become more sensitive and more effective in opposing contemporary abuses of women as experimental subjects.

Diana E. Axelsen is former chair of the Department of Philosophy at Spelman College and Professor of Philosophy at California Lutheran College in Thousand Oaks, California. *This paper is a revised version of one presented at a symposium on "Southern Women: From Myth to Modern Times," November 13-15, 1980 in Atlanta, Georgia. Professor Axelsen expresses gratitude to Graham Barker-Benfield for his bibliographic suggestions and for permission to quote from his book, The Horrors of the Half-Life: Male Attitudes Toward Women and Sexuality in Nineteenth-Century America (New York: Harper & Row, 1979).*

First, I shall look briefly at the status of health care for slaves in the 19th century. In *Black Culture and Black Consciousness*, Lawrence Levine describes the importance of folk remedies among slaves, and notes that slaves resisted attempts by their masters to interfere with these traditional medical practices. Many of these practices were of African origin, and the medical lore was preserved and transmitted in this country by grandmothers born in Africa. Levine also notes that "a number of slave practitioners won considerable reknown for their skills,"[1] and white patients of a Tennessee slave petitioned the state legislature to allow him to practice medicine formally. Also, white, Black, and Indian populations shared folk practices and learned from one another.[2]

On the other hand, Western medicine was also gaining a firm foothold in the South. The Alabama Medical Association was organized in 1846, and there were significant numbers of physicians in Alabama. Ten years later, the legislature passed an act authorizing the establishment of a state medical college, which was incorporated as the Medical College of Alabama by the Alabama General Assembly on January 30, 1860.[3] According to Eugene Genovese, "Most slaveholders provided physicians' services for their slaves at an average cost of three dollars per slave per year, and many spent large numbers—ten dollars to more than a hundred—to provide medical care for slaves."[4] However, since slaveholders' practices varied, since Western medicine was often dangerous and even deadly rather than helpful, and since it is difficult to assess the overall impact of folk medicine, the actual health of slaves remains a matter of controversy. However, for our purposes, it is important primarily to be aware of both the presence of the folk medical tradition and the availability of some Western medical care to slaves, though the provision of medical care as simply an economic investment must also be acknowledged.

I turn now to Sims' role in southern medical care. The sources which refer to him often quote from his autobiography, especially descriptions of his own bout with malaria. He is known as a pioneer in the treatment of clubfoot, as well as in "women's medicine." His early years of practice included surgery on the mouth and jaw. His role in founding the Women's Hospital in New York, where for many years he was chief surgeon, is the focus of attention with respect to his career outside the South. He has been praised by colleagues and medical historians as the "father of American gynecology."[5]

Until 1950, the primary source of information about Sims' work was his own autobiography, called *The Story of My Life*,[6] though there were some medical biographies in the early

1900's, including one by his son-in-law.[7] In 1950, a physician, Seale Harris, published a biography of Sims, *Woman's Surgeon*, which is one of the most important sources of information concerning Sims' life and work. Harris regards Sims' most notable surgical contribution as the repair of vesicovaginal fistula, i.e., a tear in the vaginal wall resulting in chronic leakage from the bladder. Though today this condition occurs primarily as a congenital defect, and occasionally as a result of accident or in unattended childbirth, tears in the vaginal wall were not uncommon results of childbirth in Sims' time. Sims also developed the speculum, pioneered in the use of wire sutures, and developed the "Sims" position for pelvic examination and surgery. Sims' attention to sanitary procedures during surgery is note worthy since it preceded Listerism, and probably accounts for his unusually low mortality rate during surgery (he lost no patients during the period under discussion).

The first book to point out the abuse of persons involved in Sims' surgery was not published until 1976. The British historian Graham Barker-Benfield devotes a chapter of his book, *Horrors of the Half-known Life: Male Attitudes Toward Women and Sexuality in 19th Century America*, to Sims.[8] Except for this book, however, there seems to have been no published analysis of this important historical instance of the abuse of women as experimental subjects until quite recently.[9] My discussion is intended not only to examine these events, but also to suggest how an analysis of Sims' work and its setting can help to define areas of ethical concern in medical theory and practice today, especially as it affects women, minorities, and the poor.

James Marion Sims was born in South Carolina in 1813, and graduated from Jefferson Medical College in Philadelphia in 1835. That fall, he moved to Mount Meigs, in Montgomery County, Alabama, where he set up practice. In 1840, he moved into Montgomery. Though Sims displayed an interest in innovative surgical techniques from the beginning of his career, he did not intend to enter women's medicine, and in fact had a deep distaste for the treatment of "women's diseases." This distaste was apparently overcome by his competitiveness with men in the development of new surgical techniques and by his desire for superiority and recognition in the male medical world of the 19th century. He saw surgery as a way of proving himself, and regarded unsuccessful surgery as a personal failure. Sims also paved the way for an emphasis on invasive surgery as a treatment of preference for many "female disorders."[10] Sims also saw women as defined in large part by their capacity for reproduction; this attitude is reflected in his later preoccupation with problems of infertility in women.[11]

It was in 1845 that Sims saw his first patient with vesico-vaginal fistula. She was a slave woman known to us only as Anarcha. Sims had been asked to deliver the baby with forceps after three days of labor had elapsed, and reluctantly agreed. When he later saw her and was asked to consider surgery for the vaginal injuries she had sustained, resulting in both vesico-vaginal fistula and recto-vaginal fistula, he pronounced treatment impossible. In the next two months, he saw two other slave women, Lucy and Betsy, also patients suffering from vesico-vaginal fistula; in each case, he insisted that the situation was hopeless. Only when using atmospheric pressure to distend the uterus while manually treating a woman whose uterus had been displaced in an accident did he realize that he might be able to use atmospheric pressure to his advantage in surgery. Aware of the need for an instrument to aid in the process, he developed a forerunner of the modern speculum, using a pewter spoon and an elaborate arrangement of mirrors and lighting.[12] Convinced now of the possibility of successful surgery, he made inquiries around the countryside and found that indeed there were other Black women who had been hidden away for years, suffering from vesico-vaginal fistula. According to Harris, these women were unable to take any part in normal life; yet they never died from their affliction. Instead they allegedly lived on year after year in misery and ostracism wishing for death and sometimes committing suicide to achieve it.[13]

Sims then planned surgery for Lucy, Anarcha, and Betsy, as well as for nine other slave women, whom he agreed to support except for the provision that their masters would pay taxes and provide clothing. Though he succeeded in closing the fistulas, small perforations remained after healing, leakage continued, and infection of the sutures was a continuing problem. These difficulties were finally eliminated after he began using wire rather than silk sutures. The slave women endured operation after operation during the years between 1845 and 1849. Finally, in May, 1849, the thirtieth operation on Anarcha was successful.[14]

The history of anesthesia during this period is important in our analysis of Sims' work. He performed all of this surgery on the slave women without anesthesia, except for the ineffective use of opium, which tended to produce nausea and constipation rather than anesthesia.[15] Sims and Harris praised the endurance and stoicism of the slave women. After the successful operation on Anarcha, many white women came to Sims for treatment of vesico-vaginal fistula. However, none of them was able to endure a single operation.[16]

Although Crawford Long had used inhaled ether as an anesthetic as early as 1842, Sims was unaware of Long's work in the adjoining state of Georgia. Long had apparently gotten the idea of using ether by observing that he and others sustained cuts, bruises and other injuries during the "ether frolics" of the time, yet felt no pain at the time of injury. Long, however, apparently failed to realize the great significance of the use of ether, or had used it only in cases which he regarded as inadequate tests of its overall effectiveness.[17] Also, it appears that Long may have simply substituted ether for whiskey to meet particular emergencies. Long first read about W. T. G. Morton's work with ether in December, 1846, but Long himself did not publish an account of his own use until 1849.[18] Thus, Sims' lack of awareness of Long's work is understandable.

Less understandable, however, is Sims' continued failure to use ether or to seek out current research in the area of anesthesiology. After G. Q. Colton used nitrous oxide or "laughing gas" as entertainment in an 1844 demonstration in Hartford, Connecticut, Horace Wells used nitrous oxide in surgery; he is credited by some historians with developing the idea of anesthesia by inhalation. He continued his work with nitrous oxide in Boston in 1845. In 1846, also in Boston, W. T. G. Morton demonstrated the use of inhaled ether as an anesthetic.[19] The first published report of the discovery of surgical anesthesia in the United States appeared in the November 18, 1846 issue of *The Boston Medical and Surgical Journal*.[20] From 1846 on, the use of ether spread through America and Europe. Charles Jackson, a chemist, is also credited with the use of ether in Plymouth, Massachusetts, in 1842. He may have suggested to Morton the substitution of ether for nitrous oxide, since ether was known by chemists to have similar effects as nitrous oxide, though ether could be safely used in sufficient amounts to produce anesthesia, as nitrous oxide could not.[21] Sims developed an interest in anesthesia and in Long's part in its history sometime after 1850, and in fact published an article on its history in an 1877 issue of the *Virginia Medical Monthly*.[22] However, Sims seemed unaware of the experimentation done in this area prior to 1850. This fact seems especially striking since according to Harris, he was given to "diligent reading of the medical journals."[23]

Obviously Sims' slave patients were in no position to demand that he search for an effective anesthetic; moreover, slave women rarely used alcohol, seldom drank to excess, and did not use opium or other narcotics as did upper-class white women, so they were unlikely to have requested the use of even these substances. Even after his unsuccessful attempts to operate on white women emphasized the pain associated with the surgery, apparently Sims continued to ignore the issue of pain control for at least a year. This aspect of his work is reflective of the dehumanizing and imperceptive manner in which Sims treated his patients.

Moreover, both Harris and Sims over-emphasized the severity of the condition Sims was treating. While certainly a source of chronic discomfort and possible secondary irritation, and while obviously embarrassing in many contexts, vesico-vaginal fistula is not a disorder involving chronic or severe pain. As we saw above, Harris suggests that some slave women found their condition so unbearable that it drove them to suicide; however, this seems simply to be part of the unjustified exaggeration with which both Sims and Harris portrayed the condition. According to Genovese, there was a low incidence of suicide among the slave population generally; most, he says, "seem to have resorted to suicide to escape capture after having run away or to avoid punishment after sale."[24] In any case, the discomfort of vesico-vaginal fistula, in comparison to the effects of excessive beatings, chronic malnutrition, and other forms of physicial and psychological aggression, hardly constitutes a probable motive for suicide. Moreover, that slave women would have been allowed to retreat as invalids because of this condition is also a statement which should be questioned, though no specific sources are available on this issue.

Sims' attitude toward pain management and his exaggeration of the severity of his patients' condition are striking dimensions of the larger issue of control over his patients. Obviously, the powerlessness of the slaves in seeking alternative medical care or in objecting to any aspect of Sims' practice must be seen as central to the coercive nature of this surgery. According to Barker-Benfield, Sims bought slaves for his use as patients;[25] Harris does not mention this, but he does state that temporary control over the first twelve slaves was given to Sims by the women's masters, with the provision that the masters pay the taxes and provide clothing.[26] Since they had no opportunity to refuse consent, to describe the "cooperativeness" of the patients is meaningless. Sims failed utterly to recognize his patients as autonomous persons, and his insensitivity, heightened by his own personal drive for success, cannot be minimized, especially as a balance to the enormous amount of praise accorded Sims for this work and for subsequent applications of the technique developed in Montgomery. Harris describes the numerous memorials to Sims, in Montgomery and elsewhere, and adds:

> Montgomery has not forgotten the heroic roles of the three slaves, Anarcha, Lucy, and Betsy, who suffered, not only that they themselves might be cured, but that women injured in childbirth in future generations might be saved from lives of misery and invalidism. A movement has been begun, sponsored by leading women in Montgomery to establish a memorial to the three slave heroines.[27]

Thus, Harris perpetuates a view of these women not only as choosing freely to participate in their own treatment but as volunteers in experimental surgery intended to help future generations. It is obvious that these women, admirable though they may be, were simply not able to make such choices because they were not accorded the freedom of choosing or refusing participation.

Sims, however, was very much a product of his own professional training and of his culture. His surgery occurred in the 19th century South, where racial, sexual, political, and economic power structures were uniquely suited to provide an opportunity for an abuse of human subjects such as Sims'. A society in which being white and male was a general source of power, and in which being a physician carried special prestige, explains much of Sims' behavior. In this period, too, stoic acceptance of pain was seen as "natural" for women in childbirth and was also attributed to slaves generally. Sims' work should be understood not only as an expression of his own values, but, more broadly, as an example of the ways in which social values can deprive whole groups of persons of the right to participate in decisions concerning their own health. Today, the medical issues are different, but the need to look closely at the impact of societal values on the treatment of women in medicine remains. There is still a need to be on guard against invasive surgery, including Caesarean sections and hysterectomies, and against various forms of experiments with both contraception and reproduction.[28] As in Sims' time, poor and non-white women are especially vulnerable. Only when all women are free to choose whether to participate in research, and only when all are free to choose from the best forms of gynecological and obstetrical care, can we claim to have used the lessons of the 19th century to free women from male-controlled research and practice in "women's medicine." A real societal commitment to the health of Black women thus will require a major change in the values which underlie the entire system of the development and provision of health care in America.

NOTES

[1] Lawrence W. Levine, *Black Culture and Black Consciousness* (New York: Oxford University Press, 1977), p. 64.

[2] Levine, pp. 64-65.

[3] Lucille Griffith, *History of Alabama* (Northport, Alabama: Colonial Press, 1962), p. 146, and Saffold Bernay, *Handbook of Alabama* (Birmingham: Roberts and Son, 1892), p. 211. See also Lucille Griffith, *Alabama: A Documentary History to 1900* (University, Alabama: University of Alabama Press, 1972).

[4] Eugene D. Genovese, *Roll, Jordan, Roll: The World the Slaves Made* (New York: Pantheon, 1974), p. 62.

[5] Seale Harris, *Woman's Surgeon* (New York: Macmillan, 1950), p. 374, p. 392.

[6] J. Marion Sims, *The Story of My Life*, ed. H. Marion-Sims (New York: Appleton, 1884, 1885, 1888). Incomplete.

[7] John Allan Wyeth, *With Sabre and Scapel* (New York: Harper and Brothers, 1914).

[8] G.J. Barker-Benfield, *The Horrors of the Half-known Life: Male Attitudes Toward Women and Sexuality in Nineteenth Century America* (New York: Harper and Row, 1976).

[9] One recent discussion of Sims' experimental surgery is in Robert S. Mendelsohn, *Male Practice: How Doctors Manipulate Women* (Chicago: Contemporary Books, 1981).

[10] Harris, p. 82; Barker-Benfield, pp. 92-94.

[11] Barker-Benfield, pp. 117-199.

[12] Harris, pp. 82-86.

[13] Harris, p. 87.

[14] Harris, pp. 100-102.

[15] Harris, pp. 100-102, pp. 108-109.

[16] Harris, p. 109.

[17] Harris, pp. 312-313.

[18] Victor Robinson, *Victory Over Pain: A History of Anesthesia* (New York: Henry Schuman, 1946), pp. 90-91.

[19] Howard Riley Raper, *Man Against Pain: The Epic of Anesthesia* (New York: Prentice-Hall, 1945), pp. 151-154. See also Raper, pp. 142-154, and Robinson, pp. 83-140.

[20] Smithsonian Institute, Museum of History and Technology, Medical History Section. (Washington, D.C.)

[21] Robinson, p. 109.

[22] Harris, pp. 311-315. Sims' article, titled "The Discovery of Anesthesia," appeared in the *Virginia Medical Monthly* 4 (1877), 81-100. The point of the article was to establish the priority of the role of Sims' fellow southerner, Crawford Long, as the discoverer of anesthesia.

[23] Harris, p. 81.

[24] Genovese, p. 639.

[25] Barker-Benfield, p. 101.

[26] Harris, p. 87.

[27] Harris, pp. 375-376.

[28] For a discussion of contemporary value conflicts in obstetrical care, see Jeanne Guillemin, "Babies by Cesarean: Who Chooses, Who Controls?" *The Hastings Center Report* 11 (June, 1981), 15-18.

THE HYSTERICAL WOMAN: SEX ROLES AND ROLE CONFLICT IN 19th-CENTURY AMERICA*

BY CARROLL SMITH-ROSENBERG

HYSTERIA was one of the classic diseases of the nineteenth century. It was a protean ailment characterized by such varied symptoms as paraplegia, aphonia, hemi-anaesthesia, and violent epileptoid seizures. Under the broad rubric of hysteria, nineteenth-century physicians gathered cases which might today be diagnosed as neurasthenia, hypochondriasis, depression, conversion reaction, and ambulatory schizophrenia. It fascinated and frustrated some of the century's most eminent clinicians; through its redefinition Freud rose to international fame, while the towering reputation of Charcot suffered a comparative eclipse. Psychoanalysis can historically be called the child of the hysterical woman.

Not only was hysteria a widespread and—in the intellectual history of medicine—significant disease, it remains to this day a frustrating and ever-changing illness. What was diagnosed as hysteria in the nineteenth century is not necessarily related to the hysterical character as defined in the twentieth century, or again to what the Greeks meant by hysteria when they christened the disease millennia ago. The one constant in this varied history has been the existence in virtually every era of Western culture of some clinical entity called hysteria; an entity which has always been seen as peculiarly relevant to the female experience, and one which has almost always carried with it a pejorative implication.

* This project was supported in part by grant No. 7 FO2 HD48800–01A1 from the National Institutes of Health and by a grant from the Grant Foundation, New York.

For the past half century and longer, American culture has defined hysteria in terms of individual psychodynamics. Physicians and psychologists have seen hysteria as a "neurosis" or character disorder, the product of an unresolved Oedipal complex. Hysterical women, fearful of their own sexual impulses—so the argument went—channeled that energy into psychosomatic illness. Characteristically, they proved unable to form satisfying and stable relationships.[1] More recently psychoanalysts such as Elizabeth Zetzel have refined this Freudian hypothesis, tracing the roots of hysteria to a women's excessively ambivalent preoedipal relation with her mother and to the resulting complications of oedipal development and resolution.[2] Psychologist David Shapiro has emphasized the hysterical woman's impressionistic thought pattern.[3] All such interpretations focus exclusively on individual psychodynamics and relations within particular families.

Yet hysteria is also a socially recognized behavior pattern and as such exists within the larger world of cultural values and role relationships. For centuries hysteria has been seen as characteristically female—the hysterical woman the embodiment of a perverse or hyper femininity.[4] Why has this been so? Why

[1] For a review of the recent psychiatric literature on hysteria see Aaron Lazare, "The Hysterical Character in Psychoanalytic Theory: Evolution and Confusion," *Archives of General Psychiatry*, XXV (August, 1971), pp. 131–137; Barbara Ruth Easser and S. R. Lesser, "Hysterical Personality: A Reevaluation," *Psychoanalytic Quarterly*, XXXIV (1965), pp. 390–405, and Marc H. Hollander, "Hysterical Personality," *Comments on Contemporary Psychiatry*, I (1971), pp. 17–24.

[2] Elizabeth Zetzel, *The Capacity for Emotional Growth. Theoretical and Clinical Contributions to Psychoanalysis, 1943–1969* (London: Hogarth Press, 1970), Chap. 1-f, "The So-Called Good Hysteric."

[3] David Shapiro, *Neurotic Styles*, (New York: Basic Books, 1965).

[4] The argument can be made that hysteria exists among men and therefore is not exclusively related to the female experience; the question is a complex one, and I am presently at work on a parallel study of male hysteria. There are, however, four brief points concerning male hysteria that I would like to make. First, to this day hysteria is still believed to be principally a female "disease" or behavior pattern. Second, the male hysteric is usually seen by physicians as somehow different. Today it is a truism that hysteria in males is found most frequently among homosexuals; in the nineteenth century men diagnosed as hysterics came almost exclusively from a lower socio-economic status than their physicians—

did large numbers of women "choose" the character traits of hysteria as their particular mode of expressing malaise, discontent, anger or pain? [5] To begin to answer this question, we must explore the female role and role socialization. Clearly not all women were hysterics; yet the parallel between the hysteric's behavior and stereotypic femininity is too close to be explained as mere coincidence. To examine hysteria from this social perspective means necessarily to explore the complex relationships that exist between cultural norms and individual behavior, between behavior defined as disease and behavior considered normal.

Using nineteenth-century America as a case study,[6] I propose to explore hysteria on at least two levels of social interaction. The first involves an examination of hysteria as a social role

immigrants, especially "new immigrants," miners, railroad workers, blacks. Third, since it was defined by society as a female disease, one may hypothesize that there was some degree of female identification among the men who assumed a hysterical role. Lastly, we must recall that a most common form of male hysteria was battle fatigue and shell shock. I should like to thank Erving Goffman for the suggestion that the soldier is in an analogous position to women regarding autonomy and power.

[5] The word choose, even in quotes, is value-laden. I do not mean to imply that hysterical women consciously chose their behavior. I feel that three complex factors interacted to make hysteria a real behavioral option for American women: first, the various experiences that caused a woman to arrive at adulthood with significant ego weaknesses; second, certain socialization patterns and cultural values which made hysteria a readily available alternate behavior pattern for women, and third, the secondary gains conferred by the hysterical role in terms of enhanced power within the family. Individual cases presumably each represented their own peculiar balance of these factors, all of which will be discussed in this paper.

[6] Nineteenth-century hysteria has attracted a good number of students: two of the most important are Henri F. Ellenberger, *The Discovery of the Unconscious* (New York: Basic Books, 1970), and Ilza Veith, *Hysteria: The History of a Disease* (Chicago: University of Chicago Press, 1965). Ellenberger and Veith approach hysteria largely from the framework of intellectual history. For a review of Veith see Charles E. Rosenberg, "Historical Sociology of Medical Thought," *Science*, CL (October 15, 1965), p. 330. For two studies which view nineteenth-century hysteria from a more sociological perspective see Esther Fischer-Homberger, "Hysterie und Misogynie: Ein Aspekt der Hysteriegeschichte," *Gesnerus*, XXVI (1969), pp. 117–127, and Marc H. Hollander, "Conversion Hysteria: A Post-Freudian Reinterpretation of Nineteenth-Century Psychosocial Data," *Archives of General Psychiatry*, XXVI (1972), pp. 311–314.

within the nineteenth-century family. This was a period when, it has been argued, social and structural change had created stress within the family and when, in addition, individual domestic role alternatives were few and rigidly defined. From this perspective hysteria can be seen as an alternate role option for particular women incapable of accepting their life situation. Hysteria thus serves as a valuable indicator both of domestic stress and of the tactics through which some individuals sought to resolve that stress. By analyzing the function of hysteria within the family and the interaction of the hysteric, her family, and the interceding—yet interacting—physician, I also hope to throw light upon the role of women and female-male relationships within the larger world of nineteenth-century American society. Secondly, I will attempt to raise some questions concerning female role socialization, female personality options, and the nature of hysterical behavior.[7]

I

It might be best to begin with a brief discussion of three relatively well known areas: first, the role of women in nineteenth-century American society; second, the symptoms which hysterical women presented and which established the definition of the disease, and lastly, the response of male physicians to their hysterical patients.

The ideal female in nineteenth-century America was expected to be gentle and refined, sensitive and loving. She was the guardian of religion and spokeswoman for morality. Hers was the task of guiding the more worldly and more frequently tempted

[7] I would like to thank Renée Fox, Cornelia Friedman, Erving Goffman, Charles E. Rosenberg and Paul Rosenkrantz for having read and criticized this paper. I would also like to thank my clinical colleagues Philip Mechanick, Henry Bachrach, Ellen Berman, and Carol Wolman of the Psychiatry Department of the University of Pennsylvania for similar assistance. Versions of this paper were presented to the Institute of the Pennsylvania Hospital, the Berkshire Historical Society, and initially, in October 1971, at the Psychiatry Department of Hannehmann Medical College, Philadelphia.

male past the maelstroms of atheism and uncontrolled sexuality. Her sphere was the hearth and the nursery; within it she was to bestow care and love, peace and joy. The American girl was taught at home, at school, and in the literature of the period, that aggression, independence, self-assertion and curiosity were male traits, inappropriate for the weaker sex and her limited sphere. Dependent throughout her life, she was to reward her male protectors with affection and submission. At no time was she expected to achieve in any area considered important by men and thus highly valued by society. She was, in essence, to remain a child-woman, never developing the strengths and skills of adult autonomy. The stereotype of the middle class woman as emotional, pious, passive and nurturant was to become increasingly rigid throughout the nineteenth century.[8]

There were signficant discontinuities and inconsistencies between such ideals of female socialization and the real world in which the American woman had to live. The first relates to a dichotomy between the ideal woman and the ideal mother. The ideal woman was emotional, dependent and gentle—a born follower. The ideal mother, then and now, was expected to be strong, self-reliant, protective, an efficient caretaker in relation to children and home. She was to manage the family's day-to-day finances, prepare foods, make clothes, compound drugs, serve as family nurse—and, in rural areas, as physician as well.[9] Espe-

[8] This summary of woman's role and role socialization is drawn from a larger study of male and female gender roles and gender role socialization in the United States from 1785 to 1895 on which I am presently engaged. This research has been supported by both the Grant Foundation, New York City and the National Institute of Child Health and Human Development, N.I.H. It is difficult to refer succinctly to the wide range of sources on which this paragraph is based. Such a role model appears in virtually every nineteenth-century woman's magazine, in countless guides to young women and young wives and in etiquette books. For a basic secondary source see Barbara Welter, "The Cult of True Womanhood," *American Quarterly*, XVIII (1966), pp. 151–174. For an excellent over-all history of women in America see Eleanor Flexner, *Century of Struggle*, (Cambridge, Massachusetts: Harvard University Press, 1959).

[9] For the daily activities of a nineteenth-century American housewife see, for example, *The Maternal Physician: By an American Matron* (New York: Isaac Riley, 1811. Reprinted New York: Arno Press, 1972); Hugh Smith, *Letters to Married*

cially in the nineteenth century, with its still primitive obstetrical practices and its high child mortality rates, she was expected to face severe bodily pain, disease and death—and still serve as the emotional support and strength of her family.[10] As S. Weir Mitchell, the eminent Philadelphia neurologist wrote in the 1880's, "We may be sure that our daughters will be more likely to have to face at some time the grim question of pain than the lads who grow up beside them . . . . To most women . . . there comes a time when pain is a grim presence in their lives." Yet, as Mitchell pointed out, it was boys whom society taught from early childhood on to bear pain stoically, while girls were encouraged to respond to pain and stress with tears and the expectation of elaborate sympathy.[11]

Contemporaries noted routinely in the 1870's, 1880's and 1890's that middle-class American girls seemed ill-prepared to assume the responsibilities and trials of marriage, motherhood and maturation. Frequently women, especially married women with children, complained of isolation, loneliness, and depression. Physicians reported a high incidence of nervous disease and hysteria among women who felt overwhelmed by the burdens of frequent pregnancies, the demands of children, the daily exertions of housekeeping and family management.[12] The realities

Ladies (New York: Bliss, White and G. & C. Carvill, 1827); John S. C. Abbott, *The Mother at Home* (Boston: Crocker and Brewster, 1833); Lydia H. Sigourney, *Letters to Mothers* (New York: Harper & Brothers, 1841); Mrs. C. A. Hopkinson, *Hints for the Nursery or the Young Mother's Guide* (Boston: Little, Brown & Company, 1836); Catherine Beecher and Harriet Beecher Stowe, *The American Woman's Home* (New York: J. B. Ford & Company, 1869). For an excellent secondary account of the southern woman's domestic life see Anne Firor Scott, *The Southern Lady* (Chicago: University of Chicago Press, 1970).

10 Nineteenth-century domestic medicine books, gynecological textbooks, and monographs on the diseases of women provide a detailed picture of women's diseases and health expectations.

11 S. Weir Mitchell, *Doctor and Patient* (Philadelphia: J. B. Lippincott Company, 1887), pp. 84, 92.

12 See among others Edward H. Dixon, *Woman and Her Diseases* (New York: Charles H. Ring, 1846), pp. 135–136; Alice Stockham, *Tokology: A Book for Every Woman* (Chicago: Sanitary Publishers, 1887), p. 83; Sarah A. Stevenson, *Physiology of Women*, 2nd edn. (Chicago: Cushing, Thomas & Co., 1881), p. 91; Henry Pye Chavasse, *Advice to a Wife and Counsel to a Mother* (Philadelphia: J. B. Lippin-

of adult life no longer permitted them to elaborate and exploit the role of fragile, sensitive and dependent child.

Not only was the Victorian woman increasingly ill-prepared for the trials of childbirth and childrearing, but changes were also at work within the larger society which were to make her particular socialization increasingly inappropriate. Reduced birth and mortality rates, growing population concentration in towns, cities and even in rural areas, a new, highly mobile economy, as well as new patterns of middle class aspiration—all reached into the family, altering that institution, affecting domestic relations and increasing the normal quantity of infra-familial stress.[13] Women lived longer; they married later and less often. They spent less and less time in the primary processing of food, cloth and clothing. Increasingly, both middle and lower class women took jobs outside the home until their marriages—or permanently if unable to secure a husband.[14] By the post-Civil War years, family limitation—with its necessary implication of altered domestic roles and relationships—had become a real option within the decision-making processes of every family.[15]

cott, 1891), p. 97. A Missouri physician reported the case of a twenty-eight year old middle class woman with two children. Shortly after the birth of her second child, she missed her period, believed herself to be pregnant for a third time and succumbed to hysterical symptoms: depression, headaches, vomiting and seizures. Her doctor concluded that she had uterine disease, exacerbated by pregnancy. He aborted her and reported a full recovery the following day. George J. Engelmann, "A Hystero-Psychosis Epilepsy Dependent upon Erosions of the Cervix Uteri," *St. Louis Clinic Record* (1878), pp. 321–324. For similar cases, see A. B. Arnold, "Hystero-Hypochondriasis," *Pacific Medical Journal,* XXXIII (1890), pp. 321–324, and George J. Engelmann, "Hystero-neurosis," *Transactions of the American Gynecological Association,* II (1877), pp. 513–518.

[13] For a study of declining nineteenth-century American birth rates see Yasukichi Yasuba, *Birth Rates of the White Population in the United States, 1800–1860* (Baltimore: Johns Hopkins University Press, 1962) and J. Potter, "American Population in the Early National Period," in *Proceedings of Section V of the Fourth Congress of the International Economic History Association,* Paul Deprez, ed., (Winnipeg, 1970), pp. 55–69.

[14] For a useful general discussion of women's changing roles see Eleanor Flexner, *op. cit.*

[15] For a discussion of birth control and its effect on domestic relations see Carroll Smith-Rosenberg and Charles E. Rosenberg, "The New Woman and the

Despite such basic social, economic and demographic changes, however, the family and gender role socialization remained relatively inflexible. It is quite possible that many women experienced a significant level of anxiety when forced to confront or adapt in one way or another to these changes. Thus hysteria may have served as one option or tactic offering particular women otherwise unable to respond to these changes a chance to redefine or restructure their place within the family.

So far this discussion of role socialization and stress has emphasized primarily the malaise and dissatisfaction of the middle class woman. It is only a covert romanticism, however, which permits us to assume that the lower class or farm woman, because her economic functions within her family were more vital than those of her decorative and economically secure urban sisters, escaped their sense of frustration, conflict or confusion. Normative prescriptions of proper womanly behavior were certainly internalized by many poorer women. The desire to marry and the belief that a woman's social status came not from the exercise of her own talents and efforts but from her ability to attract a competent male protector were as universal among lower class and farm women as among middle and upper class urban women. For some of these women—as for their urban middle class sisters—the traditional female role proved functional, bringing material and psychic rewards. But for some it did not. The discontinuity between the child and adult female roles, along with the failure to develop substantial ego strengths, crossed class and geographic barriers—as did hysteria itself. Physicians connected with almshouses, and later in the century with urban hospitals and dispensaries, often reported hysteria among immigrant and tenement house women.[16] Sex differentiation and class distinc-

Troubled Man: Medical and Biological Views of Women in Nineteenth-century America," *Journal of American History* (in press).

[16] William A. Hammond, *On Certain Conditions of Nervous Derangement* (New York: G. P. Putnam's Sons, 1881), p. 42; S. Weir Mitchell, *Lectures on the Diseases of the Nervous System, Especially in Women*, 2nd edn. (Philadelphia, Lea Brothers & Co., 1885), pp. 114, 110; Charles K. Mills, "Hysteria," in *A System of Practical Medicine by American Authors*, William Pepper, ed., assisted by Louis Starr, vol. V,

tions both play a role in American social history, yet hysteria seems to have followed a psychic fault line corresponding more to distinctions of gender than to those of class.

Against this background of possible role conflict and discontinuity, what were the presenting symptoms of the female hysteric in nineteenth-century America? While physicians agreed that hysteria could afflict persons of both sexes and of all ages and economic classes (the male hysteric was an accepted clinical entity by the late nineteenth century), they reported that hysteria was most frequent among women between the ages of 15 and 40 and of the urban middle and upper middle classes. Symptoms were highly varied. As early as the seventeenth century, indeed, Sydenham had remarked that "the frequency of hysteria is no less remarkable than the multiformity of the shapes it puts on. Few maladies are not imitated by it; whatever part of the body it attacks, it will create the proper symptom of that part." [17] The nineteenth-century physician could only concur. There were complaints of nervousness, depression, the tendency to tears and chronic fatigue, or of disabling pain. Not a few women thus afflicted showed a remarkable willingness to submit to long-term, painful therapy—to electric shock treatment, to blistering, to multiple operations, even to amputations.[18]

"Diseases of the Nervous System" (Philadelphia: Lea Brothers & Co., 1883), p. 213; Charles E. Lockwood, "A Study of Hysteria and Hypochondriasis," *Transactions of the New York State Medical Association*, XII (1895), pp. 340–351. E. H. Van Deusen, Superintendent of the Michigan Asylum for the Insane reported that nervousness, hysteria and neurasthenia were common among farm women and resulted, he felt, from the social and intellectual deprivation of their isolated lives. Van Deusen, "Observations on a Form of Nervous Prostration," *American Journal of Insanity*, XXV (1869), p. 447. Significantly most English and American authorities on hysteria were members of a medical elite who saw the wealthy in their private practices and the very poor in their hospital and dispensary work. Thus the observation that hysteria occurred in different social classes was often made by the very same clinicians.

17 Thomas Sydenham, "Epistolary Dissertation," in *The Works of Thomas Sydenham, M.D. . . . with a Life of the Author*, R. G. Latham, ed., 2 vols. (London: New Sydenham Society, 1850), II, p. 85.

18 Some women diagnosed as hysterics displayed quite bizarre behavior—including self-mutilation and hallucinations. Clearly a certain percentage of these women would be diagnosed today as schizophrenic. The majority of the women diagnosed

The most characteristic and dramatic symptom, however, was the hysterical "fit." Mimicking an epileptic seizure, these fits often occurred with shocking suddenness. At other times they "came on" gradually, announcing their approach with a general feeling of depression, nervousness, crying or lassitude. Such seizures, physicians generally agreed, were precipitated by a sudden or deeply felt emotion—fear, shock, a sudden death, marital disappointment—or by physical trauma. It began with pain and tension, most frequently in the "uterine area." The sufferer alternately sobbed and laughed violently, complained of palpitations of the heart, clawed her throat as if strangling and, at times, abruptly lost the power of hearing and speech. A death-like trance might follow, lasting hours, even days. At other times violent convulsions—sometimes accompanied by hallucinations—seized her body.[19] "Let the reader imagine," New York physician E. H. Dixon wrote in the 1840's,

> the patient writhing like a serpent upon the floor, rending her garments to tatters, plucking out handsful of hair, and striking her person with violence—with contorted and swollen countenance and fixed eyes resisting every effort of bystanders to control her . . .[20]

Finally the fit subsided; the patient, exhausted and sore, fell into a restful sleep.

During the first half of the nineteenth century physicians described hysteria principally though not exclusively in terms of such episodes. Symptoms such as paralysis and contracture were believed to be caused by seizures and categorized as infraseizure symptoms. Beginning in mid-century, however, physicians became

as hysterical, however, did not display such symptoms, but rather appear from clinical descriptions to have had a personality similar to that considered hysterical by mid-twentieth-century psychiatrists.

[19] For three typical descriptions of such seizures, see Buel Eastman, *Practical Treatise on Diseases Peculiar to Women and Girls* (Cincinnati: C. Cropper & Son, 1848), p. 40; Samuel Ashwell, *A Practical Treatise on the Diseases Peculiar to Women* (London: Samuel Highley, 1844), pp. 210–212; William Campbell, *Introduction to the Study and Practice of Midwifery and the Diseases of Children* (London: Longman, Rees, Orme, Brown, Green & Longman, 1833), pp. 440–442.

[20] E. H. Dixon, *op. cit.*, p. 133.

increasingly flexible in their diagnosis of hysteria and gradually the fit declined in significance as a pathognomonic symptom.[21] Dr. Robert Carter, a widely-read British authority on hysteria, insisted in 1852 that at least one hysterical seizure must have occurred to justify a diagnosis of hysteria. But, he admitted, this seizure might be so minor as to have escaped the notice even of the patient herself; no subsequent seizures were necessary.[22] This was clearly a transitional position. By the last third of the nineteenth century the seizure was no longer the central phenomenon defining hysteria; physicians had categorized hysterical symptoms which included virtually every known human ill. They ranged from loss of sensation in part, half or all of the body, loss of taste, smell, hearing, or vision, numbness of the skin, inability to swallow, nausea, headaches, pain in the breast, knees, hip, spine or neck, as well as contracture or paralysis of virtually any extremity.[23]

Hysterical symptoms were not limited to the physical. An hysterical female character gradually began to emerge in the nineteenth-century medical literature, one based on interpretations of mood and personality rather than on discrete physical symptoms—one which grew closely to resemble twentieth-century definitions of the "hysterical personality." Doctors commonly described hysterical women as highly impressionistic, suggestible, and narcissistic. Highly labile, their moods changed suddenly, dramatically, and for seemingly inconsequential reasons. Doctors complained that the hysterical woman was egocentric in the extreme, her involvement with others consistently superficial and

[21] For examples of mid-nineteenth-century hysterical symptoms see Colombat de L'Isère, *A Treatise on the Diseases and Special Hygiene of Females*, trans. with additions by Charles D. Meigs, (Philadelphia: Lea and Blanchard, 1845), pp. 522, 527–530; Gunning S. Bedford, *Clinical Lectures on the Diseases of Women and Children* (New York: Samuel S. & W. Wood, 1855), p. 373.

[22] Robert B. Carter, *On the Pathology and Treatment of Hysteria* (London: John Churchill, 1853), p. 3.

[23] See, for example, F. C. Skey, *Hysteria* (New York: A. Simpson, 1867), pp. 66, 71, 86; Mary Putnam Jacobi, "Hysterical Fever," *Journal of Nervous and Mental Disease*, XV (1890), pp. 373–388; Landon Carter Grey, "Neurasthenia: Its Differentiation and Treatment," *New York Medical Journal*, XLVIII (1888), p. 421.

tangential. While the hysterical woman might appear to physicians and relatives as quite sexually aroused or attractive, she was, doctors cautioned, essentially asexual and not uncommonly frigid.[24]

Depression also appears as a common theme. Hysterical symptoms not infrequently followed a death in the family, a miscarriage, some financial setback which forced the patient to become self-supporting; or they were seen by the patient as related to some long-term, unsatisfying life situation—a tired school teacher, a mother unable to cope with the demands of a large family.[25] Most of these women took to their beds because of pain, paralysis or general weakness. Some remained there for years.

The medical profession's response to the hysterical woman was at best ambivalent. Many doctors—and indeed a significant proportion of society at large—tended to be caustic, if not punitive towards the hysterical woman. This resentment seems rooted in two factors: first, the baffling and elusive nature of hysteria itself, and second, the relation which existed in the physicians' minds between their categorizing of hysteria as a disease and the role women were expected to play in society. These patients did not function as women were expected to function, and, as we shall see, the physician who treated them felt threatened both as a professional and as a rejected male. He was the therapist thwarted, the child untended, the husband denied nurturance and sex.

During the second half of the nineteenth century, the newly established germ theory and discoveries by neurologists and anatomists for the first time made an insistence on disease spec-

[24] See, for example, George Preston, *Hysteria and Certain Allied Conditions*, (Philadelphia: P. Blakiston, Son & Co., 1897), pp. 31, 53; Charles E. Lockwood, *op. cit.* p. 346; Buel Eastman, *op. cit.*, p. 39; Thomas More Madden, *Clinical Gynecology*, (Philadelphia: J. B. Lippincott, 1895), p. 472.

[25] See W. Symington Brown, *A Clinical Handbook on the Diseases of Women*, (New York: William Wood & Company, 1882); Charles L. Dana, "A Study of the Anaesthesias of Hysteria," *American Journal of the Medical Sciences* (October, 1890), p. 1; William S. Playfair, *The Systematic Treatment of Nerve Prostration and Hysteria*, (Philadelphia: Henry C. Lea's Son & Co., 1883), p. 29.

ificity a *sine qua non* for scientific respectability. Neurology was just becoming accepted as a speciality, and in its search for acceptance it was particularly dependent on the establishment of firm, somatically-based disease entities.[26] If hysteria *was* a disease, and not the imposition of self-pitying women striving to avoid their traditional roles and responsibilities—as was frequently charged, it must be a disease with a specific etiology and a predictable course. In the period 1870 to 1900, especially, it was felt to be a disease rooted in some specific organic malfunction.

Hysteria, of course, lacked all such disease characteristics. Contracture or paralysis could occur without muscular atrophy or change in skin temperature. The hysteric might mimic tuberculosis, heart attacks, blindness or hip disease, while lungs, heart, eyes and hips remained in perfect health.[27] The physician had only his patient's statement that she could not move or was wracked with pain. If concerned and sympathetic, he faced a puzzling dilemma. As George Preston wrote in his 1897 monograph on hysteria:

> In studying the . . . disturbances of hysteria, a very formidable difficulty presents itself in the fact that the symptoms are purely subjective. . . . There is only the bald statement of the patient. . . . No confirming symptoms present themselves . . . and the appearance of the affected parts stands as contradictory evidence against the patient's word.[28]

Equally frustrating and medically inexplicable were the sudden

[26] For a discussion of the importance of creating such organic etiologies in the legitimization of an increasingly large number of such "functional" ills, see Charles E. Rosenberg, "The Place of George M. Beard in Nineteenth-Century Psychiatry," *Bulletin of the History of Medicine*, XXXVI (1962), pp. 245–259. See also Owsei Temkin's discussion in his classic history of epilepsy, *The Falling Sickness*, 2nd edn., rev. (Baltimore: Johns Hopkins University Press, 1971), of the importance placed by neurologists in the late nineteenth century upon the differentiation of epilepsy and hysteria.

[27] William Campbell, *op. cit.*, pp. 440–441; Walter Channing, *Bed Case: Its History and Treatment* (Boston: Ticknor and Fields, 1860), pp. 41–42, 49. Charles L. Mix, "Hysteria: Its Nature and Etiology," *New York Medical Journal*, LXXII (August, 1900), pp. 183–189.

[28] George Preston, *op. cit.*, pp. 96–97.

changes in the hysteric's symptoms. Paralysis or anaesthesia could shift from one side of the body to the other, from one limb to another. Headaches would replace contracture of a limb, loss of voice, the inability to taste. How could a physician prescribe for such ephemeral symptoms? "Few practitioners desire the management of hysterics," one eminent gynecologist, Samuel Ashwell, wrote in 1833. "Its symptoms are so varied and obscure, so contradictory and changeable, and if by chance several of them, or even a single one be relieved, numerous others almost immediately spring into existence." [29] Half a century later, neurologist Charles K. Mills echoed Ashwell's discouraging evaluation. "Hysteria is pre-eminently a chronic disease," he warned. "Deceptive remissions in hysterical symptoms often mislead the unwary practitioner. Cures are sometimes claimed where simply a change in the character of the phenomena has taken place. It is a disease in which it is unsafe to claim a conquest." [30]

Yet physicians, especially newly established neurologists with urban practices, were besieged by patients who appeared to be sincere, respectable women sorely afflicted with pain, paralysis or uncontrollable "nervous fits." "Looking at the pain evoked by ideas and beliefs," S. Weir Mitchell, America's leading expert on hysteria wrote in 1885, "we are hardly wise to stamp these pains as non-existent." [31] Despite the tendency of many physicians to contemptuously dismiss the hysterical patient when no organic lesions could be found, neurologists such as Mitchell, George M. Beard, or Charles L. Dana sympathized with these patients and sought to alleviate their symptoms.

Such pioneer specialists were therefore in the position of having defined hysteria as a legitimate disease entity, and the hysterical woman as sick, when they were painfully aware that no organic etiology had yet been found. Cautiously, they sought to formally define hysteria in terms appropriately mechanistic. Some late

[29] Samuel Ashwell, *op. cit.*, p. 226.
[30] Charles K. Mills, *op. cit.*, p. 258.
[31] S. Weir Mitchell, *Lectures on the Diseases of the Nervous System*, *op. cit.*, p. 66.

nineteenth-century physicians, for example, still placing a traditional emphasis on hysteria's uterine origins, argued that hysteria resulted from "the reflex effects of utero-ovarian irritation."[82] Others, reflecting George M. Beard's work on neurasthenia, defined hysteria as a functional disease caused either by "metabolic or nutritional changes in the cellular elements of the central nervous system." Still others wrote in terms of a malfunction of the cerebral cortex.[83] All such explanations were but hypothetical gropings for an organic explanation—still a necessity if they were to legitimate hysteria as a disease.[84]

The fear that hysteria might after all be only a functional or "ideational" disease—to use a nineteenth-century term—and therefore not really a disease at all, underlies much of the writing on hysteria as well as the physicians' own attitudes toward their patients. These hysterical women might after all be only clever frauds and sensation-seekers—morally delinquent and, for the physician, professionally embarrassing.

Not surprisingly, a compensatory sense of superiority and hostility permeated many physicians' discussions of the nature and etiology of hysteria. Except when called upon to provide

[82] Thomas More Madden, *op. cit.*, p. 474. The uterine origin of hysteria was by far the most commonly held opinion throughout the eighteenth and nineteenth centuries. Some believed it to be the exclusive cause, others to be among the most important causes. For three typical examples see: Alexander Hamilton, *A Treatise on the Management of Female Complaints and of Children in Early Infancy* (Edinburgh: Peter Hill, 1792), pp. 51–53. George J. Engelmann, "Hystero-Neurosis," *op. cit.*, note 12; Augustus P. Clarke, "Relations of Hysteria to Structural Changes in the Uterus and its Adnexa," *American Journal of Obstetrics*, XXXIII (1894), pp. 477–483. The uterine theory came under increasing attack during the late nineteenth century. See Hugh J. Patrick, "Hysteria; Neurasthenia," *International Clinics*, III (1898), pp. 183–184; F. C. Skey, *op. cit.*, p. 68.

[83] Robert Barnes, *Medical and Surgical Diseases of Women*, (Philadelphia: H. C. Lea, 1874), p. 101; S. D. Hopkins, "A Case of Hysteria Simulating Organic Disease of the Brain," *Medical Fortnightly*, XI (July 1897), p. 327; C. K. Mills, *op. cit.*, p. 218; J. Leonard Corning, *A Treatise on Hysteria and Epilepsy* (Detroit: George S. Davis, 1888), p. 2; August A. Eshner, "Hysteria in Early Life," read before the Philadelphia County Medical Society, June 23, 1897.

[84] For examples of such concern and complexity, see A. A. King, "Hysteria," *The American Journal of Obstetrics*, XXIV (May, 1891), pp. 513–515; Marshall Hall, *Commentaries Principally on the Diseases of Females* (London: Sherwood, Gilbert and Piper, 1830), p. 118; C. L'Isère, *op. cit.*, p. 530.

a hypothetical organic etiology, physicians saw hysteria as caused either by the indolent, vapid and unconstructive life of the fashionable middle and upper class woman, or by the ignorant, exhausting and sensual life of the lower or working class woman. Neither were flattering etiologies. Both denied the hysteric the sympathy granted to sufferers from unquestionably organic ailments.

Any general description of the personal characteristics of the well-to-do hysteric emphasized her idleness, self-indulgence, her deceitfulness and "craving for sympathy." Petted and spoiled by her parents, waited upon hand and foot by servants, she had never been taught to exercise self-control or to curb her emotions and desires.[35] Certainly she had not been trained to undertake the arduous and necessary duties of wife and mother. "Young persons who have been raised in luxury and too often in idleness," one late-nineteenth-century physician lectured, "who have never been called upon to face the hardships of life, who have never accustomed themselves to self-denial, who have abundant time and opportunity to cultivate the emotional and sensuous, to indulge the sentimental side of life, whose life purpose is too often an indefinite and self-indulgent idea of pleasure, these are the most frequent victims of hysteria."[36] Sound education, outside interests such as charity and good works, moral training, systematic outdoor exercise and removal from an overly sympathetic family were among the most frequent forms of treatment recommended. Mothers, consistently enough, were urged to bring up daughters with a strong sense of self-discipline, devotion to family needs, and a dread of uncontrolled emotionality.[37]

Emotional indulgence, moral weakness and lack of will power characterized the hysteric in both lay and medical thought. Hys-

[35] Robert B. Carter, *op. cit.*, p. 140; J. L. Corning, *op. cit.*, p. 70; Mills, *op. cit.*, p. 218.

[36] Preston, *op. cit.*, p. 36.

[37] See, for example: Mitchell, *Lectures on the Diseases of the Nervous System*, p. 170; Rebecca B. Gleason, M.D., of Elmira, New York, quoted by M. L. Holbrook, *Hygiene of the Brain and Nerves and the Cure of Nervousness* (New York: M. L. Holbrook & Company, 1878), pp. 270–271.

teria, S. Weir Mitchell warned, occurred in women who had never developed habitual restraint and "rational endurance"—who had early lost their power of "self rule."[38] "The mind and body are deteriorated by the force of evil habit," Charles Lockwood wrote in 1895, "morbid thought and morbid impulse run through the poor, weak, unresisting brain, until all mental control is lost, and the poor sufferer is . . . at the mercy of . . . evil and unrestrained passions, appetites and morbid thoughts and impulses."[39]

In an age when will, control, and hard work were fundamental social values, this hypothetical etiology necessarily implied a negative evaluation of those who succumbed to hysteria. Such women were described as weak, capricious and, perhaps most important, morbidly suggestible.[40] Their intellectual abilities were meager, their powers of concentration eroded by years of self-indulgence and narcissistic introspection.[41] Hysterical women were, in effect, children, and ill-behaved, difficult children at that. "They have in fact" Robert Carter wrote, "all the instability of childhood, joined to the vices and passions of adult age. . . .[42]

Many nineteenth-century critics felt that this emotional regression and instability was rooted in woman's very nature. The female nervous system, doctors argued, was physiologically more sensitive and thus more difficult to subject to the will. Some physicians assumed as well that woman's blood was "thinner" than man's, causing nutritional inadequacies in the central nervous system and an inability to store nervous energy—a weakness, Mary Putnam Jacobi stressed, women shared with children. Most commonly, a woman's emotional states generally, and hysteria in particular, were believed to have the closest ties to her reproduc-

[38] S. Weir Mitchell, *Fat and Blood* (Philadelphia: J. B. Lippincott, 1881), pp. 30–31.

[39] Lockwood, *op. cit.*, pp. 342–343; virtually every authority on hysteria echoed these sentiments.

[40] Alexander Hamilton, *op. cit.*, p. 52; Dixon, *op. cit.*, pp. 142–143; Ashwell, *op. cit.*, p. 217; Mills, *op. cit.*, p. 230.

[41] Walter Channing, *op. cit.*, p. 28.

[42] Robert B. Carter, *op. cit.*, p. 113.

tive cycle.[43] Hysteria commenced with puberty and ended with menopause, while ailments as varied as menstrual pain and irregularity, prolapsed or tipped uterus, uterine tumor, vaginal infections and discharges, sterility, could all—doctors were certain—cause hysteria. Indeed, the first question routinely asked hysterical women was "are your courses regular?"[44] Thus a woman's very physiology and anatomy predisposed her to hysteria; it was, as Thomas Laycock put it, "the natural state" in a female, a "morbid state" in the male.[45] In an era when a sexual perspective implied conflict and ambivalence, hysteria was perceived by physician and patient as a disease both peculiarly female and peculiarly sexual.

Hysteria could also result from a secret and less forgivable form of sexuality. Throughout the nineteenth century, physicians believed that masturbation was widespread among America's females and a frequent cause of hysteria and insanity. As early as 1846, E. H. Dixon reported that masturbation caused hysteria "among females even in society where physical and intellectual culture would seem to present the strongest barriers against its incursions. . . ." Other physicians concurred, reporting that harsh public and medical reactions to hysterical women were

[43] Mary P. Jacobi, *op. cit.*, pp. 384–388; M. E. Dirix, *Woman's Complete Guide to Health* (New York: W. A. Townsend & Adams, 1869), p. 24; E. B. Foote, *Medical Common Sense* (New York: Published by the author, 1864), p. 167.

[44] Reuben Ludlum, *Lectures, Clinical and Didactic, on the Diseases of Women* (Chicago: C. S. Halsey, 1872), p. 87; Robert Barnes, *op. cit.*, p. 247. In 1847, the well-known Philadelphia gynecologist, Charles D. Meigs, had asked his medical school class the rhetorical question: "What is her erotic state? What the protean manifestations of the life force developed by a reproductive irritation which you call hysteria." Meigs, *Lectures on the Distinctive Characteristics of the Female*, delivered before the Class of Jefferson Medical College, January 5, 1847 (Philadelphia: T. K. & P. G. Collins, 1847), p. 20.

[45] Thomas Laycock, *Essay on Hysteria*, pp. 76, 103, 105. See also Graham J. Barker-Benfield, "The Horrors of the Half-Known Life" (unpublished Ph.D. thesis, University of California at Los Angeles, 1969) and Ann Douglas Wood, "The Fashionable Diseases: Women's Complaints and Their Treatment in Nineteenth Century America," *Journal of Interdisciplinary History* (in press) for a speculative psychoanalytic approach to gynecological practice in nineteenth-century America.

often based on the belief that masturbation was the cause of their behavior.[46]

Masturbation was only one form of sexual indulgence. A number of doctors saw hysteria among lower class women as originating in the sensuality believed to characterize their class. Such tenement-dwelling females, doctors reported, "gave free reign to . . . 'passions of the baser sort,' not feeling the necessity of self-control because they have to a pitiably small degree any sense of propriety or decency." Hysteria, another physician reported, was found commonly among prostitutes, while virtually all physicians agreed that even within marriage sexual excess could easily lead to hysteria.[47]

Expectedly, conscious anger and hostility marked the response of a good many doctors to their hysterical patients. One New York neurologist called the female hysteric a willful, self-indulgent and narcissistic person who cynically manipulated her symptoms. "To her distorted vision," he complained, "there is but one commanding personage in the universe—herself—in comparison with whom the rest of mankind are nothing." Doctors admitted that they were frequently tempted to use such terms as "willful" and "evil," "angry" and "impatient" when describing the hysteric and her symptoms.[48] Even the concerned and genteel S. Weir Mitchell, confident of his remarkable record in curing hysteria, described hysterical women as "the pests of many households, who constitute the despair of physicians, and who furnish those

[46] Dixon, *op. cit.*, p. 134; J. Leonard Corning, *op. cit.*, p. 70; William Murray, *A Treatise on Emotional Disorders of the Sympathetic System of the Nerves*, (London: John Churchill, 1866). An extensive nineteenth-century masturbation literature exists. See, for example, Samuel Gregory, *Facts and Important Information for Young Women on the Self-Indulgence of the Sexual Appetite* (Boston: George Gregory, 1857), and Calvin Cutter, *The Female Guide: Containing Facts and Information upon the Effects of Masturbation* (West Brookfield, Mass.: Charles A. Mirick, 1844). Most general treatises on masturbation refer to its occurrence in females.

[47] Preston, *op. cit.*, p. 37; Carter, *op. cit.*, pp. 46, 90. Nineteenth-century physicians maintained a delicate balance in their view of the sexual etiology of hysteria. Any deviation from moderation could cause hysteria or insanity: habitual masturbation, extended virginity, over-indulgence, prostitution, or sterility.

[48] Skey, *op. cit.*, p. 63.

annoying examples of despotic selfishness, which wreck the constitutions of nurses and devoted relatives, and in unconscious or half-conscious self-indulgence destroy the comfort of everyone about them." He concluded by quoting Oliver Wendell Holmes' acid judgment that "a hysterical girl is a vampire who sucks the blood of the healthy people about her."[49]

Hysteria as a chronic, dramatic and socially accepted sick role could thus provide some alleviation of conflict and tension, but the hysteric purchased her escape from the emotional—and frequently—from the sexual demands of her life only at the cost of pain, disability, and an intensification of woman's traditional passivity and dependence. Indeed a complex interplay existed between the character traits assigned women in Victorian society and the characteristic symptoms of the nineteenth-century hysteric: dependency, fragility, emotionality, narcissism. (Hysteria has, after all, been called in that century and this a stark caricature of femininity.) Not surprisingly the hysteric's peculiar passive aggression and her exploitive dependency often functioned to cue a corresponding hostility in the men who cared for her or lived with her. Whether father, husband, or physician, they reacted with ambivalence and in many cases with hostility to her aggressive and never-ending demands.

II

What inferences concerning woman's role and female-male relationships can be drawn from this description of nineteenth-century hysteria and of medical attitudes toward the female patient? What insights does it allow into patterns of stress and resolution within the traditional nuclear family?

Because traditional medical wisdom had defined hysteria as a disease, its victims could expect to be treated as sick and thus to elicit a particular set of responses—the right to be seen and treated by a physician, to stay in bed and thus be relieved of their

[49] Mitchell, *Lectures on the Diseases of the Nervous System*, p. 266; S. Weir Mitchell, *Fat and Blood*, *op. cit.*, p. 37.

normal day-to-day responsibilities, to enjoy the special prerogatives, indulgences, and sympathy the sick role entailed. Hysteria thus became one way in which conventional women could express—in most cases unconsciously—dissatisfaction with one or several aspects of their lives.

The effect of hysteria upon the family and traditional sex role differentiation was disruptive in the extreme. The hysterical woman virtually ceased to function within the family. No longer did she devote herself to the needs of others, acting as self-sacrificing wife, mother, or daughter. Through her hysteria she could and in fact did force others to assume those functions. Household activities were reoriented to answer the hysterical woman's importunate needs. Children were hushed, rooms darkened, entertaining suspended, a devoted nurse recruited. Fortunes might be spent on medical bills or for drugs and operations. Worry and concern bowed the husband's shoulders; his home had suddenly become a hospital and he a nurse. Through her illness, the bedridden woman came to dominate her family to an extent that would have been considered inappropriate—indeed shrewish—in a healthy woman. Taking to one's bed, especially when suffering from dramatic and ever-visible symptoms, might also have functioned as a mode of passive aggression, especially in a milieu in which weakness was rewarded and in which women had since childhood been taught not to express overt aggression. Consciously or unconsciously, she had thus opted out of her traditional role.

Women did not accomplish this redefinition of domestic roles without the aid of the men in their family. Doctors commented that the hysteric's husband and family often, and unfortunately, rewarded her symptoms with elaborate sympathy. "The hysteric's credit is usually first established," as one astute mid-century clinician pointed out, "by those who have, at least, the wish to believe them." [50] Husbands and fathers were not alone in their cooperation; the physician often played a complex and in a sense emo-

[50] Carter, *op. cit.*, p. 58.

tionally compromising role in legitimizing the female hysteric's behavior. As an impartial and professionally skilled observer, he was empowered to judge whether or not a particular woman had the right to withdraw from her socially allotted duties. At the same time, these physicians accepted as correct, indeed as biologically inevitable, the structure of the Victorian family and the division of sex roles within it. He excused the woman only in the belief that she was ill and that she would make every effort to get well and resume her accustomed role. It was the transitory and unavoidable nature of the sick role that made it acceptable to family and physician as an alternate mode of female behavior.[61]

The doctor's ambivalence toward the hysterical woman, already rooted as we have seen in professional and sexual uncertainties, may well have been reinforced by his complicitory role within the family. It was for this reason that the disease's erratic pattern, its chronic nature, its lack of a determinable organic etiology, and the patient's seeming failure of will, so angered him. Even if she were not a conscious malingerer, she might well be guilty of self-indulgence and moral delinquency. By diagnosing her as ill, he had in effect created or permitted the hysterical woman to create a bond between himself and her. Within the family configuration he had sided with her against her husband or other male family members—men with whom he would normally have identified.[62]

The quintessential sexual nature of hysteria further complicated the doctor's professional stance. As we have already seen, the hysterical patient in her role as woman may well have mobilized whatever ambivalence towards sex a particular physician felt. In a number of cases, moreover, the physician also played the role of oedipal father figure to the patient's child-woman role, and in such instances his complicity was not only moral and

[61] For an exposition of this argument see Erving Goffman, "Insanity of Place," *Psychiatry*, XXXII (1969), pp. 357–388.

[62] Such complaints are commonplace in the medical literature. See Mitchell, *Lectures*, p. 67; Mitchell, *Doctor and Patient*, *op. cit.*, p. 117; Robert Thornton, *The Hysterical Women: Trials, Tears, Tricks and Tantrums*, (Chicago: Donohue & Henneberry, 1893), pp. 97–98; Channing, *op. cit.*, pp. 35–37; L'Isère, *op. cit.*, p. 534.

intellectual but sexual as well. These doctors had become part of a domestic triangle—a husband's rival, the fatherly attendant of a daughter. This intra-family role may therefore go far to explain the particularly strident and suspicious tone which characterized much of the clinical discussion of hysteria. The physician had, by his alertness to deception and self-indulgence and by his therapeutic skills, to prevent the hysterical woman from using her disease to avoid her feminine duties—and from making him an unwitting accomplice in her deviant role. While tied to her as physician and thus legitimizer of her sick role, he had also to preserve his independence.

Although much of this interpretation must remain speculative, both the tone and substance of contemporary medical reaction to the female hysteric tends to confirm these inferences. Physicians were concerned with—and condemned—the power which chronic illness such as hysteria gave a woman over her family. Many women, doctors noted with annoyance, enjoyed this power and showed no inclination to get well: it is hardly coincidental that most late-nineteenth-century authorities agreed that removal from her family was a necessary first step in attempting to cure the hysterical patient.[58]

Not only did the physician condemn the hysteric's power within her family, he was clearly sensitive to her as a threat to his own prestige and authority. It is evident from their writings that many doctors felt themselves to be locked in a power struggle with their hysterical patients. Such women, doctors claimed, used their symptoms as weapons in asserting autonomy in relation to their physician; in continued illness was their victory. Physicians perceived hysterical women as unusually intractable and self-assertive. Although patients and women, they reserved the right to judge and approve their male physician's every action.

[58] The fact that the physician was at the same time employed and paid by the woman or her family—in a period when the profession was far more competitive and economically insecure than it is in mid-twentieth century—implied another level of stress and ambiguity.

Indeed, much of the medical literature on hysteria is devoted to providing doctors with the means of winning this war of wills. Physicians felt that they must dominate the hysteric's will; only in this way, they wrote, could they bring about her permanent cure. "Do not flatter yourselves . . . that you will gain an easy victory," Dr. L. C. Grey told a medical school class in 1888:

> On the contrary, you must expect to have your temper, your ingenuity, your nerves tested to a degree that cannot be surpassed even by the greatest surgical operations. I maintain that the man who has the nerve and the tact to conquer some of these grave cases of hysteria has the nerve and the tact that will make him equal to the great emergencies of life. Your patient must be taught day by day . . . by steady resolute, iron-willed determination and tact—that combination which the French . . . call "the iron hand beneath the velvet glove."[54]

"Assume a tone of authority which will of itself almost compel submission," Robert Carter directed. "If a patient . . . interrupts the speaker, she must be told to keep silence and to listen; and must be told, moreover, not only in a voice that betrays no impatience and no anger, but in such a manner as to convey the speaker's full conviction that the command will be immediately obeyed."[55]

Much of the treatment prescribed by physicians for hysteria reflects, in its draconic severity, their need to exert control—and, when thwarted, their impulse to punish. Doctors frequently recommended suffocating hysterical women until their fits stopped, beating them across the face and body with wet towels, ridiculing and exposing them in front of family and friends, showering them with icy water. "The mode adopted to arrest this curious malady," a physican connected with a large mental hospital wrote,

> consists in making some strong and sudden impression on the mind through . . . the most potent of all impressions, fear. . . .

[54] Channing, *op. cit.*, p. 22; Thomas A. Emmett, *Principles and Practices of Gynecology* (Philadelphia: H. C. Lea, 1879), p. 107; L. C. Grey, "Clinical Lecture," p. 132.

[55] Carter, *op. cit.*, p. 119; Ashwell, *op. cit.*, p. 227.

> Ridicule to a woman of sensitive mind, is a powerful weapon . . . but there is no emotion equal to fear and the threat of personal chastisement . . . They will listen to the voice of authority.[56]

When, on the other hand, the hysterical patient proved tractable, gave up her fits or paralyses and accepted the physician as saviour and moral guide, he no longer had to appear in the posture of chastising father. He could respond to his hysterical patient with fondness, sympathy, and praise. No longer was she thwarting him with "temper, tears, tricks, and tantrums"—as one doctor chose to title a study of hysteria.[57] Her cure demonstrated that he had mastered her will and body. The successful father-like practitioner had restored another wayward woman to her familial duties. Thomas Addis Emmett, pioneer gynecological specialist, recalled with ingenuous candor his mode of treating hysterics:

> the patient . . . was a child in my hands. In some respects the power gained was not unlike that obtained over a wild beast except that in one case the domination would be due to fear, while with my patient as a rule, it would be the desire to please me and to merit my approval from the effort she would make to gain her self-control. I have at times been depressed with the responsibility attending the blind influence I have often been able to gain over the nervous women under my influence.[58]

Not surprisingly, S. Weir Mitchell ended one of his treatises on hysteria with the comment that doctors, who knew and understood all women's petty weaknesses, who could govern and forgive them, made the best husbands.[59] Clearly the male physician who treated the hysterical woman was unable to escape the sex role relations that existed within nineteenth-century society generally.

[56] Skey, *op. cit.*, p. 60.

[57] Robert Thornton, *op. cit.*

[58] Thomas A. Emmett, *Incidents of My Life*, (New York: G. P. Putnam's Sons, 1911), p. 210. These are Emmett's recollections at the end of a long life. It is interesting that decades earlier Emmett, in discussing treating hysterical women, had confessed in hostile frustration that "in fact the physician is helpless. . . ." Emmett, *Principles and Practices*, *op. cit.*, p. 107.

[59] Mitchell, *Doctor and Patient*, pp. 99–100.

III

The hysterical female thus emerges from the essentially male medical literature of the nineteenth century as a "child-woman," highly impressionable, labile, superficially sexual, exhibitionistic, given to dramatic body language and grand gestures, with strong dependency needs and decided ego weaknesses. She resembled in many ways the personality type referred to by Guze in 1967 as a "hysterical personality," or by Kernberg in 1968 as an "infantile personality."[60] But in a very literal sense these characteristics of the hysteric were merely hypertrophied versions of traits and behavior commonly reinforced in female children and adolescents. At a time when American society accepted egalitarian democracy and free will as transcendent social values, women, as we have seen, were nevertheless routinely socialized to fill a weak, dependent and severely limited social role. They were sharply discouraged from expressing competition or mastery in such "masculine" areas as physical skill, strength and courage, or in academic or commercial pursuits, while at the same time they were encouraged to be coquettish, entertaining, non-threatening and nurturant. Overt anger and violence were forbidden as unfeminine and vulgar. The effect of this socialization was to teach women to have a low evaluation of themselves, to significantly restrict their ego functions to low prestige areas, to depend on others and to altruistically wish not for their own worldly success, but for that of their male supporters.

In essence, then, many nineteenth-century women reached maturity with major ego weaknesses and with narrowly limited compensatory ego strengths, all of which implies, I think, a generic relationship between this pattern of socialization and the adoption of hysterical behavior by particular individuals. It

[60] Samuel Guze, "The Diagnosis of Hysteria: What are We Trying to Do," *American Journal of Psychiatry*, CXXIV (1967), pp. 494–498; Otto Kernberg, "Borderline Personality Organization," *Journal of the American Psychoanalytical Association*, XV (1967), pp. 641–685. For a critical discussion of the entire problem of diagnosis, see Henry Bachrach, "In Defense of Diagnosis," *Psychiatry* (in press).

seems plausible to suggest that a certain percentage of nineteenth-century women faced with stress developing out of their own peculiar personality needs or because of situational anxieties might well have defended themselves against such stress by regressing towards the childish hyper-femininity of the hysteric. The discontinuity between the roles of courted woman and pain-bearing, self-sacrificing wife and mother, the realities of an unhappy marriage, the loneliness and chagrin of spinsterhood may all have made the petulant infantilism and narcissistic self-assertion of the hysteric a necessary alternative to women who felt unfairly deprived of their promised social role and who had few strengths with which to adapt to a more trying one. Society had indeed structured this regression by consistently reinforcing those very emotional traits characterized in the stereotype of the female—and caricatured in the symptomatology of the hysteric. At the same time, the nineteenth-century female hysteric also exhibited a significant level of hostility and aggression—rage—which may have led in turn to her depression and to her self-punishing psychosomatic illnesses. In all these ways, then, the hysterical woman can be seen as both product and indictment of her culture.

I must conclude with a caution. The reasons why individuals displayed that pattern of behavior called by nineteenth-century physicians "hysteria" must in individual cases remain moot. What this paper has sought to do is to suggest why certain symptoms were available and why women, in particular, tended to resort to them. It has sought as well to use the reactions of contemporaries to illuminate female-male and intrafamilial role realities. As such it has dealt with hysteria as a social role produced by and functional within a specific set of social circumstances.

Smothered Slave Infants: Were Slave Mothers at Fault?

By MICHAEL P. JOHNSON

IN THE SOUTH CAROLINA UPCOUNTRY DISTRICT OF ABBEVILLE IN 1850 a one-month-old slave girl named Harriet was reported to the census marshal Charles M. Pelot as having died in December 1849 because she was "Smothered by carelessness of [her] mother." Similar reports are scattered throughout the mortality schedules of the United States census for the southern states. Allice Burrow, a six-month-old slave girl in Henrico County, Virginia, "was Smouthered by her Mother Lying on her while asleep"; in Tippah County, Mississippi, the two-month-old slave girl Biddy was "Accidentally overlaid by [her] mother in her Sleep"; in Cobb County, Georgia, an eight-month-old slave boy was "Overlaid by [his] Mother"; in Spartanburg District, South Carolina, a five-month-old slave girl was said to have been "Overlaid by [her] mother and smothered."[1] The grim record goes on and on.

In 1860 the slave states accounted for 94 percent of the nation's 2,129 reported deaths by suffocation. Most of these victims "were probably the children of slaves," the published mortality census

[1] All citations are from Manuscript Census Returns, Seventh Census of the United States, 1850, South Carolina, Schedule 3, Mortality, South Carolina Microcopy Number 2, roll 1; and Manuscript Census Returns, Eighth Census of the United States, 1860, Georgia, Schedule 3, Mortality, National Archives Microfilm Series T-655, roll 8; Virginia, Schedule 3, Mortality, National Archives Microfilm Series T-1132, roll 5; Mississippi, Schedule 3, Mortality, Mississippi Department of Archives and History Microfilm, roll 2730; South Carolina, Schedule 3, Mortality, South Carolina Microcopy No. 2, roll 1. These are cited hereafter by state, year, and county or district. Quotations in the text are, in order of their appearance, from South Carolina Mortality Schedules, 1850, Abbeville District, frame 3; Virginia Mortality Schedules, 1860, Henrico County, 309; Mississippi Mortality Schedules, 1860, Tippah County, 2 (second paged series); Georgia Mortality Schedules, 1860, Cobb County, 162; and South Carolina Mortality Schedules, 1860, Spartanburg District, frame 378. I am indebted to the late Andrew B. Appleby, Joyce O. Appleby, Carl N. Degler, Jonathan S. Dewald, Stanley L. Engerman, Karl G. Hufbauer, and Jonathan M. Wiener for their critical reading of an earlier version of this article.

MR. JOHNSON is associate professor of history at the University of California at Irvine.

THE JOURNAL OF SOUTHERN HISTORY
Vol. XLVII, No. 4, November 1981

TABLE 1

SMOTHERING DEATHS IN 1860

State	*Whites*	*Slaves*	*White Death Rate*	*Slave Death Rate*	*Slave Death Rate/White Death Rate*
Georgia	10	259	0.5	18.5	37
Mississippi	6	213	0.6	17.5	29
South Carolina	2	122	0.2	10.8	54
Virginia	5	230	0.2	16.6	83
Totals	23	824	0.3	16.0	53

speculated.[2] In 1850, when the published census made a separate calculation of slave and white deaths, 82 percent of the victims of suffocation were slaves.[3] According to a calculation in the 1860 published census slaves were nine times more likely than whites to die of suffocation, a larger interracial gap than for any other cause of death.[4] However, all these figures drastically understate the difference between slaves and whites in the reported incidence of smothering. The appropriate comparison is between death rates. The number of smothered slaves per 1,000 living slave infants should be compared with the number of smothered whites per 1,000 white infants. In 1850 the death rate for smothered slaves was 28 times larger than that for whites.[5] In 1860, according to data from the manuscript mortality schedules of Georgia, Mississippi, South Carolina, and Virginia summarized in Table 1, slave infants were 53

[2] The 1860 published mortality census did not separate slave deaths from white deaths. U. S. Census Office, *Statistics of the United States (Including Mortality, Property, &c.,) in 1860* . . . (Washington, 1866), 252.

[3] There were 934 reported suffocation deaths in 1850, of which 764 were slaves. J. D. B. De Bow, *Mortality Statistics of the Seventh Census of the United States, 1850* (Washington, 1855), 28.

[4] The calculation was based on the 1850 federal mortality data and mortality statistics from Kentucky, New York City, South Carolina, and New Orleans. U. S. Census Office, *Statistics of the United States . . . in 1860*, 281–83.

[5] The 1850 death rate for slave infants who died by smothering was 8.4; that for whites was 0.3. Of course, many deaths from all causes were not reported. Several census marshals made notes similar to that of B. F. Buckner, the marshal in Beaufort District, South Carolina, in 1860, who wrote, "Difficult to obtain correct returns of mortality—few Records of same being kept—and in many instances changes of Overseers & Agents the first of the year—Consequently many deaths unreturned." South Carolina Mortality Schedules, 1860, Beaufort District (St. Peter's Parish), frame 246. The result, as the published 1860 census made clear, was that many deaths were unreported. The exact extent of underenumeration varied widely from place to place, depending both on the reports made to the census marshals and the diligence and expertise of the marshals themselves. Given this underenumeration, any calculation of a death rate is at best an approximation of the actual rate. For the best estimates of death rates for the black population see Jack E. Eblen, "New Estimates of the Vital Rates of the United States Black Population During the Nineteenth Century," *Demography*, XI (May 1974), 301–19.

times more likely to die of smothering than were southern white infants.[6] Between 1790 and 1860 smothering was responsible for the deaths of over 60,000 slave infants.[7]

The reason so many slave children were smothered was quite clear to contemporaries. Slave mothers were careless. As they slept with their infants, they accidentally overlaid and smothered them. The fault clearly lay with the mothers. ". . . I wish it to be distinctly understood that nearly all the accidents occur in the negro population," wrote Pelot, adding, "which goes clearly to prove their great carelessness & total inability to take care of themselves."[8] Although many southerners would have considered Pelot's statement an exaggeration, virtually all would have agreed that the smothering deaths were accidental. Again and again census marshals noted "smothered accidentally" or "overlaid by accident." None of the smothering deaths in Georgia, Mississippi, South Carolina, and Virginia in 1860 produced even a hint of infanticide. There was simply no motive. An observer "will see how very prolific the female slaves are," Pelot noted, "which shows conclusively that their minds are at ease & that they are reconciled and satisfied with the station which God has pleased to place them in."[9] A content, sleepy

[6] The data in Table 1 and in all the other tables and figures in this article, with the exception of Table 6, were collected from the manuscript mortality schedules of the 1860 federal census of Georgia, Mississippi, South Carolina, and Virginia. The data include every person in each of these states whose cause of death was listed in the 1860 mortality schedules as smothered, overlaid, or suffocated. Most of the victims were reported as having been smothered (77 percent); those reported as having been overlaid or suffocated accounted for 18 and 5 percent respectively. The death rates in Table 1 were obtained by dividing the total number of smothering deaths in each state and in the four states together by the total number of living white and slave infants in each state and in the four states together. (Infants are defined as children who are less than one year old.) Today, smothering death rates would be expressed as the number of smothering deaths per thousand live births. But since the number of live births in 1860 is unknown, the number of living infants has been used for the denominator of the death-rate calculation. This method of calculating the death rate has been used throughout this article.

[7] This is a conservative estimate based on the assumption that the 1860 smothering death rate of sixteen deaths per thousand living slave infants was constant from 1790 to 1860. The number of slave infants (again, defined as those under one year of age) was estimated for the census years from 1790 to 1840 by assuming that 7.9 percent of the slaves under ten were infants (which was the case in 1850) and by assuming that the population under ten was 34 percent of the total population in the years from 1790 to 1810. The number of slave infants in each year was estimated by a simple linear regression of the decadal infant estimates. With this procedure, the estimated number of smothering deaths between 1790 and 1860 was 62,191. Of course, a nonlinear regression procedure, different annual slave infant population estimates, and shifts in the death rate would all affect the exact numerical result. But since it is unlikely that the smothering death rate declined during this period and since the actual slave infant population was probably larger than that estimated by the linear-regression procedure, the total number of smothered slave infants was probably well over 60,000.

[8] South Carolina Mortality Schedules, 1850, Abbeville District, frames 11–12.

[9] *Ibid.*, frames 16–17.

slave mother carelessly rolled over her infant and smothered it.

Of course, carelessness could be compounded by exhaustion. Thomas Affleck, a planter in the hill country of Mississippi, reported in a southern medical journal that "not a few [slave infants] are over-laid by the wearied mother, who sleeps so dead a sleep as not to be aware of the injury to her infant . . . ."[10] Other medical writers concurred about the dangers of hard work for slave women.[11] But none of the census marshals in the states surveyed in this article recorded any remarks that suggested masters contributed to the smothering deaths by working slave women too hard. Yet the census data suggest very strongly that the heavy physical labor masters assigned to slave women—not the carelessness of the slave mothers—was the major reason so many slave infants were "smothered."

In fact, it is extremely unlikely that these slave infants were victims of smothering. Several historians have recently argued that suffocation deaths were caused by Sudden Infant Death Syndrome (SIDS). Todd L. Savitt's pioneering study of the smothered slaves listed in the death registers of twenty-four Virginia counties and two towns between 1853 and 1860 identified "a remarkable epidemiological correspondence [between smothered slaves and modern victims of SIDS], both in age and in seasonal variation." Savitt pointed out that medical scientists do not fully understand the etiology of SIDS, but he suggested that an "important factor" in the large difference between the smothering death rates of slaves and whites was "the marked underreporting of white suffocation deaths . . . , probably due in part to the social stigma associated with child smothering."[12] Robert William Fogel and Stanley L.

[10] Affleck, "On the Hygiene of Cotton Plantations and the Management of Negro Slaves," *Southern Medical Reports*, II (1851), 435. Of course, masters could blame overseers for overworking slave women, as did Thomas Jefferson: ". . . the loss of 5 little ones in 4 years induces me to fear that the overseers do not permit the [slave] women to devote as much time as is necessary to the care of their children: that they view their labor as the 1st object and the raising of their child but as secondary. I consider the labor of a breeding woman as no object, and that a child raised every 2 years is of more profit than the crop of the best laboring man. in this, as in all other cases, providence has made our interests and our duties coincide perfectly. . . . I must pray you to inculcate upon the overseers that it is not their labor, but their increase which is the first consideration with us." Jefferson to Joel Yancey, January 17, 1819, Edwin M. Betts, ed., *Thomas Jefferson's Farm Book: With Commentary and Relevant Extracts from Other Writings* (Princeton, 1953), 43.

[11] See for example John H. Morgan, "An Essay on the Causes of the Production of Abortion Among Our Negro Population," *Nashville Journal of Medicine and Surgery*, XIX (August 1860), 117, 120–21; [Edmund M. Pendleton], "On the Susceptibility of the Caucasian and African Races to the Different Classes of Disease," *Southern Medical Reports*, I (1850), 338.

[12] Savitt, *Medicine and Slavery: The Diseases and Health Care of Blacks in Antebellum*

Engerman offered a similar interpretation, arguing that deaths actually caused by "undisclosed infections" were probably more likely to be "reported as suffocation for slaves than for free men" because of "the jaundiced view of the overseers who reported the death statistics to the census takers."[13]

Although neither Savitt nor Fogel and Engerman estimated how much of the difference between white and slave smothering rates could be accounted for by white underreporting and slave overreporting, both studies emphasized that the mothers of the children were not responsible for the deaths.[14] Modern research has demonstrated, as Savitt said, "that children cannot be smothered as long as there is any circulating air available, even when the infant is beneath the covers or wedged against the sleeping mother."[15] Instead of accidental suffocation, specific mineral deficiencies may have been responsible for these deaths, Kenneth F. Kiple and Virginia H. Kiple have argued.[16] Although the Kiples acknowledged that scientists have not uncovered any compelling evidence of the role of calcium and magnesium deficiencies in SIDS, they nonetheless asserted that the similarities between SIDS and the "nutritional tetany" sometimes caused by these mineral deficiencies "strongly indicate a nutritional etiology" for SIDS and smothered slaves.[17] "Black children were victims of a conspiracy of nutrition, African environmental heritage, and North American climatic circumstances rather than planter mistreatment," they concluded.[18]

Richard Sutch suggested just the opposite conclusion in his searching critique of Fogel and Engerman's analysis of slave nutrition. "The staggering difference between slave and white infant suffocation rates . . . would appear as reflections of extreme pov-

---

Virginia (Urbana, Chicago, and London, 1978), 124 (first quotation), 126 (second and third quotations). See also Savitt, "Smothering and Overlaying of Virginia Slave Children: A Suggested Explanation," *Bulletin of the History of Medicine*, XLIX (Fall 1975), 400–404.

[13] Fogel and Engerman, *Time on the Cross: The Economics of American Negro Slavery* (Boston and Toronto, 1974), 126; cited hereinafter as *Time on the Cross*, I.

[14] However, in a note Fogel and Engerman make the confusing statement that "Virtually all of the difference between the free and slave suffocation rates might be explained by what has recently been identified as the 'sudden infant death' syndrome." *Time on the Cross: Evidence and Methods—A Supplement* (Boston and Toronto, 1974), 101, note 4.5.4; cited hereinafter as *Time on the Cross*, II.

[15] Savitt, *Medicine and Slavery*, 124.

[16] Kiple and Kiple, "Slave Child Mortality: Some Nutritional Answers to a Perennial Puzzle," *Journal of Social History*, X (Spring 1977), 284–309.

[17] *Ibid.*, 296. Although one SIDS researcher, Joan L. Caddell, has argued that magnesium deprivation is related to SIDS, other scientists have failed to confirm her findings and are skeptical about the significance of mineral deficiencies. See Marie Valdes-Dapena, "Sudden Unexplained Infant Death, 1970 Through 1975: An Evolution in Understanding," *Pathology Annual*, XII, Pt. 1 (1977), 139–40.

[18] Kiple and Kiple, "Slave Child Mortality," 299.

erty, low birth weights, and poor postnatal care," Sutch argued.[19] Although the close association of these factors with SIDS is undisputed, Sutch did not develop further his implication that the planters were responsible for their lethal impact on slave children.[20] All these scholars agreed that smothered slaves were actually victims of SIDS but differed sharply over the significance and explanation of the high incidence of smothering among slaves. The conflicting interpretations and their rather narrow empirical base warrant a step-by-step reconsideration of the evidence that smothered slaves were SIDS victims, of the difference between slave and white smothering rates, and of the implications of recent medical research for understanding why so many slaves were "smothered."

First, consider the evidence of smothering. The remarks of the census marshals suggest that infants whose deaths were attributed to smothering were in fact found dead in bed. Usually census marshals simply recorded the cause of death as "smothered" or "overlaid." But in Fauquier County, Virginia, the marshal reported two slave infants who were "Supposed to have been smothered in bed . . . ."[21] In Carroll County, Georgia, a slave girl three months old was reported "Smothered probably."[22] The tentative nature of these remarks suggests that smothering was not observed or certain but inferred from the circumstances in which the dead child was found. James Kincannon, the census marshal in Noxubee County, Mississippi, listed "Found dead" as the cause of death of a nine-month-old slave girl and noted: "Supposed to have been Smothered."[23] Even more detailed notes were made by Thomas R. Nisbet, the marshal in Lancaster District, South Carolina. Alongside the report of a slave infant whose cause of death he listed as "Sudden," Nisbet noted, "found Dead in the Bed." Another slave infant who was "overlaid" was, Nisbet wrote, "found Dead in the morning."[24] Indeed, according to D. W. Johnson, the marshal in Union District, South Carolina, in 1850, the actual number of

[19] Sutch, "The Care and Feeding of Slaves," in Paul A. David *et al., Reckoning with Slavery: A Critical Study in the Quantitative History of American Negro Slavery* (New York, 1976), 292.

[20] The best overviews of recent SIDS research are Richard L. Naeye, "Sudden Infant Death," *Scientific American*, CCXLII (April 1980), 56–62; Marie A. Valdes-Dapena, "Sudden Infant Death Syndrome: A Review of the Medical Literature, 1974-1979," *Pediatrics*, LXVI (October 1980), 597–614; Valdes-Dapena, "Sudden Unexplained Infant Death," 117–45; and J. Bruce Beckwith, *The Sudden Infant Death Syndrome* (Rockville, Md., 1975). The history of SIDS research is analyzed in Karl G. Hufbauer and Michael P. Johnson, "The Social History of SIDS Research in the United States, 1945–1974," unpublished manuscript in possession of the author. A version of the paper was presented at the October 1979 meeting of the Society for the Social Studies of Science.

[21] Virginia Mortality Schedules, 1860, Fauquier County, 214.

[22] Georgia Mortality Schedules, 1860, Carroll County, 75.

[23] Mississippi Mortality Schedules, 1860, Noxubee County, 1 (seventh paged series).

[24] South Carolina Mortality Schedules, 1860, Lancaster District, frames 237, 235.

smothered slave infants was much larger than that reported: "A very large proportion of the Deaths of Infant Slaves [whose cause of death was] reported as Unknown Sudden were supposed to have been caused by their mothers' overlying them during Sleep. The presumptive evidence of this fact was of the strongest character."[25]

Taken together, these fragmentary notes of the census marshals suggest that slave infants who were reported to have been smothered, suffocated, or overlain by their mothers were actually found dead in bed. Since a mother slept with her infant, she was presumed to be responsible for smothering it. The death was presumed to be accidental because there was no evidence that the child was sick—in which case death would have been attributed to another cause. The slave mother's grief probably persuaded her master that the death was indeed accidental and that she was responsible.[26] And in fact, the slave mother probably felt responsible for the tragedy.

Ex-slave Tabby Abbey's testimony is compelling. Born in Virginia in 1833, Tabby Abbey was sold at the age of sixteen and taken to Mississippi, near Tunica. "I never did work 'round de white folks' house but always done field work, mostly clarin' new groun'," she told her interviewer in 1936. "I had one baby in my life, a long time ago; but I went to sleep one day when I wuz nussin' him and rolled over on him and smothered him to death. I like to went crazy for a long time atter dat."[27] How many other slave mothers "like to went crazy" after their babies were discovered dead in their beds cannot be known. But it is possible to establish that it is extremely unlikely that the slave infants were actually smothered by their mothers.

The mortality data provide three important kinds of evidence that most of the smothered slaves were actually SIDS victims: the circumstances in which the dead child was discovered, the child's age, and the month of death. It is well established that SIDS victims die during sleep and are typically discovered dead in their bed, their parents having had no warning that they were seriously ill or distressed.[28] The same circumstances that led masters and slave

[25] South Carolina Mortality Schedules, 1850, Union District, frame 199.

[26] Savitt quotes a master's letter to his brother: "Last week Tilla overlaid /when asleep/ and killed her youngest child—a boy 6 or 7 months old. This was no doubt caused by her own want of care and attention." *Medicine and Slavery*, 124.

[27] George P. Rawick, Jan Hellegas, and Ken Lawrence, eds., *The American Slave: A Composite Autobiography, Supplement*, Series I (12 vols., Westport, Conn., and London, Eng., 1977), VI: *Mississippi Narratives*, Pt. 1, pp. 3–4. Volumes in this series are cited hereinafter as Rawick *et al.*, eds., *American Slave*.

[28] Indeed, "sleep apnea," or the cessation of breathing during sleep, is currently thought to be the final episode before death. See Naeye, "Sudden Infant Death," 56; and Naeye, "The Sudden Infant Death Syndrome: A Review of Recent Advances," *Archives of Pathology and Laboratory Medicine*, CI (April 1977), 165–67; Valdes-Dapena, "Sudden Unexplained Infant Death," 133; and Beckwith, *Sudden Infant Death Syndrome*, 27.

FIGURE 1. AGE AT DEATH: SMOTHERED SLAVES

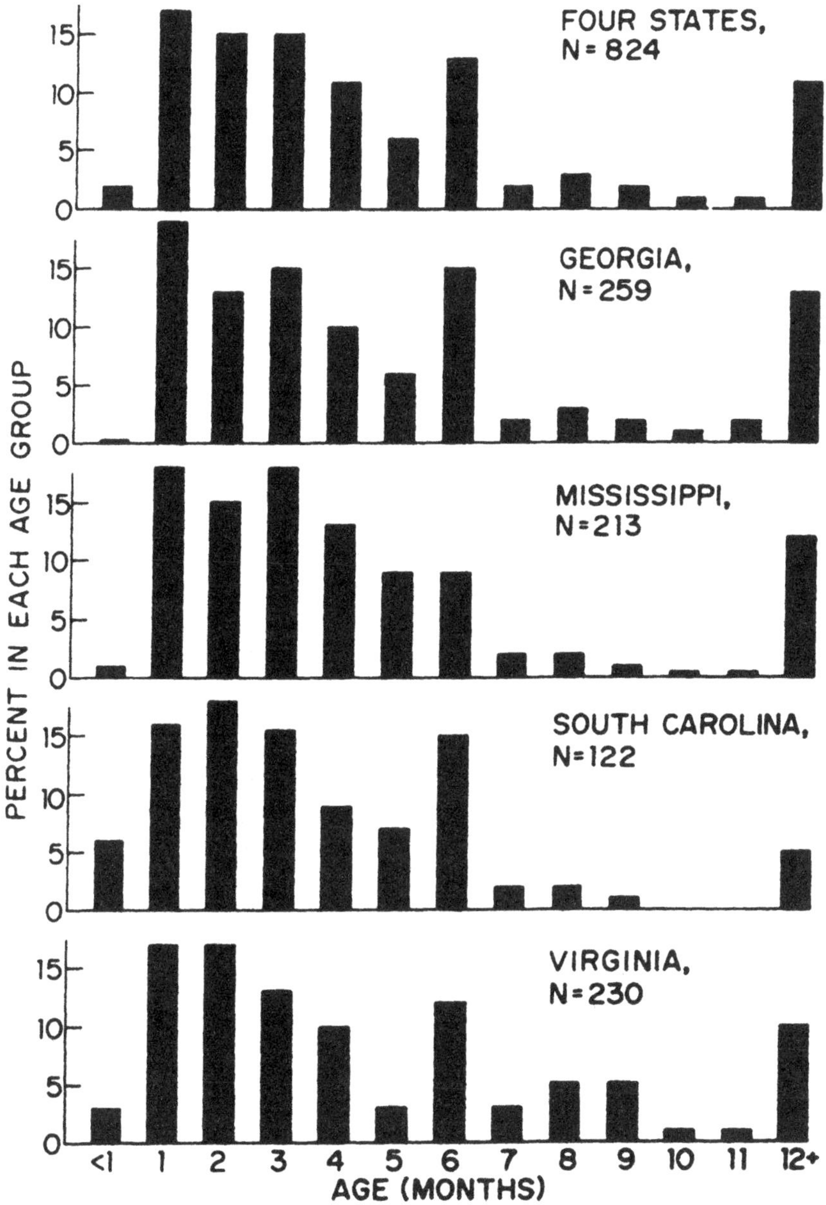

mothers to conclude that the slave infants had been smothered strongly suggest, in light of modern medical knowledge, that the infants succumbed to SIDS. But the most conclusive evidence comes from the age distribution of "smothered" slaves.

According to Dr. J. Bruce Beckwith, an authority on SIDS, "The sparing of very young infants, peak incidence between 2 and 4 months, and rapid decline before the age of 6 months are common to virtually all studies [of SIDS]. We are aware of no other condition with this unique age distribution."[29] As Figure 1 demonstrates, the age distribution of smothered slaves in all four states was quite close to the unique SIDS pattern. Overall, only 2 percent of the smothered slaves were less than one month old, over three-quarters were between one and six months old, and nearly 90 percent were less than one year old.

The discrepancies between the smothered slaves' age distribution and the SIDS pattern are relatively easy to explain. The ages of smothered slaves were not reported as accurately as the ages of SIDS victims. When an infant dies of SIDS today, its age is reported at the time of death. In contrast, the smothered slave infants' deaths were reported by either the master or an overseer up to a year after the slave infant had died. Even if the precise age of the infant had been known to the master or overseer at the time of death, it is likely that it was remembered less accurately when it was reported to the census marshal. For example, the large proportion of six-month-old smothered slaves is almost certainly an artifact of inaccurate age reporting. Many masters apparently responded to a census marshal's question about the age of a slave infant with, "Oh, about six months." This sort of imprecision in the age reports makes the conformity of the age distribution of the smothered slaves to the unique pattern of SIDS all the more remarkable. Of course, the death of some of the smothered slave infants was probably caused by something other than SIDS. As Beckwith explains, "Any sizeable series of sudden, unexpected infant deaths will include a number of cases in which generally acceptable causes for death will be uncovered by postmortem study."[30] A careful study of five hundred such infants in the state of Washington found that 15 percent of the deaths could be explained by causes other than SIDS.[31] Since none of the slave infants was autopsied, there is every reason to

[29] Beckwith, *Sudden Infant Death Syndrome*, 9.

[30] *Ibid.*, 2. An analysis of 59,379 pregnancies which resulted in 125 SIDS deaths is reported in Richard L. Naeye, Bertha Ladis, and Joseph S. Drage, "Sudden Infant Death Syndrome: A Prospective Study," *American Journal of Diseases of Children*, CXXX (November 1976), 1207–10. See also Naeye, "Sudden Infant Death," 56–62.

[31] Beckwith, *Sudden Infant Death Syndrome*, 2–3.

FIGURE 2. AGE AT DEATH: ALL SLAVE INFANTS and SMOTHERED SLAVE INFANTS

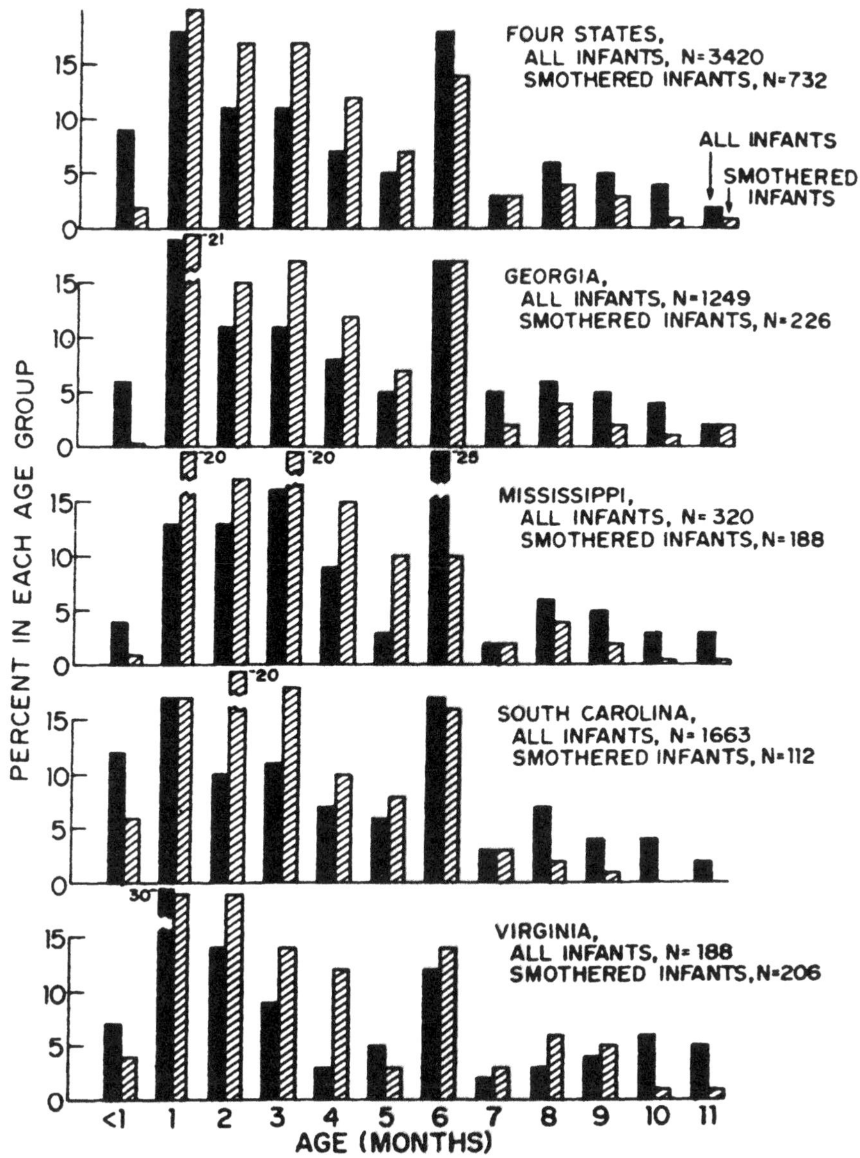

expect that at least a similar fraction of their deaths might have causes other than SIDS. That would probably account for many of the smothered slaves who were over one year old.[32]

[32] However, the age of SIDS victims in the Naeye, Ladis, and Drage study ranged from two weeks to eighteen months.

But before the age distribution of the smothered slaves can be used as evidence that the infants were actually victims of SIDS, we must make certain that the age distribution is not simply an artifact of the mortality reports. Perhaps, for example, the ages of all slave infants whose deaths were reported to the census marshals show the same pattern as the smothered slave infants. If this were true, then the smothered slave infants' age distribution was not evidence of a unique disease syndrome but simply part of a larger pattern of unreliable age reporting. Figure 2 demonstrates that the age distribution of smothered slave infants was in fact different from that of all slave infants whose deaths were reported in 1860.[33] In the four states together the proportion of deaths below one month of age among all slave infants was more than four times that among smothered infants; between one and four months of age—the peak months of SIDS incidence—smothered infant deaths exceeded all infant deaths 66 percent to 47 percent; and from six months on the pattern reversed, the proportion of all infant deaths being greater than that of smothered infants. Chi-square tests comparing the age distribution of smothered slave infants and all slave infant deaths in the four states together and in each state individually had p values of less than 0.001.

The similarity of the age distribution of smothered slaves to the unique SIDS age pattern makes it extremely likely that the slave infants were victims of SIDS. If the age distribution does nothing else, it virtually disproves the notion that these deaths were caused by smothering or suffocation. If that was indeed the cause, as is often assumed by laymen even today in SIDS cases, then, as Beckwith notes, "Why is the very young infant spared, at a time when he seems most vulnerable, yet by the time of peak incidence, between 2 and 3 months, good head control has been achieved?"[34] The same

[33] The age distribution of all slave infant deaths reported in Figure 2 was determined by analyzing all reported slave infant deaths in the 1860 federal mortality schedules of fifty-nine Georgia counties, thirteen Mississippi counties, six Virginia counties, and all South Carolina districts. In each state, the victims of smothering in the sample counties (that is, those counties for which all infant deaths were analyzed) were included among all infant deaths. Therefore, the difference between the age distribution of smothered infants and all *other* infants was more pronounced than that shown in Figure 2, which makes the strongest test for the difference. Since the number of sample counties was relatively small in Mississippi and Virginia, the number of smothering deaths included in the sample of all infant deaths in these states was also small; most of the smothering deaths in these states were not included in the sample of all infant deaths. The chi-square test employed below is a measure of the likelihood that the pattern observed with the smothered slave infants could have arisen by chance from the larger population of all slave infant deaths, even though in actuality the age distribution pattern of smothered slaves was not different from the larger pattern. The probability that the observed difference occurred by chance is expressed by p. For example, if p is equal to 0.001, then there is one chance in a thousand that the observed difference arose by chance.

[34] Beckwith, *Sudden Infant Death Syndrome*, 25. Important early studies that challenged the suffocation interpretation include Paul V. Woolley, Jr., "Mechanical Suffocation

FIGURE 3. DEATH MONTH: SMOTHERED SLAVES

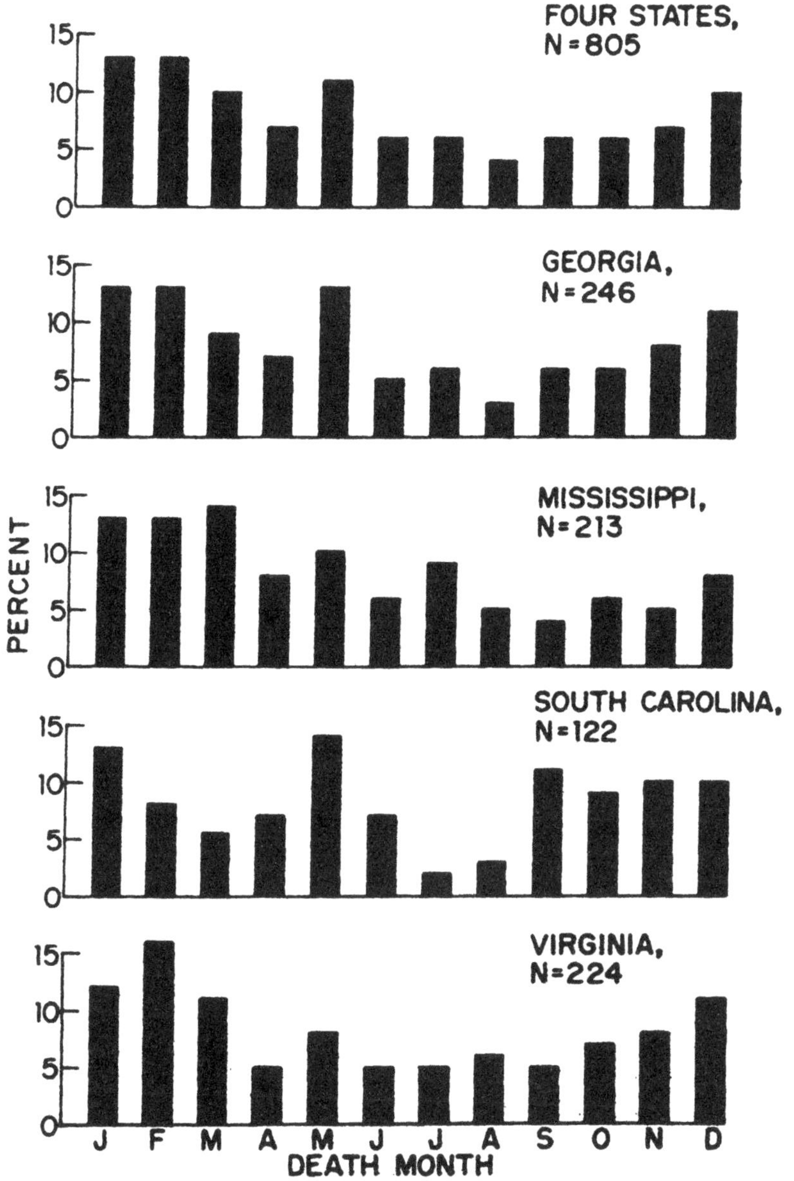

During Infancy: A Comment on Its Relation to the Total Problem of Sudden Death," *Journal of Pediatrics*, XXVI (June 1945), 572–75; and Jacob Werne and Irene Garrow, "Sudden Deaths of Infants Allegedly Due to Mechanical Suffocation," *American Journal of Public Health*, XXXVII (April 1947), 675–87.

FIGURE 4. DEATH MONTH: ALL SLAVE INFANTS and SMOTHERED SLAVES, FOUR STATES

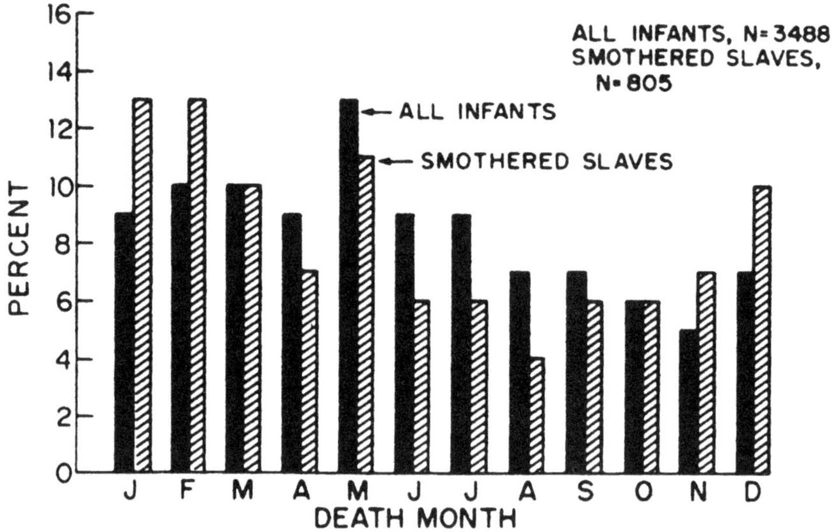

question applies to the infanticide interpretation of these deaths.[35] If slave mothers were bent on infanticide, why did they wait so long? In short, whatever caused the deaths of these slave infants, they were not smothered intentionally or accidentally by their mothers.

Additional evidence that these slave infant deaths were caused by SIDS comes from the death-month distribution. "Nearly all workers have observed seasonal variations in SIDS incidence, with fewer cases occurring in the summer months," Beckwith reports.[36] Figure 3 shows that the same pattern characterized the smothered slaves. In each state the summer months had a lower incidence of smothering deaths.

Since the census was taken during the summer of 1860 it is possible that the dip in incidence during the summer was an artifact of memory. If a slave had suffocated in August 1859 his master would have had to remember the death for a year to report it the following June. For example, the high incidence of smothering reported for the month of May was almost certainly the result of masters' fresh memory of the recent past. Perhaps masters' faulty memories accounted for the low summertime incidence of smothering.

[35] For a refutation of the infanticide interpretation of SIDS proposed by S. S. Asch, "Crib Deaths: Their Possible Relation to Postpartum Depression and Infanticide," *Mt. Sinai Journal of Medicine*, XXXV (May–June 1968), 214–20, see Walter A. Kukull and Donald R. Peterson, "Sudden Infant Death and Infanticide," *American Journal of Epidemiology*, CVI (December 1977), 485–86.

[36] Beckwith, *Sudden Infant Death Syndrome*, 11.

This possibility is ruled out by the monthly distribution of deaths of all slave infants. If memory were the only explanation for the summertime decline in smothering incidence, then the decline should also exist for the incidence of all other slave infant deaths. There is no reason to suppose that masters would selectively forget the summertime deaths of smothered infants. Figure 4 demonstrates that masters did remember summertime deaths. Compared to smothered slaves, a disproportionate number of all slave infants died between April and September. A disproportionate share of smothered slaves died in the winter months of November, December, January, and February. Chi-square tests comparing the death-month distribution of smothered slaves and all slave infant deaths gave *p* values of less than 0.001 for all four states together and for South Carolina and Virginia and values of less than 0.002 for Mississippi and of 0.056 for Georgia. In short, this is very strong evidence that the incidence of smothering was, like that of SIDS, actually lower in the summer.

The death-month and age distributions combined with the citations from the census marshals make it very difficult to construct a persuasive case that smothered slaves were not SIDS victims. Instead, the mortality data strongly support the conclusion of Savitt and others that the slaves died of SIDS. Although slave mothers did not literally smother these infants, as contemporaries believed, perhaps they did or neglected to do something else that was responsible for the deaths. How else can one account for the large difference between the death rates of smothered slave and white infants?

One of the possibilities mentioned earlier is that more white infants were "smothered" than the census manuscripts indicate. The twenty-three white smothering deaths reported to the census marshals in Georgia, Mississippi, South Carolina, and Virginia in 1860 conformed closely to the age and death-month distributions of the smothered slaves, as Figure 5 shows. Although the number of deaths is too small to conclude with certainty that these white infants died of SIDS, the peak incidence at two months of age and the disproportionate number of wintertime deaths suggest very strongly that they did. Additional evidence comes from Calhoun County, Mississippi, where census marshal W. R. Sykes recorded the death of the two-month-old white infant James W. Smith, whose cause of death was "Smothered by mother," Sykes adding "overlayed by whilst asleep."[37] Other white parents may have refused to admit

[37] Mississippi Mortality Schedules, 1860, Calhoun County, 5.

FIGURE 5. SMOTHERED WHITES, N=23

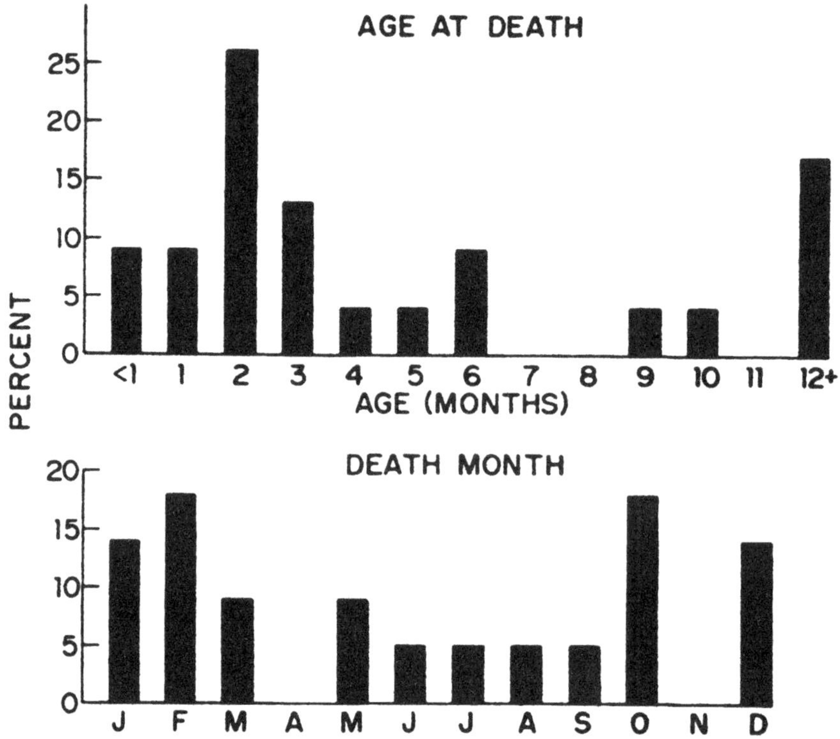

such deaths to the census marshals, or smothering may have been suspected as a cause of death less often because fewer white mothers slept with their infants. Or maybe white parents attributed the death of a "smothered" infant to another cause. If we pursue the hint of census marshal D. W. Johnson that many infants whose deaths were probably caused by "overlaying" were reported as having died suddenly of unknown cause, then it appears that whites were indeed more subject to "overlaying" than is suggested by the data on smothered infants alone.

The 1860 manuscript mortality schedules of the four states studied in this article contain reports of 171 white infants who died suddenly of unknown cause.[18] Predictably, many more such deaths were reported for slave infants, 652 in all. It is quite possible that

[18] That is, these infants are all those in the 1860 federal mortality schedules of these states who were listed by the census marshal with a cause of death of either "unknown" or "sudden" and with zero or "sudden" listed in the length of illness. Of course, older children also died suddenly of no known cause, but they were not included in these calculations.

FIGURE 6. AGE AT DEATH: SUDDEN INFANT DEATHS, OF UNKNOWN CAUSE IN FOUR STATES, WHITES (N=171) and SLAVES (N=652)

some of these deaths were caused by SIDS. But many of them were not, according to the age distribution of the deaths shown in Figure 6. Unlike the victims of SIDS, infants who died suddenly of unknown cause were likely to be one month old or younger. These very young infants probably did not die of SIDS. Many of the older infants may have died of SIDS, but it is impossible to be certain from this evidence alone. At least these data prove that white infants were indeed subject to dying suddenly and unexpectedly for no known reason. That syndrome was not confined as exclusively to slave infants as suggested by the data on smothering deaths alone.

Nonetheless, slave infants were much more subject than white infants to sudden, unexpected death, whether or not it was called smothering. The death rate for sudden death of unknown cause for white infants was 2.5; the rate for slave infants was five times greater, 12.7. Although this is much smaller than the fifty-three-fold difference between white and slave death rates for smothering, it is clear that slave infants were much more subject to sudden, unexpected death than whites. It is very unlikely that there were enough unreported white deaths to equalize these differences. Instead, being a slave somehow increased an infant's risk of dying suddenly and unexpectedly because it was "smothered" by its mother. But why?

Modern studies have consistently found that "SIDS victims have a greater proportion of young mothers of low socioeconomic and educational level, who live in crowded housing and have little prenatal care."[39] The most recent research also indicates that the SIDS victims are not normal, healthy infants. Instead, SIDS victims exhibit a variety of "neurologic abnormalities" which constitute "multiple evidences of probable neonatal brain dysfunction . . . ."[40] The exact relationship between the SIDS infant's neurological abnormalities and the mother and her environment is not clear. In a report on the most recent research Dr. Richard L. Naeye points out that four of the six factors that have been identified as contributing to SIDS "have been shown to either damage the fetus or place it at increased risk of damage"; in particular, "(1) a bacterial infection of the amniotic fluid, (2) anemia in the mother and (3) the use by the mother of cigarettes or (4) barbiturates."[41] Although these factors will only account for about a third of all sudden infant deaths, Naeye believes that, "Their greatest significance may be their indication that fetal life is a fruitful area in which to continue the search for the origins of the syndrome." The respiratory control centers in the brain are located in the brain stem which, according to Naeye, "is a particularly vulnerable target for

[39] Naeye, Ladis, and Drage, "Sudden Infant Death Syndrome," 1210. Of course, this statement should not be misconstrued to mean that all SIDS victims come from poor families. As Beckwith notes, "Despite its greater attack rate among the underprivileged, SIDS is in fact no respecter of class or social position." *Sudden Infant Death Syndrome*, 11. See also Valdes-Dapena, "Sudden Unexplained Infant Death," 124–27; P. Froggatt, Margaret A. Lynas, and G. MacKenzie, "Epidemiology of Sudden Unexpected Death in Infants ('Cot Death') in Northern Ireland," *British Journal of Preventive and Social Medicine*, XXV (August 1971), 119–34; Robert Strimer, Lester Adelson, and Robert Oseasohn, "Epidemiologic Features of 1,134 Sudden, Unexpected Infant Deaths: A Study in the Greater Cleveland Area from 1956 to 1965," *Journal of the American Medical Association*, CCIX (September 8, 1969), 1493–97; and Marie Valdes-Dapena *et al.*, "Sudden Unexpected Death in Infancy: A Statistical Analysis of Certain Socioeconomic Factors," *Journal of Pediatrics*, LXXIII (September 1968), 387–94.

[40] Naeye, Ladis, and Drage, "Sudden Infant Death Syndrome," 1209; quotations in text and this note. In particular, the infants who became SIDS victims exhibited "abnormalities in respiration, feeding, temperature regulation, and specific neurologic tests." However, none of these abnormalities was great enough to allow physicians to identify the infants who were likely to die of SIDS. Several research teams are currently working on methods of identifying high-risk infants; see for example R. G. Carpenter *et al.*, "Multistage Scoring System for Identifying Infants at Risk of Unexpected Death," *Archives of Disease in Childhood*, LII (August 1977), 606–12.

[41] The other two factors, not specifically related to pregnancy, are infant blood type *B* and crowded housing. The latter has been shown to contribute to mild respiratory infections which "increase the frequency and duration of apneic spells in infants who are prone to apnea." Naeye, "Sudden Infant Death," 60–61; includes quotations both in text and this note. The environmental and demographic characteristics of mothers of SIDS victims are also "associated with excessive fetal injury and perinatal mortality" in general. Naeye, Ladis, and Drage, "Sudden Infant Death Syndrome," 1210. See also Naeye and William A. Blanc, "Influences of Pregnancy Risk Factors on Fetal and Newborn Disorders," *Clinics in Perinatology*, I (September 1974), 187–95.

damage during fetal life because it has a higher metabolic rate than other areas of the brain have. Specifically, the brain stem is vulnerable to damage by low levels of both oxygen and glucose in the blood."[42] This modern knowledge of the general significance of fetal neurological development and the specific risks associated with amniotic fluid infections, maternal anemia, and poor nutrition suggests why so many slave infants were "smothered."

The hard physical labor required of pregnant slave women is the most promising explanation for the high incidence of SIDS among slave infants. Recent research has demonstrated that hard work can have serious consequences for pregnant women. Naeye's study of fetal amniotic fluid infections in Ethiopia, for example, found that the frequency of infections "was greater in the poorest gravid women, in those engaged in hard physical labor, and in twins." "Poverty restricts the quantity and quality of food intake in Ethiopian pregnant women while hard physical labor has a caloric cost," Naeye explains, adding that "The nutritional requirements of pregnancy are greater with twins than with single born infants."[43] A similar relationship between hard work and nutrition probably prevailed among pregnant slave women in the antebellum South.

The nutritional value of the slave diet has been the subject of intense controversy.[44] The best recent evidence indicates that the typical slave diet may have been adequate in caloric quantity but deficient in nutritional quality.[45] The nutritional requirements of a pregnant slave woman were obviously greater both in calories and in specific nutrients. In particular, a pregnant woman required about 65 percent more dietary protein, two and one-half times as much calcium, and three hundred more calories per day than a nonpregnant, nonlactating woman.[46] Sutch has pointed out that a slave "could subsist" on a typical slave ration if the assigned work in-

[42] Naeye, "Sudden Infant Death," 61.

[43] Naeye *et al.*, "Amniotic Fluid Infections in an African City," *Journal of Pediatrics*, XC (June 1977), 969. "Many other factors associated with the [sudden infant death] syndrome appear to lose their high risk in the absence of an infection of the amniotic fluid," Naeye reports. "Sudden Infant Death," 61. For a comparison of SIDS death rates in countries throughout the world see Valdes-Dapena, "Sudden Unexplained Infant Death," 123–24.

[44] See Savitt, *Medicine and Slavery*, 90–103; Fogel and Engerman, *Time on the Cross*, I, 109–15; II, 87–98; Sutch, "Care and Feeding of Slaves," 231–301; Leslie H. Owens, *This Species of Property: Slave Life and Culture in the Old South* (New York, 1976), 50–69; Eugene D. Genovese, *Roll, Jordan, Roll: The World the Slaves Made* (New York, 1974), 62–63, 540–49, 603–604, 638–39; John W. Blassingame, *The Slave Community: Plantation Life in the Antebellum South* (New York and other cities, 1972), 158–59; Kenneth M. Stampp, *The Peculiar Institution: Slavery in the Ante-Bellum South* (New York, 1956), 282–89.

[45] Savitt, *Medicine and Slavery*, 92; Sutch, "Care and Feeding of Slaves," 233–82; Kiple and Kiple, "Slave Child Mortality," 294–99.

[46] Savitt, *Medicine and Slavery*, 92.

cluded such "'light' to 'moderate'" tasks as cooking, house cleaning, hoeing, plowing, or clearing brush. "Heavy" work, including "such plantation-type activities as dragging logs, felling trees, and digging ditches," greatly increased a slave's caloric needs.[47] Although direct evidence of the rations for pregnant slave women is lacking, the high caloric cost of hard work had to have an adverse effect unless the diet was adjusted accordingly. Even if one assumes the very best about the diet of pregnant slave women—namely that they had the same diet as pregnant white women—it is clear that pregnant slave women had to do more hard physical labor than pregnant white women. That was probably why the incidence of SIDS was higher among slave infants.[48]

Several antebellum medical writers commented on the dangers of hard work for pregnant slave women. A Tennessee physician, John H. Morgan, wrote that "the exposure to which negro women are subjected as field hands during menstruation and pregnancy," along with "The promiscuous and excessive intercourse of the sexes" were "among the principal causes of sterility and abortion." "And many diseases to which they are incident arise from the same cause," he added. In particular, he argued that "The functions of menstruation and pregnancy being so peculiarly delicate, negroes suffer seriously during those periods from hard labor and exposure in bad weather, frequently being badly fed and badly clothed . . . ."[49] A Georgia physician, Edmund Monroe Pendleton, wrote that the much greater incidence of abortion and miscarriage among slaves "either teaches that slave labor is inimical to the procreation of the species from exposure, violent exercise, &c., or, as the planters believe, the blacks are possessed of a secret by which they destroy the foetus at an early stage of gestation." Pendleton did not doubt the existence of abortifacients, but he considered it a "question for the philosopher and the philanthropist" whether slave

[47] Sutch, "Care and Feeding of Slaves," 267–68.

[48] Modern studies have uniformly reported a higher incidence of SIDS among blacks. For example, a recent study of SIDS in North Carolina found that the SIDS death rate for whites was 1.23 per thousand live births, while that for blacks was 3.75. Other studies have reported similar differences. However, there is no evidence to suggest that this is the result of a specific genetic heritage. Jack H. Blok, "The Incidence of Sudden Infant Death Syndrome in North Carolina's Cities and Counties: 1972–1974," *American Journal of Public Health*, LXVIII (April 1978), 367–72; Thaddeus J. Bell, Joel S. Sexton, and Sandra E. Conradi, "The Status of Sudden Infant Death Syndrome (1974), and SIDS in Charleston County, South Carolina," *Journal of the South Carolina Medical Association*, LXXI (October 1975), 312–15; Valdes-Dapena, "Sudden Unexplained Infant Death," 124–26; Naeye, Ladis, and Drage, "Sudden Infant Death Syndrome," 1207–1208, 1210; Sutch, "Care and Feeding of Slaves," 287–92; Naeye, "Sudden Infant Death," 60.

[49] Morgan, "An Essay on the Causes of the Production of Abortion Among Our Negro Population," 117 (first three quotations), 121 (last two quotations).

women were "acquainted with them . . . and whether the natural instinct of the mother to love and protect her offspring should be overruled so frequently by the moral obtundity of this class of people . . . ."[50] To the question, "Are negro women, under the ordinary regime of plantations, as prolific as white?", a Mississippi observer answered: "Yes: more so, when not overworked."[51] These experienced and informed observers clearly recognized the dangers of hard work for pregnant slave women.

Some masters were equally aware of the risks of hard work. James R. Sparkman wrote that on the South Carolina rice plantation he managed "Allowance is invariably made for the women so soon as they report themselves *pregnant* they being appointed to such light work as will insure a proper consideration for the offspring."[52] Ex-slave Polly Turner Cancer reported that on the Mississippi cotton plantation where she worked around the house "Ole Marster wudn't let de wimmen do no heavy liftin' coz he wanted dem de have big fine babies; he always sed, 'I don't want no runts.' When we picked cotton he always made de men tote de sacks."[53] Lula Flannigan remembered that her Georgia master "wuz watchful ter see dat 'omans had good keer when dey chilluns wuz bawned. Dey let dese 'omans do easy, light wuk towuds de last fo' de chilluns is bawned, en den atter wuds dey doan do nuffin' much twel dey is well en strong ergin."[54] Although slaveowners clearly benefited from the birth of healthy slave children this testimony suggests that those who took steps to limit the work of pregnant slave women did so late in pregnancy, usually in the last trimester and often in the last few weeks. Such practices may have forestalled premature delivery, but they were too late to have had a significant effect on the influence of hard work on fetal development. And according to slaves many masters did not even observe these precautions.

Harry McMillan, a forty-year-old South Carolina field hand, was asked by the American Freedmen's Inquiry Commission in 1863, "The women had the same day's work as the men; but suppose a woman was in a family way was her task less?" "No, sir," McMillan replied; "most of times she had to do the same work. Sometimes the wife of the planter learned of the condition of the woman and

[50] [Pendleton], "On the Susceptibility of the Caucasian and African Races to the Different Classes of Disease," 338.

[51] Affleck, "On the Hygiene of Cotton Plantations and the Management oı Negro Slaves," 434.

[52] Sparkman to Benjamin Allston, March 10, 1858, J. Harold Easterby, ed., *The South Carolina Rice Plantation as Revealed in the Papers of Robert F. W. Allston* (Chicago, 1945), 346. Italics in the original.

[53] Rawick *et al.*, eds., *American Slave*, VII: *Mississippi Narratives*, Pt. 2, p. 350.

[54] *Ibid.*, III: *Georgia Narratives*, Pt. 1, p. 248.

said to her husband you must cut down her day's work. Sometimes the women had their children in the field."[55] Madison Jefferson, a slave from a large Virginia estate, reported to the British and Foreign Antislavery Society in 1841 that "He has known women who were *enceinte,* employed in plantation labour until within a few hours of their delivery; and in some cases the children have been actually brought forth in the field."[56] James Lucas told an interviewer in 1936 of his birth 103 years earlier on a big cotton plantation along the Mississippi River, "Trufe is I wuz bawn in a cotton field during cotton pickin time. De wimmin fixed my mammy up so she didn't lose no time."[57] Jennie Webb, another former slave on a Mississippi cotton plantation, recalled, "My ma wuked in de fiel's up to de day I was born. I wuz born 'twix de fiel's an' de cabins. Ma wuz tooken to de house on a ho'se."[58]

Additional evidence of the common practice of working slave women until late in pregnancy comes from slave testimony about whipping. Former Virginia slave Jordan Johnson told an interviewer about Charlie Jones and his wife who were working in a tobacco field together. "Was plantin' tobacco—he was settin' out an' she was hillin'. Annie was big wid chile an' gittin' near her time, so one day she made a slip an' chopped a young shoot down. Ole man Diggs, de overseer, come runnin' up screamin' at her an' it made her mo' nervous, an she chopped off 'nother one. Ole overseer lif' up dat rawhide an' beat Annie 'cross de back an shoulders 'till she fell to de groun'."[59] Lizzie Williams remembered that on the Mississippi cotton plantation where she worked "I[']s seen nigger women dat was fixin' to be confined do somethin' de white folks didn't like. Dey [the white folks] would dig a hole in de ground just big 'nuff fo' her stomach, make her lie face down an whip her on de back to keep from hurtin' de child."[60] South Carolina slave Solomon Bradley told the American Freedmen's Inquiry Commission, "I have seen a woman in the family way punished by making a hole in the ground for her stomach when she was stretched out for whipping."[61] Clara Young, a former field hand on a plantation near

[55] John W. Blassingame, ed., *Slave Testimony: Two Centuries of Letters, Speeches, Interviews, and Autobiographies* (Baton Rouge, 1977), 380.

[56] *Ibid.*, 221. Italics in the original.

[57] Rawick *et al.*, eds., *American Slave*, VIII: *Mississippi Narratives*, Pt. 3, p. 1337.

[58] *Ibid.*, X: *Mississippi Narratives*, Pt. 5, p. 2250.

[59] Charles L. Perdue, Jr., Thomas E. Barden, and Robert K. Phillips, eds., *Weevils in the Wheat: Interviews with Virginia Ex-Slaves* (Charlottesville, 1976), 160.

[60] She also reported that "Lots o' times de women in dat condition [pregnant] would be plowin', hit a stump, de plow jump an' hurt de child to where dey would loose it an law me, such a whippin as dey would get!" Rawick *et al.*, eds., *American Slave*, X: *Mississippi Narratives*, Pt. 5, p. 2337.

[61] Blassingame, ed., *Slave Testimony*, 372. For other instances see *ibid.*, 220, 380.

Aberdeen, Mississippi, recalled that her cousin had been whipped so severely by the overseer that she died the next morning. ". . . she was jest sebenteen years ol' and was in de fambly way for de fust time, and could't work as hard as de rest."[62] Although many overseers and masters may not have been so cruel, far too many were. Yet the most significant disclosure in the slaves' testimony is that it was not at all uncommon for pregnant slave women to do the same tasks as other slaves and to be expected to perform them as efficiently.

Annie Coley's mother was a field hand whose master rewarded her for having twelve children by taking her out of the fields and assigning her to weaving. But Annie Coley remembered an incident which proved that slave women did not simply depend on the self-interest of the master for their protection:

> But ole Boss Jones had a mean overseer who tuk 'vantage of the womens in the fiel's. One time he slammed a niggah woman down that was heavy, en cause her to hev her baby—dead. The niggah womens in the Quarters jumped on 'im and say they gwine take him to a brushpile and burn him up. But their men hollered for 'em to turn him loose. Then Big Boss Jones came en made the womens go back to the Quarters. He said, "I ain' whipped these wretches fer a long time, en I low to whip 'em dis evenin'." But all de womens hid in the woods dat evenin', en Boss never say no more about it. He sent the over seer away en never did hev no more overseers.[63]

The slave women on Annie Coley's plantation courageously and successfully resisted the overseer's cruelty. Yet it is significant that what aroused their hostility was not that a pregnant slave woman was working in the fields but that she was horribly abused. Even a "reasonable" master like Boss Jones expected pregnant slave women to work hard; the women in his quarters must have realized the futility of protesting that. Many other masters apparently did not lighten the work routine of pregnant slave women soon enough to diminish the effects of hard work on the developing fetus. "All my child hood life I can never remember seeing my pa or ma gwine to wuk or coming in from wuk in de day light as dey went to de fiel's fo' day an' wuked 'til after dark," Jennie Webb recalled. "It wuz wuk, wuk, all de time."[64]

Evidence that "smothered" slave infants were among the consequences of hard work for pregnant slave women comes from the different death rates in the rice, cotton, tobacco, and upcountry

[62] Rawick *et al.*, eds., *American Slave*, X: *Mississippi Narratives*, Pt. 5, p. 2402. For another similar incident see *ibid.*, 1927.
[63] *Ibid.*, VII: *Mississippi Narratives*, Pt. 2, pp. 441–42.
[64] *Ibid.*, X: *Mississippi Narratives*, Pt. 5, p. 2250. See also *ibid.*, 2199.

TABLE 2

GEORGIA, 1860: DEATH RATES OF SMOTHERED SLAVES AND ALL SLAVE INFANTS

	Cotton Counties	*Piedmont and Pine Barrens Counties*	*Coastal Rice Counties*	*State*
Death Rate of Smothered Slaves	21.0	10.7	4.6	18.5
(N)	(233)	(22)	(4)	(259)
Death Rate of All Slave Infants	158	128	203	156
(N)	(1,068)	(86)	(96)	(1,250)

NOTE: The death rates for all slave infants were derived from the deaths of all slave infants in fifty-nine sample counties. The rate for the entire state was calculated by weighting the death rate for each region by the relative share of the state's slave infants.

TABLE 3

SOUTH CAROLINA, 1860: DEATH RATES OF SMOTHERED SLAVES AND ALL SLAVE INFANTS

	Low Country	*Middle Districts*	*Upcountry*	*State*
Death Rate of Smothered Slaves	7.6	13.2	11.1	10.8
(N)	(21)	(40)	(61)	(122)
Death Rate of All Slave Infants	150	147	146	147
(N)	(414)	(443)	(808)	(1,665)

NOTE: The death rates for all slave infants were computed from the deaths of all slave infants in the state.

regions of the South. In general, where the production of staple crops for market was primary and where gang labor prevailed, the death rates for smothered slave infants were highest. Georgia is an excellent example, as Table 2 demonstrates. In the cotton counties of central and southwest Georgia—which contained 78 percent of the state's slaves and produced 94 percent of the state's cotton—the smothering death rate was almost twice that in the less market-oriented Piedmont and Pine Barrens counties—which produced only 6 percent of the state's cotton although they contained nearly a third of the state's population. This contrast between regions of maximum and minimum staple-crop production was not simply the result of a higher overall death rate for slave infants in the cotton counties. The death rate for all slave infants in the cotton counties

TABLE 4

MISSISSIPPI, 1860: DEATH RATES OF SMOTHERED SLAVES AND ALL SLAVE INFANTS

	River and Black-Belt Counties	*Pine-Hills Counties*	*State*
Death Rate of Smothered Slaves	16.6	20.2	17.5
(N)	(153)	(60)	(213)
Death Rate of All Slave Infants	120	94	114
(N)	(287)	(33)	(320)

NOTE: The death rates for all slave infants were derived from the deaths of all slave infants in thirteen sample counties. The rate for the entire state was calculated by weighting the death rate for each region by the relative share of the state's slave infants.

was only 20 percent higher than that in the Piedmont and Pine Barrens. An even sharper contrast existed between Georgia's cotton and rice counties. In the coastal counties that produced 99 percent of the state's rice, the smothering death rate was less than one-fourth that in the cotton counties.[63] But the coastal counties were not a healthier environment for slave infants; the death rate for all slave infants in the coastal counties was nearly a third higher than that in the cotton counties. Although slaves in both regions were producing staple crops for market, in the rice region their work was organized largely by the task system, while gang labor prevailed in cotton areas.

A similar pattern existed in South Carolina as Table 3 illustrates. In the cotton-producing middle districts and upcountry—which respectively accounted for 33 percent and 56 percent of the cotton produced in the state and which contained 25 percent and 45 percent of the state's slaves—the smothering death rate was significantly higher than in the rice-growing low country. The smothering death rate in the middle districts was 74 percent higher than in the low country; the upcountry rate was 46 percent higher. Yet the death

[63] The obvious climatic difference between the regions does not appear to be a likely explanation for the different smothering death rates. Modern studies have discounted the effect of climate on SIDS. For example, the death rate from SIDS in Stockholm, Sweden, in 1974 was 0.06, while the rate in Memphis, Tennessee, between 1965 and 1974 ranged between 3.10 and 0.9. See Valdes-Dapena, "Sudden Unexplained Infant Death," 123–24; Beckwith, *Sudden Infant Death Syndrome*, 11; Philip S. Spiers, James J. Schlesselman, and Stephen G. Wright, "Sudden Infant Death Syndrome in the United States: A Study of Geographic and Other Variables," *American Journal of Epidemiology*, C (November 1974), 380–89; and Donald R. Peterson, Donovan J. Thompson, and Nina M. Chinn, "A Method for Assessing the Geographic Distribution and Temporal Trends of the Sudden Infant Death Syndrome in the United States from Vital Statistics Data," *ibid.*, 373–79.

TABLE 5

VIRGINIA, 1860: DEATH RATES OF SMOTHERED SLAVES AND ALL SLAVE INFANTS

	Tidewater Counties	*Piedmont Counties*	*Western Counties*	*State*
Death Rate of Smothered Slaves	12.9	22.6	4.1	16.6
(N)	(61)	(161)	(8)	(230)
Death Rate of All Slave Infants	227	222	338	228
(N)	(35)	(131)	(65)	(231)

NOTE: The death rates for all slave infants were derived from the deaths of all slave infants in six sample counties. The rate for the entire state was calculated by weighting the death rate for each region by the relative share of the state's slave infants.

rate for all slave infants in the low country was virtually identical to the rates in the state's cotton regions.

In Mississippi, as Table 4 shows, the pattern was similar to that in the cotton regions of South Carolina. The cotton counties along the Mississippi River and in the black belt adjoining Alabama actually had a slightly lower smothering death rate than the pine hills. Yet, what is striking about the death rates for these two regions is not their difference but their similarity, like that between the South Carolina middle districts and upcountry. The similarity probably arose from a common commitment to cotton cultivation for market. The ratio of slaves to cotton production in the two regions was identical; the river and black-belt counties contained 78 percent of the state's slaves and produced 78 percent of the state's cotton, while the pine-hills counties produced 22 percent of the state's cotton with the same proportion of the state's slaves.

In Virginia, where the staple crop was tobacco and where there was considerable regional variation in the devotion to its production for market, the pattern of smothering death rates resembled that in Georgia. Although the Tidewater counties contained 36 percent of the state's slaves, they produced only 15 percent of the state's tobacco and, as Table 5 shows, the death rate of smothered slaves in the Tidewater was much less than that in the Piedmont. In fact, the smothering death rate in the market-oriented Piedmont counties—which contained 51 percent of the state's slaves and produced 84 percent of the state's tobacco—was 75 percent higher than that in the Tidewater. In the less market-oriented western counties—which contained 13 percent of the state's slaves but produced only 1 percent of the state's tobacco—the smothering death rate was less than one-fifth of that in the Piedmont. Yet the death rate for all slave infants in the western counties was over 50 percent higher than that in the Piedmont.

Overall, the highest regional smothering death rates were in areas devoted to staple-crop production with gang labor. In rice areas, where the task system was employed, or in regions less intensely devoted to staple-crop production, the smothering death rates were lower. This is a pattern one would expect to find if the hard work that masters assigned to pregnant slave women were the major cause of slave smothering deaths. But whether market-oriented production, cotton or tobacco cultivation, gang labor, and close white supervision conspired to make heavier demands on pregnant slave women than a more diversified and less intensely market-oriented production or than rice cultivation and the task system cannot be irrefutably proved. However, the different smothering death rates in the South's agricultural regions make this possibility plausible and worth accepting as somewhat more than a tentative hypothesis.

If the labor that masters assigned to pregnant slave women was the major explanation for the high incidence of SIDS among slave infants, then the smothering death rates should have dropped dramatically after emancipation. Freedmen and freedwomen successfully resisted the planters' efforts to reestablish gang labor. Black women withdrew from the heavy, closely supervised field work they had done as slaves.[66] The family sharecropping system still required black women to work in the fields. But precisely because the sharecroppers' labor was organized by black family members rather than by masters, pregnant black women could be sheltered from the heaviest, most exhausting tasks. And indeed, after emancipation the smothering death rates plummeted.

According to mortality data collected in the 1880 federal census the death rate for smothered black infants in the South was only one-fifth of that in 1860. As Table 6 shows, the smothering rates along the South Atlantic and Gulf coasts remained lower than those of the interior, but all the rates had fallen precipitously compared to 1860. In fact, they had fallen to a level indistinguishable from rates for blacks in the northern regions, although they remained over four times greater than the white rates. Perhaps part of the decline was caused by black parents' reticence about admitting to a census

[66] See Jonathan M. Wiener, "Class Structure and Economic Development in the American South, 1865–1955," *American Historical Review*, LXXXIV (October 1979), 973–76; Wiener, *Social Origins of the New South: Alabama, 1860–1885* (Baton Rouge and London, 1978), 36–38, 42–47, 66–69; Herbert G. Gutman, *The Black Family in Slavery and Freedom, 1750–1925* (New York, 1976), 167–68; Roger L. Ransom and Richard Sutch, *One Kind of Freedom: The Economic Consequences of Emancipation* (Cambridge and other cities, 1977), 44–47.

TABLE 6

DEATH RATES OF SMOTHERED INFANTS IN 1880

Region	Smothered White Infants	Smothered Black Infants	All Black Infants
South Atlantic[1]	0.4	1.7	144
Gulf Coast[2]	0.4	1.1	119
Piedmont[3]	1.0	3.4	157
Black Belt[4]	0.7	3.0	143
South Appalachian[5]	0.5	3.9	111
The South[6]	0.7	3.2	127
Northern Mississippi River Belt[7]	0.6	3.4	112
Missouri River Belt[8]	0.9	3.9	152

NOTE: These regional subdivisions are the only ones for which the mortality data are reported in categories appropriate for the calculation of death rates of smothered black and white infants. For a map of these regions see John S. Billings, *Report on the Mortality and Vital Statistics of the United States as Returned at the Tenth Census (June 1, 1880)* (2 parts in 3 vols., Washington, 1885-1886), Pt. II, between pages x and xi. For the exact counties included in each region see *ibid.*, Pt. I, xiv-xvi.

[1] Includes coastal and Tidewater counties from Virginia to Georgia.
[2] Includes all of Florida and Gulf Coast counties of Alabama, Louisiana, Mississippi, and Texas.
[3] Includes the Piedmont region of Virginia and North Carolina.
[4] Includes the Black Belt and cotton counties of South Carolina, Georgia, Alabama, and Mississippi.
[5] Includes the hill regions of Virginia, West Virginia, Kentucky, North Carolina, Tennessee, Georgia, and Alabama.
[6] Includes the five regions listed above.
[7] Includes the counties along the northern Mississippi from its confluence with the Ohio River north to Minnesota.
[8] Includes counties along the Missouri River from just west of St. Louis north and west to North Dakota.

official that one of their children had been smothered. That possibility cannot be ruled out, but it seems unlikely that reticence alone would account for such a dramatic decrease in the smothering death rate.

Of course, neither slave women nor their masters could have known about the connection between hard work, pregnancy, and smothering. Medical writers agreed, and masters were well aware, that hard work was not good for pregnant slave women. But the large number of smothered slave infants and the testimony of the slaves themselves are powerful evidence that many masters found it easier to ignore the risks of hard work for pregnant slave women than the promise of a cash crop safely harvested. Masters may not have acted any differently had they known better. Not knowing, they easily blamed slave mothers for smothering their infants. Slave women had to do the master's work and to bear the shame and guilt for one of its tragic consequences. At least, Tabby Abbey did.

MAKING WOMEN MODERN: MIDDLE CLASS WOMEN AND HEALTH REFORM IN 19TH CENTURY AMERICA

Regina Markell Morantz

Social historians have yet to explore adequately either the connection between health reform and advances in 19th-century medicine or the role of women in the active promotion and adoption of rationalistic health practices. As life expectancy increased and infant mortality declined, sickness gradually ceased to be endemic. More important, fatalistic attitudes toward death and disease gave way to the conviction that good health was within the reach of each and every citizen. The nature and impact of these changes cannot be explained merely by recounting the heroic strides made by medical scientists during these years. While the work of Pasteur, Koch, and others was vitally important, advances in bacteriology and medical therapeutics do not tell the whole story. The 19th-century revolution in health was far more pervasive; its advocates were not only great men of science, but ordinary men and women who promulgated and implemented new attitudes toward public and personal cleanliness.

Beginning in the ante-bellum period, self-help in health matters, public hygiene, dietary reform, temperance, hydro-therapy and physiological instruction merged as ingredients in a coherent and articulate campaign to save the nation by combating the ill-health of its citizenry. Although such attention to personal health and hygiene was not wholly original, never before had the regard for good health given rise to such widespread public activity.[1]

In the modernizing world of the 19th century, health reformers played a critical role in transforming traditional attitudes toward sickness and death. They promoted the active assumption by men and women of the responsibility for their own health, the health of their families, and the health of society at large. Itinerant speakers lecturing to enthusiastic audiences and dedicated to furthering common knowledge of health and hygiene traversed the cities and towns of the North and West. Hundreds of heuristic tracts instructed eager readers in the "laws of life." A handful of journals kept men and women informed of new developments. The popular *Water Cure Journal*, for example, boasted 10,000 subscribers in 1849, the second year of its publication.[2]

Although the movement held attractions for both men and women, and, as we shall see, the contributions of male spokesmen were vital, middle-class women, by virtue of their new roles in an increasingly complex society, became the health reformers' primary constituency. Because the changing structure of the 19th-century family increasingly required women to school their children in "modern" values, they welcomed with relief the practical solutions to bewildering problems offered in health reform journals and tracts.

The concern with hygiene was an integral part of the ante-bellum reformist world view. Indeed, the health crusade converged with several better known radical concerns. Historians have been quick to point out this identity of ideas and personnel. No study of ante-bellum reform can ignore the fundamental role of hygienic and physiologic concepts. Abolitionist speakers, for example, lodged at health reform boarding houses, and a large number of women's rights advocates followed some form of Sylvester Graham's vegetarian diet. Oberlin College, familiar as a breeding ground for abolitionism and women's rights, adopted strict vegetarianism in its dining room in 1835. Asa Mahan, the college's president, put a "reformation in food, drink, and dress" high on the list of important causes.[3]

Moreover, a cursory glance at the men and women who actively promoted the health revolution suggests that, like other reformers, they came from the Northeastern, predominantly middle-class sectors of the American population. Sylvester Graham began his career in New Jersey as a Presbyterian minister and temperance lecturer. William A. Alcott, cousin of Bronson, was a thoughtful, Yale-trained physician. Joel Shew and Russell Trall graduated from regular medical schools in New York. James Caleb Jackson, a self-made man, was the son of a yeoman farmer in upstate New York. Mary Gove Nichols became a teacher in Maine. Rachel Brooks Gleason graduated from New York's Central Eclectic School of Medicine and ran a water cure establishment with her physician husband. Paulina Wright Davis and Elizabeth Oakes Smith both hailed from prominent New York landholding families. Harriot Hunt's father, a skilled navigator, invested his small capital in Boston's commerical shipping industry. Lydia Folger Fowler, wife of the phrenologist publisher Lorenzo, was the second woman to receive a medical degree in the United States. A descendant of the Puritan settlers of Nantucket Island and distant cousin of the astronomer Maria Mitchell, Lydia's father was a manufacturer, a shipowner, and a selectman of his native town. Recently, an intensive study of the rank and file of the Boston Ladies Physiological Society found that the large majority were predominantly the wives and mothers of Boston's middle class.[4]

Previous students of the health reform movement have offered us a number of useful insights. We know, for example, that health crusaders shared with other reformers of the period a fundamental Enlightenment rationalism. Implicit in their theory of sickness was a concept of self-help and a conviction that disease could be prevented by teaching people the "laws" of physiology and hygiene. Other scholars suggest that the rationalistic impulse in health reform rhetoric was overshadowed by heavy doses of Christian perfectionism. Preaching the interconnectedness of the moral and physical life, health reformers agreed that man could not achieve success in the one without total control over the other. Medical historians, in contrast, have emphasized a causal relationship between the rise of health reform and the decline of heroic medical therapeutics. Health crusaders stood united in their criticism of the bleeding, purging and dosing of the professional practice of the day. Finally, a few scholars attribute the rise of the movement to the pervasive anti-elitism characteristic of the ante-bellum period, an atmosphere which fueled the public animus against established medical practice.[5]

While earlier work has been informative, two crucial questions remain virtually unexplored in the historiographical literature. The first concerns the relationship of health reform to modernization; the second relates to the connection between women's interest in health reform and changes in their status.[6] Although this essay will make some brief and admittedly speculative observations concerning the first of these problems, its primary focus will be to suggest a tentative framework for explaining women's role in the health reform movement. It is hoped that such a framework will aid others in further explorations of the subject.

Former accounts have only briefly acknowledged and never analyzed women's participation. We know a great deal about Sylvester Graham, William A. Alcott, and James Harvey Kellogg, but our information about the many women who preached, implemented and occasionally elaborated on the ideas of these more prominent health reformers remains sketchy.[7] Yet a number of the most outspoken of the health crusaders were female, and women swelled the ranks of the new movement.

In 1837 the American Physiological Society was founded in Boston to foster health by teaching physiology. Almost a third of its members were women and at its second annual meeting the new organization acknowledged women's central role in promoting good health in the following resolution:

> *Resolved,* That woman in her character as wife and mother is only second to the Deity in the influence that she exerts on the physical, the intellectual, and the moral interests of the human race, and that her education should be adapted to qualify her in the highest degree to cherish those interests in the wisest and best manner.[8]

Women took to the field as lecturers. Ladies' Physiological Societies appeared throughout the Northeast. The names of Mary Gove Nichols, Harriot Hunt, and Lydia Folger Fowler are only the most familiar of the dozens of women who taught enthusiastic female audiences the "laws of life."

Profound changes in women's roles underlay their active interest in health reform. The social transformation touched off by industrialization and urbanization gradually forced them to redefine their responsibilities in an altered family setting. Since colonial times traditional verities had suggested that woman's place was in the home. But women had experienced family, home and work as an integrated, stable whole. The heavy burden of household production and the immediate concern with economic subsistence left them little time and less inclination to question their duties. Moreover, social roles for women in the 17th and 18th centuries in reality remained quite fluid and imperfectly defined. It was left to the 19th century to institutionalize the concept of "woman's sphere."

As productive labor shifted from the home to the factory, men, acting on premodern conceptions of men's and women's responsibilities, increasingly sought outside employment. Masculine and feminine spheres became more rigidly separated. This development quickly colored 19th-century cultural expectations.

Economic changes suddenly made it possible for the first time for large numbers of women to become primarily wives and mothers. No longer did playing a vital role in the family economy compete for their time and attentiom. The ideal of the modern family – small in size, emotionally intense, and woman supervised – made its appearance as a distinctive emblem of middle-class culture.

Contemporaries noted these changes with satisfaction. In a letter to the *Water Cure Journal* in 1854, the reformer Frances Dana Gage observed:

> Steam power suggested steam power, [sic] and one invention gave leisure for another; mind was released from physical labor, and gained time and leisure for higher and nobler development; woman was obliged to keep sight of the age. She was a help-meet, suggesting, striving, planning, and executing; thinking for the young, and leading them to the depots of usefulness.... Woman ... thirty years ago seldom went from the home, because she *could not be spared*, now that spinning-jennies and patent looms do the spinning and weaving, and sewing machines are doing the needle-work, steam-power does the knitting, and garments are made so cheap... it seems an idle waste of time to use 'Her needle'...[9]

Paralleling these economic developments was the desire to educate women to their duties as mothers which sparked the spread of female education in the first half of the 19th century. Enlightenment theorists had been the first to propose that, within the home, women should have primary responsibility for rearing the nation's young. Only an astute mother, they argued, could raise her sons to be proper citizens of the Republic. Health reformers merely eleaborated on this theme. "Now who," asked a typical contributor to the *Practical Educator and Journal of Health* in 1847, "is the best qualified to supervise a household? She who has been thoroughly trained... or she who knows practically nothing about it.... Let woman be intellectually educated as highly as possible."[10]

Educational opportunity brought middle-class women into contact with Enlightenment ideas about progress and individual freedom. Such concepts colored their adjustments to underlying social changes and helped produce a talented minority with rising status expectations who came to feel frustration, distate, anger, even desperation at the severe limitations imposed on them by the growing popularity of the "cult of the lady." Trained in a more ascetic Protestant tradition of usefulness, strength, duty, and good works, many middle-class women rejected the fashionable, indolent life of the leisured wife. Gradually two competing images of the ideal 19th-century woman emerged. On the one hand, woman was described as weak, sickly, dependent and ornamental. On the other she was exalted as highly spiritual and morally superior – confined to the home, yet invested with genuine power and responsibility within her sphere. Both health reformers and women's rights advocates would reject the first and seize on the second ideal – that of woman's moral power – using it effectively in this century to explore significant and divergent outlets for female energies. These women would practice domesticity, not as a cult, but as a science. Responding to changes in women's traditional role which left them devoid of adequate models and established forms of behavior, they sought to elevate and professionalize the domestic sphere as a means of seeking an effective and practical role for women in a new and unpredictable social setting.[11]

The middle-class woman's new domestic orientation required a single-minded concern with the problems of health and hygiene. Her own good health became a matter of conscious choice. She took an assiduous interest in questions concerning marriage, childbearing and childrearing, family health, sexuality and family limitation. Health reformers, both men and women, shared these interests and attempted to provide practical solutions to unsettling problems. Indeed, health reformers gave to the majority of their female constituents a justification for devoting their fulltime efforts to woman's traditional role of homemaking, recast, it is important to note, in a modern and scientific setting.

For the ordinary woman, the health revolution became a fundamental ingredient in women's modernization, allowing her to cope with the problems created by industrial and urban living and easing her transition into a more complex and modern world. Yet the movement also produced a smaller number of female activists who linked their concern with health problems to a more aggressive feminism. The health reform movement thus touched the average woman and the feminist in slightly different ways. Ironically, even as health reformers aided in readjusting female roles to coincide with traditional values concerning woman's place, they helped, sometimes unwittingly, to lay the groundwork for the eventual erosion of ancient pieties. To the female leaders of the campaign health reform offered a path out of the home and a more active role in social change.

II

Because woman's procreative role often made her health more precarious than man's, it seemed natural for the health reformers to begin their efforts with an aggressive concern for the state of female health. "If a plan for *destroying female health,* in all the ways in which it could be most effectively done, were drawn up," announced Catherine Beecher, "it would be exactly the course which is now pursued by a large portion of this nation, especially in the more wealthy classes." Dr. James C. Jackson, founder of the Danville water cure agreed. "American girls," he lamented, "are all sickly." "You are sick," wrote Mrs. S.M. Estee to the feminine readers of the *Water Cure Journal,* "and have been for months, years, and some of you your whole lives."[12]

We cannot know for sure whether or not this generation of women was sicker than their grandmothers. What is certain, however, is that they *thought* they were. Indeed, they well may have been. Fashionable dress took its toll on female health; the corset and tight lacing did much to damage female anatomy. Increased urbanization brought crowded and unsanitary living conditions. More and more middle-class women denied themselves the fresh air and exercise experienced by the rural housewife out of necessity rather than by choice. And the psychological strains of dislocation may have prompted some women to opt for ill-health, rather than stand and face changes which they could still barely comprehend.[13]

It soon became apparent that only healthy vigorous women could meet the challenges thrust upon them by a society in transition. Health reformers believed that woman was in the process of creating a new role for herself. "Woman . . . is a new element in society," wrote Dr. James Jackson to his associate Dr. Harriet A. Judd, "just emerging from her hybernation. . . and so much better fitted to take to herself *new* ideas, and develop them. . . ."[14] Good health was essential to woman's new self-expression and improved status. "Let mothers be educated in all that concerns life and health. . . ." insisted Mrs. Eliza de La Vergue, M.D. "Let them learn that *knowledge gives the highest order of power."*[15]

Good health became a prerequisite to woman's new place in the world. "Woman was neither made a toy nor a slave, but a help-meet to man," wrote "A Bloomer to Her Sisters," "and as such devolves upon her very many important duties and obligations which cannot be met so long as she is the puny, sickly, aching, weakly, dying creature that we find her to be; and woman must, to a very considerable extent, redeem herself – she must throw off the shackles that have hitherto bound both body and mind, and rise into the newness of life."[16]

Women could achieve none of these goals until they learned to dress properly. Health reformers made dress reform a symbol of women's new aspirations. Impractical clothes immobilized women and kept them from their responsibilities. Some regular physicians had linked fashionable dress to female ill health, but health reformers succeeded in making dress reform a moral imperative. Good health was doomed, they argued, as long as women clung to the dictates of French fashion. They called upon women to liberate their sould by freeing their bodies from the harmful effects of tight lacing and long, heavy unhygienic skirts. "How. . . glorious, "mused Rachel Brooks Gleason, M.D. "would it be to see every woman free from *every* fetter that fashion has imposed! Such a day of 'universal emancipation' of the sex would worthy of a celebration through all coming time." "We can expect but small achievement from women," warned Mary Gove Nichols, "so long as it is the labor of their lives to carry about their clothes." "How in the name of common sense," asked Edith Denner, "is a woman with long, full skirts, ever to become a practical Ornithologist, Geologist, or Bontanist. . .?[17]

Health reform journals pressed the issue. Lengthy technical descriptions of the damage wrought on female anatomy by the corset appeared, complete with diagrams. Pictures entitled the "Allopathic Lady, or Pure Cod Liver Oil Female, Who Patronizes a Fashionable Doctor, And Considers It Decidedly Vulgar to Enjoy Good Health," were published side by side with those of women in reformed dress. A typical caption read "A Water-Cure Bloomer, Who Believes In The Equal Rights Of Men And Women To Help Themselves And Each Other, And Who Thinks It Respectable, If Not Genteel, To Be Well." Not content merely to admonish their readers, some journals printed sewing instructions. For a modest sum, the *Laws of Life* sold patterns to its subscribers.[18]

In a society where women were expected to play an increasingly complex role in the nurture of children and the organization of family life, health crusaders brought to the bewildered housewife, not just sympathy and compassion, but a structured regimen and way of life. William A. Alcott, as early as 1839, took for granted the mother's primary responsibility in childrearing and the father's extended absence from the home. "All, or nearly all," he wrote in his book *The Young Mother,* "must devolve on the mother. The father has not time to attend to his children."[19]

Burdened by this reorientation toward their family responsibilities, many ordinary women found in the health reform movement a means of coping with an imprecise, undependable and often hostile environment. Lectures, journals and domestic tracts provided friendly advice and companionship in an era characterized by weakening ties between relatives and neighbors. Women found a means to end their isolation and make contact with others of their sex. In study groups and through letters to the various journals, they shared their common experiences with other women. No longer must woman bear her burden alone. This collective sensitivity to the community among women was symbolized by the frequent references to "sisterhood" in health reform literature.[20]

"I wish," wrote Mary Gove Nichols of her motives in becoming a health reformer, "to teach mothers how to cure their own diseases, and those of their children; and to increase health, purity, and happiness in the family and the home."[21] For some women, Mrs. Nichols and her fellow reformers achieved these goals.[22] Numerous articles on Cookery, Bathing, Teething, Care of Infants, Childhood Sexuality, Cleanliness, and Domestic Economy carefully taught women how to manage their households properly. Itinerant physiological lecturers assaulted women's widespread ignorance of their bodies. Nichols relied heavily on discussion of anatomy and physiology in her lectures. She instructed her listeners in the formation of bone structure, the role of respiration and circulation, the anatomy and physiology of the stomach. The process of digestion was described in detail. The remainder of her course involved information on dietetics and the importance of physical education. The evils of "tight lacing," and dire warnings against the harmful effects of the "solitary vice" also proved popular topics for discussion.[23]

Advice on the supervision of pregnancy and childbirth was strikingly prophetic of today's feminist critique of professional obstetrical practice. Health reformers questioned regular physicians' very approach to the process of parturition, calling their treatment "unnatural and often outrageous." "Here," observed Thomas Low Nichols,

> where august nature should reign supreme, her laws are too often violated, and all her teachings set at naught. Instead of preparing a woman to go through the process of labor with all the energy of her vitality, she is weakened by medication and blood-letting. Instead of being put upon a proper regimen, and a diet suited to her condition, she is more than ever pampered and indulged. And when labor comes on, the chances are that it will be interfered with in the most mistaken, the most unjustifiable . . . manner. The uterus will be stimulated into excessive and spasmodic action by the deadly ergot; the mother, at this most interesting and sacred hour of life, will be made dead drunk with ether or chloroform . . .and if a weakened and deranged system does not act as promptly as the doctor wishes, he proceeds to deliver with instruments, with the risk, often the certainty of destroying the child, and very often inflicting upon the mother irreparable injury.

"Under the popular medical orders of the day," agreed Russell Trall, "pregnant females are regarded as invalids, and are bled, paregoric'd, magnesia'd, stimulated, mineralized and poisoned, just as though they were going through a regular course of fever."[24] In contrast, health reformers viewed conception, gestation, and parturition as natural functions. They rejected the notion that pain in childbirth was inevitable, labeling such a belief "an insult to Providence." They urged exercise, fresh air, proper diet, and cleanliness. Daily bathing was advised for infants, who were to be dressed in loose-fitting, comfortable garments to give plenty of opportunity for movement. No drugs were allowed for mother or child. Such attention to hygiene and diet probably improved the health of many, if we can believe the numerous testimonials from satisfied individuals to be found in the back pages of health reform journals.[25]

When the middle-class woman took possession of her life and the lives of those around her in the area of health, she also provided herself with a platform from which to effect other changes, both within the family constellation and in society at large. One doubts if this process was always conscious. Yet it seems equally clear that her psychological acceptance of various domestic responsibilities often led to subtle shifts in the power relationship between the sexes, giving rise to new attitudes toward what was, and what was not acceptable in marriage. Nowhere was this process more apparent than in the health reformers' attitudes toward sexual intercourse.[26]

Health reformers were among the first 19th-century thinkers to prescribe restraint in sexual matters. Believing that good health required constant control, vigilant self-discipline, and vigorous dominion over man's animal nature, they warned that of all the sensual passions, "the sexual element" was the most difficult to subdue. "No other element in our own nature," wrote Henry C. Wright, "has so much to do in . . . forming our character and shaping our destiny . . . But what is done . . . to bring the sexual element under the control of an enlightened reason and a tender conscience?"[27]

Reformers clearly intended sexual restraint to benefit women and urged them to assert their rights in the sexual sphere. Much of female ill-health and infant mortality, they argued, could be attributed to husbands' sexual abuse of their wives. Believing that the male's passion for copulation far outdistanced his wife's, thinkers and educators urged men to follow the sexual rhythms of their more delicate spouses.[28]

Excessive childbearing endangered female health while it drained most women of the energy needed to perform the duties of scientific motherhood. Hence, health reformers linked their insistence on sexual restraint to family limitation. They were among the first to advocate birth control publicly. Children, they argued, must never be the result "of chance, of mere reckless, selfish passion." When, they asked "will men and women show a rational, conscientious, loving forethought, in giving existence to their children as they do in commerce, politics, and religion?" Every child should be a welcome child. "Welcome" became a code word for "planned." The "great object" of sexual intercourse, declared Henry C. Wright, was the *"perpetuation and perfection of the race."* Couples not ready to have children should remain sexually continent.[29]

In an era still largely ignorant of mechanical means of contraception, women benefitted from such cautious attitudes in numerous ways. Historians have already documented women's profound fears of pregnancy in this period. Less frequent childbearing did improve female health. Furthermore, the desire to avoid conception probably colored women's enjoyment of coitus. Some undoubtedly followed the common belief that failure to achieve orgasm would prevent pregnancy. Moreover, lovemaking techniques were often brutal and aggressive.[30] Even 19th-century physicians, although aware of female orgasm, knew very little else about the intricate nature of female sexual response. One suspects that middle-class women instructed their husbands and sons in the laws of sexual continence with a degree of enthusiasm and a measure of self-defense.[31]

While exalting the rewards of parenthood and elevating the motherly role, health reformers enjoined couples to limit their offspring. The contradiciton in such views remains more apparent than real. The ideal of educated motherhood eventually proved antithetical to large families. Women were simply incapable of achieving either the emotional intensity or the domestic expertise required of them when caring for a large brood. Margaret Sanger's injunction that parents should have "fewer and better babies" had its origins in the ante-bellum period, among these "enlightened" sections of the middle class.[32]

III

Rarely in any century have human beings been content to view health and disease as matters of mere chance. The health reformers' approach, however, was distinctly novel. To the Puritans and other colonials, sickness had been primarily a moral and spiritual dilemma which called for introspection and soul searching. But the 19th-century health reformers insisted that it resulted from a violation of God's and Nature's laws. Such laws were eminently sensible, and the individual could, indeed, he *must*, keep himself well. No longer was sickness and death to be tolerated with the stoicism and resignation that contrasted the limited moral choices of man with the all-powerful inscrutability of God. "Many people," observed Mary Gove Nichols, "seem to think that all diseases are immediate visitations from the Almighty, arising from no cause but his *immediate* dispensation . . . Many seem to have no idea that there are established laws with respect to life and health, and that the transgression of these laws is followed by disease." Man, agreed Marie Louise Shew, was designed to live in good health to a ripe old age. Disease was man's doing, not God's. The prevention of disease and premature death was indeed within the control of mankind.[33]

The emergence of health reform as a coherent crusade cannot be understood apart from the gradual appearance of a novel set of assumptions about the world – an attitude which historians, for want of a more precise theoretical model, have attributed to the modernization process. Health reformers insisted upon the efficacy of individual action. They were certain that human beings could affect the future by manipulating the environment and controlling themselves. This was a conviction that they shared with all other reformers of the ante-bellum period. Yet this common outlook was itself a reflection of a more fundamental change in thought and feeling.

Even many critics of the concept of modernization agree that if used carefully it can serve as a helpful organizing principle for studying the social, political, and cultural fragmentation which accompanied industrialization.[34] The modernization model can be of aid in relating changes in individual and family dynamics to other aspects of social history.

Although we may differ as to the cause, most of us would agree that modern men and women behave differently from their ancestors: they exhibit high occupational and educational goals, they value mobility, personal freedom, and self-improvement, and their fundamental belief in progress leads to an implicit abandonment of passivity in the face of life's difficulties.[35] Health reformers filled their literature with such themes. Indeed, one could argue that health reform facilitated the adjustment of men and women in the 19th century to industrialization and urbanization.

Occasionally health tracts revealed the reformers' profound ambivalence toward social and economic change, and such equivocation was itself significant. By no means did all health crusaders welcome the new order with unbridled enthusiasm.[36] As other historians have shown, many individuals looked nostalgically backward to an idealized "republic of virtue" where the mutual interdependency of family members and society at large promoted "good health" in the form of physical and spiritual unity.[37] While they desired "progress," health reformers did not always realize that it would lead inevitably to changes in values. Arguing, on the one hand, that an excessive application to business led to insanity in men, while luxury and idleness produced nervousness in women, they simultaneously sought the creation of a personality type remarkably well-suited to the competitive atmosphere of the industrial order.[38] Preaching moderation and self-control, reformers strove to provide men and women with a coherent mode of adjustment to the physical and psychological demands of an urbanizing environment. By helping, willy-nilly, to effect a transformation of personality which equipped individuals to deal with other aspects of modernization, health reform itself became a part

By the end of the 19th century, reform ideas about personal cleanliness, public health, and family hygiene had become familiar axioms of middle-class American culture – a badge of distinction by which members set themselves off from "illegitimate" immigrant groups, many of whom retained distinctly premodern daily habits and attitudes toward disease. Indeed, those health reformers primarily concerned with public health had long been aware of the relationship between ignorance, immoral habits, poverty and sickness. The allegedly "filthy" and "depraved" customs attributed to the immigrant poor proved particularly vexing. Health reformers of all persuasions believed that they worked to make good health a measure of middle-class respectability.[39]

To the middle-class women, troubled by the contradictory demands of urbanization and industrialization, health reform offered both physical and psychological relief. Holding out to confused wives and mothers the prospect of improving the quality of life, not merely by changing the environment, but by gaining control of themselves, health reformers promised women that they could raise their children healthy in mind and clean in body. Reformers offered wives the possibility of keeping their husbands moral by cooking the right foods. Preaching sexual continence and physiological knowledge, they helped to legitimate female rights in the bedroom at a time when sexual contact need not universally have been a positive experience. Indeed, health reform manuals supported women's right to limit the number of their children and control their own bodies, though they accepted only sexual continence as a moral means of birth control. Nevertheless, the idea that fertility should, or even could be consistently tampered with was distinctly modern, and neatly complemented other social and economic developments.[40]

For a minority of brave, ambitious and talented women health reform also provided an outlet and an escape from an intolerably narrow and confining role. Health reformers shared with other 19th-century Americans the belief that woman's role was invested with cosmic moral significance. But unlike many of their contemporaries, female health activists subscribed to the widest possible definition of woman's sphere. They understood that to purify society, women would indeed have to enter it. Admitting women into the masculine sphere, even in a limited way, would eventually have profound effects on future definitions of sex roles.

Most middle-class women, however, were not feminists. Health reform gave them a coherent program to ease their adjustment to a society in transition. Over and over again the reformers identified poor female health with underemployment and idleness. This familiar refrain suggests a lack of integration in the lives of middle-class women, a tenuousness and uncertainty about their role. Female health reformers especially addressed themselves to this problem. Elevating the art of domesticity to a science, they restored to their followers a sense of purpose and direction, while they preserved in a new form traditional assumptions about woman's role which were deeply imbedded in the culture. The health reform regimen established new standards by which ordinary women could measure their own respectability and worth.[41]

Reformers underscored woman's importance by emphasizing her central role in the task of human betterment. Improvement of female health, they argued, would lead to social regeneration. Woman was invested with awesome responsibilities. "There are no duties on earth so nearly angelic as those which devolve upon woman. . . ." declared Alcott. "If all wives loved and delighted in their homes as Solomon would have them, few husbands would go down to a premature grave through the avenues of intemperance and lust, and their kindred vices." *The Lily,* a feminist and temperance journal, emphasized woman's moral power. "Woman's influence is truly kingly [sic] in general society. It is powerful in a daughter and a sister; but it is the mother who weaves the garlands that flourish in eternity." The gravity of woman's influence went even beyond her own family, for health reformers shared a contemporary belief in the inheritance of acquired characteristics. "For the sake of the race," explained Mary Gove Nichols, "I ask that all be done for woman that can be done, for it is an awful truth that fools are the mothers of fools." James C. Jackson was even more blunt: "God punishes as well as rewards mankind *through woman*. . . . She is appointed to dispense divine retributions as well as divine blessings... through her does God visit the iniquities of the father on the children to the third and fourth generations."[42]

Though such attitudes gave women genuine responsibility and power, they also exacted a large measure of anxiety and even guilt. "Women are answerable, in a very large degree," admonished Paulina Wright Davis, "for the imbecilities of disease, mental and bodily, and for the premature deaths prevailing throughout society – for the weakness, wretchedness, and shortness of life – and no remedy will be radical till reformation of life and practice obtains among our sex. . . ."[43] Such a psychological burden might well have been unbearable had not health reformers given to women fellowship, moral support, and practical information.

The health reformers' emphasis on educated motherhood and scientific domesticity in a sense helped make middle-class women modern. But being modern did not necessarily mean being equal. If the concept of female moral superiority was a source of *power* for women in the 19th century, it cannot be confused with *liberation*.[44] Indeed, it may have merely guaranteed the perpetuation and elaboration of traditional assumptions about mothering and housekeeping in an altered social setting. Full equality for women continued to be underminded by a single-minded concern with woman's maternal role. Even the most feminist of health reformers failed to realize that women would never be equal as long as they remained confined to a sphere – no matter how expansively that sphere was defined.

University of Kansas Regina Markell Morantz

FOOTNOTES

This article grew out of a paper presented at a symposium on "Medicine Without Doctors: Home Health Care in American History," sponsored by the Department of the History of Medicine, University of Wisconsin, Madison, April 14, 1975. The author is grateful to Ellen Chesler, Rita Napier, Cliff Griffin, Eric Foner, John Clark and Martin Pernick for reading and criticizing the manuscript.

1. The most recent treatments of the health reform movement include William B. Walker, "The Health Reform Movement in the United States, 1830-1870" (Ph.D. Thesis, John Hopkins, 1955); Richard Shryock, "Sylvester Graham and the Popular Health Movement, 1830-1870," in *Medicine in America, Historical Essays* (Baltimore, 1966), 111-125; John Blake, "Health Reform," in E.S. Gaustad, ed., *The Rise of Adventism: Religion and Society in Mid-Nineteenth Century America* (New York, 1974), 30-49; H.E. Hoff and J. Fulton, "The Centenary of the First American Physiological Society Founded at Boston by William A. Alcott and Sylvester Graham," *Bull. Hist. Med.*, 5, (Oct., 1937) 687-734; Stephen Wilner Nissenbaum, "Careful Love: Sylvester Graham and the Emergence of Victorian Sexual Theory in America, 1830-1840" (Ph.D. Thesis, University of Wisconsin, 1968); James C. Whorton, "Christian Physiology: William Alcott's Prescription for the Millenium," *Bull. Hist. Med.*, 49, (Winter, 1975) 466-481. Two lively popular works are James H. Young, *The Toadstool Millionaires: A Social History of Patent Medicines in America Before Federal Regulation* (Princeton, 1961) and Gerald Carson *Cornflake Crusade* (New York, 1967). The public health movement is dealt with in Charles and Carroll Smith-Rosenberg, "Pietism and the Origins of the American Public Health Movement: A Note on John H. Griscom and Robert W. Hartley," *Jour. Hist. Med.* 23 (1968) 16-35; Richard H. Shryock, "The Early American Public Health Movement," in *Medicine in America*, 126-138. John D. Davies skillfully chronicles the phrenology movement in *Phrenology, Fad and Science* (New Haven, 1955).

2. *Water Cure Journal*, 7 (1849), 18. (Hereafter cited as *WCJ.*) The Seventh Day Adventist publication, *The Health Reformer* claimed 11,000 subscribers in 1868. See Ronald L. Numbers "Health Reform on the Delaware," *New Jersey History*, 92 (Sept., 1974), 7.

3. For the convergence of health reform with other reform movements see Robert S. Flectcher, "Bread and Doctrine at Oberlin," *Ohio State Archeological and Historical Quarterly*, 49 (Jan., 1940), 58; Sidonia E. Taupin, " 'Christianity in the Kitchen,' or A Moral Guide for Gourmets," *American Quarterly*, 15 (1963), 85-89; Thomas H. LeDuc, "Grahamites and Garrisonites," *New York History*, 20 (April, 1939), 189-191; Michael Katz, *The Irony of Early School Reform* (Boston, 1968). For a thoughtful and highly provocative recent treatment see Ronald G. Walters, "The Erotic South: Civilization and Sexualtiy in American Abolitionism," *American Quarterly*, 25 (May, 1973), 177-201.

4. See Martha Verbrugge, "The Ladies Physiological Institute: Health Reform and Women in Ante-bellum Boston" (Paper delivered at Third Annual Berkshire conference on Women's History, Brvn Mawr, June, 1976). The one exception to this middle-class analysis may have been the Thomsonians, a health reform sect which has been tentatively linked to working-class elements. I would contend that the Thomsonians do not fall out of the mainstream of the movement I am discussing, because health reform could very well have played a similar role in "modernizing" native American workers in the ante-bellum period as I will argue it played for the middle class. As Paul Faler and Alan Dawley have recently shown, the internalization of "modern" values often transcended class divisions. See "Working Class Culture and Politics in the Industrial Revolution: Sources of Loyalism and Rebellion," *Journal of Social History*, 9 (June, 1976) 466-79. I am indebted to Irene Javors of City College for discussing her preliminary findings on the Thomsonians with me.

5. For the influence of the Enlightenment see Alice Felt Tyler, *Freedom's Ferment* (New York, 1944). For Christian perfectionism see James C. Whorton, " 'Christian Physiology:' William Alcott's Prescription for the Millenium," *Bull. Hist. Med.*, 49, (Winter, 1975), 466-81. For the decline of heroic therapeutics see Shryock, op cit. For anti-elitism see Richard Shryock, "Cults and Quackery in American Medical History," Middle States Association of History and Social Studies Teachers, *Trans*, 37 (1939), 19-30.

6. The most recent treatment of modernization in America does not refer to health reform at all. See Richard D. Brown, *Modernization, The Transformation of American Life, 1600-1865*, (New York, 1976).

7. The one exception is John Blake's excellent article on Mary Gove Nichols, "Mary Gove Nichols, Prophetess of Health," in *Proceedings of the American Philosophical Society*, 106 (June, 1962), 219-234.

8. Hebbel and Hoff, *op cit*, 701.

9. On changes, particularly in New England, which touched the lives of many in the reform leadership see the thoughtful introduction by Michael Katz to *The Irony of Early School Reform* (Boston, 1968). Also Stanley Engerman, Ed., *The Reinterpretation of American Economic History*, (New York, 1971), Stephen Thernstrom, *Poverty and Progress* (Cambridge, 1964); Stephen Thernstrom and Richard Sennett, eds., *Nineteenth Century Cities* (New Haven, 1969). Two recent articles on women and work before industrializaition are Joan Scott and Louise Tilly, "Women's Work and Family in 19th Century Europe," *Comparative Studies in History & Society*, 17 (Jan., 1975) 36-64; Alice Kessler-Harris, "Stratifying by Sex: Understanding the History of Working Women," *Labor Market Segmentation*, ed. by Richard Edwards, *et. al* (Lexington, Mass., 1975). For quote from Frances Dana Gage see *WCJ*, 17 (1854), 35.

10. Rev. H. Winslow, "Domestic Education in Females," I (1847), 259-61.

11. The concept of the "republican mother," which was given life during the ante-bellum period, gained momentum through several permutations until progressive era reformers and social workers recast it in the 20th-century notion of "educated motherhood." See Linda Kerber, "Daughters of Columbia: Educating Women for the Republic, 1787-1805," in Stanley Elkins and Eric McKitrick, *The Hofstadter Aegis*, (New York, 1974), and "The Republican Mother" (Paper read at the Southern Historical Association Meeting, November, 1975); Jill Conway, "Perspectives on the History of Women's Education in the United States," *Hist. of Ed. Quart.* 14 (Spring, 1974), 1-12. For the progressive period see Sheila Rothman, "Social History and Social Policy: The Case of Women, Children & the Family" (Paper read at the meeting of the Organization of American Historians, April, 1976, St. Louis). For an excellent discussion of the social and economic roots of American feminism, particularly the influence of education see Keith Melder, "The Beginning of the Women's Rights Movement in the United States, 1800-1840" (Ph.D. Thesis, Yale, 1964); Gerda Lerner, "The Lady and the Mill Girl: Changes in the Status of Women in the Age of Jackson," *American Studies*, 10 (Spring, 1969), 5-15.

12. *Letters to the People on Health and Happiness* (New York, 1856), 7. "Shall Our Girls Live or Die," *Laws of Life*, 10 (1867), 2; "To Sick Women," *WCJ*, 26 (1858), 96. See also Augustus K. Gardner, "The Physical Decline of American Women," *WCJ*, 29 (1860), 21-22, 50-51.

13. Striking evidence for the conviction of many women writers that their grandmothers enjoyed better health can be found in Catherine Beecher, *Housekeeper and Healthkeeper* (New York, 1873), 424-428. Another possible explanation for the increase in complaints is that women were no longer willing to tolerate their ill health. See also Carroll Smith-Rosenberg, "The Hysterical Woman: Sex Roles and Role Conflict in Nineteenth-Century America," *Social Research*, 39 (Winter, 1972), 652-678.

14. *WCJ*, 15 (1854), 74, 94.

15. Italics mine. *WCJ*, 20 (1855), 74.

16. *WCJ*, 15 (1853), 131. See also Harriet Austin, "Woman's Present and Future," *WCJ*, 16 (1853), 57.

17. "Woman's Dress," *WCJ*, 11 (1851), 30: "The New Costume," *WCJ*, 12 (1851) 30; Science and Long Skirts," *WCJ*, 20 (1855), 7.

18. *WCJ*, 16 (1853), 120; 11 (1851) 96, and *passim*. Most of the water-cure establishments encouraged their female patients to wear reformed dress. Almost every issue of any health reform journal had something about dress: *The Water Cure Journal* and *The Laws of Life* showed special interest in dress reform; the *Graham Journal* and the *American Vegetarian and Health Journal* less frequently. Dress reform was also a popular topic in women's rights journals like *The Una*, *The Lily*, and later *The Revolution*. Many of the articles in these journals pertaining to dress were written by health reformers. See especially *WCJ*, 12 (1851), 33 58; *WCJ*, 34 (1862), 1-2; *WCJ*, 15 (1853), 7, 10, 32, 34, 35, 131; *WCJ*, 13 (1852), 111; *The Laws of Life*, 10 (1867), 93-94, 129-130, 145-146; *The Revolution*, 3 (1869), 149-50; *Graham Journal*, 3 (1839), 301-2.

19. Boston, 1839, 265-266.

20. *WCJ*, 1 (1846), 29.

21. See "To Her Sick Sisters," *WCJ*, 26 (1858), 96. "A Bloomer to Her Sisters," *WCJ*, 15 (1853), 131. There are many examples. For a possible meaning to this sense of community see Carroll Smith-Rosenberg "The Female World of Love and Ritual: Relations Between Women in 19th Century America," *Signs*, I (A'1975), 1-29. For Nichols quote see *A*

Woman's Work in Water Cure, 14. See also Mary Gove Nichols, "To the Women Who Read the Water Cure Journal," *WCJ*, 14 (1852), 68: "We do not consider ourselves doctors in the common understanding of the word – though we shall not neglect to do the highest good in this department, but we consider ourselves educators – set apart and qualified by Providence for the work. We will educate men and women for Physicans and Teachers of health, and young women to be wise wives and mothers. We will make the most beneficial impression on the world that is possible to us."

22. See Martha Verbrugge, *op cit.* Hers is the first local study we have of the rank and file. One suspects others will yield similar conclusions.

23. Chapters on Food, Cooking and Domestic Economy in William A. Alcott, *The Young Housekeeper* (Boston, 1849); *Graham Journal*, "Keep Your Children Clean," I (1837), 176; Masturbation and Its Effect on Health," 2 (1838), 23. Mary Gove Nichols, *Lectures to Women*, passim. See also advertisement in the *Graham Journal*, II (1838), 288. For articles on fresh air and bathing: *WCJ*, (1847), 161-68, 177; *WCJ*, 4 (1847), 193; pregnancy, exercise and childbirth: *WCJ*, 3 (1847), 145, 151, 183-84; "Our New Cookbook," "How to Can a Fruit," *Laws of Life*, 10 (1867), 12: "Cleanliness and Healthfulness," *Laws of Life*, 10 (1867), 16; "Teething and Its Management," "Children's Dress," *WCJ*, 12 (1851), 101, 104. Martha Verbrugge has emphasized this practical dimension of the health reform program. She contends that the Ladies' Physiological Institute helped ordinary middle-class women adjust to the opportunities and the limitations imposed on them by modern life. Verbrugge is impressed less with the radical elements of the Boston group and more with the organization's goal of easing women into traditional role patterns potentially disturbed by changing social conditions. Her study is significant because it suggests that health reform appealed to several different types of women. She argues, for example, that only a small minority of the members of the Boston society were outspoken feminists. See Verbrugge, *op cit.*

24. Thomas Low Nichols, *"The Curse Removed; The Efficacy of Water-Cure in the Treatment of Uterine Disease and the Removal of the Pains and Perils of Pregnancy and Childbirth,"* (New York, 1850), 13; Trall, "Allopathic Midwifery," *WCJ*, 9 (1850), 121; Mary Gove Nichols, "Maternity and the Water Cure for Infants," *WCJ*, 11 (1851), 57-9; Eliza de la Vergue, M.D. "Infants, Their Improper Nursing and Meication," *WCJ*, 20 (1855).

25. See an interesting autobiographical sketch by Mrs. Mary A. Torbit, "Reasons for Becoming a Lecturer," *WCJ*, 14 (1851), 91. One of the health reformers' favortie arguments – that women had natural abilities to cure – led them to a desire to teach women medicine. Indeed, the entrance of women into the medical profession grew out of the cult of scientific domesticity popularized by the health reform movement. Reformers applauded the acceptance of women as medical students, chiding the regulars for their conservatism. In time these early female pioneers, who entered medicine convinced of their natural abilities, would be transformed into full-fledged professionals by their contact with an increasingly scientific and empirical discipline. They became exposed to a more modern system of values, their outlook permanently altered in the process. See Regina Markell Morantz, "Daughters of Aesculapius: The Entrance of Women into the Medical Profession in 19th Century America, Ideology and Social Setting" (Paper delivered at Minneapolis, Women Historians of the Midwest Conference, October, 1975).

26. Indeed, the attitude of the health reformers toward the relations between the sexes was innovative. They preached a version of companionate marriage. See Morantz, "Health Reform and Women: An Ideology of Self Help" (Paper presented at the symposium on "Medicine Without Doctors, Home Health Care in American History," Department of the History of Medicine, University of Wisconsin, Madison, April 14, 1975).

27. Henry C. Wright, *Marriage and Parentage* (Boston, 1855, Arno reprint, 1974), 5.

28. *Ibid.*, 91, 257. See also Orson Fowler, *Love and Parentage* (New York, 1847), 272-274,

passim. See Linda Gordon, "Voluntary Motherhood: The Beginnings of Feminist Birth Control Ideas in the United States," in L. Banner and M. Hartman, *Clio's Consciousness Raised: New Perspectives on the History of Women* (New York, 1974), 54-71. Not all advisors proscribed sexual intercourse without procreation. However all agreed that coitus should be approached with caution. Mechanical means of contraception were an anathema because such methods degraded women by encouraging overindulgence.

29. Wright, *Ibid.*

30. See Eliza B. Duffey, *The Relations of the Sexes* (New York, 1879), especially Chapter 13, "The Limitation of Offspring."

31. Although Carl Degler has rightly pointed out that at least some women did have orgasms in the 19th century, a fact which it would be silly to dispute, I would suggest that female orgasm was inherently more problematical than that of the male, and that the 19th century was generally ignorant of the more subtle nature of female sexual response. Marriage counselors in the 1920's and 1930's documented this widespread ignorance and tried to correct it. Alfred Kinsey's statistics show a gradual increase in the number of married women achieving orgasm in the years after 1900. Carroll Smith-Rosenberg has examined possible differences in male and female approaches to sexuality in the 19th century in greater detail in a recent paper, "A Gentle and A Richer Sex: Female Perspectives on Nineteenth Century Sexuality" (Third Berkshire Conference on Women's History, Bryn Mawr, June, 1976). See also Regina Markell Morantz, "The Scientist as Sex Crusader: Alfred Kinsey and American Culture," *American Quarterly* (Fall, 1977) See Duffey, Ch. 13. It should be pointed out that most health reformers were also eugenicists. See Henry C. Wright, *The Empire of the Mother Over the Character and Destiny of the Race* (Boston, 1863).

32. Moreover, social reformers of all types recognized that large families hampered upward mobility. The reputation of the Irish for their alleged indulgence of the sensual passions was widespread. They had nothing but "large," dirty" families to show for it:" Did wealth consist in children," asserted the *Common School Journal*, "it is well known, that the Irish would be a rich people; and if the old Roman law prevailed here, which granted special privilege to every man who had more than three, this people would be elevated into an aristocracy." Quoted in Katz, *The Irony of Early School Reform*, 123. Many of the early school reformers, including Horace Mann, had a lively interest in health reform. Largely because of this interest the Massachusetts legislature passed a law in 1850 requiring physiological instruction in the schools.

33. *Lectures to Women*, 20. *Water Cure for Ladies*, Preface, iii. See Charles Rosenberg, *The Cholera Years* (Chicago, 1962).

34. See Christopher Lasch on the problems of the modernization model in the first of three articles on the historiography of the family in *New York Review of Books*, (Nov. 13, 1975).

35. James T. Fawcett, "Modernization, Individual Modernity, and Fertility," in J.T. Fawcett, ed. *Studies in the Psychology of Population* (New York, 1973); Alex Inkeles, "The Modernization of Man," in *Modernization, the Dynamics of Growth* New York, 1966), 138-150, and "Making Men Modern: on the Causes and Consequences of Individual Change in Six Developing Countries," *Am. Jour. of Soc*, 75 (1969), 208-225; also Richard D. Brown, "Modernization and the Modern Personality in America, 1600-1865," *Jour. of Interdisc. Hist.* 2 (W' 1972), 201-227.

36. See for example, David J. Rothman, *The Discovery of the Asylum* (Boston, 1971)

37. "Excessive Application: A Cause of Insanity," *Monthly Miscellany and Journal of Health 1 (1846) 212.* See also Barbara Sicherman, "Paradox of Prudence; Mental Health in the gilded Age," *Journ. of Amer. Hist.* 62 (Mar., 1976), 890-912.

38. For other discussions of this personality type see Peter Cominos, "Late Victorian Respectability and the Social System," *Int. Rev. of Soc. Hist.* 8 (1963), 18-48, 216-50; Herbert Gutman, "Work, Culture, and Society in Industrializing America," *AHR*, 78 (June, 1973), 531-587; Michael Katz, *The Irony of Early School Reform;* Alan Dawley and Paul Faler, "Working Class Culture and Politics in the Industrial Revolution: Sources of Loyalty and Rebellion," *Journal of Social History* 9 (June, 1976), 466-79.

39. "Looking. . . at the social habits of the working people in some of our densely populated districts, it does indeed appear a hopeless effort to attack their vices, unless one could at the same time pull down their houses, and build them others adapted to a more perfect state of bodily and mental health," "Sanitary and Social Reform Coeval," by Mrs. Ellis in *Practical Educator and Journal of Health*, 1 (1847) 354-5. Charles Rosenberg has made this same point in connection with 19th-century prescriptions for male sexual purity. See "Sexuality, Class, Role," *American Quarterly* 25 (May, 1973), 131-153; also William Coleman, "Health and Hygiene in the Encyclopedie: A Medical Doctrine for the Bourgeoisie," *Jour. Hist. Med.* 29 (Oct., 1974), 339-412, applies a similar argument to the French bourgeoisie. See S. Weir Mitchell, "So great is my reverence for supreme wholesomeness, that I should almost be tempted to assert that perfect health is virtue." *Address on Opening of the Institute of Hygiene of the University of Pennsylvania.* (Phil., 1892), 4. A few health reformers merged the moral injunction to "guard the health of the race" with overt nativism. "Already," warned James C. Jackson,

> the decay of our women and the delicate constitutions of our young men are forcing the latter to seek revitalization by intermarriage with immigrant women from Europe. What with the decline of the Puritan and Cavilier stock on the one hand, and the great influx of foreign born on the other, it is not difficult to predict *our future.* In less than fifty years the New England type of manhood will have ceased to govern this Republic, and when once it ceases to govern it will cease to exist. . . . *Nothing but a bold and faithful advocacy of the laws of health can stop this ebbtide of human life.*

See *WCJ* 26 (1858), 4.

40. See James T. Fawcett, "Modernization, Individual Modernity, and Fertility." Also see Robert V. Wells, "Family History and Demographic Transition," *Jour. Soc. Hist.*, 9 (Fall, 1975), 1-20.

41. It should be pointed out that the domestic ideal had very different effects on working-class women. By encouraging them to aspire to an often impossible goal, the cult of domesticity helped keep married women out of the work force, or at least aspiring to be idle. This insured that working women would often be undependable allies in labor disputes. Believing that their primary commitment should be to the family, they accepted low pay and low status jobs, viewing their situation as only temporary. See Alice Kessler-Harris, "Stratifying by Sex." The domestic ideology also increased women's perceptions of class differences among themselves. Middle-class women were often advised to be cautious about the health of hired servants. Advice literature warned of the dangers of immigrant girls infecting the household. I am indebted to my colleague David Katzman for this information. For a stimulating discussion of the middle-class English woman's involvement in health reform see Patricia Branca, *Silent Sisterhood, Middle Class Women in the Victorian Home* (Pittsburgh, 1976), especially Parts II and III. Branca argues that middle-class Victorian women were the first large group to establish a modern outlook toward life and death.

42. William Alcott, *The Young Wife* (Boston, 1837), 87-89; *The Lily*, I (1849), 52; Nichols, *Lectures to Women*, 212, and "Woman the Physician," *WCJ*, 12 (1851), 75; Jackson, "The Women of the United States," *WCJ* 26 (1858), 3, and "Women's Rights," *WCJ*, 31 (1861), 61. For an excellent summary of hereditarian views in this period see Charles Rosenberg, "The Bitter Fruit: Heredity, Disease, and Social Thought in Nineteenth Century America," *Perspectives in American History*, 7 (1974), 189-238.

43. *WCJ*, 1(1846), 29.

44. See Christopher Lasch, "The Woman Reformers' Rebuke," in *The World of Nations*, (New York, 1974).

From Maidenhood To Menopause: Sex Education For Women in Victorian America

By JOHN S. HALLER, JR.

The "twilight talks" for American women during the Victorian era, concealed in manuals of hygiene and ethics, religious pamphlets, medical articles, and etiquette books, reflected the late nineteenth century's conspicuous mask of prudery. Sex, like nature, proceeded according to an established set of laws or principles which, when carefully observed, would prevent women from yielding to the lower passions. Sex had a certain order and harmony which manifested the infinite wisdom of the Deity, but seldom did the concept include the words beauty and goodness. The sex-in-life manuals were calculated to impress the feminine mind with sentiments of virtue and chastity, and the notion that sex had somehow interfered with the realization of those objectives. Intelligent discussion of sex predisposed the Victorian woman to an assortment of inferences in which sex was somehow at variance with the search for morality and the proper definition of virtue. The same Providence that watched over America in its victories and peace was similarly engaged in the management of the American woman and her capacity as preserver of the species. In this fashion, American manners and morals became the darlings of religious and medical tracts which found in sex the pernicious spectre of Satan and the engine of immorality. Deeply Protestant in tone, with a strong undercurrent of Old Testament vengeance, nineteenth century manuals portrayed sex as the basest of human tendencies, the aberrations of which were invariably detected and punished through disease and mental anguish. Sex as described in the manuals became middle-class, with all the marks of sobriety, propriety, modesty, and conformity, and provided for rural America much the same function it provided for urban America looking across the Atlantic for cues for correct behavior. American sexual morality consisted of—and reflected—middle class prejudices, sentimentality, romanticized expectations, the workings of Divine Providence, and pseudo-scientific sophistication.

From another point of view, the sex-in-life manuals were a carry-over from the dabblers of the mid-nineteenth century society in the area of pseudo-science, liberal Christianity, Transcendentalism, and perfectionist tendencies. It was with the sex manuals that the clergy, who were declining in their function as medical advisors, and the physicians, who were attempting to widen their function as spiritual as well as physical healer, met to reform both medicine and morals. Strands of Thomsonianism, sentimentalism, Swedenborgianism, homeopathy, phrenology, and animal magnetism converged to create a congenial atmosphere for reconciling the spiritual affectations of middle class morality with matters of the flesh.[1]

The sex-in-life manuals gave to the American woman a common body of ideals to be taken seriously, out of which she was to shape the manner and morals of her class. Here was a pedagogical apparatus molded to direct her duties as maiden and anxious parent in the area of personal conduct. The empirical data from which the manuals drew their social and moral fabric came from a body of middle-class fictions—myths which sought to explain the discrepancy between middle-class principles and the reality of sin, disease, poverty and immorality. A sense of pretention, along with a very real sense of educational, ethical, and economic superiority to the rawness of working-class America, combined to create a thinly concealed romantic moral code, steeped in fictitious parables and impossible ideals, struggling to assert a new and imaginative perspective for the American class structure. The aspirations of the middle class form a vital link in a proper understanding of sexual attitudes of the late nineteenth century.

The proper training of girls, their personal hygiene, their relations with other children, their reading habits, and the embarrassing problem of masturbation (variously called the "solitary vice," "self-pollution," or the "soul-and-body-destroyer") dominated a major portion of the sex manuals of the day. Girls were cautioned never to handle their sexual organs, for, while it gave a temporary pleasure, the habit left "its mark upon the face so that those who are wise may know what the girl is doing."[2] The misuse of the sexual organs brought an inevitable threat of disease and severe complications in later life. "The infliction of the penalty may be somewhat delayed," wrote one physician, "but it will surely come, sooner or later." The young girl who practiced the solitary vice would never escape the consequences of her indiscretion. All through life, "the penalty of unlawful transgression [would] be visited upon her," and when she became a wife and mother, her earlier abuse would make the "perils incident to [her present role] be vastly increased."[3] She would become subject to a multitude of disorders such as backaches, tenderness of the spine, nervousness, indolence, pale cheeks, hollow eyes and a generally "languid manner." Her attitude, once pure and innocent, would turn peevish, irritable, morose, and disobedient; furthermore, she would suffer loss of memory, appear "bold in her manner instead of being modest," and manifest unnatural appetites for mustard, pepper, vinegar, cloves, clay, salt, chalk, and charcoal.[4] One writer conjectured that her eyes became dull (with bluish rings), that she would have difficulty in concentration and in study, and that blindness, stupidity, and even idiocy could occur.[5]

Nearly all manuals condemned the romantic novel as the villain behind the increased evidence of sexual neurasthenia, hysteria, and generally poor health in American women. Not only did sentimental literature tempt them to impurity, but the emotional stimulation that accompanied novel reading tended "to develop the passions prematurely, and to turn the thoughts into a channel which leads in the direction of the formation of vicious habits."[6] Whatever stimulated emotions in the young girl caused a corresponding development in her sexual organs. Overindulgence in romantic stories produced a flow of blood to certain body organs causing "excessive excitement" and finally disease.[7] For this reason, children's parties, staying up late, puppy love, hot drinks, "boarding-school fooleries," loose conversation, "the drama of the ballroom," talk of beaux, of love, or marriage, were contributing causes to unnatural sexual development.[8] "I want you to be my little girl as long as you can," wrote one mother in *What a Young Girl Ought to Know*, and therefore, "I ask you not to read love-stories and silly books of romance."[9]

> We wish [added one doctor] to put ourself upon record as believing firmly that the practice of novel reading is one of the greatest causes of uterine disease in young women. There is no doubt but that the influence of the mind upon the sexual organs and functions is such that disease may be produced in this way. . . . Reading of a character to stimulate the emotions and rouse the passions may produce or increase a tendency to uterine congestion, which may in turn give rise to a great variety of maladies, including all the different forms of [womb] displacement, the presence of which is indicated by weak backs, painful menstruation, leucorrhoea, etc.[10]

Thousands of women who had erred in their youth by "intently poring over the vulgar poems of Chaucer or the amorous ditties of Burns or Byron" were subsequently forced "to wage a painful warfare for years to banish from their minds the impure imagery generated by the perusal of books of this character." Most of their complications during pregnancy and menopause were traced to this source.[11] For this reason, writers cautioned parents to examine carefully every piece of literature placed in their daughter's hands, even to the extent of editing prurient Sunday-school books.[12]

Parents were also advised to prevent the phase of "silly letter writing" that occurred between boys and girls in their early school years. "We have known of several instances," warned Dr. J. H. Kellogg in his *Ladies Guide in Health and Disease* (1883), " in which the minds of pure girls became contaminated through this channel." He campaigned for "eternal vigilance" and enjoined parents to guard the chastity of daughters in all their relations. This vigilance included the prohibition of tea and coffee until they were at least eighteen years of age. These "comforting properties" were addictive and led the young female down the road to perdition to seek stronger tonics to satisfy her craving for stimulants.[13]

Like novels and letter-writing, the dance was another source of impurity. Dr. Kellogg, for example, claimed that the dance had caused the ruin of three-fourths of the degenerate women in New York city.[14] One young lady confessed that the waltz had awakened a "strange pleasure" in her constitution—her pulse fluttered, her cheeks glowed with the approach of her partner, and she "could not look him in the eye with the same frank gayety as before." According to Sylvanus Stall in *What a Young Husband Ought to Know*, the male transferred his physical emotions to the woman through animal-magnetism. It was not the dance itself, nor even the intentions of the male dance partner; rather, the female absorbed the male's more domineering and passionate nature through the magnetic contact. Thus, wrote a ruined and repentant girl, "I became abnormally developed in my lowest nature."[15]

The manuals passed hurriedly over another nasty habit—the display of unnatural affection of girls for other girls. The custom of holding each other's hands, of kissing and caressing "should be kept for . . . hours of privacy, and never indulged in before gentlemen." The reasons for this admonition "readily suggest themselves," and there were other motives "known to those well acquainted with the world."[16]

In one of her more important functions, the young lady was to provide a constant source of idealism to her brothers. "So many temptations beset young men of which young women know nothing," wrote the author of *The Young Lady's Friend* (1860), that it was of utmost concern that the sister tend to her brothers' needs. Her evenings should be devoted to their happiness, encouraging them to spend more time at home, and to make their friends her own friends; furthermore, she should encourage "innocent amusements" within the family circle for their benefit. In this manner, brothers could pass "unharmed through the temptations of youth," and would owe their purity to the "intimate companionship of affectionate and pure-minded sisters." Once having enjoyed the influence of the "home engagement," brothers would refrain from "mixing with the unpure." Because of the loving attentions of sisters, many a brother would lay aside the wine-cup and even stronger tonics "because they would not profane with their fumes the holy kiss, with which they were accustomed to bid their sisters good-night."[17]

In her relations with the male of the species, girls were advised constantly to play a passive role. "The safest and happiest way for women," wrote one author, was "to leave the matter [of courtship] entirely in his hands." Though matrimony was a great and noble vocation, it was "an incident in life, which, if it comes at all, must come without any contrivance of [the woman]."[18] And in all relations with the wooer, the girl must maintain a strict modesty in order to guard against all personal familiarity. She was never to participate in any "rude plays" that would make her vulnerable to a kiss. She was not to permit men to squeeze or hold her hands "without showing that it displeases [her], by instantly withdrawing it." Accept no unnecessary assistance, the author cautioned, "sit not with another in a place that is too narrow; read not out of the same book; let not your eagerness to see anything induce you to place your head close to another person's."[19]

Girls were to carefully guard themselves from strangers. More important, they were to have little confidence in men. "Watch them, and be ever on your guard," wrote Henry S. Cunningham in his *Lectures on the Physiological Laws of Life* (1882), "never give them ANY chance to abuse your confidence."[20] According to Dr. H. N. Guernsey, author of *Plain Talks on Avoided Subjects* (1882), young women should have no "sexual propensity, or amorous thoughts or feelings." If properly educated, he wrote, women would live through the years before marriage "perfect strangers to any sensations" and would develop such feelings only when a suitable gentleman proclaimed his intentions.

> After this acquaintance has ripened into love, and when she has become convinced of the purity of his heart, [the woman] enjoys being with him, in sitting by his side, and is unhappy in his absence. When betrothed, owing to her great and pure love for him, she takes pleasure in receiving such marks of affection from him as are shown by a tender father or brother, but nothing more. After marriage, she feels that she is really his and that he has become a part of herself–that they are no more twain but one flesh. All this has transpired without her hardly suspecting such a quality in herself as an amorous affection.[21]

Women were to passively await the male's declaration of matrimonial intentions before expressing even the slightest evidence of reciprocating love. To allow even a "partially animal basis" to appear, or to fall prey to the evils of blighted love, fomented horrible physical and mental deterioration. Blighted love weakened not only the charms of the girl but also her most important organs. Trifling with a woman's love was unethical if not wholly damaging to the physical and mental balance of her delicate structure. "It may be sport to your fiendish soul," wrote O. S. Fowler to the man, "but it is death to her and her prospective issue, or at least an essential damage to both, and if not literal death, no thanks to you." In recognition of this, many manuals addressed themselves to the young man:

> Engage her affections, and you thereby quicken the action of all the organs, all the functions of her sex proper; and thereby enhance her every female charm and virtue. . . . Then break that love, AND YOU CRIPPLE ALL THE FEMALE FUNCTIONS AND ORGANS, and of course break down the very elements of female attractiveness, because of the perfect reciprocity which exists between the mental and physical sexuality. This reciprocity compels you, when you blight her love, thereby and therein to impair the PHYSICAL organs of her sex.[22]

Young girls were also to avoid the hazards of early marriage. Premature love robbed the nerve and brain of their natural needs and blighted the organs of sex. It was consummate folly, wrote one author, for girls to "rush into the hymenial embrace" since it would only encourage exhaustion of the life powers, disease, and an early grave. In order to prevent this from occurring, young women should place themselves "on high ground" apart from "gushing affections." They should hold their love as the "choicest treasure" and not confer even the smallest degree of affection to the male wooer. This etiquette would promote in the male a higher understanding of love, expressing "upon the bended knees of confession and solicitation" only the purest form of veneration. Girls became "dog-cheap" when they yielded to the feelings of the male.[23]

While it was not the purpose of nineteenth century manuals to make the woman unaware of the differences between male and female, they did little to inform her, in other than derisive terms, of the sexual relations in married life. A large number of women entered marriage ignorant of sex; indeed, one writer said that there were some women "into whose minds the thought of coition has never once entered."[24] The honeymoon, therefore, was the focus of much of the marriage counselor's attention. Many marriages which would normally have developed into lasting relationships, wrote Dr. Emma Drake, professor of obstetrics at the Denver Homeopathic Medical School and Hospital, were ruined in the very first days of married life due to the thoughtless passions of the male. "Frightened and timid, and filled with a vague unrest at the mysteries of marriage which await their revelation," innocent brides not infrequently put their lives in the possession of husbands who "thought that every right is theirs immediately." Their "rapacious passion" wrecked whatever love and honor the young bride had developed for her husband. Manuals advised young brides to avoid these problems by introducing, through the intervention of a friend, such books that the bridegroom might wisely read for the good of the marriage.[25]

Because of the aggressive nature of the male, it was necessary and natural for women to remain cold, passive, and indifferent to the husband's sexual impulses. Careless and amative acts by the female destroyed the "innate dignity" of the wifely role and led to the misuse of the sexual function in irresponsible and immodest responses in the male.[26] It was part of nature's plan that women "have comparatively little sexual passion." Though women loved, and while they gladly embraced their husbands, they did so "without a particle of sex desire." For Mrs. Mary Wood-Allen, national superintendent of the Purity Department of the Woman's Christian Temperance Union, the most genuine sort of love between man and wife existed in the lofty beauty of platonic embrace.[27]

It should also be pointed out that the woman was not advised to experience the same pleasures as the male in the sexual union. As a passive creature, she was to endure the attentions of her husband in a negative sense, if only to deter the greater weakening of the "vital forces" in the male. Writers also believed that if women experienced "any spasmodic convulsion" in coition it would interfere with the possibility of conception—the primary function of the marriage act. "Voluptuous spasms," wrote one author of a manual in 1850, caused a weakness and relaxation in the woman which tended to make her barren.[28]

Reflecting the efforts of urban Americans to imitate Britain's Victorian mood, the sex-in-life manuals pointed out that the English people had the most reasonable understanding of marriage. It was the custom in English homes to have separate bedrooms for the husband and wife. Though "freedom-loving" Americans might think it a rather "cold custom," separate bedrooms provided the perfect environment when "proper self-control seems difficult," and when too much freedom "degenerates into license."[29] According to Dr. Mary Wood-Allen in *Marriage: Its Duties and Privileges* (1901), if the husband found sleeping with his wife a source of great temptation, then, for the sake of chastity, he must take a bed to himself.[30] While the doors separating the two rooms should "seldom be shut," nonetheless, the custom relieved the married couple of temptation and "prevent[ed] the familiarity, which even in married life, breeds contempt."[31] Furthermore, the exposure to undressing in one another's presence caused excessive emotion that harmed lasting marital relations. "If the husband cannot properly control his amorous propensitites," wrote one author, "they had better by all means occupy separate beds and different apartments, with a lock on the communicating door, the key in the wife's possession."[32] The male body, wrote Sylvanus Stall in *What a Young Man Ought to Know*, is "like a cage that encloses a beast, an angel and a devil, and no young man can afford to arouse the beast."[33] Part of the pseudo-scientific reasoning behind separate beds (like the dance) grew out of speculation regarding animal-magnetism and the belief that the vital forces of both the husband and wife would change from too frequent intimacy—the wife becoming masculine in her cravings, and the husband showing signs of peevishness, fretfulness and faultfinding.[34]

The separation of bedrooms was an important goal of late nineteenth century sex-in-life manuals. It represented a major effort to contain the evils of man's appetites. The double bed, wrote physician J. H. Greer, was a relic of a primitive age. "No matter who else may sleep together," he wrote, "husband and wife should not."[35]

> [The bed] is the most ingenious of all possible devices to stimulate and inflame the carnal passion. No bed is large enough for two persons. If brides only knew the great risk they run of losing the most precious of all earthly possessions—the love of their husbands—they would struggle as resolutely to secure extreme temperance after marriage as they do to maintain complete abstinence before the ceremony. The best means to this end is the separate bed.[36]

Since the husband was seldom strong-willed enough to master his appetites, this custom encouraged him to subordinate the bestial nature and allow his thoughts to "soar above the earth, even unto the region of the heavens."[37]

Since the sex manuals stated that conception could result at any time, they advised coition only when there was a desire for parenthood. There was to be "no pandering to sexual indulgence" or "gratification of the lower nature" as long as the slightest unwillingness for parenthood existed. Those not wishing to have children had to have a "proper manly and womanly Christian temperance in those things." Too many marriages were nothing more than licensed prostitution where the lower natures of both man and wife were "petted and indulged at the expense of the higher."[38] Since the sexual act caused an expenditure of vital force in the male body, the release of seminal fluid which was "prostituted to the simple gratification of fleshy desire" weakened the husband and endangered the well being of his physical and mental state. The husband should conserve his seminal fluid for only limited coition–the implication being that the vital energy expended in the sexual act could be better diverted to the "mental and moral force of the man." According to Dr. J. H. Greer, author of *Woman Know Thyself; Female Diseases, Their Prevention and Cure* (1902), the conservation of sperm by the male caused its assimilation by the brain, where it was expended in thought.[39]

Many manuals expressed the hope that married couples would accept strict continence as the standard in marital relations. If parents would assure their children that sexual powers in the human species were properly used only for reproduction, then "the whole veil of mystery would be blown away and the subject would then be presented in a beautiful and ennobling light." There would be no further need of prostitution; no need for "governmental regulation of vice," no white slave traffic, nor any further reason for the degradation of women. The world would be safe from the greatest social evil of life, and men and women would meet "upon the basis of intellectual congeniality" without the perplexing issue of sex, and for the first time, "the delight of friendship, now practically unknown, could be enjoyed to the fullest extent." If sexual continence prevailed in marriage, the husband and wife would not have to live as "comparative strangers" in separate bedrooms, in constant fear of inflammatory desires. "If the human body were always held in thought as a sacred temple," wrote Dr. Wood-Allen, "its outlines would be suggestive of nothing but the purest and holiest feelings." The acceptance of marital continence would eliminate forever the thought that the woman was "the means of gratifying desire," and her figure would cease to inflame the passions of the opposite sex.[40]

Nineteenth century manuals quoted extensively from ministers on the subject of sexual relations. "I firmly believe," wrote one minister, "that the purpose of the Creator in the institution of the marital relation can be fulfilled only when the two parties in the relation are agreed to *make no provision for the flesh* in thought, desire or practice." It was his belief that true marital bliss could only be achieved by perfect marital continence. There was a loss of dignity of both husband and wife if either thought of the other as a "sexual being." No matter what "pet names" be given to the sexual appetite, it was none other than lust of the basest sort. Any use of the sexual act other than for the expressed purpose of procreation was "a waste of vital energy," deteriorating the conservation of necessary forces in the body and depriving the system of its "legitimate demands." Perfect continence in marriage did not mean mere moderation in sexual relations; moderation was a casuist rationalization for the gratification of the physical appetites.[41] Sex, argued Wood-Allen, was not located entirely in the sexual organs, but permeated the entire body. Hence, a "social mingling of men and women without a thought of sex in their minds" could be a valid and proper substitute for physical pleasure.[42]

In 1900, Delos F. Wilcox wrote *Ethical Marriage*, which he dedicated to youths and maidens "who do what they think they ought to do, admitting no ideal that is impractical, and omitting no duty that is seen." Using a Spencerian formula, he argued that the institution of marriage had undergone an evolution from brute savagery to nomadic marriage, and finally into ethical marriage. The new ethical family was founded on the principles of love, intelligence, and duty, and intended to perpetuate only those traits which it considered of "superior social value."[43] According to Wilcox, nature ruled that sexual intercourse "should be had at long intervals and during a limited portion of adult life." Any sexual union other than for the expressed desire for procreation was contrary to nature's laws. In practice, this meant that married couples ought to be "loyally affectionate" until they chose to have children, at which time "they should have a single complete sexual congress."

> Time should then be given to ascertain whether or not conception has taken place. Normally menstruation ceases

> during pregnancy. If the menses are not interrupted, the probabilities are strong that conception has not taken place, and then another copulation will be necessary. Intercourse may take place once a month until there is reason to believe that the woman is pregnant, or until the season favorable to reproduction has passed. After impregnation has been secured there should be no more intercourse until another child is desired.[44]

Wilcox believed that continence was a practical answer to the sexual passions in marriage. Speaking from his own experience, he argued that the desire for sexual continence alone was not sufficient. Married couples needed to take specific steps to prevent the unleashing of passions. These steps included an understanding that marriage "should make no more immediate difference in their lives than the taking of a roommate does to a student," the avoidance of a honeymoon, the use of separate beds or sleeping quarters, the avoidance of stimulants, the emphasis upon exercise, and finally the education of children to prevent sexual curiosity or abnormal habits.[45] The benefits from marital continence were self-evident—the abandonment of habits that encouraged passion, the conservation of vital energies in the male, increased love and respect, and fewer doctor's bills.[46] Women would be freed from the "taxes of lust," they would develop a higher sense of social responsibility, marriage "would no longer be to [them] the bartering of [their] freedom for a mess of pottage," and they could enjoy a far greater freedom in dress. If men accepted the ideal of continence women could wear shorter skirts "without the sensuous desires of men being aroused." Women, whose clothes had been styled in order to prevent the "prurient curiosity of men" from creating a sense of shame in the virtuous woman, could now cast off the oppressive garments of defensive purity.[47]

In marriage, wrote Gustavus Cohen in his *Helps and Hints to Mothers and Young Wives*, "principle should be the controlling power of every thought and action." The law of continence was one of the more important principles that governed every relationship. Cohen urged every husband to permit his wife to decide when to have intercourse. A horrible blight to the marriage contract could be removed if women had the right "to deny all approaches, save and only when [they] desired maternity."[48]

Manuals for men also suggested the use of strict continence in married life. Sylvanus Stall's book, *What a Young Husband Ought to Know*, pointed out that many married couples who had chosen strict continence secured "not only greater strength and better health, but greater happiness also."[49] The passions, "the controlling organ of which lies at the very bottom and lowest part of the brain," degraded both the mind and morals of the individual. Stall advised the young husband not to eat foods such as eggs and oysters, pepper and condiments, to avoid theater-going, the reading of "salacious books," viewing nude statuary and pictures, and to "avoid such bodily exposure and postures as mar the modesty of both man and woman."[50] Dr. J. H. Kellogg, famous for his health foods and rest homes for the century's neurasthenics in Battle Creek, Michigan, suggested that many of the problems of intemperance in sex habits grew out of an improper diet, and particularly, from the use of meats and stimulating foods. The too liberal use of animal foods had encouraged "unrestrained indulgence of the passions" in both men and women. It is not too surprising that Kellogg recommended a diet of his own cereals.[51]

Physician J. H. Greer, in his *Woman Know Thyself* advocated two interesting alternatives to marital continence, called "Dianism" or love-union, and "Zugassent's Discovery." In Dianism, the husband and wife embraced each other in a state of nudity with only an "interchange of magnetic elements" which tranquilized the husband and strengthened the wife. In Zugassent's Discovery, the husband and wife united as in intercourse but refrained from orgasm. The intention here was, again, to exchange only magnetic currents and achieve a "magnetic harmony." Since complete intercourse expended a large amount of vital force in both husband and wife, Greer suggested Dianism and Zugassent's Discovery as acts which would help to replenish the waning vitality without gratification of the animal instinct.[52]

While not all manuals subscribed fully to strict marital continence, the majority certainly sanctioned it as the ideal marriage relationship. Many were content to accept a moderate sexual indulgence, after first establishing certain restrictions. For example, nearly all manuals restricted sexual relations during pregnancy. The very fundamentals of science ruled against this practice. "The submission of an unwilling wife or the sexual irritability that may be engendered through the mother who gives herself up the the indulgence of desire" might jeopardize the physical and moral future of the child. The upheaval of the child's embryonic home "through gusts of passion," left an indelible mark on the child's character.[53] Coition during pregnancy, according to one physician, predisposed children to epilepsy. "The natural excitement of the nervous system in the mother by such a cause," he wrote, "cannot operate otherwise than inflicting injury upon the tender germ in the womb." Dr. Kellogg believed that the mental and nervous sensations of the mother molded the brain of the prenatal child, and that when the mother indulged in sexual relations with her husband, she increased the chance of the child's developing an abnormal sexual instinct. "Here is the key to the origin of much of the sexual precocity and depravity which curse humanity," wrote Kellogg.[54] "Every pang of grief [or passion] you feel," added O. S. Fowler in *Maternity*, "will leave its painful scar on the forming disk of their souls."[55]

The child's future depended upon the proper conduct of the mother during pregnancy, a conduct that concerned not only her diet, but also her reading material, relations with her husband, and her most private thoughts. Dr. Holbrook, in his book *Stirpiculture*, explained why some children were more virtuous and beautiful than others. The child's character, morals, and even physical appearance, he wrote, depended largely upon the manner in which his parents conducted themselves during the pregnancy.

> In my early married life [confessed one mother] my husband and I learned how to live in holy relations, after God's ordinance. My husband lovingly consented to let me live apart from him during the time I carried this little daughter under my heart, and also while I was nursing her. These were the happiest days of my life. . . . My husband and I were never so tenderly, so harmoniously, or so happily related to each other, and I never loved him more deeply than during these blessed months.

As a result of the parents' relationship, the child born at this time was beautifully formed, and grew to be virtuous, healthy, and extremely happy. Several years later, wrote Holbrook, the same mother became pregnant with her second child, but during that pregnancy, her husband "had become contaminated with the popular idea that even more frequent relations were permissible during pregnancy." Yielding to her husband's rapacious demands, the wife became "nervous and almost despairing." The child was born sickly and nervous, and after five years of constant difficulty, died "leaving [them] sadder and wiser."[56]

A woman during her pregnancy was a "soul-gardener." The beauty and virtue of her children depended ultimately upon the manner in which she acted during her nine months of pregnancy. Since she had the duty of providing the "good soil" in which the child grew during its prenatal life, the pregnant woman was to direct herself to the single goal of creating the best possible child. She must change her dress, allowing no weight to hang around her hips. "The union suit of underclothing, the union skirt and waist combined, and the gown," wrote Dr. Drake, "are all that should be worn throughout the entire period."[57] Most important, however, the expectant mother must cultivate her mind with only the highest thoughts. Mind engendered physiological and psychological character upon the unborn child. It was common knowledge, wrote Drake, that Italian children bore "a striking resemblance to the pictures of the child Jesus, from the veneration which the mothers give to the Madonnas." From this, Drake concluded that "we not only become like what we most love, and think most about, but that we may transmit this likeness to our little ones." In order to ensure beautiful and vigorous children, the woman was to observe beautiful pictures, study statuary, yet "forbid as far as possible the contemplation of unsightly and imperfect models."[58] In particular, wives were warned to avoid the alcoholic and tobacco breath of their husbands during this period.

> Many wives are struggling alone in ill health that is directly traceable to the inhaling, night after night, of the breath of the husband, poisoned with nicotine. Many a little one is wailing through its infancy, and if it have strength sufficient, inherited from its remote ancestors, to pull it through, yet will it all its life suffer from its antenatal and postnatal poisoning; and the chances are that as soon as it is old enough it will take up the habit which is already acquired, to pass down along the line a more enfeebled heritage.[59]

Some manuals advised only the presence of a midwife in the delivery of children. The reason for this, as O. S. Fowler wrote, was to prevent the possibility of the mother's relaxing the "bars of virtue" by disclosing her particular female complaints to the male physician. Besides, there was always the added possibility that such talks and examinations by the male physician would "excite impure desires" in either of the two parties.[60]

Just as the mothers' emotions during pregnancy went into the making of the child's emotional system, so the nursing period was extremely important to the child's mental development. For this reason, sexual intercourse was also restricted during the time of nursing. There was no doubt in Kellogg's mind, for example, that the gratification of passions during the nursing period would cause "the transmission of libidinous tendencies to the child."[61] For the same reasons, mothers were continually warned of the evils of the wet-nurse. Too often, mothers employed wet-nurses with bad habits, women who drank or carried on affairs in secret. (Invariably, the examples listed in the manuals were of Irish wet-nurses.) In any case, the child suffered irreparable harm in that the mentality as well as the emotional deficiencies of the wet-nurse transferred to the child in feeding.[62] Physician Gustavus Cohen believed that mothers who neglected this important function would invite disease and any number of constitutional disorders. The failure of women to nurse their own babies, he wrote, caused eventual barrenness, premature aging, and even early death.[63]

Although the manuals strongly denounced the practice of birth control, there were indications that the practice was accepted in extreme cases where the life of the woman was in peril. But before even broaching the subject, authors were insistent upon censuring those with sordid intentions. In *The Married Woman's Private Medical Companion* (1847), for example, the author publicly rebuked a segment of his audience.

> Libertines and debauchees! these pages are not for you. You have nothing to do with the subject of which they treat. Bringing to its discussion, as you do, a distrust or contempt of the human race—accustomed as you are to confound liberty with license, and pleasure with debauchery, it is not for your palled feelings and brutalized senses to distinguish moral truth in its purity and simplicity. I never discuss this subject with such as you.

Just as readily as the author refused to enlighten the libertines of society with contraceptive knowledge, so he also restricted it verbally from those "prudes and hypocrites" which Christ had likened to "whited sepulchres," and who "at dinner, ask to be helped to the bosom of a duck, lest by mention of the word breast, [they] call up improper associations."[64] After these proper restrictions, the author then offered to his reader packages of contraceptives that could be obtained from his New York office at prices ranging from five to ten dollars, and which included, so he advertised, the baudruche, or "French secret."[65]

Manual writers advised endlessly on the dangers attendant to the woman's change of life. Physicians invariably characterized menopause as the "Rubicon" in a woman's life, and they measured the extent of discomfort and disease by the degree of abuse women had allowed their constitutions to suffer. In typically Calvinistic terms, manuals blamed the frequency and seriousness of disease upon the "indiscretions" of earlier life. Excesses of any kind, whether in sexual passion, dress, reckless use of stimulating foods, prurient reading, contraception, or solitary vice, accentuated the hardships of this period of change. The woman who transgressed nature's laws, wrote Kellogg, "will find this period a veritable 'Pandora's box' of ills, and may well look forward to it with apprehension and foreboding."[66] "Many things that have been laid to our ancestors remotely distant," wrote Dr. Drake, "are really the results of wrong-doing and living in the first decade and a half of our lives."[67] Dr. Charles D. Meigs, for example, in his *Females and Their Diseases* (1848), a book which was extensively quoted in the manuals of the time, described a young woman's efforts to prevent her monthly period in order that she might go to a ball. To achieve this, she accepted the advice of her "confidential servant" and took a hip-bath in cold water. While she succeeded in stopping the flow, she suffered an attack of "brain fever" and in her later years "felt the effects of the dereliction of duty." As a result of that single breach of nature's law, her life "was rendered a scene of bitterness, of vapours, of caprices."[68] "Nature," wrote Drake, "rebels and compels the payment of her violated laws." Usually, nature accomplished this through malignant disease, or "failing in this, a slow and dangerous change is likely to be experienced, followed by years of discomfort or invalidism."[69]

There seemed to be a certain status-suffix to every aspiring view of the role of sex. In a sense, the manuals attempted to interpret and grapple with the lack of tradition in the urban life, and to reach for an understanding of sexual relationships in a way that would give added relevance to the aspiring urban society of America. The sex-in-life manuals were an arena for imaginative writing in this period, and seem, at times, to shroud the urban middle class in a romantic arcadia set apart from the lusty vernacular of urban immigrants and city slums. The manuals were choice caricatures of subjective prejudices and assumptions concerning middle-class values. In a sense, the romantization of family and marriage portrayed in the manuals was not so much a plea for re-shaping the marriage relationship as it was a technique for explaining the incongruity that existed between middle-class "principles" and reality. The middle class measured their greatness not by their achievements but by their principles—a situation which allowed them to blame the discrepancy upon a gallery of villains. Manual writers sought out the victims of sexual deviation in the empirical reality of the city slums where sex, disease, poverty and depravity seemed to spawn the nations's problems. Acting as moral judges of society, the sex-in-life manuals became documentaries of middle-class myths seeking not only to justify their own social and moral fabric, but to explain, without the sense of personal guilt, the survival of a less imaginative reality.

NOTES

[1]For an excellent treatment of medicine, pseudo-science, and the perfectionist tendencies of 19th century American society, see Joseph F. Kett, *The Formation of the American Medical Profession, The Role of Institutions 1780-1860* (New Haven, 1968), chaps. 4, 5, and 6.

[2]Mary Wood-Allen, *What a Young Girl Ought to Know* (Philadelphia, 1897), 106; S. B. Woodward, *Hints for the Young in Relation to the Health of Body and Mind* (Boston, 1856); E. B. Lowry, *Herself; Talks with Women Concerning Themselves* (Chicago, 1911), 137-48.

[3]J. H. Kellogg, *Ladies Guide in Health and Disease. Girlhood, Maidenhood, Wifehood, Motherhood* (Iowa, 1883), 146-47, 154; Catherine Ester Beecher, *Letters to the People on Health and Happiness* (New York, 1855), 12-13; Alexander Walker, *Intermarriage: or the Mode in Which, and the Causes Why, Beauty, Health, and Intellect Result from Certain Unions, and Deformity, Disease, and Insanity from Others* (n.p., 1850), 35.

[4]Wood-Allen, *What a Young Girl Ought to Know*, 106-107; Kellogg, *Ladies Guide in Health and Disease*, 152; Lowry, *Herself; Talks with Women Concerning Themselves*, 140-41.

[5]Henry S. Cunningham, *Lectures on the Physiological Laws of Life, Hygiene and a General Outline of Diseases Peculiar to Females, Embracing a Revival of the Rights and Wrongs of Women, and a Treatise on Disease in General, with Explicit Directions How to Nurse, Nourish and Administer Remedies to the Sick* (Indianapolis, 1882), 98.

[6]Kellogg, *Ladies Guide in Health and Disease*, 208-209. See also John S. Haller, Jr., "Neurasthenia: The Medical Profession and the 'Urban Blahs' of the 19th Century," *New York Journal of Medicine*, LXX (Oct. 1970), 2489-2497.

[7]Beecher, *Letters to the People on Health and Happiness*, 45; J. H. Greer, *Woman Know Thyself; Female Diseases, Their Prevention and Cure* (Chicago, 1902), 90-92.

[8]O. S. Fowler, *Maternity; or the Bearing and Nursing of Children Including Female Education and Beauty* (New York, 1856), 16; Anna M. Galbraith, *The Four Eopchs of Woman's Life; a Study in Hygiene* (Philadelphia, 1904), 28; Helen Maria (Fiske) Hunt Jackson, *Bits of Talk about Home Matters* (Boston, 1873), 184-88.

[9]Wood-Allen, *What a Young Girl Ought to Know*, 173.

[10]Kellogg, *Ladies Guide in Health and Disease*, 208-209.

[11]*Ibid.*, 209-210; George M. Beard, *American Nervousness* (New York, 1881), 111; George F. Comfort and Anna M. Comfort, *Woman's Education and Woman's Health; Chiefly in Reply to "Sex in Education"* (Syracuse, 1874), 116.

[12]Kellogg, *Ladies Guide in Health and Disease*, 157-58. Curiously, however, manuals advised that the young girl's room should be furnished with pastoral pictures, as well as flowers and musical instruments, preferably the mandolin. See Gordon Stables, *The Girl's Own Book of Health and Beauty* (London, 1891), 191-92.

[13]Marion Harland, *Eve's Daughters; or, Common Sense for Maid, Wife, and Mother* (New York, 1882), 116; Kellogg, *Ladies Guide in Health and Disease*, 160; Stables, *The Girl's Own Book of Health and Beauty*, 49, 139.

[14]Kellogg, *Ladies Guide in Health and Disease*, 214.

[15]Sylvanus Stall, *What a Young Husband Ought to Know* (Philadelphia, 1807), 244-45; Stall, *What a Young Man Ought to Know* (Philadelphia, 1897), 243; Beecher, *Letters to the People on Health and Happiness*, 18-19; Fowler, *Maternity*, 130-32.

[16]Mrs. John Farrar, *The Young Lady's Friend* (New York, 1860), 241-42; Wood-Allen, *What a Young Girl Ought to Know*, 173.

[17]Farrar, *The Young Lady's Friend*, 201-04; [WCTU], *Physiology for Young People* (New York, 1884), 13-17.

[18]Farrar, *The Young Lady's Friend*, 258-59.

[19]*Ibid.*, 263.

[20]Cunningham, *Lectures on the Physiological Laws of Life*, 100-101.

[21]H. N. Guernsey, *Plain Talks on Avoided Subjects* (Philadelphia, 1882), 78-79.

[22]Fowler, *Maternity*, 75-79; Lowry, *Herself; Talks with Women Concerning Themselves*, 157-62.

[23]Fowler, *Maternity*, 78-79; Lowry, *Herself; Talks with Women Concerning Themselves*, 155.

[24]Stall, *What a Young Husband Ought to Know*, 126.

[25]Emma F. Angell Drake, *What a Young Wife Ought to Know* (Philadelphia, 1908), 54.

[26] *Ibid.*, 85.

[27] Wood-Allen, *Marriage; Its Duties and Privileges* (Chicago, 1901), 194.

[28] Walker, *Intermarriage*, 256; William M. Capp, *The Daughter: Her Health, Education and Wedlock* (Philadelphia, 1891), 94.

[29] Drake, *What a Young Wife Ought to Know*, 85; Greer, *Woman Know Thyself; Female Diseases, Their Prevention and Cure*, 67.

[30] Wood-Allen, *Marriage; Its Duties and Privileges*, 49.

[31] Drake, *What a Young Wife Ought to Know*, 85.

[32] Stall, *What a Young Husband Ought to Know*, 94-96.

[33] Stall, *What a Young Man Ought to Know*, 241.

[34] Gustavus Cohen, *Helps and Hints to Mothers and Young Wives*, (London, 1880), 88.

[35] Greer, *Woman Know Thyself; Female Diseases, Their Prevention and Cure*, 186.

[36] Dio Lewis, quoted in Stall, *What a Young Husband Ought to Know*, 95; Dio Lewis, *Our Girls* (New York, 1871).

[37] Drake, *What a Young Wife Ought to Know*, 86.

[38] *Ibid.*, 87-8.

[39] *Ibid.*, 88-89; Greer, *Woman Know Thyself; Female Diseases, Their Prevention and Cure*, 110-13, 153-54.

[40] Wood-Allen, *Marriage; Its Duties and Privileges*, 196-97.

[41] *Ibid.*, 201-03.

[42] *Ibid.*, 208-09. One of the few exceptions to this interpretation is found in Dr. A. J. Ingersoll, *In Health* (New York, 1884). While strongly religious, Ingersoll blamed most marital problems on the "fear" of the sexual appetite—the woman's fear of having desires and her efforts to thwart natural inclinations.

[43] Delos F. Wilcox, *Ethical Marriage* (Michigan, 1900), 56-57.

[44] *Ibid.*, 82-84. Because the child's character was greatly influenced by the intentions of the parents at the moment of conception, physician J. H. Greer advised intercourse in the morning, since "The best qualities of each parent . . . have been refreshed by rest." Greer, *Woman Know Thyself; Female Diseases, Their Prevention and Cure*, 194.

[45] Wilcox, *Ethical Marriage*, 124-25.

[46] *Ibid.*, 133-34.

[47] *Ibid.*, 137-39.

[48] Cohen, *Helps and Hints to Mothers and Young Wives*, 83; Greer, *Woman Know Thyself; Female Diseases, Their Prevention and Cure*, 206-08.

[49] Stall, *What a Young Husband Ought to Know*, 81.

[50] *Ibid.*, 93-94.

[51] Kellogg, *Ladies Guide in Health and Disease*, 142, 342-43.

[52] Greer, *Woman Know Thyself; Female Diseases, Their Prevention and Cure*, 188-89.

[53] Wood-Allen, *Marriage; Its Duties and Privileges*, 207.

[54] Stall, *What a Young Husband Ought to Know*, 200-01; Kellogg, *Ladies Guide in Health and Disease*, 425-26.

[55]Fowler, *Maternity*, 16, 124; Aimée Raymond Schroeder, *Health Notes for Young Wives* (New York, 1895), 31.

[56]Holbrook quoted in Drake, *What a Young Wife Ought to Know*, 91-93; Greer, *Woman Know Thyself; Female Diseases, Their Prevention and Cure*, 182-83.

[57]Drake, *What a Young Wife Ought to Know*, 101-02; Kellogg, *Ladies Guide in Health and Disease*, 294-95.

[58]Drake, *What a Young Wife Ought to Know*, 105-109; Lowry, *Herself; Talks with Women Concerning Themselves*, 98-100.

[59]Drake, *What a Young Wife Ought to Know*, 118; Kellogg, *Ladies Guide in Health and Disease*, 309.

[60]Fowler, *Maternity*, 183; Beecher, *Letters to the People on Health and Happiness*, 160.

[61]Kellogg, *Ladies Guide in Health and Disease*, 425-26.

[62]Harland, *Eve's Daughters*, 22-35.

[63]Cohen, *Helps and Hints to Mothers and Young Wives*, 57.

[64]A. M. Mauriceau, *The Married Woman's Medical Companion* (New York, 1847), 110-12.

[65]*Ibid.*, 143-44.

[66]Kellogg, *Ladies Guide in Health and Disease*, 372-73.

[67]Drake, *What a Woman of Forty-Five Ought to Know*, (Philadelphia, 1902), 39, 137.

[68]Meigs quoted in Cohen, *Helps and Hints to Mothers and Young Wives*, 6; Edward H. Dixon, *Woman and Her Diseases, From the Cradle to the Grave* (Philadelphia, 1860), 156.

[69]Drake, *What a Woman of Forty-Five Ought to Know*, 55.

John S. Haller, Jr. is an Associate Professor of History at Indiana University Northwest. His recent book, *Outcasts From Evolution* (Urbana, 1971) received the Anisfeld-Wolf Award in Race Relations for 1971. He is the author of numerous articles in the history of medicine and anthropology, and is currently working on a medical history of Victorian sexuality.

Birthing and Anesthesia: The Debate over Twilight Sleep

Judith Walzer Leavitt

"At midnight I was awakened by a very sharp pain," wrote Mrs. Cecil Stewart, describing the birth of her child in 1914. "The head nurse . . . gave me an injection of scopolamin-morphin. . . . I woke up the next morning about half-past seven . . . the door opened, and the head nurse brought in my baby. . . . I was so happy."[1] Mrs. Stewart had delivered her baby under the influence of scopolamine, a narcotic and amnesiac that, together with morphine, produced a state popularly known as "twilight sleep." She did not remember anything of the experience when she woke up after giving birth. This 1914 ideal contrasts with today's feminist stress on being awake, aware, and in control during the birthing experience. In 1914 and 1915, thousands of American women testified to the marvels of having babies without the trauma of childbirth. As one of them gratefully put it, "The night of my confinement will always be a night dropped out of my life."[2]

I am grateful to William J. Orr, Jr., and Susan Duke for their assistance in the preparation of this study. I would also like to thank Mari Jo Buhle, Norman Fost, Susan Friedman, Lewis Leavitt, Elaine Marks, Regina Morantz, and Ronald Numbers for their comments on earlier drafts of this paper.

1. Testimony quoted in Marguerite Tracy and Mary Boyd, *Painless Childbirth* (New York: Frederick A. Stokes Co., 1915), pp. 188–89. For a thorough account of the twilight sleep controversy in America, see Lawrence G. Miller, "Pain, Parturition, and the Profession: The Twilight Sleep in America," in *Health Care in America: Essays in Social History*, ed. Susan Reverby and David Rosner (Philadelphia: Temple University Press, 1979), pp. 19–44.

2. Tracy and Boyd, p. 198.

From the perspective of today's ideology of woman-controlled births, it may appear that women who want anesthesia sought to cede control of their births to their doctors. I will argue however, that the twilight sleep movement led by women in 1914 and 1915 was not a relinquishing of control. Rather, it was an attempt to gain control over the birthing process. Feminist women wanted the parturient, not the doctor or attendant, to choose the kind of delivery she would have. This essay examines the apparent contradiction in the women's demand to control their births by going to sleep.

The Process

The attendants, location, and drugs or instruments used in American women's birthing experiences varied in the early decades of the twentieth century. America's poorer and immigrant women delivered their babies predominantly at home, attended by midwives who seldom administered drugs and who called physicians only in difficult cases. A small number of poor women gave birth in charity or public hospitals where physicians attended them. Most upper- and middle-class women, who had more choice, elected to be attended by a physician, usually a general practitioner but increasingly a specially trained obstetrician, rather than a midwife. At the turn of the twentieth century, these births, too, typically took place in the woman's home; however, by the second decade of the century, specialists, aided partly by the twilight sleep movement, were moving childbirth from the home to the hospital.[3]

Physicians used drugs and techniques of physical intervention in many cases, although the extent cannot be quantified accurately. In addition to forceps, physicians relied on opium, chloroform, chloral, cocaine, quinine, nitrous oxide, ergot, and ether to relieve pain, expedite labor, prevent injury in precipitous labors, control hemorrhage, and prevent sepsis.[4] In one study of 972 consecutive births in Wisconsin, physicians used chloroform during the second stage of labor in half of their cases and forceps in 12 percent.[5] The reports indicate that drugs and instruments may have made labors shorter but not necessarily more enjoyable. Because most drugs could not be used safely throughout the labor and delivery, either because they affected muscle function or because they were dangerous for the baby, women still experienced pain. The use of forceps frequently added to discomfort and caused perineal tears, complicating postdelivery recovery. Maternal mortality remained

3. For more information on childbirth practices in this period, see Judy Barrett Litoff, *American Midwives: 1860 to the Present* (Westport, Conn.: Greenwood Press, 1978).

4. J. F. Ford, "Use of Drugs in Labor," *Wisconsin Medical Journal* 3 (1904–5): 257–65.

5. Ibid.

high in the early decades of the twentieth century, and childbirth, whether attended by physicians or midwives, continued to be risky.[6]

Most women described their physician-attended childbirths as unpleasant at best. Observers of the declining birthrates among America's "better" classes worried that the "fear of childbirth has poisoned the happiness of many women"[7] and caused them to want fewer children. One woman told her doctor that her childbirth had been "hell. . . . It bursts your brain, and tears out your heart, and crashes your nerves to bits. It's just like hell, and I won't stand it again. Never."[8] In scopolamine deliveries, the women went to sleep, delivered their babies, and woke up feeling vigorous. The drug altered their consciousness so that they did not remember painful labors, and their bodies did not feel exhausted by their efforts.[9] Both the women who demanded scopolamine and the doctors who agreed to use it perceived it as far superior to other anesthesia because it did not inhibit muscle function and could be administered throughout the birthing process. It was the newest and finest technique available—"the greatest boon the Twentieth Century could give to women," in the words of Dr. Bertha Van Hoosen, one of its foremost medical advocates.[10]

However, women's bodies experienced their labors, even if their minds did not remember them. Thus observers witnessed women screaming in pain during contractions, thrashing about, and giving all the outward signs of "acute suffering." Residents of Riverside Drive in New York City testified that women in Dr. William H. W. Knipe's twilight sleep hospital sent forth "objectionable" noises in the middle of the night.[11]

A successful twilight sleep delivery, as practiced by Dr. Van Hoosen at the Mary Thompson Hospital in Chicago, required elaborate facilities and careful supervision. Attending physicians and nurses gave the first

6. See, e.g., Dorothy Reed Mendenhall ("Prenatal and Natal Conditions in Wisconsin," *Wisconsin Medical Journal* 15 [1917]: 353–69), who reported, "The death rate from maternity is gradually increasing in Wisconsin, as it is throughout the United States" (p. 364). Dr. Mendenhall also noted that death rates for physician-attended births were higher than for midwife-attended births in Wisconsin (p. 353). I would like to thank Dale Treleven for calling this article to my attention.

7. Mary Boyd, "The Story of Dammerschlaf: An American Woman's Personal Experience and Study at Freiburg," *Survey* 33 (1915): 129.

8. Quoted in Russell Kelso Carter, *The Sleeping Car "Twilight," or Motherhood without Pain* (Boston: Chapple Publishing Co., 1915), pp. 10–11.

9. Scopolamine is an alkaloid found in the leaves and seeds of solanaceous plants. It is a sedative and a mild analgesic as well as an amnesiac, causing forgetfulness of pain rather than blocking the pain sensation. For obstetrical twilight sleep, scopolamine was administered with morphine—the most active alkaloid of opium—in the first dose and alone for subsequent doses.

10. Bertha Van Hoosen, *Scopolamine-Morphine Anaesthesia* (Chicago: House of Manz, 1915), p. 101.

11. *New York Times* (June 9, 1917), p. 13.

injection of scopolamine as soon as a woman appeared to be in active labor and continued the injections at carefully determined intervals throughout her labor and delivery. They periodically administered two tests to determine the effectiveness of the anesthesia: the "calling test," which the parturient passed if the doctor could not arouse her even by addressing her in a loud voice, and the "incoordination test," which she passed if her movements were uncoordinated. Once the laboring woman was under the effects of scopolamine, the doctors put her into a specially designed crib-bed to contain her sometimes violent movements (see fig. 1). Van Hoosen described the need for the bed screens: "As the pains increase in frequency and strength, the patient tosses or throws herself about, but without injury to herself, and may be left without fear that she will roll onto the floor or be found wandering aimlessly in the corridors. In rare cases, where the patient is very excitable and insists on getting out of bed. . . . I prefer to fasten a canvas cover over the tops of the screens, thereby shutting out light, noise and possibility of leaving the bed.[12] When delivery began, attendants took down the canvas crib and positioned the patient in stirrups, familiar in modern obstetrical services. Van Hoosen advised the use of a continuous sleeve to ensure that patients did not interfere with the sterile field (see fig. 2). The canvas crib and the continuous sleeve were Van Hoosen's response to a common need in twilight sleep deliveries: a secure, darkened, quiet, contained environment.

The Events

Twilight sleep became a controversial issue in American obstetrics in June 1914, when *McClure's Magazine* published an article by two laywomen describing this newly popular German method of painless childbirth.[13] In the article, Marguerite Tracy and Constance Leupp, both visitors at the Freiburg women's clinic, criticized high-forceps deliveries (which they called the common American technique) as dangerous and conducive to infection. They contrasted these imperfect births to the safety and comfort of twilight sleep. The new method was so wonderful that women, having once experienced it, would "walk all the way [to Germany] from California" to have their subsequent births under twilight sleep. The physicians at the Freiburg clinic thought the method was best suited for the upper-class "modern woman . . . [who] responds to the stimulus of severe pain . . . with nervous exhaustion and paralysis of the will to carry labor to conclusion." They were less certain

12. Van Hoosen, p. 42.

13. Marguerite Tracy and Constance Leupp, "Painless Childbirth," *McClure's Magazine* 43 (1914): 37–51.

FIG. 1.—Patient in crib-bed waiting for examination. (Source: Bertha Van Hoosen. *Scopolamine-Morphine Anaesthesia* [Chicago: House of Manz, 1915], p. 48.)

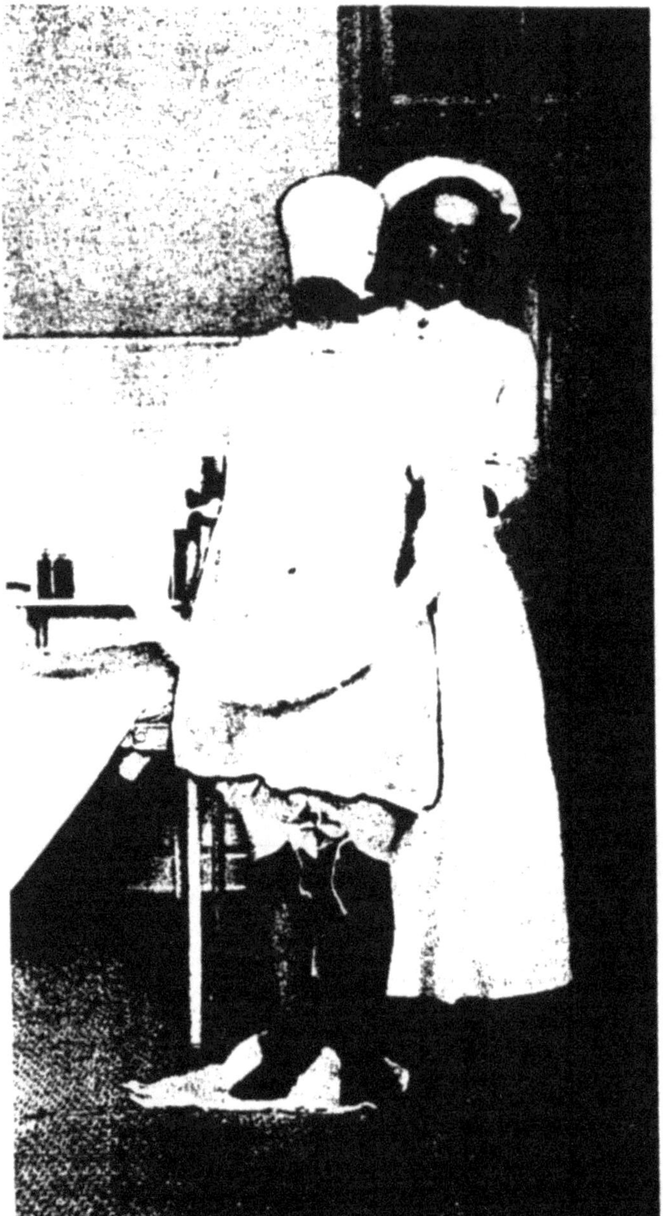

FIG. 2.—Gown with continuous sleeve. (Source: Bertha Van Hoosen, *Scopolamine-Morphine Anaesthesia* [Chicago: House of Manz, 1915], p. 88.)

about its usefulness for women who "earn their living by manual labor" and could tolerate more pain.[14]

The women who took up the cause of twilight sleep concluded that it was not in general use in this country because doctors were consciously withholding this panacea. Physicians have "held back" on developing painless childbirth, accused Mary Boyd and Marguerite Tracy, two of the most active proponents, because it "takes too much time." "Women alone," they asserted, "can bring Freiburg methods into American obstetrical practice."[15] Others echoed the call to arms: journalist Hanna Rion urged her readers to "take up the battle for painless childbirth. . . . Fight not only for yourselves, but fight for your . . . sex."[16] Newspapers and popular magazines joined the chorus, advocating a widespread use of scopolamine in childbirth.[17]

The lay public's anger at the medical profession's apparent refusal to adopt a technique beneficial to women erupted into a national movement. The National Twilight Sleep Association, formed by upper-middle-class clubwomen,[18] was best epitomized by its leaders. They included women such as Mrs. Jesse F. Attwater, editor of *Femina* in Boston; Dr. Eliza Taylor Ransom, active women's rights advocate and physician in Boston; Mrs. Julian Heath of the National Housewife's League; author Rheta Childe Dorr of the Committee on the Industrial Conditions of Women and Children; Mary Ware Dennett of the National Suffrage Association (and later the National Birth Control League); and Dr. Bertha Van Hoosen, outspoken women's leader in medical circles in Chicago.[19] Many of these leaders saw the horrors of childbirth as an

14. Ibid., p. 43. For the same sentiment among American physicians, see, e.g., John O. Polak, "A Study of Scopolamin and Morphine Amnesia as Employed at Long Island College Hospital," *American Journal of Obstetrics* 71 (1915): 722; and Henry Smith Williams, *Painless Childbirth* (New York: Goodhue Co., 1914), pp. 90–91. The classic descriptions of the ideal scopolamine delivery are Bernhard Kronig, "Painless Delivery in Dammerschlaf" (1908); and Carl J. Gauss, "Births in Artificial Dammerschlaf" (1906) and "Further Experiments in Dammerschlaf" (1911), all translated and reprinted in Tracy and Boyd (n. 1 above), pp. 205–308.

15. Mary Boyd and Marguerite Tracy, "More about Painless Childbirth," *McClure's Magazine* 43 (1914): 57–58.

16. Hanna Rion, *Painless Childbirth in Twilight Sleep* (London: T. Werner Laurie Ltd., 1915), p. 239; see also her "The Painless Childbirth," *Ladies Home Journal* 31 (1914): 9–10.

17. See, e.g., "Is the Twilight Sleep Safe—for Me?" *Woman's Home Companion* 42 (1915): 10, 43; William Armstrong, "The 'Twilight Sleep' of Freiburg: A Visit to the Much Talked of Women's Clinic," *Woman's Home Companion* 41 (1914): 4, 69; *New York Times* (September 17, 1914), p. 8; (November 28, 1914), p. 2.

18. On women's clubs and clubwomen, see Mary P. Ryan, *Womanhood in America: From Colonial Times to the Present* (New York: New Viewpoints, 1975), pp. 227–32; Edith Hoshino Altbach, *Women in America* (Lexington, Mass.: D.C. Heath & Co., 1914), pp. 114–21; William L. O'Neill, *Everyone Was Brave: A History of Feminism in America* (Chicago: Quadrangle Books, 1969), pp. 107–68; Sheila M. Rothman, *Woman's Proper Place: A History of Changing Ideals and Practices, 1870 to the Present* (New York: Basic Books, 1978), pp. 63–93.

19. Carter, pp. 174–75.

experience that united all women: "Childbirth has for every woman through all time been potentially great emergency."[20] Dr. Ransom thought that the use of twilight sleep would "create a more perfect motherhood" and urged others to work "for the betterment of womenkind."[21] Because they saw it as an issue for their sex, not just their class, and because many of the twilight sleep leaders were active feminists, they spoke in the idiom of the woman movement.[22]

The association sponsored rallies in major cities to acquaint women with the issue of painless childbirth and to pressure the medical profession into adopting the new method. In order to broaden their appeal, the association staged meetings "between the marked-down suits and the table linen" of department stores where "the ordinary woman" as well as the activist clubwoman could be found.[23] At these rallies, women who had traveled to Freiburg testified to the wonders of twilight sleep (see fig. 3). "I experienced absolutely no pain," claimed Mrs. Francis X. Carmody of Brooklyn, displaying her healthy baby at Gimbels. "An hour after my child was born I ate a hearty breakfast. . . . The third day I went for an automobile ride. . . . The Twilight Sleep is wonderful." Mrs. Carmody ended with the familiar rallying cry: "If you women want it you will have to fight for it, for the mass of doctors are opposed to it."[24]

Department-store rallies and extensive press coverage brought the movement to the attention of a broad segment of American women. Movement leaders rejoiced over episodes such as the one in which a "tenement house mother . . . collected a crowd" on a street corner where she joyfully told of her twilight sleep experience.[25] Many working-class women were attracted to twilight sleep not only because it made childbirth "pleasanter" but because they saw its use as "an important cause of decreased mortality and increased health and vitality among the mothers of children."[26] Some feared, however, that twilight sleep would remain a "superadded luxury of the wealthy mother" because it involved so much physician time and hospital expense.[27] Although different motivations propelled the physician-advocates who believed twilight sleep was safe, middle- and upper-class women who wanted the newest

20. Tracy and Boyd, p. 145.

21. Eliza Taylor Ransom, "Twilight Sleep," *Massachusetts Club Women* 1 (1917): 5. I am grateful to Regina Markell Morantz for this reference.

22. The connections between clubwomen and suffrage or other women's issues are explored in Altbach, pp. 114–15; O'Neill, pp. 49–76, 146–68; Ryan, pp. 230–49; and Eleanor Flexner, *Century of Struggle: The Woman's Rights Movement in the United States* (New York: Atheneum Publishers, 1970), pp. 172–92. The term "woman movement," in the nineteenth and early twentieth centuries, described the movement to better women's condition, including, but not limited to, the drive for suffrage.

23. Tracy and Boyd, p. 145.

24. Quoted in *New York Times* (November 18, 1914), p. 18.

25. Tracy and Boyd, p. 145.

26. Clara G. Stillman, "Painless Childbirth," *New York Call* (July 12, 1914), p. 15.

27. Sam Schmalhauser, "The Twilight Sleep for Women," *International Socialist Review* 15 (1914): 234–35. I am grateful to Mari Jo Buhle for this and the previous reference.

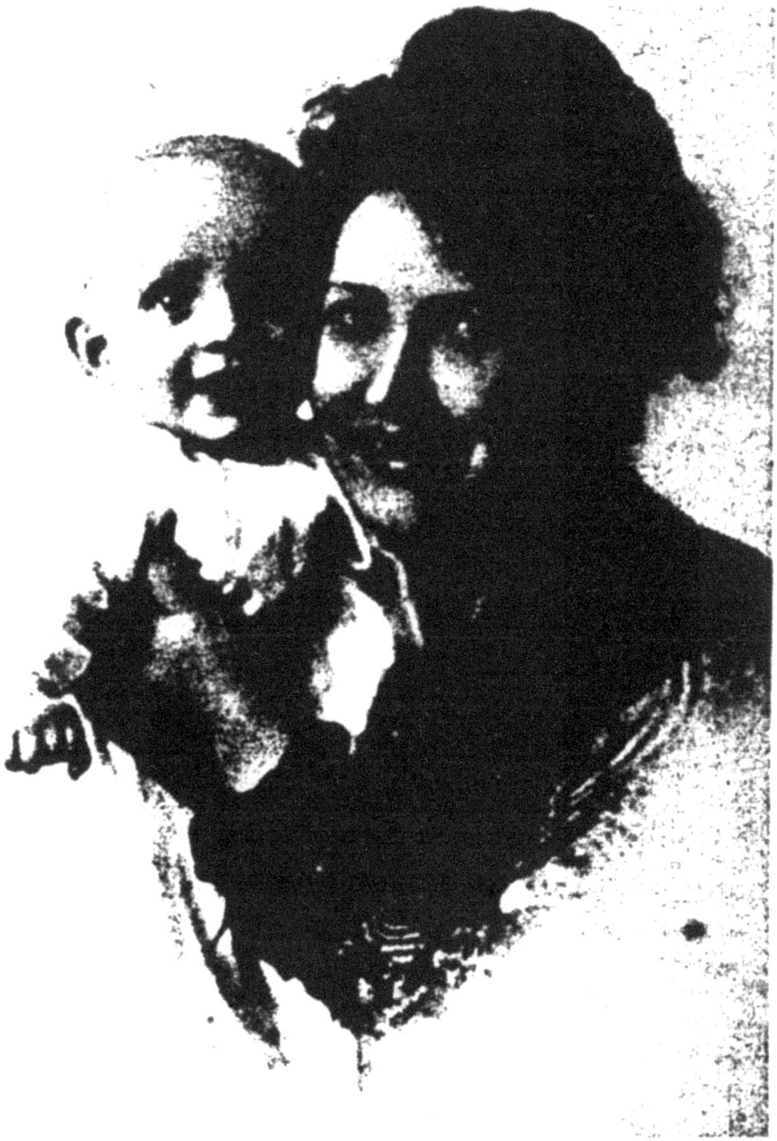

FIG. 3.—Mrs. Francis Xavier Carmody and "Charlemagne," born in Freiburg. (Source: Marguerite Tracy and Mary Boyd, *Painless Childbirth* [New York: Frederick A. Stokes Co., 1915], p. 143.)

thing medicine had to offer, and working-class women who wanted simple relief from childbed suffering, they were all united by their common desire to make childbirth safer and easier for women.

Van Hoosen emerged as the most avid advocate of twilight sleep in the Midwest. She received her M.D. from the University of Michigan

Medical School and worked at the New England Hospital for Women and Children in Boston before setting up practice in Chicago in 1892. Her enthusiasm for the method came from two sources: her strong commitment to the best in obstetrical care and her equally strong commitment to women's rights. Through her use of scopolamine in surgery and obstetrics, she became convinced that twilight sleep offered women a "return of more physiological births" at the same time that it increased the efficiency of physicians, giving them "complete control of everything."[28] She guided many other physicians to the twilight sleep method.[29] In terms of safety and comfort, she could not imagine a better method of birthing.

Increasingly, doctors began to deliver twilight sleep babies. Some traveled to Germany to learn the Freiburg technique and subsequently offered it to both private and charity patients.[30] A few physicians even became enthusiastic about the possibilities of twilight sleep. "If the male had to endure this suffering," said Dr. James Harrar of New York, "I think he would resort very precipitously to something that might relieve the . . . pain."[31] Dr. W. Francis B. Wakefield of California went even further, declaring "I would just as soon consider performing a surgical operation without an anesthetic as conducting a labor without scopolamin amnesia. Skillfully administered the best interest of both the mother and the child are advanced by its use."[32] Another physician listed its advantages: painless labor, reduction of subsequent "nerve exhaustion that comes after a prolonged hard labor," better milk secretion, fewer cervical and perineal lacerations, fewer forcep deliveries, less strain on the heart, and a "better race for future generations" since upper-class women would be more likely to have babies if they could have them painlessly.[33] There was also, it was claimed, an "advantage to

28. Bertha Van Hoosen, *Petticoat Surgeon* (Chicago: Pellegrini & Cudahy, 1947), pp. 282–82.

29. See, e.g., Bertha Van Hoosen, "A Fixed Dosage in Scopalamine-Morphine Anaesthesia," *Woman's Medical Journal* 26 (1916): 57–58; and "Twilight Sleep in the Home," ibid., p. 132.

30. For early American trials, see William H. Wellington Knipe, "'Twilight Sleep' from the Hospital Viewpoint," *Modern Hospital* 2 (1914): 250–51; A. M. Hilkowich, "Further Observations on Scopalamine-Narcophin Anesthesia during Labor with Report of Two Hundred (200) Cases," *American Medicine* 20 (1914): 786–94; William H. Wellington Knipe, "The Freiburg Method of Dammerschlaf or Twilight Sleep," *American Journal of Obstetrics* 70 (1914): 364–71; and James A. Harrar and Ross McPherson, "Scopolamine-Narcophin Seminarcosis in Labor," *Transactions of the American Association of Obstetricians and Gynecologists* 27 (1914): 372–89.

31. Quoted during discussion of Rongy, Harrar, and McPherson papers, *Transactions of the American Association of Obstetricians and Gynecologists* 27 (1914): 389.

32. W. Francis B. Wakefield, "Scopolamine Amnesia in Labor," *American Journal of Obstetrics* 71 (1915): 428. For more of this kind of enthusiasm, see also Elizabeth R. Miner, "Letter and Report of Nineteen Cases in Which 'Twilight' Was Used," *Woman's Medical Journal* 26 (1916): 131.

33. Ralph M. Beach, "Twilight Sleep," *American Medicine* 21 (1915): 40–41.

the child: To give it a better chance for life at the time of delivery; a better chance to have breast-feeding; a better chance to have a strong, normal mother."[34]

Despite the energy and enthusiasm of the twilight sleep advocates, many American doctors resisted the technique. They lashed out against the "pseudo-scientific rubbish" and the "quackish hocus-pocus" published in *McClure's*[35] and simply refused to be "stampeded by these misguided ladies."[36] These physicians did not believe that nonmedical people should determine therapeutic methods; it was a "question of medical ethics."[37] Other physicians refused to use scopolamine because they feared its dangers either to the mother or the child. The *Journal of the American Medical Association* concluded that "this method has been thoroughly investigated, tried, and found wanting, because of the danger connected with it."[38]

Because the evidence about safety was mixed, many doctors were frustrated in their attempts to find out whether scopolamine was harmful or safe for use in obstetrics. Earlier experience with the unstable form of the drug led some to refuse to try scopolamine again, although at least one pharmaceutical company had solved the problem of drug stability by 1914. "The bad and indifferent results which were at first obtained by the use of these drugs we now know to have been due entirely to overdosage and the use of impure and unstable preparations," concluded one physician in a report on his successful results with 1,000 twilight sleep mothers in 1915.[39] Dr. Van Hoosen had successfully performed surgery on 2,000 patients with the help of scopolamine by 1908[40] and began using the drug routinely in deliveries in 1914. She concluded after 100 consecutive cases that scopolamine, properly administered, "solves the problems of child-bearing" and is safe for mother and child.[41] But the medical literature continued to express concern

34. Bertha Van Hoosen, *Scopolamine-Morphine Anaesthesia*, p. 101. Some physicians reported success using twilight sleep at home, but most thought the method best suited to hospital deliveries.

35. Quoted from the *Journal of the American Medical Association* in "Another 'Twilight Sleep,'" *Literary Digest* 50 (1915): 187; W. Gillespie, "Analgesics and Anesthetics in Labor, Their Indication and Contra-Indications," *Ohio Medical Journal* 11 (1915): 611.

36. "Twilight Sleep Again," *American Medicine* 21 (1915): 149.

37. "'Twilight Sleep' in the Light of Day," *Scientific American* 79, suppl. 2041 (1915): 112. See also the *New York Times* (October 20, 1914), p. 12; (November 28, 1914), p. 12; (February 5, 1915), p. 10; (February 11, 1915), p. 8.

38. *Journal of the American Medical Association* (June 6, 1914), quoted in "'Twilight Sleeps' and Medical Publicity," *Literary Digest* 49 (1914): 60.

39. Ralph M. Beach, "Twilight Sleep: Report of One Thousand Cases," *American Journal of Obstetrics* 71 (191): 728.

40. Frederick A. Stratton, "Scopolamine Anesthesia," *Wisconsin Medical Journal* 8 (1908–9): 27.

41. Van Hoosen, *Scopolamine-Morphine Anaesthesia*, p. 101

about the possible ill effects of a breathing irregularity in babies whose mothers had been given scopolamine and morphine late in labor.[42] Doctors trying to understand the evaluation of twilight sleep must have been confused. In one journal, they read that the procedure was "too dangerous to be pursued," while another journal assured them that scopolamine, when properly used during labor, "has no danger for either mother or child."[43] Increasingly, by 1915, medical journals published studies that at least cautiously favored twilight sleep (the January 1915 issue of *American Medicine* published nine such articles),[44] although they frequently ran editorials warning of the drug's potential dangers and stressing the need for caution. Practicing physicians faced a dilemma when pregnant women demanded painless childbirth with scopolamine.[45]

While physicians debated the desirability of using scopolamine in 1914 and 1915, the public, surer of its position, demanded that twilight sleep be routinely available to women who wanted it. Hospitals in the major cities responded to these demands and to physicians' growing interest in the method by allowing deliveries of babies the Freiburg way.[46] In order to gain additional clinical experience, and possibly in response to some women's requests, some doctors used twilight sleep in hospital charity wards. But the technique was most successful in the specialty wards there upper- and middle-class patients increasingly gave birth and hospital attendants and facilities were available. By May 1915, *McClure's Magazine*'s national survey reported that the use of twilight

42. This condition, called "oligopnea," usually resolved after a few hours, but it was frightening to observe, especially for attendants who had no experience with it (Gauss, "Further Experiments in Dammerschlaf," p. 302).

43. See discussion of the Polak paper (n. 14 above) in *American Journal of Obstetrics* 7 (1915): 798; and Hilkowich, p. 793.

44. *American Medicine* 21 (1915): 24–70.

45. See, e.g., the discussion following Knipe's paper (n. 30 above) in the *American Journal of Obstetrics* 70 (1914): 1025. For articles with positive conclusions, see John Osborn Polock, "A Study of Twilight Sleep," *New York Medical Journal* 101 (1915): 293; Robert T. Gillmore, "Scopolamine and Morphine in Obstetrics and Surgery," *New York Medical Journal* 102 (1915): 298; William H. Wellington Knipe, " 'Twilight Sleep' from the Hospital Viewpoint," p. 250; W. Francis B. Wakefield, "Scopolamin-Amnesia in Labor," *American Journal of Obstetrics* 71 (1915): 428; Samuel J. Druskin and Nathan Ratnoff, "Twilight Sleep in Obstetrics—with a Report of 200 Cases," *New York State Journal of Medicine* 15 (1915): 152; Charles B. Reed, "A Contribution to the Study of 'Twilight Sleep,' " *Surgery, Gynecology and Obstetrics* 22 (1916): 656. For a negative conclusion, see Joseph Louis Baer, "Scopolamin-Morphin Treatment in Labor," *Journal of the American Medical Association* 64 (1915): 1723–28. The actual dangers of the drug varied according to dosage and timing, and it is impossible for the historian to assess the events accurately without individual case records. Any drug can be dangerous if misused, and the variability in advance about scopolamine suggests that some disasters occurred with it.

46. E.g., see *New York Times* (August 22, 1914), p. 9; and (September 10, 1914); and the American hospitals mentioned in Tracy and Boyd.

sleep, although still battling for acceptance, "gains steadily" around the country.[47]

Because of the need for expertise and extra care in administration of scopolamine, the twilight sleep movement easily fed into widespread efforts in the second decade of the twentieth century to upgrade obstetrical practice and eliminate midwives.[48] Both the women who demanded the technique and the doctors who adopted it applauded the new specialty of obstetrics. Mary Boyd desired to put an end to home deliveries when she advocated twilight sleep for charity patients: "Just as the village barber no longer performs operations, the untrained midwife of the neighborhood will pass out of existence under the effective competition of free painless wards."[49] Not only did scopolamine advocates try to displace midwives, but they also regarded general practitioners as unqualified to deliver twilight sleep babies. "The twentieth century woman will no more think of having an ordinary practitioner attend her in childbed at her own home," said two supporters, "she will go to a [twilight sleep] hospital as a matter of course."[50] Specialists agreed that "the method is not adapted for the general practitioner, but should be practiced only by those who devote themselves to obstetrics."[51] Eliza Taylor Ransom went so far as to recommend the passage of a federal law forbidding "anyone administering scopolamine without a course of instruction and a special license."[52]

Some obstetricians used this issue to discredit their general practitioner colleagues and the midwives who still delivered large numbers of America's babies. Another factor that might have pushed obstetricians to support twilight sleep was that births under scopolamine could be managed more completely by the physician. As one succinctly put it, anesthesia gave "absolute control over your patient at all stages of the game. . . . You are 'boss.' "[53] Physicians' time at the bedside could even be used for other pursuits. "I catch up on my reading and writing," testified one practitioner, "I am never harassed by relatives who want me to tell them things."[54]

47. Anna Steele Richardson's survey was reported in the *New York Times* (May 10, 1915), p. 24.

48. Litoff (n. 3 above), pp. 69–70.

49. Mary Boyd, "The Story of Dammerschlaf," *Survey* 33 (1914): 129. See the same statement in Boyd and Tracy, p. 69.

50. Constance Leupp and Burton J. Hendrick, "Twilight Sleep in America," *McClure's Magazine* 44 (1915): 172–73. The argument about expertise appeared repeatedly (see, e.g., William H. W. Knipe, "The Truth about Twilight Sleep," *Delineator* 85 [1914]: 4). Twilight sleep women were aware that theirs was an expensive demand. They expected the cost of physician-attended childbirth to jump from twenty-five to eighty-five dollars (Tracy and Boyd, p. 180).

51. Druskin and Ratnoff, p. 1520.

52. *New York Times* (April 30, 1915), p. 8.

53. Quoted from the *New Orleans Medical and Surgical Journal* in Miller (n. 1 above), p. 24.

54. Van Hoosen, *Petticoat Surgeon*, p. 282.

The Issue of Control

How do we explain the seeming contradictions in this episode in medical history? Why did women demand to undergo a process which many physicians deemed risky and in which parturients lost self-control? Why did some physicians resist a process that would have given women an easier birthing experience and would have reinforced physicians' control over childbirth in a hospital environment?

Several factors contributed to the open tensions about the use of twilight sleep. One was safety. Many physicians rejected scopolamine because they did not have access to facilities like those at the Mary Thompson Hospital or because they believed the drug too risky under any circumstances. Because of the variability among physicians' use of scopolamine and the contradictory evidence in the professional journals, we know that safety was a guiding motivation of many physicians. However, this is not enough to explain physician reluctance since so many doctors administered other drugs during labor despite questionable safety reports.[55] Differing perceptions about pain during childbirth also contributed to the intensity of feeling about twilight sleep in 1914 and 1915. Although many physicians believed that women's "extremely delicate nervous sensibilities" needed relief, others were reluctant to interfere with the natural process of childbirth. One anti–twilight sleep physician argued, "when we reflect that we are dealing with a perfectly healthy individual, and an organ engaged in a purely physiological function . . . I fail to see the necessity of instituting such a measure in a normal labor and attempt[ing] to bridge the parturient woman over this physiological process in a semi-conscious condition."[56] Women perceived, too, that some physicians used anesthesia only for "suffering when it becomes a serious impediment to the birth process."[57] However, women who had suffered greatly, or whose friends had suffered greatly, actively sought relief from their "physiological" births: They thought pain in itself a hindrance to a successful childbirth experience and "demanded" that their physicians provide them with more positive, less painful, experiences in the future.[58]

Both sides in the twilight sleep debate grappled with a third important question: whether the women or the attendants should determine

55. Fifty percent of 100 general practitioners surveyed in rural districts and small towns in Wisconsin indicated that they used ergot during labor, although its use was blamed for "a very large per cent of necessary operations for repair of injuries to the floor and pelvic organs of the female patient" (Ford [n. 4 above], p. 257).

56. Dr. Francis Reder, during a discussion of Rongy, Harrar, and MacPherson papers, *Transactions of the American Association of Obstetricians and Gynecologists* 27 (1914): 386.

57. Tracy and Boyd, p. 149.

58. For physicians' perceptions of "demanding" women, see, e.g., the discussion following the Rongy and Harrar papers, *Transactions of the American Association of Obstetricians and Gynecologists* 27 (1914): 382–83.

and control the birthing process.[59] The women who demanded that doctors put them to sleep were partially blind to the safety issue because the issue of control (over pain, bodily function, decision making) was so important to them. Control became important when doctors refused to allow women "to receive the same benefits from this great discovery that their sisters abroad are getting."[60] Twilight sleep advocates demanded their right to decide how they would have their children. Tracy and Boyd articulated this issue: "Women took their doctor's word before. They are now beginning to believe . . . that the use of painlessness should be at *their* discretion."[61] Although women were out of control during twilight sleep births—unconscious and needing crib-beds or constant attention to restrain their wild movements—this loss of control was less important to them than their determination to control the decision about what kind of labor and delivery they would have. Hanna Rion, whose influential book and articles had garnered support for the method, wrote:

> In the old-fashioned days when women were merely the blindfolded guardians of the power of child-bearing, they had no choice but to trust themselves without question in the hands of the all-wise physician, but that day is past and will return no more. Women have torn away the bandages of false modesty; they are no longer ashamed of their bodies; they want to know all the wondrous workings of nature, and they demand that they be taught how best to safeguard themselves as wives and mothers. When it comes to the supreme function of childbearing every woman should certainly have the choice of saying *how* she will have her child.[62]

Twilight sleep women wanted to control their own births by choosing to go to sleep. They were not succumbing to physicians or technology but were, they thought, demanding the right to control their own birthing experiences.

This feminist emphasis on control over decision making appears in the writings and lectures of the twilight sleep movement; its followers sought simple relief from pain.[63] Many leaders were active suffragists

59. Other contributing factors cannot be developed here. Growing professionalization and specialization with medicine produced tensions among groups of doctors that surfaced during this debate. The method's German "origins" invalidated it with many Americans during the war years. My emphasis here on the issue of control is not meant to minimize these and other factors. However, because others, especially Lawrence Miller (n. 1 above) have explored the general outlines, I have focused on the previously unanalyzed question of decision-making power. Its importance, I think, is indicated by the intensity in the women's arguments on this issue.

60. Letter from "Ex-M licus" in *New York Times* (November 28, 1914), p. 12.

61. Tracy and Boyd, p. 147 (emphasis in original).

62. Rion (n. 16 above), p. 47.

63. Tracy and Boyd claimed "four to five million" twilight sleep followers, obviously an exaggeration (p. 144).

whose commitment to twilight sleep was rooted in their belief in women's rights.[64] Although these activists agreed with most physicians that birth should increasingly be the domain of the obstetricians and that women should not suffer unnecessarily, they disagreed vehemently about who should decide what the birthing woman's experience would be. They clearly and adamantly wanted women to have the right to decide their own method of birthing.[65]

In the face of advancing obstetrical technology, many physicians wanted to retain their traditional professional right and duty to decide therapy on the basis of their judgment about the medical indications. They refused to be "dragooned" into "indiscriminate adoption" of a procedure that they themselves did not choose.[66] Even the doctors who supported twilight sleep believed that in the final analysis, the method of childbirth was "a question for the attending man and not the patient to decide."[67] It was principally this question of power over decision making that separated the movement's proponents from its opponents.

The Decline

In the very successes of the twilight sleep movement lay the seeds for its demise. Pressured by the clubwomen's associations and their own pregnant patients, doctors who had not been trained in the Freiburg method delivered babies with scopolamine. There was an enormous variation in the use of the drug, its timing through labor, the conditions in which the woman labored, and the watchfulness of attendants. As its advocates had feared, problems emerged when scopolamine was not properly monitored in a hospital setting. Following reports of adverse effects on the newborn, the drug fell into ill repute, and some hospitals that had been among the first to use it stopped administering it routinely.[68]

Those physicians who continued to advocate twilight sleep believed that accidents were due to misuse of the Freiburg method and not to the drug itself. Commenting on its discontinuation at Michael Reese Hospital in Chicago, Dr. Bertha Van Hoosen noted that "it is . . . probable that this adverse report demonstrates nothing more than the inexperience of the people using this anesthetic."[69] Dr. Ralph Beach agreed that "there is no doubt that all of the bad results which have been reported due to this

64. See, e.g., *New York Times* (November 28, 1914), p. 12.

65. See esp. Tracy and Boyd, Rion, Ransom (n. 21 above), and Van Hoosen (n. 10 above).

66. *New York Times* (September 26, 1914), p. 10.

67. Dr. Arthur J. Booker in his remarks defending Van Hoosen's use of scopolamine, quoted in Van Hoosen, *Scopolamine-Morphine Anaesthesia*, p. 12.

68. *New York Times* (April 24, 1915), p. 10; (April 30, 1915), p. 8; (May 29, 1915), p. 20; (August 25, 1915), p. 10; (August 16, 1916), p. 7.

69. Van Hoosen, "A Fixed Dosage" (n. 29 above), p. 57.

method, are due to an improper technic, or the administration of unstable preparations."[70] Simultaneously, in 1915, some hospitals expanded their obstetric services to offer twilight sleep, and others began cutting back its use. Either because they judged the drug dangerous or because they did not use it correctly, some hospitals found the method too troublesome to administer on a routine basis to all patients. Most reached a compromise and continued to use scopolamine during labor's first stage (when it was deemed safe), thus preempting their patients' protests without compromising their medical beliefs. A second inhibitory factor appeared in August 1915 when Mrs. Francis X. Carmody, one of the country's leading exponents of twilight sleep, died during childbirth at Long Island College Hospital in New York. Although doctors and her husband insisted that her death was unrelated to scopolamine, it nonetheless harmed the movement.[71] Mrs. Carmody's neighbor started a new movement to oppose twilight sleep, and women became more alert to the question of safety than they had been.[72] Doctors and some former twilight sleep advocates, emphasizing the issues of safety and difficulty of administration, began exploring other methods of achieving painless childbirth.[73]

The obstetric literature after 1915 indicates that twilight sleep did not die in that year. The women's movement may have failed to make scopalamine routinely available to all laboring women, but it succeeded in making the concept of painless childbirth more acceptable and in adding scopolamine to the obstetric pharmacopoeia. In fact, obstetricians continued to use scopolamine into the 1960s during the first stage of hospital births.[74] The use of anesthesia (including scopolamine) in childbirth grew in the years after 1915, since women, aware of the possibility of painlessness, continued to want "shorter and less painful parturition" and since physicians felt they could disregard these desires "only at great risk to [their] own practice."[75]

The attempt by a group of women, including some feminists, to control their birthing experiences backfired. The medical profession retained the choice of birth procedures and perhaps gained additional

70. Beach (n. 33 above), p. 43.

71. *New York Times* (August 24, 1915), p. 7.

72. Ibid. (August 31, 1915), p. 5.

73. See, e.g., Frank W. Lynch, "Nitrous Oxide Gas Analgesia in Obstetrics," *Journal of the American Medical Association* 64 (1915): 813.

74. See, e.g., Henry Schwarz, "Painless Childbirth and the Safe Conduct of Labor," *American Journal of Obstetrics and Diseases of Women and Children* 79 (1919): 46–63; and W. C. Danforth and C. Henry Davis, "Obstetric Analgesia and Anesthesia," *Journal of the American Medical Association* 81 (1923): 1090–96.

75. See the assessment of anesthesia used in childbirth in New York Academy of Medicine Committee on Public Health Relations, *Maternal Mortality in New York City: A Study of all Puerperal Deaths 1930–1932* (New York: Commonwealth Fund, 1933), p. 113; see also Joyce Antler and Daniel M. Fox, "Movement toward a Safe Maternity: Physician Accountability in New York City, 1915–1940," *Bulletin of the History of Medicine* 50 (1976): 569–95.

control as a result of this episode. Partial acceptance by the profession quieted the lay revolt, and women lost the power they had sought. Ironically, by encouraging women to go to sleep during their deliveries, the twilight sleep movement helped to distance women from their bodies. Put to sleep with a variety of drugs, most parturient women from the 1920s to the 1960s did not experience one of their bodies' most powerful actions and thus lost touch with their own physical potential.[76] The twilight sleep movement helped change the definition of birthing from a natural home event, as it was in the nineteenth century, to an illness requiring hospitalization and physician attendance. Parturient feminists today, seeking fully to experience childbirth, paradoxically must fight a tradition of drugged, hospital-controlled births, itself the partial result of a struggle to increase women's control over their bodies.

History of Medicine Department and *Women's Studies Program*
University of Wisconsin—Madison

76. The legacy for the parent-infant bond and for subsequent child development is explored in M. H. Klaus and J. H. Kennell, *Maternal Infant Bonding: The Impact of Early Separation or Loss on Family Development* (St. Louis: C. V. Mosby Co., 1976). For a feminist perspective on women's missing their deliveries, see Adrienne Rich, *Of Woman Born: Motherhood as Experience and Institution* (New York: W. W. Norton & Co., 1976).

VOLUNTARY MOTHERHOOD; THE BEGINNINGS OF FEMINIST BIRTH CONTROL IDEAS IN THE UNITED STATES

Linda Gordon

Voluntary motherhood was the first general name for a feminist birth control demand in the United States in the late nineteenth century.* It represented an initial response of feminists to their understanding that involuntary motherhood and child-raising were important parts of woman's oppression. In this paper, I would like to trace the content and general development of "voluntary-motherhood" ideas and to situate them in the development of the American birth-control movement.

The feminists who advocated voluntary motherhood were of three general types: suffragists; people active in such moral reform movements as temperance and social purity, in church auxiliaries, and in women's professional and service organizations (such as Sorosis); and members of small, usually anarchist, Free Love groups. The Free Lovers played a classically vanguard role in the development of birth-control ideas. Free Love groups were always small and sectarian, and they were usually male-dominated, despite their extreme ideological feminism. They never coalesced into a movement. On the contrary, they were the remnants of a dying tradition of utopian socialist and radical protestant religious dissent. The Free Lovers, whose very self-definition was built around a commitment to iconoclasm and to isolation from the masses, were precisely the group that could offer intellectual leadership in formulating the shocking arguments that birth control in the nineteenth century required.[1]

*The word "feminist" must be underscored. Since the early nineteenth century, there had been developing a body of population-control writings, which recommended the use of birth-control techniques to curb nationwide or worldwide populations; usually called neo-Malthusians, these writers were not concerned with the control of births as a means by which women could gain control over their own lives, except, very occasionally, as an auxiliary argument. And of course birth control practices date back to the most ancient societies on record.

The suffragists and moral reformers, concerned to win mass support, were increasingly committed to social respectability. As a result, they did not generally advance very far beyond prevalent standards of propriety in discussing sexual matters publicly. Indeed, as the century progressed the social gap between them and the Free Lovers grew, for the second and third generations of suffragists were more concerned with respectability than the first. In the 1860s and 1870s the great feminist theoreticians had been much closer to the Free Lovers, and at least one of these early giants, Victoria Woodhull, was for several years a member of both the suffrage and the Free Love camps. But even respectability did not completely stifle the mental processes of the feminists, and many of them said in private writings—in letters and diaries—what they were unwilling to utter in public.

The similar views of Free Lovers and suffragists on the question of voluntary motherhood did not bridge the considerable political distance between the groups, but did show that their analyses of the social meaning of reproduction for the women were converging. The sources of that convergence, the common grounds of their feminism, were their similar experiences in the changing conditions of nineteenth-century America. Both groups were composed of educated, middle-class Yankees responding to severe threats to the stability, if not dominance, of their class position. Both groups were disturbed by the consequences of rapid industrialization—the emergence of great capitalists in a clearly defined financial oligarchy, and the increased immigration which threatened the dignity and economic security of the middle-class Yankee. Free Lovers and suffragists, as feminists, looked forward to a decline in patriarchal power within the family, but worried, too, about the possible desintegration of the family and the loosening of sexual morality. They saw reproduction in the context of these larger social changes, and in a movement for women's emancipation; and they saw that movement as an answer to some of these large social problems. They hoped that giving political power to women would help to reinforce the family, to make the government more just and the economy less monopolistic. In all these attitudes there was something traditional as well as something progressive; the concept of voluntary motherhood reflected this duality.

Since we all bring a twentieth-century understanding to our concept of birth control, it may be best to make it clear at once that neither Free Lovers nor suffragists approved of contraceptive devices. Ezra Heywood, patriarch and martyr, thought "artificial" methods "unnatural, injurious, or offensive."[2] Tennessee Claflin wrote that the "washes, teas, tonics and various sorts of appliances known to the initiated" were a "standing reproach upon, and a permanent indictment against, American women. . . . No woman should ever hold sexual relations with any man from the possible consequences of which she might desire to escape."[3] *Woodhull and Claflin's Weekly* editorialized: "The means they (women) resort to for . . . prevention is sufficient to disgust every natural man. . . ."[4]

On a rhetorical level, the main objection to contraception * was that it was "unnatural", and the arguments reflected a romantic yearning for the "natural," rather pastorally conceived, that was typical of many nineteenth-century reform movements. More basic, however, particularly in women's arguments against contraception, was an underlying fear of the promiscuity that it could permit. The fear of promiscuity was associated less with fear for one's virtue than with fear of other women—the perhaps mythical "fallen" women—who might threaten a husband's fidelity.

To our twentieth-century minds a principle of voluntary motherhood that rejects the practice of contraception seems so theoretical as to have little real impact. What gave the concept substance was that it was accompanied by another, potentially explosive, conceptual change: the reacceptance of female sexuality. As with birth control, the most open advocates of female sexuality were the Free Lovers, not the suffragists; nevertheless both groups based their ideas on the traditional grounds of the "natural." Free Lovers argued, for example, that celibacy was unnatural and dangerous—for men and women alike. "Pen cannot record, nor lips express, the enervating, debauching effect of celibate life upon young men and women. . . ."[5] Asserting the existence, legitimacy and worthiness of female sexual drive was one of the Free Lovers' most important contributions to sexual reform; it was a logical correlate of their argument from the "natural" and of their appeal for the integration of body and soul.

Women's rights advocates, too, began to demand recognition of female sexuality. Isabella Beecher Hooker wrote to her daughter: "Multitudes of women in all the ages who have scarce known what sexual desire is—being wholly absorbed in the passion of maternity, have sacrificed themselves to the beloved husbands as unto God—and yet these men, full of their human passion and defending it as righteous & God-sent lose all confidence in womanhood when a woman here and there betrays her similar nature & gives herself soul & body to the man she adores."[6] Alice Stockham, a Spiritualist Free Lover and feminist physician, lauded sexual desire in men and women as "the prophecy of attainment." She urged that couples avoid reaching sexual "satiety" with each other, in order to keep their sexual desire constantly alive, for she considered desire pleasant and healthful.[7] Elizabeth Cady Stanton, commenting in her diary in 1883 on the Whitman poem, "There is a Woman Waiting for Me," wrote: "he speaks as if the female must be forced to the creative act, apparently ignorant of the fact that a healthy woman has as much passion as a man, that she needs nothing stronger than the law of attraction to draw her to the male."[8] Still, she loved Whitman, and largely because of that openness about sex that made him the Free Lovers' favorite poet.

According to the system of ideas then dominant, women, lacking sexual drives, submitted to sexual intercourse (and notice how Beecher Hooker

*Contraception will be used to refer to artificial devices used to prohibit conception during intercourse, while birth control will be used to mean anything, including abstinence, which limits pregnancy.

continued the image of a woman "giving herself", never taking) in order to please their husbands and to conceive children.The ambivalence underlying this view was expressed in the equally prevalent notion that women must be protected from exposure to sexuality lest they "fall" and become depraved, lustful monsters. This ambivalence perhaps came from a subconscious lack of certainty about the reality of the sex-less woman, a construct laid only thinly on top of the conception of woman as highly sexed, even insatiably so, that prevailed up to the eighteenth century. Victorian ambivalence on this question is nowhere more tellingly set forth than in the writings of physicians, who viewed woman's sexual organs as the source of her being, physical and psychological, and blamed most mental derangements on disorders of the reproductive organs.[9] Indeed, they saw it as part of the nature of things, as Rousseau had written, that men were male only part of the time, but women were female always.[10] In a system that deprived women of the opportunity to make extra-familial contributions to culture, it was inevitable that they should be more strongly identified with sex than men were. Indeed, females were frequently called "the sex" in the nineteenth century.

The concept of maternal instinct helped to smooth the contradictory attitudes about woman's sexuality. In many nineteenth-century writings we find the idea that the maternal instinct was the female analog of the male sex instinct; it was as if the two instincts were seated in analogous parts of the brain, or soul. Thus to suggest, as feminists did, that women might have the capacity for sexual impulses of their own automatically tended to weaken the theory of the maternal instinct. In the fearful imaginations of self-appointed protectors of the family and of womanly innocence, the possibility that women might desire sexual contact not for the sake of pregnancy—that they might even desire it at a time when they positively did not want pregnancy—was a wedge in the door to denying that women had any special maternal instinct at all.

Most of the feminists did not want to open that door either. Indeed, it was common for nineteenth-century women's-rights advocates to use the presumed "special motherly nature" and "sexual purity" of women as arguments for increasing their freedom and status. It is no wonder that many of them chose to speak their subversive thoughts about the sexual nature of women privately, or at least softly. Even among the more outspoken Free Lovers, there was a certain amount of hedging. Lois Waisbrooker and Dora Forster, writing for a Free Love journal in the 1890s, argued that while men and women both had an "amative" instinct, it was much stronger in men; and that women—only women—also had a reproductive, or "generative" instinct. "I suppose it must be universally conceded that men make the better lovers," Forster wrote. She thought that it might be possible that "the jealousy and tyranny of men have operated to suppress amativeness in women, by constantly sweeping strongly sexual women from the paths of life into infamy and sterility and death," but she thought also that the suppression, if it existed, had been permanently inculcated in woman's character.[11]

Modern birth control ideas rest on a full acceptance, at least quantitatively, of female sexuality. Modern contraception is designed to permit sexual intercourse as often as desired without the risk of pregnancy. Despite the protestations of sex counsellors that there are no norms for the frequency of intercourse, in the popular view there are such norms. Most people in the mid-twentieth century think that "normal" couples have intercourse several times a week. By twentieth-century standards, then, the Free Lovers' rejection of artificial contraception and "unnatural" sex seems to preclude the possibility of birth control at all. Nineteenth-century sexual reformers, however, had different sexual norms. They did not seek to make an infinite number of sterile sexual encounters possible. They wanted to make it possible for women to avoid pregnancy if they badly needed to do so for physical or psychological reasons, but they did not believe that it was essential for such women to engage freely in sexual intercourse.

In short, for birth control, they recommended periodic or permanent abstinence. The proponents of voluntary motherhood had in mind two distinct contexts for abstinence. One was the mutual decision of a couple. This could mean continued celibacy, or it could mean following a form of the rhythm method. Unfortunately all the nineteenth-century writers miscalculated women's fertility cycle. (It was not until the 1920s that the ovulation cycle was correctly plotted, and until the 1930s it was not widely understood among American doctors.)[12] Ezra Heywood, for example, recommended avoiding intercourse from 6 to 8 days before menstruation until 10 to 12 days after it. Careful use of the calendar could also provide control over the sex of a child, Heywood believed: conception in the first half of the menstrual cycle would produce girls, in the second half, boys.[13] These misconceptions functioned, conveniently, to make practicable Heywood's and others' ideas that celibacy and contraceptive devices should *both* be avoided.

Some of the Free Lovers also endorsed male continence, a system practiced and advocated by the Oneida community, in which the male avoids climax entirely.[14] (There were other aspects of the Oneida system that antagonized the Free Lovers, notably the authoritarian quality of John Humphrey Noyes's leadership.)[15] Dr. Stockham developed her own theory of continence called "Karezza," in which the female as well as the male was to avoid climax. Karezza and male continence were whole sexual systems, not just methods of birth control. Their advocates expected the self-control involved to build character and spiritual qualities, while honoring, refining and dignifying the sexual functions; and Karezza was reputed to be a cure for sterility as well, since its continued use was thought to build up the resources of fertility in the body.[16]

Idealizing sexual self-control was characteristic of the Free Love point of view. It was derived mainly from the thought of the utopian communitarians of the early nineteenth century,[17] but Ezra Heywood elaborated the theory. Beginning with the assumption that people's "natural" instincts, left untrammeled, would automatically create a harmonious, peaceful society—an assumption certainly derived from liberal philosophical faith in the innate goodness of man—Heywood applied it to sexuality, arguing that the natural sexual instinct was innately moderated, self-regulating. He did not imagine, as did Freud, a powerful, simple libido that could be checked only by an equally powerful moral and rational will. Heywood's theory implicitly contradicted Freud's description of inner struggle and constant tension between the drives of the id and the goals of the super-ego; Heywood denied the social necessity of sublimation.

On one level Heywood's theory may seem inadequate as a psychology, since it cannot explain such phenomena as repression and the strengthening of self-control with maturity. It may, however, have a deeper accuracy. It argues that society and its attendant repressions have distorted the animal's natural self-regulating mechanism, and have thereby created excessive and obsessive sexual drives. It offers a social explanation for the phenomena that Freud described in psychological terms, and thus holds out the hope that they can be changed.

Essentially similar to Wilhelm Reich's theory of "sex-economy," the Heywood theory of self-regulation went beyond Reich's in providing a weapon against one of the ideological bastions of male supremacy. Self-regulation as a goal was directed against the prevalent attitude that male lust was an uncontrollable urge, an attitude that functioned as a justification for rape specifically and for male sexual irresponsibility generally. We have to get away from the tradition of "man's necessities and woman's obedience to them," Stockham wrote.[18] The idea that men's desires are irrepressible is merely the other face of the idea that women's desires are non-existent. Together, the two created a circle that enclosed woman, making it her exclusive responsibility to say No, and making pregnancy her God-imposed burden if she didn't, while denying her both artificial contraception and the personal and social strength to rebel against male sexual demands.

Heywood developed his theory of natural sexual self-regulation in answer to the common anti-Free Love argument that the removal of social regulation of sexuality would lead to unhealthy promiscuity: ". . . in the distorted popular view, Free Love tends to unrestrained licentiousness, to open the flood gates of passion and remove all barriers in its desolating course; but it means just the opposite; it means the *utilization of animalism*, and the triumph of Reason, Knowledge, and Continence."[19] He applied the theory of self-regulation to the problem of birth control only as an afterthought, perhaps when women's concerns with that problem reached him. Ideally, he trusted, the amount of sexual intercourse that men and women desired would be exactly commensurate with the number of children that were wanted. Since sexual repression had had the boomerang effect of intensifying our sexual drives far beyond "natural" levels, effective birth control now would require the development of the inner self-control to contain and repress sexual urges. But in time he expected that sexual moderation would come about naturally.

Heywood's analysis, published in the mid-1870s, was concerned primarily with excessive sex drives in men. Charlotte Perkins Gilman, one of the leading theoreticians of the suffrage movement, reinterpreted that analysis two decades later to emphasize its effects on women. The economic dependence of woman on man, in Gilman's analysis, made her sexual attractiveness necessary not only for winning a mate, but as a means of getting a livelihood too. This is the case with no other animal. In the human female it had produced "excessive modification to sex," emphasizing weak qualities characterized by humans as "feminine." She made an analogy to the milk cow, bred to produce far more milk than she would need for her calves. But Gilman agreed completely with Heywood about the effects of exaggerated sex distinction on the male; it produced excessive sex energy and excessive indulgence to an extent debilitating to the whole species. Like Heywood she also belived that the path of progressive social evolution moved toward monogamy and toward reducing the promiscuous sex instinct.[20]

A second context for abstinence, in addition to mutual self-regulation by a couple, was the right of the wife unilaterally to refuse her husband. This idea is at the heart of voluntary motherhood. It was a key substantive demand in the mid-nineteenth century when both law and practice made sexual submission to her husband a woman's duty.[21] A woman's right to refuse is clearly the fundamental condition of birth control—and of her independence and personal integrity.

In their crusade for this right of refusal the voices of Free Lovers and suffragists were in unison. Ezra Heywood demanded "Woman's Natural Right to ownership and control over her own body-self—a right inseparable from Woman's intelligent existence. . . ."[22] Paulina Wright Davis, at the National Woman Suffrage Association in 1871, attacked the law "which makes obligatory the rendering of marital rights and compulsory maternity." When, as a result of her statement she was accused of being a Free Lover, she responded by accepting the description.[23] Isabella Beecher Hooker wrote her daughter in 1869 advising her to avoid pregnancy until "you are prepared in body and soul to receive and cherish the little one. . . ."[24] In 1873 she gave similar advice to women generally, in her book *Womanhood*.[25] Elizabeth Cady Stanton had characteristically used the same phrase as Heywood: woman owning her own body. Once asked by a magazine what she meant by it, she replied: ". . . womanhood is the primal fact, wifehood and motherhood its incidents . . . must the heyday of her existence be wholly devoted to the one animal function of bearing children? Shall there be no limit to this but woman's capacity to endure the fearful strain on her life?"[26]

The insistence on women's right to refuse often took the form of attacks on men for their lusts and their violence in attempting to satisfy them. In their complaints against the unequal marriage laws, chief or at least loudest among them was the charge that they legalized rape.[27] Victoria Woodhull raged, "I will tell the world, so long as I have a tongue and the strength to move it, of all the infernal misery hidden behind this horrible thing called marriage, though the Young Men's Christian Association sentence me to prison a year for every word. I have seen horrors beside which stone walls and iron bars are heaven. . . ."[28] Angela Heywood attacked men incessantly and bitterly; if one were to ignore the accuracy of her charges, she could well seem ill-tempered. "Man so lost to himself and woman as to invoke legal *violence* in these sacred nearings, *should have solemn meeting with, and look serious at his own penis until he is able to be lord and master of it, rather than it should longer rule, lord and master, of him and of the victims he deflowers.*"[29] Suffragists spoke more delicately, but not less bitterly. Feminists organized social purity organizations and campaigns, their attacks on prostitution based on a critique of the double standard, for which their proposed remedy was that men conform to the standards required of women.[30]

A variant of this concern was a campaign against "sexual abuses"—a Victorian euphemism for deviant sexual practices, or simply excessive sexual demands, not necessarily violence or prostitution. The Free Lovers, particularly, turned to this cause, because it gave them an opportunity to attack marriage. The "sexual abuses" question was one of the most frequent subjects of correspondence in Free Love periodicals. For example, a letter from Mrs. Theresa Hughes of Pittsburgh described:

> . . . a girl of sixteen, full of life and health when she became a wife . . . . She was a slave in every sense of the word, mentally and sexually, never was she free from his brutal outrages, morning, noon and night, up almost to the very hour her baby was born, and before she was again strong enough to move about . . . Often did her experience last an hour or two, and one night she will never forget, the outrage lasted exactly four hours.[31]

Or from Lucinda Chandler, well-known moral reformer:

> This useless sense gratification has demoralized generation after generation, till monstrosities of disorder are common. Moral education, and healthful training will be requisite for some generations, even after we have equitable economics, and free access to Nature's gifts. The young man of whom I knew who threatened his bride of a week with a sharp knife in his hand, to compel her to perform the office of 'sucker,' would no doubt have had the same disposition though no soul on the planet had a want unsatisfied or lacked a natural right.[32]

From an anonymous woman in Los Angeles:

> I am nearly wrecked and ruined by . . . nightly intercourse, which is often repeated in the morning. This and nothing else was the cause of my miscarriage . . . he went to work like a man a-mowing, and instead of a pleasure as it might have been, it was most intense torture. . . .[33]

Clearly these remarks reflect a level of hostility toward sex. The observation that many feminists hated sex has been made by several historians,[34] but they have usually failed to perceive that feminists' hostility and fear of it came from the fact that they were women, not that they were feminists. Women in the nineteenth century were, of course, trained to repress their own sexual feelings, to view sex as a duty. But they also resented what they experienced, which was not an abstraction, but a particular, historical kind of sexual encounter—intercourse dominated by and defined by the male in conformity with his desires and in disregard of what might bring pleasure to a woman. (That this might have resulted more from male ignorance than malevolence could not change women's experiences.) Furthermore, sexual intercourse brought physical danger. Pregnancy, child-birth and abortions were risky, painful and isolating experiences in the nineteenth century; venereal diseases were frequently communicated to women by their husbands. Elmina Slenker, a Free Lover and novelist, wrote, "I'm getting a host of stories (truths) about women so starved sexually as to use their dogs for relief, and finally I have come to the belief that a CLEAN dog is better than a drinking, tobacco-smelling, venerally diseased man!"[35]

"Sex-hating" women were not just misinformed, or priggish, or neurotic. They were often responding rationally to their material reality. Denied the possibility of recognizing and expressing their own sexual needs, denied even the knowledge of sexual possibilities other than those dictated by the rhythms of male orgasm, they had only two choices: passive and usually pleasureless submission, with high risk of undesirable consequences, or rebellious refusal. In that context abstinence to ensure voluntary motherhood was a most significant feminist demand.

What is remarkable is that some women recognized that it was not sex per se, but only their husbands' style of making love, that repelled them. One of the women noted above who complained about her treatment went on to say: "I am undeveloped sexually, never having desires in that direction; still, with a husband who had any love or kind feelings for me and one less selfish it *might* have been different, but he cared nothing for the torture to *me* as long as *he* was gratified."[36]

Elmina Slenker herself, the toughest and crustiest of all these "sex-haters," dared to explore and take seriously her own longings, thereby revealing herself to be a sex-lover in disguise. As the editor of the *Water-Cure Journal*, and a regular contributor to *Free Love Journal*,[37] she expounded a theory of "Dianaism, or Non-procreative Love," sometimes called "Diana-love and Alpha-abstinence." It meant free sexual contact of all sorts except intercourse.

> We want the sexes to love more than they do; we want them to love openly, frankly, earnestly; to enjoy the caress, the embrace, the glance, the voice, the presence & the very step of the beloved. We oppose no form or act of love between any man & woman. Fill the world as full of genuine sex love as you can . . . but forbear to rush in where generations yet unborn may suffer for your unthinking, uncaring, unheeding actions.[38]

Comparing this to the more usual physical means of avoiding conception—*coitus interruptus* and male continence—reveals how radical it was. In modern history, awareness of the possibilities of nongenital sex, and of forms of genital sex beyond standard "missionary-position" intercourse has been a recent, post-Freudian, even post-Masters and Johnson phenomenon. The definition of sex as heterosexual intercourse has been one of the oldest and most universal cultural norms. Slenker's alienation from existing sexual possibilities led her to explore alternatives with a bravery and a freedom from religious and psychological taboos extraordinary for a nineteenth-century Quaker reformer.

In the nineteenth century, neither Free Lovers nor suffragists ever relinquished their hostility to contraception. But among the Free Lovers, free speech was always an overriding concern, and for that reason Ezra Heywood agreed to publish some advertisements for a vaginal syringe, an instrument the use of which for contraception he personally deplored, or so he continued to assure his readers. Those advertisements led to Heywood's prosecution for obscenity, and he defended himself with characteristic flair by making his position more radical than ever before. Contraception was moral, he argued, when it was used by women as the only means of defending their rights, including the right to voluntary motherhood. Although "artificial means of preventing conception are not generally patronized by Free Lovers," he wrote, reserving for his own followers the highest moral ground, still he recognized that not all women were lucky enough to have Free Lovers for their sex partners.[39]

> Since Comstockism makes male will, passion and power absolute to *impose* conception, I stand with women to resent it. The man who would legislate to choke a woman's vagina with semen, who would force a woman to retain his seed, bear children when her own reason and conscience oppose it, would waylay her, seize her by the throat and rape her person.[40]

Angela Heywood enthusiastically pushed this new political line.

> Is it "proper", "polite", for men, real *he* men, to go to Washington to say, by penal law, fines and imprisonment, whether woman may continue her natural right to wash, rinse, or wipe out her own vaginal body opening—as well legislate when she may blow her nose, dry her eyes, or nurse her babe. . . .Whatever she may have been pleased to receive, from man's own, is his gift and her property. Women do not like rape, and have a right to resist its results.[41]

Her outspokenness, vulgarity in the ears of most of her contemporaries, came from a substantive, not merely a stylistic, sexual radicalism. Not even the heavy taboos and revulsion against abortion stopped her: "To cut a child up in woman, procure abortion. is a most fearful, tragic deed; but *even that* does not call for man's arbitrary jurisdiction over woman's womb."[42]

It is unclear whether Heywood, in this passage, was actually arguing for legalized abortion; if she was, she was alone among all nineteenth-century sexual reformers in saying it. Other feminists and Free Lovers condemned abortion, and argued that the necessity of stopping its widespread practice was a key reason for instituting voluntary motherhood by other means. The difference on the abortion question between sexual radicals and sexual conservatives was in their analysis of its causes and remedies. While doctors and preachers were sermonizing on the sinfulness of women who had abortions,[43] the radicals pronounced abortion itself an undeserved punishment, and a woman who had one a helpless victim. Woodhull and Claflin wrote about Madame Restell's notorious abortion "factory" in New York City without moralism, arguing that only voluntary conception would put it out of business.[44] Elizabeth Cady Stanton also sympathized with women who had abortions, and used the abortion problem as an example of women's victimization by laws made without their consent.[45]

Despite stylistic differences, which stemmed from differences in goals, nineteenth-century American Free Love and women's rights advocates shared the same basic attitudes toward birth control: they opposed contraception and abortion, but endorsed voluntary motherhood achieved through periodic abstinence; they believed that women should always have the right to decide when to bear a child: and they believed that women and men both had natural sex drives and that it was not wrong to indulge those drives without the intention of conceiving children. The two groups also shared the same appraisal of the social and political significance of birth control. Most of them were favorably inclined toward neo-Malthusian reasoning (at least until the 1890s, when the prevailing concern shifted to the problem of under-population rather than over-population).[46] They were also interested, increasingly, in controlling conception for eugenic purposes.[47] They were hostile to the hypocrisy of the sexual double standard and, beyond that, shared a general sense that men had become become over-sexed and that sex had been transformed into something disagreeably violent.

But above all their commitment to voluntary motherhood expressed their larger commitment to women's rights. Elizabeth Cady Stanton thought voluntary motherhood so central that on her lecture tours in 1871 she held separate afternoon meetings for *women only* (a completely unfamiliar practice at the time) and talked about "the gospel of fewer children & a healthy, happy maternity."[48] "What radical thoughts I then and there put into their heads & as they feel untrammelled, these thoughts are permanently lodged there! That is all I ask."[49] Only Ezra Heywood had gone so far as to defend a particular contraceptive device—the syringe. But the principle of woman's right to choose the number of children she would bear and when was accepted in the most conservative sections of the women's rights movement. At the First Congress of the Association for the Advancement of Women in 1873, a whole session was devoted to the theme "Enlightened Motherhood," which had voluntary motherhood as part of its meaning.[50]

The general conviction of the feminist community that women had a right to choose when to conceive a child was so strong by the end of the nineteenth century that it seems odd that they were unable to overcome their scruples against artificial contraception. The basis for the reluctance lies in their awareness that a consequence of effective contraception would be the separation of sexuality from reproduction. A state of things that permitted sexual intercourse to take place normally, even frequently, without the risk of pregnancy, inevitably seemed to nineteenth-century middle-class women as an attack on the family, as they understood the family. In the mid-Victorian sexual system, men normally conducted their sexual philandering with prostitutes; accordingly prostitution, far from being a threat to the family system, was a part of it and an important support of it. This was the common view of the time, paralleled by the belief that prostitutes knew of effective birth-control techniques. This seemed only fitting, for contraception in the 1870s was associated with sexual immorality. It did not seem, even to the most sexually liberal, that contraception could be legitimized to any extent, even for the purposes of family planning for married couples, without licensing extra-marital sex. The fact that contraception was not morally acceptable to respectable women was, from a woman's point of view, a guarantee that those women would not be a threat to her own marriage.

The fact that sexual intercourse often leads to conception was also a guarantee that men would marry in the first place. In the nineteenth century women needed marriage far more than men. Lacking economic independence, women needed husbands to support them, or at least to free them from a usually more humiliating economic dependence on fathers. Especially in the cities, where women were often isolated from communities, deprived of the economic and psychological support of networks of relatives, friends and neighbors, the prospect of dissolving the cement of nuclear families was frightening. In many cases children, and the prospect of children, provided that cement. Man's responsibilities for children were an important pressure for marital stability. Women, especially middle-class women, were also dependent on their children to provide them with meaningful work. The belief that motherhood was a woman's fulfillment had a material basis: parenthood was often the only creative and challenging activity in a woman's life, a key part of her self-esteem.

Legal, efficient birth control would have increased men's freedom to indulge in extra-marital sex without greatly increasing women's freedom to do so. The pressures enforcing chastity and marital fidelity on middle-class women were not only fear of illegitimate conception but a powerful combination of economic, social and psychological factors, including economic dependence, fear of rejection by husband and social support networks, internalized taboos and, hardly the least important, a socially conditioned lack of interest in sex that may have approached functional frigidity. The double standard of the Victorian sexual and family system, which had made men's sexual freedom irresponsible and oppressive to women, left most feminists convinced that increasing, rather than releasing, the taboos against extra-marital sex was in their interest, and they threw their support behind social-purity campaigns.

In short, we must forget the twentieth-century association of birth control with a trend toward sexual freedom. The voluntary motherhood propaganda of the 1870s was associated with a push toward a more restrictive, or at least a more rigidly enforced, sexual morality. Achieving voluntary motherhood by a method that would have encouraged sexual license was absolutely contrary to the felt interests of the very group that formed the main social basis for the cause—middle-class women. Separating these women from the early-twentieth-century feminists, with their interest in sexual freedom, were nearly four decades of significant social and economic changes and a general weakening of the ideology of the Lady. The ideal of the Free Lovers—responsible, open sexual encounters between equal partners—was impossible in the 1870s because men and women were not equal. A man was a man whether faithful to his wife or not. But women's sexual activities divided them into two categories—wife or prostitute. These categories were not mere ideas, but were enforced in reality by severe social and economic sanctions. The fact that so many, indeed most, Free Lovers in practice led faithful, monogamous, legally-married lives is not insignificant in this regard. It suggests that they instinctively understood that Free Love was an ideal not be realized in that time.

As voluntary motherhood was an ideology intended to encourage sexual purity, so it was also a pro-motherhood ideology. Far from debunking motherhood, the voluntary motherhood advocates consistently continued the traditional Victorian mystification and sentimentalization of the mother. It is true that at the end of the nineteenth century an increasing number of feminists and elite women—that is, still a relatively small group—were choosing not to marry or become mothers. That was primarily because of their increasing interest in professional work, and the difficulty of doing such work as a wife and mother, given the normal uncooperativeness of husbands and the lack of social provisions for child care. Voluntary motherhood advocates shared the general belief that mothers of young children ought not to work outside their homes but should make mothering their full-time occupation. Suffragists argued both to make professions open to women and to ennoble the task of mothering; they argued for increased rights and opportunities for women *because* they were mothers.

The Free Lovers were equally pro-motherhood; they only wanted to separate motherhood from legal marriage.[51] They devised pro-motherhood arguments to bolster their case against marriage. Mismated couples, held together by marriage laws, made bad parents and produced inferior offspring, Free Lovers said.[52] In 1870 *Woodhull and Claflin's Weekly* editorialized, "Our marital system is the greatest obstacle to the regeneration of the race."[53]

This concern with eugenics was characteristic of nearly all feminists of the late nineteenth century. At the time eugenics was mainly seen as an implication of evolutionary theory and was picked up by many social reformers to buttress their arguments that improvement of the human condition was possible. Eugenics had not yet become a movement in itself. Feminists used eugenics arguments as if they instinctively felt that arguments based solely on women's rights had not enough power to conquer conservative and religious scruples about reproduction. So they combined eugenics and feminism to produce evocative, romantic visions of perfect motherhood. "Where boundless love prevails. . .," *Woodhull and Claflin's Weekly* wrote, "the mother who produces an inferior child will be dishonored and unhappy . . . and she who produces superior children will feel proportionately pleased. When woman attains this position, she will consider superior offspring a necessity and be apt to procreate only with superior men."[54] Free Lovers and suffragists alike used the cult of motherhood to argue for making motherhood voluntary. Involuntary motherhood, wrote Harriet Stanton Blatch, daughter of Elizabeth Cady Stanton and a prominent suffragist, is a prostitution of the maternal instinct.[55] Free Lover Rachel Campbell cried out that motherhood was being "ground to dust under the misrule of masculine ignorance and superstition."[56]

Not only was motherhood considered an exalted, sacred profession, and a profession exclusively woman's reponsibility, but for a woman to avoid it was to choose a distinctly less noble path. In arguing for the enlargement of woman's sphere, feminists envisaged combining motherhood with other activities, not rejecting motherhood. Victoria Woodhull and Tennessee Claflin wrote:

> Tis true that the special and distinctive feature of woman is that of bearing children, and that upon the exercise of her function in this regard the perpetuity of race depends. It is also true that those who pass through life failing in this special feature of

> their mission cannot be said to have lived to the best purposes of woman's life. But while maternity should always be considered the most holy of all the functions woman is capable of, it should not be lost sight of in devotion to this, that there are as various spheres of usefulness outside of this for woman as there are for man outside of the marriage relation.[57]

Birth control was not intended to open the possibility of childlessness, but merely to give women leverage to win more recognition and dignity. Dora Forster, a Free Lover, saw in the fears of underpopulation a weapon of blackmail for women:

> I hope the scarcity of children will go on until maternity is honored at least as much as the trials and hardships of soldiers campaigning in wartime. It will then be worth while to supply the nation with a sufficiency of children . . . every civilized nation, having lost the power to enslave woman as mother, will be compelled to recognize her voluntary exercise of that function as by far the most important service of any class of citizens.[58]

"Oh, women of the world, arise in your strength and demand that all which stands in the path of true motherhood shall be removed from your path," wrote Lois Waisbrooker, a Free Love novelist and moral reformer.[59] Helen Gardener based a plea for women's education entirely on the argument that society needed educated mothers to produce able sons (not children, sons).

> Harvard and Yale, not to mention Columbia, may continue to put a protective tariff on the brains of young men: but so long as they must get those brains from the proscribed sex, just so long will male brains remain an 'infant industry' and continue to need this protection. Stupid mothers never did and stupid mothers never will, furnish this world with brilliant sons.[60]

Clinging to the cult of motherhood was part of a broader conservatism shared by Free Lovers and suffragists—acceptance of traditional sex roles. Even the Free Lovers rejected only one factor—legal marriage—of the many that defined woman's place in the family. They did not challenge conventional conceptions of woman's passivity and limited sphere of concern.[61] In their struggles for equality the women's-rights advocates never suggested that men should share responsibility for child-raising, housekeeping, nursing, cooking. When Victoria Woodhull in the 1870s and Charlotte Perkins Gilman in the early 1900s suggested socialized child care, they assumed that only women would do the work.[62] Most feminists wanted economic independence for women, but most, too, were reluctant to recommend achieving this by turning women loose and helpless into the economic world to compete with men.[63] This attitude was conditioned by an attitude hostile to the egoistic spirit of capitalism; but the attitude was not transformed into a political position and usually appeared as a description of women's weakness, rather than an attack on the system. Failing to distinguish, or even to indicate awareness of a possible distinction between women's conditioned passivity and their equally conditioned distaste for competition and open aggression, these feminists also followed the standard Victorian rationalization of sex roles, the idea that women were morally superior. Thus the timidity and self-effacement that were the marks of women's powerlessness were made into innate virtues. Angela Heywood, for example, praised women's greater ability for self-control, and, in an attribution no doubt intended to jar and titillate the reader, branded men inferior on account of their lack of sexual temperance.[64] Men's refusal to accept women as human beings she identified, similarly, as a mark of men's incapacity: ". . . man has not yet achieved himself to realize and meet a PERSON in woman. . . ."[65] In idealistic, abstract terms, no doubt such male behavior is an incapacity. Yet that conceit failed to remark on the power and privilege over women that the supposed "incapacity" gave men.

This omission is characteristic of the cult of motherhood. Indeed, what made it a cult was its one-sided failure to recognize the privileges men received from women's exclusive responsibility for parenthood. The "motherhood" of the feminists' writings was not merely the biological process of gestation and birth, but a package of social, economic and cultural functions. Although many of the nineteenth-century feminists had done substantial analysis of the historical and anthropological origins of woman's social role, they nevertheless agreed with the biological-determinist point of view that women's parental capacities had become implanted at the level of instinct, the famous "maternal instinct." That concept rested on the assumption that the qualities that parenthood requires—capacities for tenderness, self-control and patience, tolerance for tedium and detail, emotional supportiveness, dependability and warmth—were not only instinctive but sex-linked. The concept of the maternal instinct thus also involved a definition of the normal instinctual structure of the male that excluded these capacities, or included them only to an inferior degree; it also carried the implication that women who did not exercise these capacities, presumably through motherhood, remained unfulfilled, untrue to their destinies.

Belief in the maternal instinct reinforced the belief in the necessary spiritual connection for women between sex and reproduction, and limited the development of birth-control ideas. But the limits were set by the entire social context of women's lives, not by the intellectual timidity of their ideas. For women's "control over their own bodies" to lead to a rejection of motherhood as the *primary* vocation and measure of social worth required the existence of alternative vocations and sources of worthiness. The women's rights advocates of the 1870s and 1880s were fighting for those other opportunities, but a significant change had come only to a few privileged women, and most women faced essentially the same options that existed fifty years earlier. Thus voluntary motherhood in this period remained almost exclusively a tool for women to strengthen their positions within conventional marriages and families, not to reject them.

FOOTNOTES

1 There is no space here to compensate for the unfortunate general lack of information about the Free Lovers. The book-in-progress from which this paper is taken includes a fuller discussion of who they were, the content of their ideology and practice. The interested reader may refer to the following major works of the Free Love cause:

R. D. Chapman, *Freelove a Law of Nature* (New York: author 1881).

Tennessee Claflin, *The Ethics of Sexual Equality* (New York: Woodhull & Claflin, 1873).

———, *Virtue, What Is It and What It Isn't; Seduction, What It Is and What It Is Not* (New York: Woodhull & Claflin, 1872).

Ezra Heywood, *Cupid's Yokes: or, The Binding Forces of Conjugal Life* (Princeton, Mass.: Co-operative Publishing Co., n.d., probably 1876).

———, *Uncivil Liberty: An Essay to Show the Injustice and Impolicy of Ruling Woman Without Her Consent* (Princeton, Mass.: Co-operative Publishing Co., 1872).

C. L. James, *The Future Relation of the Sexes* (St. Louis: author, 1872).

Juliet Severance, *Marriage* (Chicago: M. Harman, 1901).

Victoria Claflin Woodhull, *The Scare-Crows of Sexual Slavery* (New York: Woodhull & Claflin, 1874).

———, *A Speech on the Principles of Social Freedom* (New York: Woodhull & Claflin, 1872).

———, *Tried as by Fire: or, the True and the False Socially* (New York: Woodhull & Claflin, 1874).

2 Heywood, *Cupid's Yokes, p. 20.*

3 Claflin, *The Ethics of Sexual Equality*, pp. 9-10.

4 *Woodhull & Claflin's Weekly* 1, no. 6 (1870): 5.

5 Heywood, *Cupid's Yokes*, pp. 17-18.

6 Letter to her daughter Alice, 1874, in the Isabella Beecher Hooker Collection. Beecher Stowe Mass. This reference was brought to my attention by Ellen Dubois of SUNY-Buffalo.

7 Alice B. Stockham, M.D., *Karezza, Ethics of Marriage* (Chicago: Alice B. Stockham & Co., 1898), pp. 84, 91-92.

8 Theodore Stanton and Harriot Stanton Blatch, eds., *Elizabeth Cady Stanton as Revealed in Her Letters, Diary and Reminiscences* (New York: Harper & Bros., 1922), 2:210 (Diary, 9-6-1883).

9 Ben Barker-Benfield, "The Spermatic Economy: A Nineteenth Century View of Sexuality," *Feminist Studies* 1, no. 1 (Summer 1972): 53.

10 J.J. Rousseau, *Emile* (New York: Columbia University Teachers College, 1967), p. 132. Rousseau was, after all, a chief author of the Victorian revision of the image of woman.

11 Dora Forster, *Sex Radicalism as Seen by an Emancipated Woman of the New Time* (Chicago: M. Harman, 1905), p. 40.

12 Norman E. Himes, *Medical History of Contraception* (New York: Gamut Press, 1963).

13 Heywood, *Cupid's Yokes*, pp. 19-20, 16.

14 Ibid., pp. 19-20; *Woodhull & Claflin's Weekly* 1, no, 18 (September 10, 1870): 5.

15 Heywood, *Cupid's Yoke*, pp. 14-15.

16 Stockham, *Karezza*, pp. 82-83, 53.

17 See for example, *Free Enquirer*, ed. Robert Owen and Frances Wright, (May 22, 1830), pp. 235-236.

18 Stockham, *Karezza*, p. 86.

19 Heywood, *Cupid's Yoke*, p. 19.

20 Charlotte Perkins Gilman, *Women and Economics* (New York: Harper Torchbooks, 1966), pp. 38-39, 43-44, 42, 47-48, 209.

21 In England, for example, it was not until 1891 that the courts first held against a man who forcibly kidnapped and imprisoned his wife when she left him.

22 Ezra Heywood, *Free Speech: Report of Ezra H. Heywood's Defense before the United States Court, in Boston, April 10, 11, and 12, 1883* (Princeton, Mass.: Co-operative Publishing Co., n.d.), p. 16.

23 Quoted in Nelson Manfred Blake, *The Road to Reno, A History of Divorce in the United States* (New York: Macmillan, 1962), p. 108, from the *New York Tribune*, May 12, 1871 and July 20, 1871.

24 Letter of August 29, 1869, in Hooker Collection, Beecher-Stowe Mss. This reference was brought to my attention by Ellen Dubois of SUNY-Buffalo.

25 Isabella Beecker Hooker, *Womanhood: its Sanctities and Fidelities* (Boston: Lee and Shepard, 1873), p. 26.

26 Elizabeth Cady Stanton Mss. No. 11, Library of Congress, undated. This reference was brought to my attention by Ellen Dubois of SUNY-Buffalo.

27 See for example, *Lucifer, The Light-Bearer*, ed. Moses Harman (Valley Falls, Kansas: 1894-1907) 18, no. 6 (October 1889): 3.

28 Victoria Woodhull, *The Scare-Crows*, p. 21. Her mention of the YMCA is a reference to the fact that Anthony Comstock, author and chief enforcer for the U.S. Post Office of the anti-obscenity laws, had begun his career in the YMCA.

29 *The Word* (Princeton, Mass.) 20, no. 9 (March 1893): 2-3. Emphasis in original.

30 See for example, the National Purity Congress of 1895, sponsored by the American Purity Alliance.

31 *Lucifer* (April 26, 1890), pp. 1-2.

32 N. a. *The Next Revolution: or Woman's Emancipation from Sex Slavery* (Valley Falls, Kansas: Lucifer Publishing Co., 1890), p. 49.

33 Ibid., pp. 8-9.

34 Linda Gordon et al., "Sexism in American Historical Writing," *Women's Studies* 1, no. 1 (Fall 1972).

35 *Lucifer* 15, no. 2 (September 1886): 3.

36 *The Word* 20 (1892-1893).

37 (Slenker) *Lucifer*, May 23, 1907; *Cyclopedia of American Boigraphy* 8: 488.

38 See for example *Lucifer* 18, no. 8 (December 1889): 3; 18, no. 6 (October 1889): 3; 18, no. 8 (December 1889): 3.

39 Heywood, *Free Speech*, pp. 17, 16.

40 Ibid., pp. 3-6. "Comstockism" also is a reference to Anthony Comstock. Noting the irony that the syringe was called by Comstock's name, Heywood continued: "To name a really good thing 'Comstock' has a sly, sinister, wily look, indicating vicious purpose; in deference to its N.Y. venders, who gave that name, the Publishers of *The Word* inserted an advertisement . . . which will hereafter appear as 'the Vaginal Syringe'; for its intelligent, humane and worthy mission should no longer be libelled by forced association with the pious scamp who thinks Congress gives him legal right of way to and control over every American Woman's Womb." At this trial, Heywood's second, he was acquitted. At his first trial, in 1877, he had been convicted, sentenced to two years, and served six months; at his third, in 1890, he was sentenced to and served two years at hard labor, an ordeal which probably caused his death a year later.

41 *The Word* 10, no. 9 (March 1893): 2-3.

42 Ibid.

43 See for example Horatio Robinson Storer, M.D., *Why Not? A Book for Every Woman* (Boston: Lee and Shepard, 1868). Note that this was the prize essay in a contest run by the A.M.A. in 1865 for the best anti-abortion tract.

44 Claflin, *Ethics*; Emanie Sachs, *The Terrible Siren, Victoria Woodhull, 1838-1927* (New York: Harper & Bros., 1928), p. 139.

45 Elizabeth Cady Stanton, Susan Anthony, Matilda Gage, eds., *History of Woman Suffrage*, 1:597-598.

46 Heywood, *Cupid's Yokes*, p. 20; see also *American Journal of Eugenics*, ed. M. Harman 1, no. 2 (September 1907); *Lucifer* (February 15, 1906; June 7, 1906; March 28, 1907; and May 11, 1905).

47 I will deal with early feminists' ideas concerning eugenics in my book.

48 Elizabeth Cady Stanton to Martha Wright, June 19, 1871, Stanton Mss. This reference was brought to my attention by Ellen Dubois of SUNY-Buffalo; see also Stanton, *Eight Years After, Reminiscences 1815-1897* (New York: Schoeken, 1971), pp. 262,297.

49 Stanton and Blatch, *Stanton as Revealed in Her Letters*, pp. 132-133.

50 *Papers and Letters*, Association for the Advancement of Women, 1873. The AAW was a conservative group formed in opposition to the Stanton-Anthony tendency. Nevertheless Chandler, a frequent contributor to Free Love journals, spoke here against undesired maternity and the identification of woman with her maternal fuction.

51 *Woodhull & Claflin's Weekly* 1, no. 20 (October 1, 1870): 10.

52 Woodhull, *Tried as by Fire*, p. 37; Lillian Harman, *The Regeneration of Society*. Speech before Manhattan Liberal Club, March 31, 1898 (Chicago: Light Bearer Library, 1900).

53 *Woodhull & Claflin's Weekly* 1, no. 20 (October 1, 1870): 10.

54 Ibid.

55 Harriot Stanton Blatch, "Voluntary Motherhood," *Transactions*, National Council of Women of 1891, ed. Rachel Foster Avery (Philadelphia: J. B. Lippincott, 1891), p. 280.

56 Rachel Campbell, *The Prodigal Daughter, or, the Price of Virtue* (Grass Valley, California, 1885), p. 3. An essay read to the New England Free Love League, 1881.

57 *Woodhull & Claflin's Weekly* 1, no. 14 (August 13, 1870): 4.

58 In addition to the biography by Sachs mentioned above, see also Johanna Johnston, *Mrs. Satan* (New York: G. P. Putnam's Sons, 1967), and M. M. Marberry, *Vicky, A Biography of Victoria C. Woodhull* (New York: Funk & Wagnalls, 1967).

59 From an advertisement for her novel, *Perfect Motherhood; Or, Mabel Raymond's Resolve* (New York: Murray Hill, 1890), in *The Next Revolution*.

60 Helen Hamilton Gardener, *Pulpit, Pew and Cradle* (New York: Truth Seeker Library, 1891), p. 22.

61 Even the most outspoken of the Free Lovers had conventional, role-differentiated images of sexual relations. Here is Angela Heywood, for example: "Men must not emasculate themselves for the sake of 'virtue,' they must, they will, recognize manliness and the life element of manliness as the fountain source of good manners. Women and girls demand strong, well-bred generative, vitalizing sex ability. Potency, virility, is the grand basic principle of man, and it holds him clean, sweet and elegant, to the delicacy of his counterpart." From *The Word* 14, no. 2 (June 1885): 3.

62 Woodhull, *The Scare-Crows;* Charlotte Perkins Gilman, *Concerning Children*.

63 See for example Blatch, "Voluntary Motherhood," pp. 283-284.

64 *The Word* 20, no. 8 (February 1893): 3.

65 Ibid.

Chlorotic Girls, 1870–1920: A Historical Perspective on Female Adolescence

Joan Jacobs Brumberg
Cornell University

BRUMBERG, JOAN JACOBS. *Chlorotic Girls, 1870–1920: A Historical Perspective on Female Adolescence.* CHILD DEVELOPMENT, 1982, **53**, 1468–1477. In light of the current interest in anorexia nervosa, this historical study explores the relationship of culture to age- and gender-specific symptomatologies. Between 1870 and 1920, chlorosis, a form of anemia, was widely reported in female adolescents in the United States. Diagnosis occurred on both the clinical and popular levels, yet neither the etiology nor the symptoms were precisely clear. Treatment generally included rest and large doses of iron salts. In large part, chlorosis was a cultural construction embedded in the context of Victorian medicine and family life. Physicians expected to see chlorosis in adolescent girls in the process of sexual maturation; girls learned to have the disease from family, friends, the popular press, and their doctors. Changes in diet and nutrition after 1900, coupled with increased understanding of ovarian function and iron deficiency anemia, provide only a partial explanation of the disease's eventual decline. By 1920, a changed social environment made chlorosis a social liability for girls and their mothers.

Students of human development generally fail to appreciate the relevance of historical study to understanding biomedical phenomena, particularly those that relate to specific stages of the life course. Our identification of contemporary female adolescence with both anorexia nervosa and bulimarexia raises larger questions about the evolution of gender- and age-specific symptomatologies, questions that may be answered in part by reference to the history of American women. Consequently, this essay poses a deceptively simple but nevertheless important question: What can we learn from the historical study of a particular disease?

Earlier versions of this paper were presented to the Department of Human Development and Family Studies and the Women's Studies Sex and Gender Study Group, both at Cornell. The author has profited from her colleagues' critical comments and from perceptive readings by Nancy Tomes and Will Provine. Address reprint requests to: Joan Jacobs Brumberg, Department of Human Development and Family Studies, Martha Van Rensselaer Hall G95, Cornell University, Ithaca, New York 14853.

[1] Female adolescence is a largely neglected area of psychological, sociological, and historical study. See Elder (1980) for commentary on this lacuna in the developmental literature. Among historians, important studies of adolescence and youth in Europe and the United States by John Gillis (1974) and Joseph Kett (1977) focus primarily on the patterns and behaviors of males. Carol Dyhouse's *Girls Growing Up in Victorian and Edwardian England* (1981) is essentially a study of the socialization of girls in English schools. The author is at work on a book that describes the changing historical experience of female adolescence in the United States, 1850 to the present.

[*Child Development*, 1982, 53, 1468–1477. 0009-3920/82/5306-0026$01.00]

The complete answer is part of a more extensive investigation of the changing symptomatology of American girlhood from 1850 to the present.[1] What you will read here is not a biomedical diagnosis or an epidemiological explanation but a historical description and analysis of chlorosis, a disease which was linked solely to female adolescence in the period 1870–1920. While there was neither a precise constellation of symptoms nor a medical consensus as to its cause, there was agreement about the constituency for this popular form of anemia. Chlorotic girls, not boys, were the focus of attention from medical men, parents, and educators. In fact, chlorosis represented an entire conception of the female adolescent rather than a simple anemia.

This analysis is guided by a set of assumptions drawn from the fields of anthropology, history, the sociology of medicine, and human development. First, since the contexts for human development invariably shape physiological, cognitive, and behavioral growth processes (Bronfenbrenner 1979), historical study can and should be enlisted in the effort to define the relationship between structural and cultural changes and the evolving psychological orientations of young women. Second, modern anthropological studies, particularly Margaret Mead's (1928) pioneering description of adolescence as a biocultural transition, clearly demonstrate that what is pathological within one cultural setting may be modal in another or vice versa. It is a logical corollary that variations with respect to what is atypical or modal can also occur over time within a single culture as well as cross-culturally. A striking case in point is the changing age of menarche in the United States; in 1833, the normative age for the onset of the menses may have been as high as 17; in 1972, it was 13 years of age (Bullough 1981; Laslett 1971; Money & Ehrhardt 1972, pp. 197–198). Third, historical and sociological study reveals that in addition to the systematic study of the physical world and its phenomena, science is also an expression of our culture and our social relations (Mishler et al. 1981; Pellegrino 1963).

Thus, the clinical object—disease—must be regarded as both cultural artifact and somatic phenomenon. Consequently, a single disease may have a biography or life history all its own, responsive to social as well as medical cure. Previous studies point to the limited duration of chlorosis (Figlio 1978; Hudson 1977; Huang, Note 1) without providing adequate cultural explanations for why it was that chlorosis was so prevalent among a single age and sex group. Hudson relates the rise of the disease to advances in laboratory medicine (particularly in the field of hematology) and the demise of the disease to a generalized improvement in nutrition (which he does not document). Siddall links the declining frequency of the disease to change in prenatal care, that is, the elimination of "blood-letting" in the care of expectant mothers (Siddall 1982). Huang, the most extensive scholarly investigation to date, attributes the decline in incidence by 1900 to increased medical acceptance of the "iron deficiency hypothesis" and the parallel development of a successful treatment, namely, iron therapy in correct dosages. In this scenario, medical men, not patients, play a primary role in the cure. Figlio attributes the origin of chlorosis and other chronic diseases in late nineteenth-century Britain to the exigencies of class. In England, chlorosis was linked to the idle daughters of the aristocracy and the bourgeoisie; yet their physicians, according to Figlio, were only "marginal members" of the middle class. As a result, both the cure and the explanatory etiology of chlorosis were shaped by class tensions. And as a cure, British doctors promoted a "medicalized condemnation" of the luxurious habits associated with the leisure of girls in the privileged classes.

In the American case, the diverse social settings in which chlorosis developed undercut a strictly class explanation. This article argues that medical pathologies linked to adolescent girls may emerge at particular moments in time, their appearance and disappearance not entirely explained by empirical factors. Moreover, adolescent girls are more directly implicated in the cure for chlorosis than either the Hudson or Huang studies allow. Certainly chlorosis cannot be understood fully without exploring its meaning for the patient. What you will read here is a rather straightforward exposition of the relationship between the biomedical diagnosis of the disease, medical conceptions of the female adolescent, and the changing social experience of girls. This essay places chlorosis in the context of its "life and times" in order to suggest the complex interplay of adolescent physiology, medicine, and social and family life.

Writing in the fifth volume of his massive medical compendium, *A System of Medicine*, T. Clifford Allbutt (1905) set forth the distinguishing characteristics of chlorosis, a form of anemia named for the greenish tinge that allegedly marked the skin of the patient. Allbutt reported that chlorosis was a "malady of women, and primarily of young women at or about the age of puberty . . . consisting in defect of the red corpuscles of the blood, a defect partly of numbers, chiefly of hemoglobin; the plasma being constant, or even enriched." The term chlorosis had been in use throughout the nineteenth century. In *Females and Their Diseases*, Charles Meigs referred to a "puberic condition" that "the French call *pâles couleurs*, and which we term green sickness or chlorosis" (Meigs 1848, p. 344). In *The Lady's Manual of Homeopathic Medicine*, written some 20 years later, E. H. Ruddock defined chlorosis as "a condition of general debility affecting young women" caused by a "deficiency" in the red corpuscles (Ruddock 1869, pp. 31–32). To the modern eye, chlorosis appears to be merely a curious, archaic name for iron deficiency anemia, yet Allbutt's comprehensive medical discussion of the etiology and symptoms of the disease suggests no easy one-to-one equivalent.

Allbutt distinguished chlorosis from other anemias by its constituency (girls between 14 and 25) and on the basis of patient reports of difficult respiration or dyspnea. "The heart is irritable," he wrote; "it often palpitates to the great distress of the patient. The palpitation makes itself felt . . . on the least exertion" (Allbutt 1905, p. 501). In addition to shortness of breath and energy, chlorotic girls were said to experience a wide variety of symptoms, including "caprices and perversions" of the appetite, amenorrhea, inertia and melancholy, headaches, "mental disposition," and a "desire for sleep and repose" (Allbutt 1905; Jones 1897; Ruddock

1869; Tait 1889). The patients' complexions, however, were not always pale or conspicuously tinted, as the name of the disease suggested. "Chlorotic girls still blush readily enough," wrote Allbutt, "and even in the height of an attack of their malady some of them never lose a vivid carmine on the malar eminences" (Allbutt 1905, p. 499).

Allbutt's synthesis of the medical literature on chlorosis suggests how popular a malady it had become during the nineteenth century. Among female adolescents, chlorosis existed on a number of different diagnostic levels that are easy enough to hypothesize but almost impossible to quantify. After about 1870, some young women, probably those of the middle and upper classes living in urban or commercial centers with a well-educated professional class, were clinically diagnosed as chlorotics on the basis of actual analysis of their blood. In these cases, hemoglobin deficiencies did exist. Many other patients, however, were called chlorotic by less careful and less knowledgeable doctors simply on the basis of symptoms described to them in a medical interview. No blood tests were made on this group of patients; rather, the age and gender of the patients triggered the diagnosis. Since the disease conveyed no particular status liabilities, it was easy enough to assign, particularly to those girls who may have used being "sickly" as a means of securing special attentions within the family or among friends. Still other girls, generally those without access to a physician or without the means to pay one, used the term chlorosis to describe their debilities and followed self-diagnosis with a home cure, that is, patent medicine designed to improve and strengthen the female constitution (Stage 1979).

Because chlorosis existed on both the clinical and popular levels, it was regarded as altogether commonplace and democratic. "The chlorotic girl," Allbutt wrote, 'is known in every consulting-room, public or private. The disease is no respector of rank or fortune" (Allbutt 1905, p. 497). Maintaining that chlorotic girls came from farms as well as urban centers, from all walks and stations of life, Allbutt claimed the broadest constituency for the disease despite evidence, drawn from his own clinical practice, that might point to a hereditary propensity for the condition. For example, Allbutt reported that he had treated at least two, and possibly three, generations of chlorotic daughters in a single family. When another doctor associated the disease with blondes, suggesting a possible link to race, Allbutt dismissed the claim with the remark that the disease was simply "more conspicuous" in fair people. A 1915 analysis of the disease by physician Richard C. Cabot, later the founder of the Department of Social Ethics at Harvard, pointed to the large number of Irish domestics in Boston who, apparently, reported the disease. Yet, Cabot could not find much additional evidence for an Irish propensity for chlorosis since factory girls of the same ethnic background seemed not to be affected. Among the Germans, Cabot noted, girls who "have moved to the city, from the country" were likely to develop chlorosis (Cabot 1915, p. 647).

Rather than scientifically refine the constituency for chlorosis by establishing its connection to specific racial or social variables, Allbutt and others advanced the notion that all adolescent girls were potentially chlorotic: "Perhaps, every girl passes as it were, through the outer court of chlorosis in her progress from youth to maturity." In fact, Allbutt suggested that even those who appeared well might be suffering from the disease: "It is a common experience that many girls otherwise healthy and living under the best conditions of life become chlorotic; perhaps, no girl escapes it altogether; some, however, show it but little and recover rapidly." Finally, Allbutt posited that the physician was needed to distinguish between the healthy and the diseased girl. If, as Allbutt maintained, "every girl may be regarded as potentially chlorotic," then the boundary between the normal and the pathological was, in his own words, an "arbitrary one" (Allbutt 1905, pp. 484, 486, 492). Every female adolescent raised the specter of chlorosis.

The actual cause of chlorosis was the subject of much debate. According to Huang (Note 1), nineteenth-century etiologies focused on three major causes: environmental, moral, and constitutional. Typical of the first is an 1869 medical guide that linked chlorosis to "confinement" in badly ventilated or poorly lighted rooms (Ruddock 1869, p. 32). In the United States these environmental causes were present in all classes. Among factory girls, chlorosis was linked to poor diet and "bad living"; among college girls, the disease was linked to excessive study and lack of outdoor exercise. Different doctors had their own favorite constitutional and moral interpretations, ranging from "derangement of the menstrual function," to "impoverished blood," to a "disease of the nervous system," to "a morbid condition of the organs of generation." Allegedly, the last of these was the result of masturbation. One medical adviser, urging mothers "to find out whether the disease may not be induced by secret habits," suggested that girls be watched "unobtrusively" and allowed "as little as possible to remain alone" (Ruddock 1869, p. 35). Although masturbation was not widely hypothesized as a direct cause of chlorosis, doctors like Allbutt were unwilling to disassociate the "master vice" completely. Allbutt advised his fellow physicians that in looking for the cause of chlorosis "if epithelial debris be found repeatedly in the urine, masturbation must not be forgotten, and corroborative evidence of the habit . . . detected" (Allbutt 1905, p. 487).

Menstruation, however, was almost always implicated in the etiology of chlorosis because the disease was associated with puberty in girls, not boys. In *Modern Medicine* readers found the following tentative analysis: "Judging from the fact that chlorosis is confined to the female, and that it occurs in the period immediately after the establishment of the function of menstruation, we can hardly help suggesting that there is some immediate relation between menstruation and chlorosis, but we can go no further. We have nothing to say as to what that relation is, or whether we are right in supposing any such relation exists. The figures suggest it; that is all we can say" (Cabot 1915, p. 648). Medical men were obviously confused by the fact that some girls developed chlorosis even before the onset of the menses, making a direct causal relationship unlikely. Consequently, popular medical tracts, such as Lucien Warner's *A Treatise on the Functions and Diseases of Women* (1875), glossed the issue of the premenstrual chlorotic girl, offering this common interpretation of the origins of the pathology: "the real seat of the disease is in the nervous system, although it manifests itself chiefly in impoverishment of the blood. It occurs most frequently at the time of puberty, because the system is then in such a transition, that it requires slighter disturbing causes for its development" (Warner 1875, pp. 68–69).

Clearly, in the transitionary period from childhood to adulthood girls were "at risk" for disease. In women, puberty and the onset of the menses marked the beginning of a period of psychological as well as physiological crisis that would continue until menstruation was regularized or "firmly established." Medical tracts urged both girls and their parents to consider the need for a special "hygiene of puberty" (Howard 1908, p. 67). Because of "large demands upon the resource of the female adolescent system," Lucien Warner advised close parental supervision of the diet, clothing, exercise, sleep, and mental and moral training of girls. In the 1870s, Dr. Edward Clarke, professor of medicine in Harvard College, argued against higher education for young women precisely because he believed that the "complicated apparatus peculiar to the female" needed time and ease to develop, free from the drain of intellectual activity. Clarke's influential but controversial book, *Sex in Education* (1873), presented case studies, allegedly drawn from clinical practice, of girls whose "catamenial function," ovarian development, and general health were ruined by inattention to the special demands of their new "periodicity."[2] In the view of many, female adolescence was especially dangerous because menstruation raised the specter of

[2] In *Adolescence* (1904), G. Stanley Hall built a psychology of adolescent development based on the law "that there is a trophic or nutritive background to everything" and that the "profound metamorphoses of puberty involve adjustments far more radical than are usually imagined" (p. 252). In a chapter entitled "Diseases of Body and Mind," Hall detailed various nosological peculiarities of adolescence including chlorosis (vol. 1, p. 260). Hall's conception of "periodicity" and the consequent crisis of female adolescence was expressed in romantic metaphors: "Puberty for a girl is like floating down a broadening river into an open sea. Landmarks recede, the water deepens and changes in its nature, there are new and strange forms of life, the currents are more complex, and the phenomena of tides make new conditions and new dangers. The bark is frail, liable to be tossed by storms of feeling, at the mercy of wind and wave, and if without chart and compass and simple rules of navigation, aimless drifting in the darkness of ignorance, amidst both rocks and shoals, may make of the weak or unadvised wrecks or castaways" (vol. 1, pp. 507–508).

multiple crises of a social as well as a medical nature. Only marriage insured a formal, guaranteed, and effective resolution of the difficult transition period. As a result, marriage was sometimes suggested as a cure for chlorosis (Huang, Note 1). Warner wrote of this kind of therapy: "It should in no case be resorted to except upon the recommendation of some responsible physician . . ." (Warner 1875, p. 74).

While most medical men implicated menstruation in the etiology of chlorosis. some did not. For example, in *Chlorosis: The Special Anemia of Young Women* (1897), E. Lloyd Jones, an instructor in pathology at Cambridge and a research scholar for the British Medical Association, reported that there simply was "not sufficient evidence to show that chlorosis is due to menstrual loss." Rather, Jones proposed an interpretation of the causes of the disease that reflected new research techniques and insights derived from the science of hematology. Chlorosis, Jones argued, was best understood in relation to the blood changes that occurred at puberty, particularly a drop in specific blood gravity among females. Using the centrifugal method (whirling tubes of blood at a speed of 1,000 rpm), Jones discovered that the average ratio between serum and corpuscles could be differentiated by gender and age. This disparity in female and male blood was presented in a number of charts and tables, which gave the treatise an empirical aura and in turn documented in chlorotic girls a reduction in the amount of hemoglobin, a diminution of the number of red corpuscles, and an increase in the proportion of serum to corpuscles. Still, like Allbutt, Jones had difficulty distinguishing the normal from the pathological: "the blood of the chlorotic subject exhibits an exaggeration of the fall in specific gravity which occurs in healthy young women about the age of puberty; and, indeed, it is likely that I included among my healthy women some who were in reality chlorotic. . . ." (Jones 1897, p. 20).

If hematology failed to establish absolute distinctions between the blood of healthy and diseased girls, diagnosis was confused even further by the fact that the pathological was also regarded as the ideal type. That is to say that girls with the disease were also the most attractive and, possibly, the best potential mothers. In fact, Jones claimed that chlorosis in adolescence was positively correlated with high fertility. "Those women who have the lowest specific gravity of the blood, and the largest number of brothers and sisters," Jones wrote, "are generally fair, with pretty pink and white complexions, blue or light eyes, fine hair, with a goodly amount of subcutaneous fat. Such women are, I believe, unusually prolific . . ." (Jones 1897, pp. 15–17). Jones's attention to the looks of the chlorotic girl was not unusual. According to one medical report, chlorosis was "the anemia of good looking girls" (Tait 1889, pp. 282–283). Medical men generally agreed with Allbutt's statement of their physiological normality: "chlorotic girls do not lack size, nor do they fall away from the main lines of development" (Allbutt 1905, p. 497). Jones, however, took the association between chlorosis and good looks a step further, claiming that while the "lips and ears" of a chlorotic girl might be "pallid," her cheeks certainly were not. Jones asserted that the face of the chlorotic girl remained a "pretty pink and white color" precisely because her blood vessels were so "well-filled."

The medical notion of the chlorotic girl as simultaneously diseased, fertile, and attractive fit within the framework of the Victorians' sentimentalization of sickly women (Bullough & Voght 1973; Ehrenreich & English 1973; Haller & Haller 1974; Morantz 1974; Rosenberg & Smith-Rosenberg 1973; Wood 1973). In the nineteenth century, adult women in the United States were prone to a generalized invalidism as well as both hysteria and neurasthenia, the latter a polite but "profound physical and mental exhaustion" (Sicherman 1977; Veith 1965). Neurasthenia, like chlorosis, had an imprecise constellation of symptoms including sick headaches, palpitations, and nervous dyspepsia. (In his classic work, *American Nervousness* [1881], George Beard called neurasthenia "slippery, fleeting, and vague.") For the study of female adolescence the crucial point is that invalidism and neurasthenia were not uncommon pathologies among mothers, aunts, teachers, and family friends who conditioned the psychological orientation and experiences of younger women. Chlorotic girls and sickly mothers did share some common symptoms and probably legitimated each others' complaints. It is also important to understand that among nineteenth-century physicians the same cluster of symptoms (e.g., exhaustion, headaches, heart palpitations, and indigestion) could result in different diagnoses depending on the age and gender of the patient. In this way, the labeling of medical conditions by nineteenth-century doctors reinforced the gender and age categories that were the basis of the Victorian social order.

The coexistence of both disease and physical attractiveness among chlorotics was also a telling reflection of the state of medical and scientific knowledge, particularly with respect to ovarian function. For example, Jones, who was typical of many late nineteenth-century physicians, attributed the chlorotic girls' good looks, that is, her rosy glow, to the fact that her vessels were "well-filled." Moreover, he maintained that girls bled from the finger more easily than boys. These claims were based on the belief that in chlorotic women there was an absolute increase in the total volume of blood. Jones and others attributed the alleged increase in blood volume to the tendency to "store up blood during the intermenstrual periods"; at each menstrual period, girls would receive "blood changes" or experience "fresh additions to the reserve laid aside." Allbutt's experience confirmed Jones's view; he posited that chlorosis was "the exaggeration of the fertile blood, of blood, that is, which has for its end the storage of nutritive materials for the foetus during pregnancy" (Allbutt 1905, pp. 483–484).

The clinical portrait of the chlorotic girl was obviously confused by a lack of understanding of menstrual physiology. Until the work of Westphalen in 1896, prevailing theory held that menstruation was set in motion by the "tubal nerve," that is, a "nerve irritation" produced by the ovary caused the blood vessels to dilate just prior to ovulation; if unfertilized, the ovum was swept away by the flow. Westphalen first described the cyclical changes in the uterine lining and the continual process of building up and breaking down of that lining (Leonardo 1944). Jones, however, who had only a rudimentary understanding of what took place in the uterus during menstruation, was able to associate chlorosis with greater blood volume and fecundity at the same time that he reported amenorrhea in his chlorotic patients. Ultimately, Jones revealed his ambivalence about the simple hematological calculus he had proposed, calling chlorosis "a chronic autointoxication brought about by some substances which are probably the products of uterine, Fallopian or ovarian metabolism, and producing effects on the blood by inducing changes in the gastrointestinal canal by the medium of the nervous system" (Jones 1897, p. 67).

In calling chlorosis an "autointoxication," Jones raised the issue of the involvement of adolescent girls in the creation of their own disease. As already noted, chlorosis was the kind of condition that depended in large measure on self-reporting or reports from parents. According to clinical observations, many adolescents presented themselves at the office of the family doctor with a diagnosis in hand. "I think my blood must be out of order," was the characteristic analysis in the experience of an Erie, Pennsylvania practitioner. Still other patients reported what their peers had said: "friends . . . commented on the lack of color in my face" (Montgomery 1919). According to Lucien Warner, concerned parents recited the sad case histories of daughters who were "unusually dull and listless," whose "fits of sadness and weeping" appeared to be without cause. Ruddock reported that his chlorotic patients were "sombre and taciturn, weeping without cause; and sighing involuntarily" (Ruddock 1869, p. 32). Generally, however, the symptoms described by late nineteenth-century physicians were physiological rather than psychological, although the doctors never promoted the notion of a happy chlorotic nor discredited the idea that the ultimate cause might be emotional (e.g., lovesickness, homesickness, shock). The most commonly reported symptoms were progressive loss of strength, difficulty in respiration, and loss of appetite.

Lethargy and shortness of breath received mention but little elaboration; Allbutt noted that girls who once could "trip upstairs" easily were reduced to a state of inactivity by chlorosis. More interesting, however, were the eating disorders associated with chlorosis, all of which acted to confirm what the 1897 *American Jour-*

nal of Medical Science called the "capricious appetite" of young women. Nearly 30 years before, a homeopathic medical guide for women noted that in the chlorotic girl the appetite was "lost or so perverted that substances such as chalk, cinders, etc. are desired" (Ruddock 1869, p. 32). In 1875, Lucien Warner's popular medical compendium associated chlorosis with "loss of appetite, loathing of food, and often a desire which almost amounts to a passion, for such indigestible and repulsive articles as charcoal, slate-stones, chalk, plaster, flies, bugs, and other similar substances" (Warner 1875, p. 70). Another report stated that the commonest dietary abnormality among chlorotics was "a special fondness for pickles and sour things" (Cabot 1915, p. 649).

In 1897, E. Lloyd Jones linked chlorosis to a less bizarre diet, but to an eating "disorder" nonetheless. Chlorotic girls, he observed, were not simply prone to the excessive consumption of carbohydrates; they eschewed an important nutritive source: "Almost all chlorotic girls are fond of biscuits, potatoes, etc. while they avoid meat on most occasions, and when they do eat meat, they prefer the burnt outside portion" (Jones 1897, p. 39). Meigs confirmed the same problem in a dialogue between a physician and an adolescent girl. " 'Oh, I like pies and preserves but I can't bear meat,' the young woman reportedly told her family doctor" (Meigs 1848, p. 361). Apparently, while many chlorotic patients assured their doctors that they ate meat, physicians regularly found that their meat eating actually involved only the scantiest quantities of burnt, overcooked parts. J. H. Montgomery, a Pennsylvania physician, observed this "disgust for meat in any form"; a medical guide reported that among chlorotics "the appetite for animal food completely ceases" (Montgomery 1919; Ruddock 1869, p. 34). In articulating his cure for chlorosis, Allbutt wrote: "it is of the first importance to overcome the common distaste for meat. Girls will say that the entry of a dish of hot meat into the room makes them feel sick. . . ." (Allbutt 1905, p. 517).

The repugnance for animal flesh among Victorian adolescents clearly had a larger cultural significance. In fact, meat eating was tied to female physiology, sexuality, and, consequently, behavior as an adult woman. In negotiating the difficult biological transition to adulthood, Warner suggested that meat eating could actually accelerate sexual development; at the same time, a restriction on the carnivorous aspect of the diet could tame premature or rampant sexuality as well as overabundant menstrual flow: "If there is any tendency to precocity in menstruation, or if the system is very robust and plethoric, the supply of meat should be quite limited. If, on the other hand, the girl is of sluggish temperament and the menses are tardy in their appearance, the supply of meat should be especially generous. . . ." (Warner 1875, p. 54). In excess, meat eating was popularly linked to nymphomania (Bullough & Voght 1973). A stimulative diet of meat and condiments was recommended only for those girls whose development of the passions seemed, somehow, "deficient."

If a meatless diet could insure their sexual morality, it is no wonder that so many middle-class girls, aspiring to be good, evidenced distaste for a food that, allegedly, increased the menstrual flow and made them more passionate. In making the refusal of meat a positive social virtue, middle- and upper-class girls increased the likelihood of their incurring iron deficits of exactly the kind that led to iron deficiency anemia. Moreover, Allbutt's important synthesis of the medical literature on chlorosis reveals that even as early as 1905, American girls had fallen victims to the grand obsession: slimness. "Many young women, as their frames develop, fall into a panic fear of obesity," Allbutt wrote, "and they not only cut down on their food, but swallow vinegar and other alleged antidotes to fatness" (Allbutt 1905, p. 485). Consequently, voluntary restrictions on diet were part of female adolescent life in the United States before the twentieth century. Whether a girl chose to avoid meat because she found its associations "disgusting" or she ate less for fear of expanding her waistline, the fact of the matter is that these cultural attitudes were in place, tying feminine goodness and attractiveness to an ideal body type. Thus, there were cultural sources as well as organic reasons for the "loss of appetite" and the "peculiarities of diet" associated with chlorotic girls.

As therapy for these patients, physicians debated the effectiveness of rest versus outdoor exercise. However, most doctors prescribed daily supplements of iron salts even though there was little consensus on how organic and inorganic iron actually affected the blood and few studies of the iron intake of chlorotics (Huang, Note 1). Blaud's Pills, a well-known patent medicine that combined iron and potassium carbonate, were frequently cited by doctors writing about the clinical treatment of chlorotic girls. Iron supplements from drug manufacturers were praised by professional medical men; Allbutt, in fact, called the patent medical business "our excellent allies." Popular advertising in newspapers and magazines promoted "blood and nerve remedies" by the score, keeping pace with both the physicians' clinical diagnosis of chlorosis and the girls' self-reporting and self-diagnosis of their weak condition. E. Lloyd Jones typically prescribed Blaud's Pills after each meal along with small doses of bismuth salicylate with morphine (to relax the stomach before eating) and a diet of underdone meat, no potatoes, and little bread. J. H. Montgomery, who also ordered sulphate of iron in doses of 6–12 grains daily, was careful to point out that the iron supplements should not be prematurely discontinued as soon as the hemoglobin reached normal. Rather, Montgomery, warning of relapse, encouraged continuation of the supplements for at least 2 months and the cultivation of "better habits." Another source estimated that "under treatment" the disease was usually relieved "well within six months" and recommended that the patient go from one 0.3-gram pill after each meal in the first week to three pills after each meal, or 2.7 grams per day, in the third week (Jones 1897, pp. 57–60). Despite medical faith in the efficacy of supplementary iron, doctors were willing to concede that "it is also true that patients will improve without the administration of iron, provided we correct their constipation and improve their general hygiene" (Allbutt 1905, p. 515). Generally, however, a regimen of Blaud's Pills accomplished a satisfactory "cure." Once past the age of 25, or at such time as they married, the risk of developing chlorosis was drastically reduced.

By 1900, chlorosis was already on the decline; by the 1930s the disease was moribund.

Statistical evidence from both the wards and the dispensary at Massachusetts General Hospital indicates that between 1898 and 1907 the number of cases declined by nearly 90% (Cabot 1915, pp. 646–647). Practicing physicians confirmed the same trend. In 1915, Dr. Richard C. Cabot reported: "We do not see chlorosis now as we used to ten years ago." Cabot carefully described how this decline in cases could not be explained away by "supposing that we now call the same cases by another name" (Cabot 1915, p. 646). In other words, chlorosis was not simply a diagnostic entity that was subsumed into a different category. By 1936, an Iowa physician, W. M. Fowler, was moved to eulogize the disease in an article entitled "Chlorosis—an Obituary," published in the *Annals of Medical History*. "What disease," Fowler asked, "can compare with chlorosis in having occupied such a prominent place in medical practice only to disappear spontaneously while we are still speculating as to its etiology?" (Fowler 1936, p. 168). Thus, the chlorotic era, which reached its peak in the last 3 decades of the nineteenth century, came to be regarded as something of a medical curiosity at the very time when massive economic deprivation, in the form of the Great Depression, should have increased the constituency for anemias of all kinds.

"Very little of the decrease in chlorosis can be attributed to direct medical intervention," writes Robert P. Hudson, a contemporary medical historian (Hudson 1977, p. 459). If the demise of chlorosis is not the self-conscious accomplishment of American medicine, how then did it occur? Hudson claims that certain changes in the day-to-day life of Americans in the first few decades of this century had consequences for the future of chlorosis, specifically, a general improvement in nutrition, diminishing prejudice against the eating of meat,[3] the abandonment of corsets or "tight lacing," and a related increase in physical activity

[3] The last decades of the nineteenth century may be an important transitional period in the history of nutrition throughout the Western world. For example, research by J. C. Toutain (1971) suggests that in France animal proteins accounted for only about 25% of the total protein intake until after 1880–1890.

among women. While all of these changes are relevant, they fail to capture the essential dynamic of the chlorotic era. That is to say, neither more effective iron therapy, improved nutritional levels, nor increased physical activity, each a legitimate biomedical factor, provides the essential cipher for decoding the social construction of chlorosis.

At a basic level, chlorosis depended for its existence on the popular notion that adolescence, marked by the onset of the menses, made a girl ripe for disease. So long as medical men misunderstood the true nature of the ovulatory cycle and the menstrual flow, women did, in fact, appear to be strangely afflicted. Important discoveries that marked the beginning of the modern endocrine perspective on menstrual physiology came only after 1900; in particular, the 1908 description of the cycle of changes in the endometrium, by Hitschmann and Adler, paved the way for a more accurate understanding of the significance of menstruation. Between 1903 and 1928, the role of ovarian hormones in triggering the cycle was established through animal experimentation (Leonardo 1944, pp. 255–258). Taken together, these and other developments in the history of gynecology finally condemned the notion of menstruation as a "crisis." Once it was discovered that the menstrual cycle actually lasted for 28 days and then routinely began again, it became difficult to argue that the process itself made adolescent girls susceptible to disease. In effect, the rise of endocrinology in the early twentieth century undercut the medical diagnosis of chlorosis. Informed and better-educated doctors were simply less likely to assume that adolescent girls were either "at risk" or sick.

Finally, the patients and their families must be implicated in the demise of chlorosis. However iatrogenic medical practice may be (Illich 1977), the prevalence of chlorosis depended both on young female patients presenting a certain set of complaints and the biomedical diagnosis and labeling by medical men. Girls who were told that they had chlorosis learned how to have it from family, friends, and the popular press as well as from their doctors; their behavior as "sick" persons was surely affected by the expectations of the people and the institutions with whom they interacted. The fact that neurasthenic conditions were fashionable among the adult women who superintended their school, church, and family life is essential to understanding the psychology of chlorotic girls. It may well be that nineteenth-century mothers and daughters, particularly among the middle and upper classes, were bonded together by their common ill health rather than their vigor.

As social and cultural values changed, American girls began to choose activity over inactivity, the meeting place over the malaise. Chlorotic girls, with their problems of respiration and limited energy, were aptly suited to a domesticated nineteenth-century environment where they could conscientiously take their iron pills and their requisite afternoon naps. As the lives of girls became more public and standardized, chlorosis became a problem. Geared increasingly to attendance in public high schools, programs of physical activity, peer-group associations beyond the home and family, as well as the "dating system" (Modell, Note 2) and the media of romance (film, radio, and popular press), girls replaced concern about their blood with a different set of anxieties about face and figure.

So, too, parents and parental expectations changed. For American mothers, the years between 1900 and 1920 were significant for the emphasis put in the popular women's press on the idea that there was a "scientific nutrition" with application to the home. Dieticians such as Sarah Tyson Rorer, domestic editor of the *Ladies' Home Journal* from 1897 to 1911, charged American mothers with "building and repairing the human body" through right diet (Boyd 1971). Other pioneers in applied nutrition addressed the general public through bulletins issued by the U.S. Department of Agriculture. In the 1890s, W. O. Atwater developed dietary guides which Ellen Swallow Richards, founder of the home economics movement, translated into family menu planning. Between 1916 and 1923, the USDA popularized the concept of five basic food groups, adapting it for kitchen use (Hertzler & Anderson 1974; Leitch 1942). Once this information was available and incorporated into the day-to-day domestic routines of American women of the middle class, mothers were simply less likely to tolerate having a nutritional disease in the home.

In effect, both mothers and daughters had moved beyond invalidism and chlorosis. Complaints of weakness and loss of appetite, as well as the notion of "rest cures," simply did not "fit" with the plethora of institutions and programs servicing American girlhood by World War I. By 1920, a girl with chlorosis was not only a social "drag" but a liability with respect to her own mother's perception of herself as a competent domestic manager and nurturer. If, as the contemporary Geritol commercials repeatedly remind us, iron deficiency anemia never disappeared, chlorosis surely did precisely because the cultural and familial context that stimulated its construction changed dramatically.

Reference Notes

1. Huang, S.-R. Chlorosis and the iron controversy: an aspect of nineteenth-century medicine. Unpublished doctoral dissertation, Harvard University, 1978.
2. Modell, J. Pre–World War II courtship patterns in the United States. Unpublished paper, Cornell University, March 1982.

References

Allbutt, T. C. Chlorosis. In T. C. Allbutt (Ed.), *A system of medicine.* New York: Macmillan, 1905.

Beard, G. *American nervousness.* New York: Putnam's 1881.

Boyd, L. Sarah Tyson Rorer. In E. T. James (Ed.), *Notable American women.* Vol. **3.** Cambridge, Mass.: Harvard University Press, 1971.

Bronfenbrenner, U. *The ecology of human development.* Cambridge, Mass.: Harvard University Press, 1979.

Bullough, V. Age at menarche: a misunderstanding *Science,* 1981, **213,** 365–366.

Bullough, V., & Voght, M. Women, menstruation and nineteenth-century medicine. *Bulletin of the History of Medicine,* 1973, **47,** 66–82.

Cabot, R. C. Chlorosis. In W. Osler & T. McCrae (Eds.), *Modern medicine.* New York: Lea & Febinger, 1915.

Clarke, E. H. *Sex in education; or, a fair chance for the girls*. Boston: Osgood, 1873.
Dyhouse, C. *Girls growing up in Victorian and Edwardian England*. London: Routledge & Kegan Paul, 1981.
Ehrenreich, B., & English, D. *Complaints and disorders: the sexual politics of sickness*. Old Westbury, N.Y.: Feminist Press, 1973.
Elder, G. H., Jr. Adolescence in historical perspective. In J. Adelson (Ed.), *Handbook of adolescent psychology*. New York: Wiley, 1980.
Figlio, K. Chlorosis and chronic disease in nineteenth-century Britain: the social constitution of somatic illness in a capitalist society. *Social History*, 1978, **3**, 167–197.
Fowler, W. M. Chlorosis—an obituary. *Annals of Medical History*, 1936, **8**, 168–177.
Gillis, J. *Youth and history—tradition and change in European age relation 1770–present*. New York: Academic Press, 1974.
Hall, G. S. *Adolescence* (2 vols.). New York: Appleton, 1904.
Haller, J., & Haller, R. *The physician and sexuality in Victorian America*. Urbana: University of Illinois Press, 1974.
Hertzler, A., & Anderson, H. L. Food guides in the United States. *Journal of the American Dietetic Association*, 1974, **64**, 18–28.
Howard, A. *Medical gynecology*. New York: Appleton, 1908.
Hudson, R. P. The biography of disease: lessons from chlorosis. *Bulletin of History of Medicine*, 1977, **51**, 448–463.
Illich, I. *Medical nemesis*. New York: Bantam, 1977.
Jones, E. L. *Chlorosis: the special anemia of young women*. London: Balliere, Tindall & Cox, 1897.
Kett, J. F. *Rites of passage: adolescence in America 1790 to the present*. New York: Basic, 1977.
Laslett, P. Age of menarche in Europe since the eighteenth century. In T. Rabb & R. Rotberg (Eds.), *The family in history*. New York: Harper & Row, 1971.
Leitch, I. The evolution of dietary standards. *Nutrition Abstracts and Reviews*, 1942, **2**, 509–521.
Leonardo, R. *History of gynecology*. New York: Froben, 1944.
Mead, M. *Coming of age in Samoa*. New York: Morrow, 1928.

Meigs, C. *Females and their diseases*. Philadelphia: Lea & Blanchard, 1848.
Mishler, E., et al. *Social contexts of health, illness and patient care*. New York: Cambridge University Press, 1981.
Money, J., & Ehrhardt, A. E. *Man and woman, boy and girl: the differentiation and dimorphism of gender identity from conception to maturity*. Baltimore: Johns Hopkins, 1972.
Montgomery, J. H. *Clinical observations on cases of simple anemia or chlorosis occurring in young women in the decade following puberty*. Erie, Pa.: Author, 1919.
Morantz, R. The lady and her physician. In M. S. Hartman & L. Banner (Eds.), *Clio's consciousness raised: new perspectives on the history of women*. New York: Harper & Row, 1974.
Pellegrino, E. D. Medicine, history and the idea of man. *Annals of the American Academy of Political and Social Science*, 1963, **346**, 9–20.
Rosenberg, C., & Smith-Rosenberg, C. The female animal: medical and biological views of woman and her role in nineteenth-century America. *Journal of American History*, 1973, **60**, 332–356.
Ruddock, E. H. *The lady's manual of homeopathic treatment*. New York: Smith, 1869.
Sicherman, B. The uses of a diagnosis: doctors, patients and neurasthenia. *Journal of the History of Medicine and Allied Sciences*, 1977, **32**, 33–54.
Siddall, A. C. Chlorosis–etiology reconsidered. *Bulletin of the History of Medicine*, 1982, **56**, 254–260.
Stage, S. *Female complaints: Lydia Pinkham and the business of women's medicine*. New York: Norton, 1979.
Tait, R. L. *Diseases of women*. Philadelphia: Lea, 1889.
Toutain, J. C. *La Consommation alimentaire en France de 1789 à 1964*. Geneva: Droz, 1971.
Veith, I. *Hysteria: the history of a disease*. Chicago: University of Chicago Press, 1965.
Warner, L. *A popular treatise on the functions and diseases of women*. New York: Manhattan, 1875.
Wood, A. D. The fashionable diseases: woman's complaints and their treatment in nineteeth-century America. *Journal of Interdisciplinary History* **4**, 1973, 25–52.

UNDER THE SHADOW OF MATERNITY: AMERICAN WOMEN'S RESPONSES TO DEATH AND DEBILITY FEARS IN NINETEENTH-CENTURY CHILDBIRTH

JUDITH WALZER LEAVITT

In 1846 a young woman in Warren, Pennsylvania, gave birth to a son and soon after was taken with "sinking spells." Her female friends and relatives were there to help her; they took encouragement when she appeared better and consoled each other when she fell into a stupor. A woman who was with her during these days wrote to a mutual friend, describing the scene around Mary Ann Ditmer's bed.

> Oh my beloved Girl – You may imagine our sorrow, for you too must weep with us – How can I tell you: I cannot realize myself – Mary Ann will soon cease to be among the living – and numbered with the dead. . . . Elizabeth, it was such a scene that is hard to be described – L and I remained until the afternoon. Mrs. Mersel came and relieved us, also Mrs. Whalen came. We took a few hours sleep and returned – She had requested us to remain as long as she lived – there was every indication of a speedy termination of her suffering – Mary had come over – Mrs. N remained to watch. . .all thought she was dying – She was very desirous of living till day light – She thought she might have some hope if she could stand it until morning – She retained her sense perfectly – She begged us to be active and not be discouraged that she might live yet – that life was so sweet – how she clung to it – Elizabeth I would wish you might be spared such a sight – we surrounded her dying bed – Each one diligent to keep life and animation in the form of one they so much loved and who at that very time was kept alive with stimulating medicines and wine – I cannot describe it for o my God the horrors of that night will ever remain in the minds of those who witnessed it – our hearts swelled at the sight.[1]

Mary Ann lingered a few days, during which time she bestowed rings and locks of hair upon her friends so they might remember her; she made her peace with God and provided for her child. Then she died. Her story, both in its recognition of the childbirth-related dangers to women's lives and in its revelations of women

Feminist Studies 12, no. 1 (Spring 1986).

helping women, represents a reality visited upon countless numbers of American women in the eighteenth and nineteenth centuries, and it is a reality with supreme significance for understanding women's lives.

In this article I will examine the meaning of maternity's influence over women's lives by analyzing specifically the physical dangers of childbearing and women's responses to those childbirth-related risks. During most of American history, women's anticipation of the possibility of dying or of being permanently injured during childbirth influenced their life expectations and experiences. But women's responses to their repeated and dangerous confinements suggest, instead of resignation to their difficulties, an active participation in shaping events in America's birthing rooms.

Feminists reject the notion that biology is destiny and deny that biological constraints themselves determine the course of women's lives. But feminist historians, looking back at women's experiences, are forced to acknowledge that biology has been a significant factor in setting the limits of life's choices for most women. Specifically, the "shadow of maternity," in the words of many nineteenth-century women,[2] provided the material conditions under which the culturally imposed social parameters of women's lives were defined. Most married women, and many unmarried women, had to face the physical and psychological effects of recurring pregnancies, childbirths, and postpartum recoveries, all of which took a toll on their time, energy, dreams, and bodies. The biological act of maternity, which carried with it severe risks, significantly marked women's lives as they made their way from birth to death. My examination of childbirth's biological domination over women's lives focuses on women's fear of the physical dangers of childbirth and examines the extent to which the fears reflected the reality of their life experiences, but I do not mean to suggest that these fears and dangers encompassed the totality of women's childbirth experiences, or that they alone determined the direction of life's choices. Childbirth had many meanings in women's lives, but this article will focus on the physical dimension of the birthing experience and on the female-centered birthing environment women developed to counteract the potentially deleterious nature of confinement.

My conclusions about biology's influence over women do not

connote biological control, inevitableness, or women's passive acceptance of their fate. In contrast to the work of Edward Shorter,[3] which posits that biology held a stranglehold over women such that they could not escape until twentieth-century medical science came to their rescue, my work emphasizes the decisions women made within their confines to break the boundaries that biology seemed to set. My research reveals women in control of many aspects of their lives, including biological aspects, and I think women's culture developed through these biological bonds – even when those bonds were limiting their other activities. Women's biological functions might have led society to try to circumscribe women's nondomestic activities, but women themselves were not bound by their biological functions. Throughout American history, women struggled to overcome their most significant biological limitations – as they perceived them – ofttimes successfully. The very processes of coping with and trying to change and expand available choices created in some cases improved conditions, but more importantly, the processes created a support system for women that opened wider worlds. Women used the strengths and help of other women to face their problems, and in their unity developed coping mechanisms that were illustrative of what I think can be called a feminist impulse embedded within traditional women's experiences. Feminism did not develop when or because modern medicine saved women from their bodies (as Shorter posits), but, rather, feminist inclinations and the collective behavior they fostered developed out of the basic and shared experiences of women's bodies at times when those bodies seemed most confining and difficult. In this sense, feminism, women grasping control and working together to overcome their commonly experienced burdens, can arise out of the very essence of biological femaleness and reside alongside the most traditional part of women's experiences.[4]

The shadow of maternity, under which so many women lived, has had numerous features, only some of which I will be able to discuss here. Underlying the shadow of maternity most significantly were high fertility rates. At the turn of the nineteenth century, American women bore an average of seven children before their fertile years ended. This implies considerably more than seven pregnancies, because many terminated before term. For many groups in the expanding American population, rates remained high throughout the nineteenth century.[5] Although control over fertility is not the subject of this article, we must view women's past life experiences within the context of limited choices over conception. Pregnancy, birth, and postpartum recovery occupied a significant portion of most women's adult lives, and the ensuing motherhood defined a major part of women's identity.

Take, for example, the life of Mary Vial Holyoke, who married into a prominent New England family in 1759. In 1760, after ten months of marriage, she gave birth to her first baby. Two years later, her second was born. In 1765 she was again "brought to bed" of a child. Pregnant immediately again, she bore another child in 1766. The following year she delivered her fifth, and in one more year delivered her sixth. Free from pregnancy and childbirth in 1769, she gave birth again in 1770. During the next twelve years, she bore five more children. The first twenty-three years of Mary Vial Holyoke's married life, the years of her youth and vigor, were spent pregnant or recovering from childbirth. Because only three of her twelve children lived to adulthood, she withstood, also, frequent tragedies. She devoted her body and her life to procreation throughout her reproductive years. Mary Holyoke had more pregnancies and suffered more child deaths than her average contemporary, and she presents a poignant example of the extreme physical trials women endured. Mary Holyoke had little choice in her frequent pregnancies: her life reveals how the biological capacity of women to bear children historically has translated into life's destiny for individual women.[6]

Mary Holyoke's experience became less common in nineteenth-century America, especially among white women, as fertility rates declined. By 1900, white women, showing the ability to cut their fertility in half over the century, averaged 3.56 children. Historians and demographers trying to understand this decline have suggested that as much as 75 percent of the dropping fertility rate can be explained by active fertility control, including abortion and birth control techniques. Some people seem to have succeeded in asserting partial control over the size of their families, but it is important to keep in mind that the fertility declines demographers have identified with nineteenth-century America apply only to white native-born women; immigrant and black women continued to have babies in larger numbers.[7]

Fertility rates explain only part of the impact of childbirth on women's lives. Maternity cast a shadow greater than its frequent repetition alone could have caused. Maternity, the creation of new life, carried with it the ever-present possibility of death. The shadow that followed women through life was the fear of the ultimate physical risk of bearing children. Young women perceived that their bodies, even when healthy and vigorous, could yield up a dead infant or could carry the seeds of their own destruction. As Cotton Mather had warned at the beginning of the eighteenth century, and as American women continued to believe, conception meant "your *Death* has Entered into you." Nine months' gestation could mean nine months to prepare for death. A possible death sentence came with every pregnancy.[8]

Many women spent considerable time worrying and preparing as if they would not survive their confinements. During Nannie Stillwell Jackson's pregnancy in 1890, she wrote in her diary: "I have not felt well today am afraid I am going to be sick I went up to Fannies a little while late this evening & was talking to her, & I told her to see after Lizzie & Sue [other children] if I was to die & not to let me be buried here . . . & I want Lizzie & Sue to have *everything that is mine,* for no one has as good a rite [*sic*] to what I have as they have."[9] A pregnant Clara Clough Lenroot confided in her diary in 1891: "It occurs to me that *possibly* I may not live. . . . I wonder if I should die, and leave a little daughter *behind* me, they would name her 'Clara.' I should like to have them." Three days later she again was worrying. "If I shouldn't live I wonder what they will do with the baby! I should want Mama and Bertha [sister] to have the bringing up of it, but I should want Irvine [husband] to see it every day and love it so much, and I should want it taught to love him better than anyone else in the world." With the successful termination of the birth, Clara's husband wrote in his wife's diary, "Dear Clara, 'mama and Bertha' won't have to take care of your baby, thank God." He continued, "Everything is all right, but at what cost. My poor wife, how you have suffered, and you have been so brave. . . . I have seen the greatest suffering this day that I have ever known or ever imagined."[10]

When her sister Emma experienced a difficult pregnancy in 1872, Ellen Regal came to be with her and found her "so patient and resigned." Ellen wrote to their brother, "It is not strange that she should tremble and shrink at the thought of that Valley of the Shadow of Death which she must so soon enter." In the middle of the nineteenth century, Lizzie Cabot wrote to her sister when she was pregnant with her first child, "I have made my will and divided off all my little things and don't mean to leave undone what I ought to do if I can help it." Sarah Ripley Stearns, returning from church near her time of confinement, wrote in her diary: "Perhaps this is the last time I shall be permitted to join with my earthly friends."[11]

The extent to which these death fears spread to other family members beyond the parturients is evident in the diary of Albina Wight, whose sister living in another state was pregnant and near confinement. In 1870 Albina wrote, "I am so affraid [*sic*] she won't live through it." Three days later, she continued to think of her sister, "I could not keep Tilda out of my thoughts It has seemed like a funeral all day . . . I fear she is not living."[12]

I could go on with examples of how much some women feared that they might die, but I think the point is made. Young, vigorous, healthy women who should have been anticipating a long life ahead instead faced the very real possibility that their pregnancies would bring their deaths, that in creating a life they would pay with their own.

Women and family members were not the only ones who anticipated maternal death. Many physicians who attended parturients through the fearful hours of labor and delivery also brooded on mortality. In the 1870s, Dr. James S. Bailey of Albany, New York, pondered the sometimes sudden and unexplained deaths of women following childbirth. He wrote: "To see a female, apparently in vigorous health until the period of accouchement, suddenly expire from some unforeseen accident, which is beyond the control of the attending physician, is well calculated to fill the mind with alarm and gloomy forebodings" and make it impossible "while attending a case of confinement, to banish the feeling of uncertainty and dread as to the result of cases which seemingly are terminating favorably."[13] Similarly, Dr. William Lusk, after relating the tragic story of a twenty-three-year-old "very beautiful young woman" who died after delivery, warned his fellow physicians that "the exhausted condition in which the woman is left after childbirth render[s] her an easy prey to the perils of the puerperal state."[14] Fort Wayne, Indiana, physician H.V. Sweringen wrote that "parturition under the most favorable circumstances is attended with great risk."[15] Most physicians and families were well aware of the possibility of death: fears of confinement's dangers permeated society.

The extent to which social fears about maternal deaths reflected a reality of high death rates is almost impossible for historians to determine with any degree of confidence. Graphs of maternal deaths, such as the one below created from New York City data, illustrate that deaths from causes associated with maternity seem to have been declining toward the last part of the nineteenth century. The statistics also show that the maternal death rate leveled out toward the end of the century and continued at a high level (and even increasing) in the twentieth century. But these figures do not tell the whole story. They record the deaths per live births that physicians or other attendents attributed to puerperal causes, but they remain silent on the deaths associated with childbirth, such as from tuberculosis, that physicians did not directly attribute to confinement-related causes. Officials might have recorded that women who died while pregnant or within a month after childbirth died from tuberculosis, which was exacerbated by maternity, when it would be accurate also to have attributed the deaths to maternity-related causes. Even the imperfectly reported maternal deaths and live births are only available for certain parts of the country for certain years in the nineteenth century.[16]

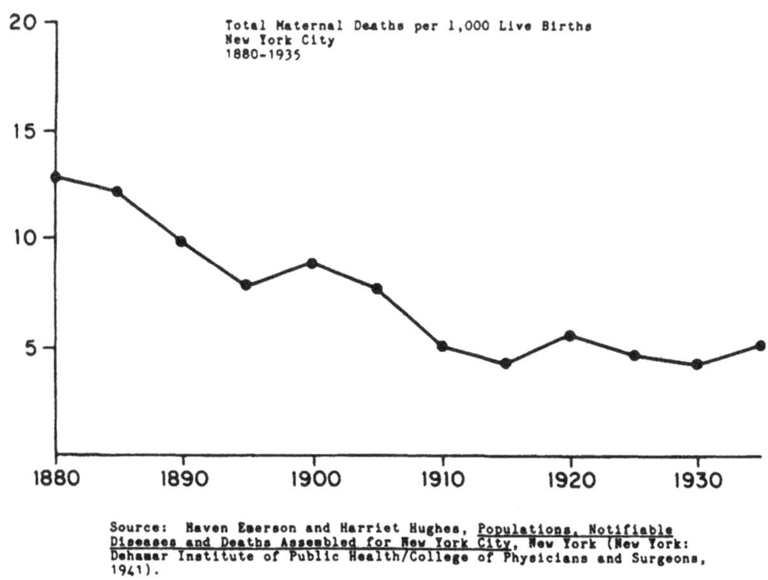

Source: Haven Emerson and Harriet Hughes, Populations, Notifiable Diseases and Deaths Assembled for New York City, New York (New York: Dehamar Institute of Public Health/College of Physicians and Surgeons, 1941).

Perhaps more valuable to our understanding of the reality of maternal death is the observation that most women seemed to know or know of other women who had died in childbirth. One woman, for example, wrote that her friend "died as she has expected to" as a result of childbirth as had six other of their childhood friends. Early in the twentieth century approximately 1 mother died for each 154 live births. If women delivered, let us estimate, an average of five live babies, these statistics can mean that over their reproductive years, one of every thirty women might be expected to die in childbirth. In another early-twentieth-century calculation, one of every seventeen men claimed they had a mother or sister who had died as the immediate results of childbirth.[17]

Despite the real decline in the number of births women endured, and a corresponding but smaller decline in the rate of maternal deaths, women remained fearful of maternity. Women might have been at risk for puerperal death fewer times during their lifetimes, but for them the fear of dying during childbirth continued to influence the possible parameters of their lives. Part of this, I believe, can be explained by the fact that maternal deaths continued at higher than acceptable (that is, preventable) levels. Physicians and women realized that by the turn of the twentieth century deaths from many infectious diseases, such as tuberculosis and diphtheria, were declining, but that deaths from childbirth-related causes remained high. Improvements in living conditions and in medical knowledge about disease transmission seemed to lead to improvements in mortality statistics, except for women in childbirth. Furthermore, maternal mortality statistics from other countries showed that women elsewhere fared better than women in the United States did. In 1910, when the United States recorded that 1 mother died for every 154 babies born alive, Sweden's record showed that 1 mother was lost for every 430 live births.[18]

In the past, the shadow of maternity extended beyond the possibility and fear of death. Women knew that if procreation did not kill them or their babies, it could maim them for life. Postpartum gynecological problems – some great enough to force women to bed for the rest of their lives, others causing milder disabilities – hounded the women who did not succumb to their labor and delivery. For some women, the fears of future debility were more disturbing than fears of death. Vesicovaginal and rectovaginal fistulas (holes between the vagina and either the bladder or the rectum caused by the violence of childbirth or by instrument damage), which brought incontinence and constant irritation to sufferers; unsutured perineal tears of lesser degree, which may have caused significant daily discomforts; major infections; and general weakness and failure to return to prepregnant physical vigor threatened young women in the prime of life. Newly married women looking forward to life found themselves almost immediately faced with the prospect of permanent physical limitations that could follow their early and repeated confinements.

Chicago physician Henry Newman believed that the "normal process of reproduction [is] a formidable menace to the after-health of the parous woman."[19] Lacerations – tears in the perineal tissues – probably caused the greatest postpartum trouble for women. The worst of these, the fistulas, which led to either urine or feces constantly leaking through the vaginal opening without the possibility of control, were, in the words of one sympathetic doctor, "the saddest of calamities, entailing. . .endless suffering upon the poor patient. . .death would be a welcome visitor."[20] Women who had to live with this condition sat sick and alone as long as they lived unless they were one of the beneficiaries of Dr. J. Marion Sims's operation in the second half of the century. Their incontinence made them unpleasant companions, and even their loved ones found it hard to keep them constant company.[21]

More frequent and less debilitating, but still causing major problems for many women, were tears in the vaginal wall or cervix that might have led to prolapsed uterus, uncomfortable sexual intercourse, or difficulties with future deliveries. One physician noted that "the wide-spread mutilation. . .is so common, indeed, that we scarcely find a normal perineum after childbirth."[22] Most perineal lacerations probably were minor and harmless; but if severe ones were not adequately repaired, women might suffer from significant postpartum discomfort.[23] Women complained most frequently of a prolapsed uterus. This displacement of the womb downwards, sometimes even through the vaginal opening, often resulted from lacerations or postpartum relaxation and consequent elongation of the ligaments. One physician noted that fallen womb is often a temporary condition, but he also found it quite common: "Any woman subject to ill turns, lassitude, and general debility will tell you that not unfrequently upon these occasions she is sensible of a falling of the womb."[24] The condition caused misery for women. Albina Wight's sister Eliza, to give just one example from the 1870s, had a difficult delivery that was followed by prolapse. Six weeks following one of her sister's confinements, Albina recorded: "Eliza is sick yet can only walk across the room and that overdoes her. She has falling of the Womb. poor girl." Eliza's medical treatment by "a calomel doctor" who gave her "blue pills" did not help. Five months following the delivery she could only "walk a few steps at a time and cannot sit up all day." A second doctor predicted that "it will be a long time before she will get around again."[25]

The typical treatment for this common female ailment was the use of a pessary, a mechanical support for the uterus inserted into the vagina and left there as long as necessary (see figure 1). Pessaries themselves often led to pelvic inflammations and pain for the women whose conditions they were designed to alleviate. In the opinion of one physician,

> I think it is indisputable that a pessary allowed to remain for a very short period will invariably produce irritation, and if continued longer, will produce almost as certainly, ulceration. I have removed many pessaries that have produced ulceration; one in particular, hollow and of silver gilt, was completely honey combed by corrosion, its interior filled with exuviae of the most horrible offensiveness, the vagina ulcerated through into the bladder, producing a vesico-vaginal fistula, and into the rectum, producing a recto-vaginal fistula; the vagina in some portion obliterated by adhesive inflammation and numerous fistulae made through the labia and around the mons veneris for the exit of the various discharges.[26]

Uterine displacements puzzled physicians and pained women throughout the nineteenth century. A midcentury physician noted that anteflexion, an abnormal forward curvature of the uterus that seemed not amenable to pessary correction, "is the dread of almost every physician, and the constant, painful perplexity of many a patient." He told of his recent case:

> In the winter of 1863, I was consulted by a young lady from a distant part of the State, on account of a disease from which she had suffered for nearly four years. She had received the advice of many a physician of high and low degree – had worn the ring pessary – the globe pessary – the horseshoe pessary – the double S pessary and the intra-uterine stem pessary – and the common sponge. . . . The patient gave a history of frequent inflammation of the uterus and ovaries, and there appeared to be quite strong adhesions

FIGURE 1

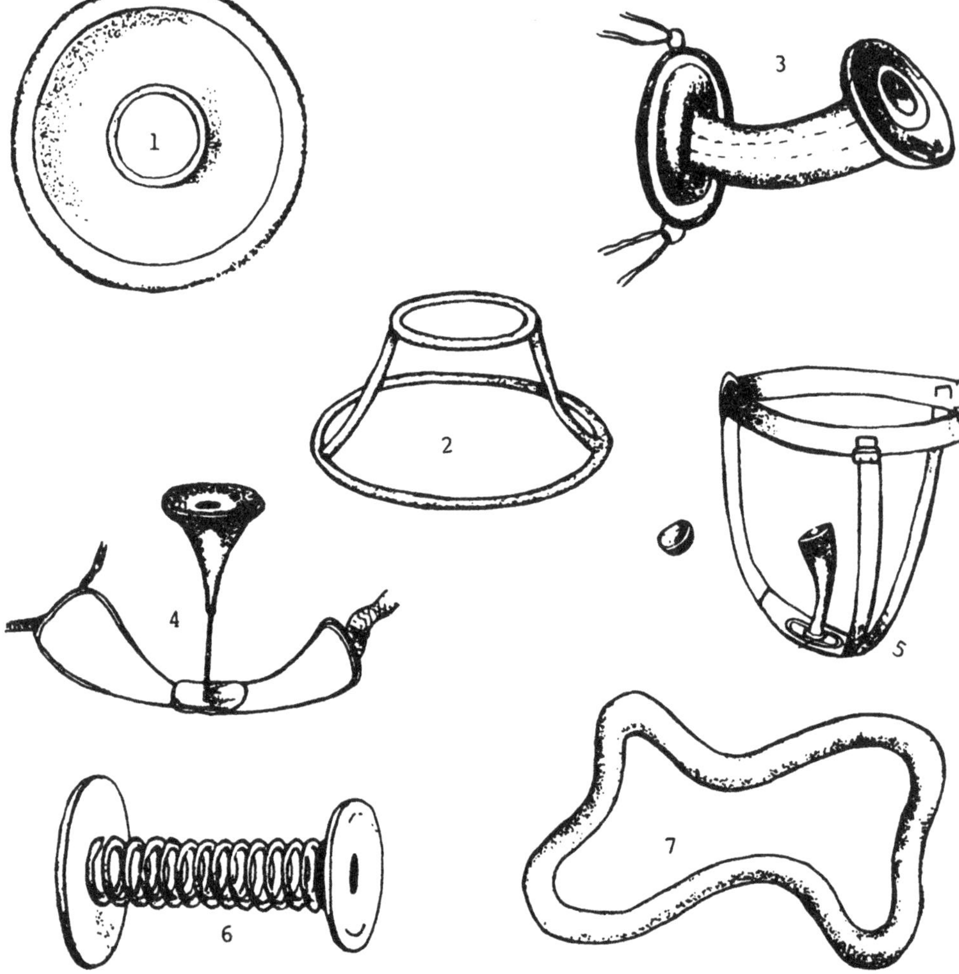

1. Smellie's ring pessary
2. Meig's double ring pessary, of gutta percha
3. Merriam's glass pessary to be fastened externally
4. O'Leary's hard rubber cup, with a screw to regulate its length, resting on a plate secured externally
5. Taft's ball and socket
6. Schaffer's spiral spring
7. Sims' pure, flexible Britannia pessary, capable of being bent in any desired form

SOURCE: Augustus K. Gardner, "On the Use of Pessaries," *Transactions of the American Medical Association* 15 (1865): (109-22).

binding the womb in its assumed place. She had had too frequent menstruation – profuse and intolerably painful – frequent and painful micturition [urination].

The physician inserted his "modified" ring pessary and reported that "the patient went to her home after a few weeks entirely relieved from all bad symptoms."[27]

In the last half of the nineteenth century, physicians reported increased incidence of perineal and cervical lacerations and their accompanying gynecological problems, attributed by many observers to increased use of forceps and other interventions in physician-directed deliveries. If it is true that physicians' interventions caused problems for women in this period (and that is a question I explore elsewhere), it is also the case that physicians became increasingly adept at repairing the problems. The medical journals are filled with case studies of women whose badly managed deliveries had caused them problems, which could then be fixed by superior medical care. For example, an Iowa physician, Dr. Nicholas Hard, reported in 1850 a case he salvaged. A thirty-five-year-old woman "with her first child, having had the forceps applied at an improper time during her labour, suffered from inflammation of the vulva, vagina, and contiguous soft parts, and had a tardy convalescence. . . . The vaginal orifice was perfectly closed. . .she suffered exceedingly from retained catamenial [menstrual] fluid." The doctor instrumentally reopened the vagina and happily reported that his patient now "walks to church, visits, and does house-work."[28]

Women who had already had children were more likely than first-time mothers to worry about the possible aftereffects of labor and delivery. They remembered how long it took them the first time to recover from the birth, they remembered how they had suffered, and they were particularly loath to repeat the ordeal. As one woman wrote about her second pregnancy: "I confess I had dreaded it with a dread that every mother must feel in repeating the experience of child-bearing. I could only think that another birth would mean another pitiful struggle of days' duration, followed by months of weakness, as it had been before."[29]

Apart from their concern about resulting death and physical debility, women feared pain and suffering during the confinement itself. They worried about how they would bear up under the pain and stress, how long the confinement might last, and whether trusted people would accompany them through the ordeal. The short hours between being a pregnant woman and becoming a mother seemed, in anticipation, to be interminably long, and they occupied the thoughts and defined the worries of multitudes of women. Women's descriptions of their confinement experiences foretold the horrors of the ordeal.

Josephine Preston Peabody wrote in her diary of the "most terrible day of [her] life," when she delivered her firstborn, the "almost inconceivable agony" she lived through during her "day-long battle with a thousand tortures and thunders and ruins." Her second confinement brought "great bodily suffering," and her third, "the nethermost hell of bodily pain and mental blankness. . . . The *will-to-live* had been massacred out of me, and I couldn't see why I *had* to."[30] Another woman remembered "stark terror was what I felt most."[31]

"Between oceans of pain," wrote one woman of her third birth in 1885, "there stretched continents of fear; fear of death and dread of suffering beyond bearing."[32] Surviving a childbirth did not allow women to forget its horrors. Lillie M. Jackson, recalling her 1905 confinement, wrote: "While carrying my baby, I was so miserable . . . . I went down to death's door to bring my son into the world, and I've never forgotten. Some folks say one forgets, and can have them right over again, but today I've not forgotten, and that baby is 36 years old."[33] Too many women shared with Hallie Nelson her feelings upon her first birth: "I began to look forward to the event with dread—if not actual horror." Even after Nelson's successful birth, she "did not forget those awful hours spent in labor."[34]

Regardless of the particular fear that women carried along with their swelling uteruses, the end result was similar for all of them. The prospect of often repeated motherhood promised hardship and anxiety. As Hannah Whitall Smith wrote in her diary in 1852:

> I am very unhappy now. The trial of my womanhood which to me is so very bitter has come upon me again. When my little Ellie is 2 years old she will have a little sister or brother. And this is the end of all my hopes, my pleasing anticipations, my returning youthful joyousness. Well, it is a woman's lot and I must try to become resigned and bear it in patience and *silence* and not make my home unhappy because I am so. But oh, how hard it is.[35]

Many women walked with Hannah Smith under the shadow of maternity, experiencing repeated and agonizing births in unrelenting succession with no relief throughout their fertile years.

Many women suffered physical complications through their confinements that stayed with them the rest of their lives. For many women the physical hardships of childbearing determined the parameters of their lives and defined their social destiny. Although it is also true that childbearing and the ensuing motherhood held many happy times for women, it is the difficult part of the experience that created the boundaries within which most women had to construct their lives. The childbirth experience was, of course, heavily influenced by cultural and economic conditions, the particular time and place in which women lived, and their socioeconomic class or ethnic group. But much of the meaning of childbirth for women was determined not by the particulars of the event, but by what women shared with each other by virtue of their common biological experience.

With all the horrors and dangers and worries, women could have easily given up hopes of improving their childbirth experiences or their hard domestic prospects. And no doubt some women did merely resign themselves to lives of invalidism and deprivation. But what comes through the written record much more strongly are the positive aspects of the experience that women chose to emphasize, the caring ways in which they tried to help each other, and the simple fact that women were able to change the childbirth experience for themselves in significant ways throughout the nineteenth century.

Let us examine first the cooperative nature of the labor and delivery experience. Throughout American history up until the twentieth century, when childbirth moved to the hospital, most women gave birth at home with the help of their female friends and relatives. Birth was a women's event, and women eagerly gave their aid when it was needed. Albina Wight, who was unable to attend her sister's confinement, wrote in her diary, "Poor poor girl how I pitty [*sic*] her. She says the two wimen [*sic*] that were there were as kind and good as Sisters could be. I am glad of that . . . Oh how I do wish I could be with her."[36] When possible, sisters and cousins and mothers came to help the parturient through the ordeal of labor and delivery, and close friends and neighbors joined them around the birthing bed. One woman who described her 1866 confinement wrote: "A woman that was expecting had to take good care that she had plenty fixed to eat for her neighbors when they got there. There was no telling how long they was in for.

There wasn't no paying these friends so you had to treat them good."[37] To this women's world, husbands, brothers, or fathers could gain only temporary entrance. In an 1836 account, the new father was invited in to see his wife and new daughter, and then: "But Mrs. Warren, who was absolute in this season of female despotism, interposed, and the happy father was compelled, with reluctant steps, to quit the spot."[38]

Most crucial to the support networks women tried to gather around themselves during and following confinement were their own mothers. "If you could but be with me now, what wouldn't I give," wrote Anita McCormick Blaine to her mother, Nettie Fowler McCormick, in 1890 as she prepared for the birth of her first child. "Dearest mother mine – all would be complete if you were here." Nettie returned the sentiment. "Dearie," she wrote, "I wish I were there to thoroughly rub olive oil upon your hips, your groin muscles, your abdominal muscles all throughout – in short all the muscles that are to be called upon to yield, and be elastic at the proper time. See how reasonable it seems that they should be helped to yield, and to do their work if they are kneaded by the strong hand of mother, while olive oil is being freely applied."[39]

Some women could marshal only one or two women to help them, but many accounts list eight or ten women helpers in addition to the midwife or physician who might be attending. Nannie Jackson, in rural Arkansas in 1890, gathered six women to help when she delivered, and her oldest daughter noted at the time that "Mama had a heap of company today."[40] Antebellum southerner Madge Preston gave birth to a child in 1849, which her husband, who waited in another room, reported this way: "At this birth were present Dr. J.H. Briscoe, Mrs. Margaret Carlon, Mrs. Connolly her friend – our servant Mary Miskel, and our Negroes Lucy and Betty. They inform me that Mrs. P. bore her protracted labor, difficulty, pain and anxiety, which endured forty eight hours, with calmness, courage, and fortitude."[41]

Women went to considerable sacrifice to help their birthing relatives and friends, interrupting their lives to travel long distances and frequently staying months before and after delivery to do the household chores. When relatives were not available, neighbors stayed for the labor and delivery and brought food and kept up with washing and other domestic duties. Christiana Holmes Tillson wrote in her journal of her second confinement in 1825: "I had made the acquaintance of Mrs. Townsend, who was with me and remained until John was a week old."[42] Ann Bolton recalled with enormous fondness and gratitude her good friend: "Of thirteen children which I brought into the world, she bore me company with ten of them."[43] Even in the relatively unusual event of a woman being alone for her delivery, her friends rallied round afterwards to make sure that she got the rest she needed.[44] Women who could not summon friends were described as in this diary entry: "[I] went thence to see Mrs. Ray who has been very ill in Childbed – Had a little girl which died in a few hours. – She is much to be pitied having no female relation or intimate friend to be with her."[45] Another woman pitied herself: "It seemed very gloomy when I found my time had come, to think that I was, as it were, destitute of earthly friends. No mother, no husband, and none of my particular friends that belong to the town; they happening to be out of town."[46]

The women's network that developed at least in part through the strong attachments formed across the childbirth bed had long-lasting effects on women's lives. When women had suffered the agonies of watching their friends die, when they had helped a friend recover from a difficult delivery, or when they had participated in a successful birthing they developed a closeness that lasted a lifetime. Surviving life's traumas together made the crises bearable and produced important bonds that continued to sustain other parts of women's lives. "It was as if mothers were members of a sorority and the initiation was to become a mother," Marilyn Clohessy wrote.[47] Nannie Jackson's female support network offers one example of the importance of good friends. Her diary, only one year of which survives, is a litany of friends helping each other. Her best friend was Fannie, who lived one-half mile away; Nannie and Fannie visited each other daily, and sometimes, two, three, and four times a day. Once, during the eighth month of her third pregnancy, Nannie visited her friend three times in one evening and her husband got angry. But, Nannie noted, "I just talk to Fannie & tell her my troubles because it seems to help me to bear it better when she knows about it. I shall tell her whenever I feel like it."[48] Indeed, in this diary fragment, there is evidence of significant rebellion against her husband's wishes and her strong reliance on her relationship with Fannie. When Nannie was confined, Fannie stayed over with her for four nights. But Fannie is only the most important in a long list of close friends. Nannie, who was white, visited daily with many other women, both white and black, cooking special things for them, sharing the limited family resources, helping them with sewing projects, sitting up with them when they were sick, helping out at births, arranging funerals. These women, whose economically limited lives left nothing for outside entertainment or expense, found rich resources within their own group.

We see that the psychological dimension of the women's network played a significant role in making the difficult lives of these women bearable. Perhaps more significant to these women, however, was the very real support friends could provide during times of crisis. During labor and delivery, when a woman might not be able to stand up for herself, she could rely on her women friends to do her talking for her. Women influenced almost every aspect of birth procedures by having very important on-the-spot input into birth practices for most of the home birth period, and they made significant changes in birth procedures through their collective behavior.

Not until the last half of the eighteenth century did some urban women begin calling in physicians early in normal labor as the major attendants. Yet even then, and throughout the nineteenth century, most women continued to call their women friends and relatives to help them and relied on the advice of the women alongside or before the advice of the physician. Sometimes the women, who were called first, advised that no medical attendant be called. As one physician realized, "A certain amount of inconvenience is anticipated, and so long as this supposed limit is not passed, the patient contrives, with the advice of her female friends, to dispense with a medical attendant."[49] At other times, the attending women suggested additional help. Many physicians attributed their obstetrics calls to midwives or to neighbor women who were already present at a progressing labor. Dr. John G. Meachem, struggling to establish himself after graduating from medical school, recorded a successful first case: "Mrs. Doolittle was present, and I always thought that she had a good deal to do with engineering this call. At least I gave her the credit."[50]

The collectivity of women gathered around the birthing bed made sure that birth attendants were responsive to their wishes. They made decisions about when and if to call physicians to births that midwives were attending; they gave or withheld permission for physicians' procedures; and they created the atmosphere of female support in a room that might have contained both women and men. The result of women's seeming lack of control over biological imperatives was in fact increased control and the ability to influence events.

Women friends were so common and so active in the birthing room that physicians tried to limit them to one or two in their efforts to gain some control over the birth process. Dr. Edward Henry Dixon, for example, wrote in his popular advice book that physicians "mildly, yet firmly exclud[e] from the room all who are not absolutely necessary as attendants."[51] Until birth moved to the hospital, however, physicians shared their authority with neighbor women, most of whom had had significant birth experience. There were times, of course, when the attending women encouraged physicians' interventions. One of Wisconsin's earliest physicians reported his first forceps operation "in the presence of all the old women of the neighbourhood." He was pleased to note that "all the relatives and friends expressed themselves quite satisfied with my exertions & skills."[52]

Often, however, physicians noted ruefully that they did not conrol events in the birthing rooms. One reported that "podalic version [turning the fetus before delivery] was again attempted but was forcibly interfered with by friends."[53] Another physician noted: "The officiousness of nurses and friends very often thwarts the best-directed measure of the physician, by an overweening desire to make the patient 'comfortable'. . . . All this should be strictly forbidden. Conversation should be prohibited the patient . . . . Nothing is more common than for the patient's friends to object to [bloodletting], urging as a reason, that 'she has lost blood enough.' Of this they are in no respect suitable judges."[54] Others wrote that they found it difficult to accomplish aseptic conditions because of the interference of the woman's friends. In fact, the record shows that the parturients' friends and family made decisions about the use of forceps, anesthesia, and other interventions usually considered to be within the control of the attending physician. Physicians went along with the women's demands or risked being removed from the case. One doctor related, for example, why he would not try to shave the pubic hair of his parturient patients. "In about three seconds after the doctor has made the first rake with his safety [razor], he will find himself on his back out in the yard with the imprint of a woman's bare foot emblazoned on his manly chest, the window sash around his neck and a revolving vision of all the stars in the firmament presented to him. Tell him not to try to shave 'em."[55] Dr. John Milton Duff of Pittsburgh unhappily recorded that "the obstetrician can not always control the general environment of his patient," and he worried about her "obstreperousness." This physician lamented the "sometimes dangerous interference of ignorant and superstitious neighbors and friends." His colleague, Dr. Joseph Price of Philadelphia, agreed that "very few households will permit the practice of well-organized and disciplined maternity work."[56]

The power that the friends had did not necessarily result in better care for the parturient, but it does indicate a level of support that the birthing woman could count on. Dr. E.L. Larkins of Terre Haute, Indiana, believed that pressures from these other birth attendants led physicians to poor practices. "The sympathy of attending friends, coupled with the usual impatience of the woman from her suffering, will too often incite even the physician, against his better judgment, to resort to means to hasten labor, resulting in disaster which time and patience would have avoided."[57] But from the birthing women's point of view, this network of women supporting each other through this difficult ordeal assisted them in getting through a situation in which they felt so powerless.[58] One woman concluded that "the most important thing is not to be left alone and to know that someone is there who cares and will help you when the going gets rough."[59] Through their social network, women were able to keep control over childbirth despite the presence and authority of male physicians.

I cannot quantify my findings to say what percentage of women found the kind of support that Nannie Jackson and others developed. Nor can I determine to what extent these friendship networks might have worked better among the middle classes. I can say that I have found them across class and ethnic lines, in the rural areas and in the cities, in the beginning of the nineteenth century and at its end. I am not positing a universal experience. I'm sure that there were countless women who underwent their severest suffering virtually alone or accompanied only by their husbands, with whom they may not have been able to share their deepest feelings. I understand that unremitting poverty took its toll on many suffering women who could not develop even the outlines of a support network. I think, also, that some rich women stood outside a meaningful network of friends, isolated perhaps by their status and background. But personal accounts of childbirth by women and birth attendants suggest that the birth experience was crucial in creating the social dimensions of most women's lives distinct from other socioeconomic factors. Anita McCormick Blaine, living an affluent life in Chicago at the end of the nineteenth century, shared in many respects the birth experience of Nannie Jackson, living in impoverished rural Arkansas at the same time. They both needed, sought, and got the help of their close women friends at the crucial time of their confinements. Although it is certainly true that Blaine had more advantages and more choice in the particulars of the birth experience, to both women the female context in which they delivered their babies was crucial to a successful experience. The biological female experience of giving birth provided women with some of their worst moments and some of their best ones, and the good and the bad were experiences that all women could share with each other.

Despite the very real changes in the technical and physical experience of birth during the nineteenth century, women's perceptions of its dangers and methods of dealing with those dangers within a female-centered protective environment remained very much the same during the course of the time that birth remained in women's homes. When birth moved to the hospital for the majority of American women in the twentieth century, women lost their domestic power base and with it lost certain controls that they had traditionally held. This is the change, as I argue elsewhere, that took away women's traditional controls over childbirth and caused a basic transformation in womens' birth experiences.[60]

The silver lining in maternity's shadow that accompanied the crisis of childbirth during the home birth period – women actively helping each other shape their childbirth experiences – enabled women to find each other, to learn to give solace and support, and to receive them back in turn. It is, in fact, in the combination of shadow and light, of despair and of hope, that we can best view women's procreative experiences. Although the fears and dangers of childbirth followed women, the experience itself opened up new vistas and created practical and emotional bonds beyond the family that sustained them throughout the rest of their lives. Participating together in the function of procreation led women to share with each other some other aspects of their lives in close intimacy. This "female world of love and ritual,"[61] as Carroll Smith-Rosenberg so aptly called it, with its strong emotional and psychological supports and its ability to produce real change in women's lives, was in large part created around women's shared biological moments including repeated confinements and procreative death and debility fears. The valley of the shadow of birth gave women the essence of a good life at the same time it contributed to a strict definition of that life's boundaries. In uniting women, it ultimately provided the ability for women to stretch the boundaries of their world.

NOTES

A grant from the University of Wisconsin Graduate School supported parts of the research for this paper. I would like to thank Evelyn Fine for her excellent research help. Nancy Schrom Dye, Susan Friedman, Ann Gordon, Gerda Lerner, Florencia Mallon, Ronald Numbers, Jane Schulenberg, Steve Stern, and Anne Stoler contributed valuable comments on earlier drafts of the paper, and for these I am very grateful. The editors and readers at *Feminist Studies* provided useful suggestions and aid. I presented a shorter version of the paper at the Sixth Berkshire Conference on the History of Women at Smith College on June 3, 1984.

1. Jane Savine (?) of Warren, Pennsylvania, to Elizabeth Gordon of Cleveland, Ohio, 26 Feb. 1846; see also letter of 10 Mar. 1846, in Elizabeth Gordon Correspondence, Wisconsin State Historical Society Archives, Madison, Wisconsin.
2. See, for example, Augustin Caldwell, *The Rich Legacy: Memories of Hannah Tobey Farmer, Wife of Moses Gerrish Farmer* (Boston: Privately Printed, 1890), 97.
3. Edward Shorter, *A History of Women's Bodies* (New York: Basic Books, 1983).
4. I use the phrases "feminist impulse" and "feminist inclinations" to differentiate this analysis from any confusion with a publicly political feminism as manifested by those women who were active in the suffrage movement or in any public advocacy for women's rights and emancipation. In my interpretation of women's activity in the birthing rooms, women consciously acted to keep childbirth within women's power, where it had traditionally been, when that power was being threatened by a medical profession growing in power and ability in the nineteenth and early twentieth centuries. By banding together to retain female traditions and values and to shape the events in their own birthing rooms, women acted in a way that acknowledged a specific women's agenda. I stop short of labeling the women as feminist, and refer instead to impulses and inclinations, because I think their actions were not consciously creating a new world so much as they were supporting an autonomous women's dimension within the existing one. For historians' debates on these issues, see Ellen DuBois, Mari Jo Buhle, Temma Kaplan, Gerda Lerner, and Carroll Smith-Rosenberg, "Politics and Culture in Women's History: A Symposium," *Feminist Studies* 6 (Spring 1980): 28-64.

5. For the history of birth control and fertility patterns in America, consult Linda Gordon, *Woman's Body, Woman's Right: A Social History of Birth Control in America* (New York: Viking, 1976); James Reed, *From Private Vice to Public Virtue: Birth Control in America* (New York: Basic Books, 1978); Robert V. Wells, *Revolutions in Americans' Lives: A Demographic Perspective on the History of Americans, Their Families, and Their Society* (Westport, Conn.: Greenwood Press, 1982). On the history of childbirth, consult Janet C. Bogdan, "Care or Cure? Childbirth Practices in Nineteenth-Century America," *Feminist Studies* 4 (June 1978): 92-99; Nancy Schrom Dye, "History of Childbirth in America: Review Essay," *Signs* 6 (1980): 97-108; Catherine M. Scholten, "'On the Importance of the Obstetrick Art': Changing Customs of Childbirth in America, 1760-1825," *William and Mary Quarterly* 34 (July 1977): 426-45; Richard W. Wertz and Dorothy C. Wertz, *Lying-In: A History of Childbirth in America* (New York: Free Press, 1977); Jane B. Donegan, *Women and Men Midwives: Medicine, Morality, and Misogyny in Early America* (Westport, Conn.: Greenwood Press, 1978); Judy Barrett Litoff, *American Midwives 1860 to the Present* (Westport, Conn.: Greenwood Press, 1978); and Judith Walzer Leavitt and Whitney Walton, "'Down to Death's Door': Women's Perceptions of Childbirth in America," in *Women and Health in America: Historical Readings*, ed. Judith Walzer Leavitt (Madison: University of Wisconsin Press, 1984), 155-65.
6. *The Holyoke Diaries, 1709-1856*, Introduction and annotations by George Francis Dow (Salem, Mass.: Essex Institute, 1911).
7. Warren C. Sanderson, "Quantitative Aspects of Marriage, Fertility, and Family Limitation in Nineteenth-Century America: Another Application of the Coale Specifications," *Demography* 11 (August 1979): 339-58; Ansley J. Coale and Melvin Zelnik, *New Estimates of Fertility and Population in the United States: A Study of Annual White Births from 1855 to 1960 and of Completeness of Enumeration in the Censuses from 1880 to 1960* (Princeton: Princeton University Press, 1963). Significant variations even among white native-born women suggest that fertility control was exceedingly variable. Southern farm women, for example, continued to bear an average of almost six children at the end of the nineteenth century. In Philadelphia in 1880, German- and Irish-born women bore over seven children during their lives. See Stewart E. Tolnay, Stephen N. Graham, and Avery M. Guest, "Own-child Estimates of U.S. White Fertility, 1886-99," *Historical Methods* 15 (Summer 1982): 127-38; Phillips Cutright and Edward Shorter, "The Effects of Health on the Completed Fertility of Nonwhite and White U.S. Women Born between 1867 and 1935," *Journal of Social History* 13 (Winter 1979): 191-217; Michael R. Haines, "Fertility and Marriage in a Nineteenth-Century Industrial City: Philadelphia, 1850-1880," *Journal of Economic History* 40 (March 1980): 151-58.
8. Cotton Mather, chap. 53, "Retired Elizabeth: A Long tho' no very Hard, Chapter for A Woman whose Travail approaches with Remedies to Abate the Sorrows of Childbearing" (1710), in *The Angel of Bethesda* (Barre, Mass.: American Antiquarian Society, 1972), 235-48; quotations from p. 237.
9. Margaret Jones Bolsterli, ed., entry for July 1890, in *Vinegar Pie and Chicken Bread: A Woman's Diary of Life in the Rural South, 1890-1891* (Fayetteville: University of Arkansas Press, 1982), 38.
10. Clara Clough Lenroot, Journals and Diaries, pt. 1, 1891 to 1929, edited by her daughter, Katharine F. Lenroot, typescript (May 1969) in family hands. My thanks to Katherine Vila, who shared copies of this diary with my class at the University of Wisconsin, Madison, "Women and Health in America" during the spring semester 1983.
11. Ellen Regal to Isaac Demmon, 13 May 1872, Regal Family Collection, Michigan Historical Collection, Bentley Historical Library, University of Michigan; quoted in Carl N. Degler, *At Odds: Women and the Family in America from the Revolution to the Present* (New York: Oxford University Press, 1980), 60. Women also wrote of joyful anticipation and looked forward to surviving their pregnancies and enjoying their

children. Fear seemed a common sentiment among those women who detailed their feelings. It should be noted here that many women chose not to talk at all about their feelings during pregnancy, and if these women differed from their more articulate sisters, their sentiments are lost. Also lost to us are the feelings of women who did not leave any written records of their lives.

12. William Wight Papers, Wisconsin State Historical Society; vols. 11-15 are the diaries of William's wife, Albina Wight, 1869-76. Quotations are from vol. 11, entries for 14, 17 Apr. 1870. See also entry for 13 May 1870.

13. James S. Bailey, "Cases Illustrating Some of the Causes of Death Ocurring Soon after Childbirth," *New York State Medical Society Transactions,* 1872, 121-29; quotation from p. 121. For more on physicians' experiences with sudden puerperal death, see James L. Taylor, "What Killed the Woman?" *Journal of the American Medical Association* 14 (14 June 1890): 876-77; Fayette Dunlap, "Sudden Death in Labor and Childbed," *Journal of the American Medical Association* 9 (1887): 330-34; Edward W. Jenks, "The Causes of Sudden Death of Puerperal Women," *Transactions of the American Medical Association* 29 (1878): 373-91.

14. William Thompson Lusk, "On Sudden Death in Labor and Childbed," *Journal of the American Medical Association* 3 (1884): 427-31.

15. H.V. Sweringen, "Laceration of the Female Perineum," *Transactions of the Indiana State Medical Society* 32 (1882): 135. I am grateful to Ann Carmichael for this reference.

16. Haven Emerson and Harriet E. Hughes, *Populations, Notifiable Diseases and Deaths, Assembled for New York City, New York* (New York: DeLamar Institute of Public Health, College of Physicians and Surgeons, 1941) and *Supplement 1936-1953* (January 1955). I would like to thank Gretchen Condran and Morris Vogel, who brought these volumes to my attention, and Evelyn Fine, who decifered the figures and drew the graph. The figures are for New York City and not meant to be representative of the rest of the country, although the trend shown in these figures was probably similar outside the city. Statistics gathered by the Metropolitan Board of Health in New York after 1866 were more complete than those gathered for other cities or states.

17. The use of the figure five births per married woman in the United States is not far off the mark, and may in fact be low, given that the 3.56 recorded average includes only white and mostly native-born women. The Northwestern Mutual Life Insurance Company recorded that of 10,000 applicants for life insurance, "one man in every 17.3 who applied for insurance had a mother or sister or both who died from the immediate effects of childbirth." The May 1920 *Crusader* noted: "It is believed that a considerable percentage of these deaths from childbirth were recorded on the death certificate as being due to tuberculosis, heart disease, etc., and that the applicant for insurance remembered the associated childbirth and not the cause of death given on the death certificate. Our present mortality records do not show the frequency with which childbirth is a contributing cause of death" (5). See also C.W. Earle's comments during a Chicago Medical-Legal Society discussion of J.H. Etheridge, "The Medico-Legal Aspect of Utterances Made in Medical Societies," *Journal of the American Medical Association* 10 (5 May 1888): 570. The quotation is Anne Lesley, in Susan Inches Lesley, *Recollections of My Mother* (Boston: Press of George H. Ellis, 1889), 306.

18. I explore this issue in "'Science' Enters the Birthing Room: Obstetrics in America since the Eighteenth Century," *Journal of American History* 70 (September 1983): 281-304. See also Janet Bogdan, "The Mortality Experience of Nineteenth-Century New York City Women" (Paper presented at the Sixth Annual Berkshire Conference on the History of Women at Smith College, 3 June 1984). International comparisons of maternal mortality can be found in Grace L. Meigs, *Maternal Mortality from All Conditions Connected with Childbirth in the United States and Certain Other Countries,* Children's Bureau Publication no. 6 (Washington, D.C.: GPO, 1917). Women became aware of continuing

high maternal deaths in part from their own experience and in part from articles appearing in popular health journals such as the *Crusader* and in women's journals. See, for example, S. Josephine Baker, "Why Do Our Mothers and Babies Die?" *Ladies' Home Journal* 39 (April 1922): 32, 174.

19. Henry Parker Newman, "Prolapse of the Female Pelvic Organs," *Journal of the American Medical Association* 21 (2 Sept. 1893): 335.

20. S.D. Gross, "Lacerations of the Female Sexual Organs Consequent upon Parturition: Their Causes and Their Prevention," *Journal of the American Medical Association* 3 (1884): 337-38.

21. J. Marion Sims developed the surgical repair of the vesicovaginal fistula through his experiments on slave women in the 1840s; it gathered adherents in the second half of the nineteenth century and relieved many women of their suffering. See, for example, J. Marion Sims, *The Story of My Life* (New York: D. Appleton & Company, 1889); Seale Harris, *Woman's Surgeon: The Life Story of J. Marion Sims* (New York: MacMillan Co., 1950); Irwin H. Kaiser, "Reappraisals of J. Marion Sims," *American Journal of Obstetrics and Gynecology* 132 (15 Dec. 1978): 878-84.

22. J. O. Malsbery, "Advice to the Prospective Mother: Assistance during Her Confinement and Care for a Few Days Following," *Journal of the American Medical Association* 28 (15 May 1897): 932.

23. On postpartum lacerations, see, for example, the following articles in the *Journal of the American Medical Association*: Charles P. Noble, "The Causation of Diseases of Women," vol. 21 (16 Sept. 1893): 410-14; John C. Da Costa, "An Easy Method of Repairing the Perineum," vol. 13 (2 Nov. 1889): 645-47; Henry T. Byford, "The Production and Prevention of Perineal Lacerations during Labor, with Description of an Unrecognized Form," vol. 6 (6 Mar. 1886): 253-57, 271; and H.V. Sweringen, "Laceration of the Female Perineum," vol. 5 (15 Aug. 1885): 173-77. See also the discussion of this last paper in the *Transactions of the Indiana State Medical Society*, 258-264, during which Dr. Woolen of Indianapolis blamed physicians' interventions for the increased rate of perineal tears in women: "The frequent use of forceps is filling the country full of cases for our gynecologists, and it does seem to me that we are making a mistake" (263). Physicians, anxious to clear themselves of possible blame, more frequently named the baby's hard head rather than the hard forceps as the principal agent. Regardless of agent, however, the state of medical knowledge about repairing such damage remained at issue.

24. Augustus K. Gardner, "On the Use of Pessaries," *Transactions of the American Medical Association* 15 (1865): 110.

25. Albina Wight Diary, vol. 11: entries of 20 Aug., 6 and 9 Oct. 1873; 18 Jan. 1874. Gerda Lerner noted that Angelina Grimke suffered from prolapsed uterus and other postpartum complications following the birth of her second child, and the biographies of numerous other famous and not famous women indicate the problem was a common one. Gerda Lerner, *The Grimke Sisters from South Carolina: Pioneers for Woman's Rights and Abolition* (New York: Houghton Mifflin, 1967), 288-92.

26. Gardner, 113.

27. Homer O. Hitchcock, "A Modified Ring Pessary for the Treatment and Cure of Anteflexion and Anteversion of the Uterus," *Transactions of the American Medical Association* 15 (1865): 103-106.

28. Reported in "Midwifery" section, *Transactions of the American Medical Association* 6 (1851): 361. I address the debate concerning physicians' blame for women's postpartum problems in "'Science' Enters the Birthing Room" and in *Brought to Bed: Birthing Women and Their Physicians in America 1750-1950* (Oxford University Press, forthcoming). For some contemporary comment, see Hiram Corson, "On the Statistics of 3,036 Cases of Labor," *Journal of the American Medical Association* 7 (31 July 1886): 138-39.

29. Agnes Just Reid, *Letters of Long Ago* (Caldwell, Idaho: Caxton Printers, 1936), 24.

30. Christina Hopkinson Baker, ed., *Diary and Letters of Josephine Preston Peabody* (Boston: Houghton Mifflin Company, 1925), 214-15, 226-29.
31. Elsa Rosenberg to the author in response to author's query in the *New York Times Book Review*, 30 July 1983.
32. Elizabeth [illegible]. Emerson, *Glimpses of a Life* (Burlington, N.C.: J.S. Sargent & Co., 1960), 4-5.
33. Lillie M. Jackson, *Fanning the Embers* (Boston: Christopher Publishing House, 1966), 90-91.
34. Hallie F. Nelson, *South of the Cottonwood Tree* (Broken Bow, Neb.: Purcells, 1977), 173.
35. This diary entry is all the more poignant because it influenced two generations in this family. Hannah Whitall Smith's niece, M. Carey Thomas, found the journal and was so moved by it that she copied it into her own diary in 1878. Marjorie Housepian Dobkin, ed., *The Making of a Feminist: Early Journals and Letters of M. Carey Thomas* (Kent, Ohio: Kent State University Press, 1979). Hannah Smith's diary entry was dated 20 Dec. 1852, and Thomas copied it on 1 Sept. 1878, p. 149.
36. Albina Wight Diary, vol. 11, 14 Apr. 1870.
37. Malinda Jenkins, *Gambler's Wife: The Life of Malinda Jenkins*, as told in conversations to Jessie Lilienthal (Boston: Houghton Mifflin Co., 1933), 48.
38. Elizabeth Elton Smith, *The Three Eras of Woman's Life* (New York: Harper & Brothers, 1836), 85.
39. Anita McCormick Blaine to Nettie Fowler McCormick; Nettie Fowler McCormick to Anita McCormick Blaine, both in August 1890. McCormick Family Papers, series 1E, box 459; series 2B, box 46, Wisconsin State Historical Society.
40. Entries for 15, 16, 17 Aug. 1890, Bolsterli, 60-61.
41. William P. Preston to his daughter, May, on her fifteenth birthday, 19 May 1864, from the collection of the McKeldin Library Archives and Manuscripts, University of Maryland, College Park. I would like to thank Virginia Beauchamp for sending me this reference from her forthcoming book, *The Language of Silence: Madge Preston's Story*.
42. Christiana Holmes Tillson, *A Woman's Story of Pioneer Illinois*, ed. Milo Milton Quaife (Chicago: Lakeside Press, 1919), 128.
43. *The Life of Mrs. Robert Clay, Afterwards Mrs. Robert Bolton (Nee Ann Curtis), 1690-1738* (Philadelphia, 1928), 154.
44. Laura B. Gaye, *Laugh on Friday, Weep on Sunday: One Woman's Reminiscence* (Calabassas, Calif.: Loma Palaga Press, 1968), 55; May Harley, *Whither Shall I Go: A Story of an Itinerant Circuit Rider's Wife* (Southold, N.Y.: Academy Printing Services, 1975), 76.
45. Anna Maria Thornton, Diary of Mrs. William Thornton, 1800-1863, *Records of the Columbia Historical Society* 10 (1907): 100.
46. *Esther Burr's Journal* (Washington, D.C.: Howard University Print, 1903).
47. Marilyn Clohessy to the author, 9 Sept. 1983, in response to author's query in the *New York Times Book Review*.
48. Entry of 27 June 1890, Bolsterli, 35.
49. Fleetwood Churchill, *The Diseases of Females: Including Those of Pregnancy and Childbed*, 4th American ed. (Philadelphia: Lea & Blanchard, 1847), 340.
50. John G. Meachem, Sr., Papers 1823-1896, State Historical Society of Wisconsin, Autobiography, box 1, p. 6. See also Carl Binger, *Revolutionary Doctor: Benjamin Rush, 1746-1813* (New York: W. W. Norton & Co., 1966), 77.
51. Edward Henry Dixon, *Woman and Her Diseases from the Cradle to the Grave*, 10th ed. (Philadelphia: G.G. Evans, 1860), 261.
52. Letter from Dr. Thomas Steel to his father, 12 Dec. 1844, in the Steel Collection at the State Historical Society of Wisconsin. I am grateful to Peter Harstad for calling my

attention to Steel's obstetrical cases. For more of this kind of evidence see Leavitt, "'Science' Enters the Birthing Room."
53. Reported in James A. Harrar, *The Story of the Lying-In Hospital of the City of New York* (New York: Society of the Lying-In Hospital, 1938), 34. On the point of rebellion of women inside the hospital as well as outside, see Nancy Schrom Dye, "Scientific Obstetrics and Working-Class Women: The New York Midwifery Dispensary" (Paper delivered at the American Historical Association, San Francisco, December 1983).
54. Dixon, 262.
55. S.H. Landrum, Altus, Oklahoma, letter to the editor, *Journal of the American Medical Association* 58 (1912): 576. I would like to thank Carolyn Hackler for calling this letter to my attention.
56. John Milton Duff, "Parturition as a Factor in Gynecologic Practice," *Journal of the American Medical Association* 35 (25 Aug. 1900): 465. Price's comment came during the discussion of Duff's paper, p. 467.
57. E.L. Larkins, "Care and Repair of the Female Perineum," *Journal of the American Medical Association* 32 (11 Feb. 1899): 284.
58. See "'Science' Enters the Birthing Room" for more examples of physicians lack of control in home deliveries.
59. Clohessy to the author.
60. Discussed in "Alone among Strangers: Childbirth Moves to the Hospital" (Paper delivered at the American Historical Association Annual Meeting, San Francisco, December 1983); and Leavitt, *Brought to Bed*.
61. Carroll-Smith Rosenberg, "The Female World of Love and Ritual: Relations between Women in Nineteenth-Century America," *Signs* 1 (1975): 1-29.

THE AMERICAN MIDWIFE CONTROVERSY: A CRISIS OF PROFESSIONALIZATION

FRANCES E. KOBRIN

Although medicine itself has long been an established profession, many of the specialties within medicine have a much shorter history. This diversification is a result not simply of developments within the field itself but has also depended upon the attitude of potential patients—their feeling of a need for such specialization and their ability to take advantage of it. The role of his external factor, however, has varied considerably in the historical development of the several specialties. Surgery became differentiated as soon as the techniques developed enabling it to be practiced safely, whereas other specialties, such as dermatology, plastic surgery, or orthodontics, had to wait until a public attitude evolved which considered ills far less serious than malaria (itself once thought a natural state) as unnatural conditions which require treatment.

Such a specialty was obstetrics, which dealt with what many still consider to be the "natural process" *par excellence.* In the obstetricians' struggle for universal acceptance they faced both medical and non-medical competition and an almost insuperable economic problem; the level of even the best obstetrical work was almost more of a hindrance than a help. The decade from about 1908 began the contest between the increasingly self-conscious obstetrical specialist and his adversaries, the midwife and her advocates. That such a debate could be carried on with great virulence is itself indicative of the importance of considerations other than the strictly medical. The result, the complete defeat of the United States' variety of midwife and the essential triumph of a "single standard of obstetrics," was not simply a function of the maturity of the obstetric profession.

In the United States in 1910, about 50% of all births were reported by midwives,[1] and the percentage for large cities was often higher. At the same time, and continuing well beyond this peak period, the maternal death rate in the United States was the third highest of countries which kept such records.[2] Midwives were employed primarily by Negroes and by the foreign-born and their children, and the midwives themselves

[1] Thomas Darlington, "The present status of the midwife," *Am. J. Obst. & Gynec.*, 1911, *63*: 870.
[2] E. R. Hardin, "The midwife problem," *South. M. J.*, 1925, *18*: 347.

usually shared race, nationality, and language with their customers.[3] Because this was a period of unrestricted and heavy immigration (one-third of the population was foreign-born or Negro),[4] the midwife population was swollen considerably.

At this time also, various local medical units in the nation began to assess the situation in their areas, and this resulted in a flood of articles and addresses on " the midwife problem in ———." The big eastern cities, most affected by the heavy immigration, were the most diligent in this regard and produced the bulk of the available data. In 1906, New York commissioned a study which revealed that the New York midwife was essentially medieval, very different from European midwives, for these did not emigrate as rapidly as those who expected such service. According to this report, fully 90% were " hopelessly dirty, ignorant, and incompetent." [5] These revelations resulted in the tightening up of existing legislation, and the creation of new, for the licensing and supervision of midwives and eventually in the establishment of the Bellevue School for Midwives, an institution which lasted for thirty years. Other areas reported similar conditions.

The major failing of the midwife, which this legislation was to correct, was responsibility for maternal deaths from puerperal sepsis and for neonatal ophthalmia, both preventable with the knowledge available at the time. But it became clear during the controversy that occurred over how to deal with this problem that the midwife was by no means the sole offender in these matters. A survey of professors of obstetrics reached the conclusion that general practitioners were at least as negligent as midwives, as well as being equally responsible for preventable deformities.[6] The overall picture of the obstetrical possibilities open to a prospective patient was not very good. Hospitalization was impossible for all but the very rich or the charity cases in the wards, obstetricians were few, and general practitioners unreliable. Use of a midwife involved many hazards, despite the fact that she was usually a sympathetic woman who would wait and work with the natural labor process (often, of course, for too long) and would also in many cases be in regular attendance for more than a week afterwards, not only caring for mother and infant, but

[3] See nearly any discussion of the subject at this period, e.g., Darlington, *loc. cit.*; J. Clifton Edgar, "The remedy for the midwife problem," *Am. J. Obst. & Gynec.*, 1911, *63*: 882.

[4] Darlington, *ibid.*

[5] Edgar, *loc. cit.*

[6] J. Whitridge Williams, "Medical education and the midwife problem in the United States," *J. A. M. A.*, 1912, *58*: 1-7.

also assuming such duties as were necessary to keep the household functioning normally.

The most obvious cause of this medically unsatisfactory situation was the general opinion that the midwife was an adequate birth attendant. Her success was due to the fact that the rigors of childbirth were still considered normal and risks in the process unavoidable. The general attitude was that nature really controlled the process so that there was little constructive assistance that could be given. This feeling was clearly dominant among the public, although there were signs of change; it was also an important attitude within the medical profession as a whole. One observer, in assessing the lack of interest in obstetrics generally, noted that the word " obstetrics " comes from a Latin word meaning " to stand before " and added, " or as a sneering colleague once said, ' to stand around.' " [7]

The best evidence that this was the judgment of the medical profession was the status of the teaching of obstetrics in United States medical schools. Dr. J. Whitridge Williams, professor of obstetrics at Johns Hopkins University, made a comprehensive report on obstetrics as it was studied in United States medical schools in 1912; he found that although medical schools had been improving rapidly, obstetrics was by far the weakest area.[8] He sent a questionnaire to professors of obstetrics of 61 schools rated by the American Medical Association as acceptable (they required entrants to have at least a high school degree) and to 59 non-acceptable schools, receiving 32 and 11 replies respectively. Among his results were the following: Of the 42 professors of obstetrics, only five limited their outside practice to obstetrics, 21 to obstetrics and gynecology, and 17 were in general practice. Only ten had served in lying-in hospitals for more than six months. Only nine had seen more than a thousand cases of labor as preparation for their post, 13 had seen fewer than 500, five fewer than 100, and one had never seen a woman deliver. Six schools had no connection whatsoever with a lying-in hospital for teaching purposes, and only nine had as many as 500 cases a year for teaching material. The average medical student witnessed but one delivery, and the average for the best 20 medical schools was still only four. Half the schools required a period of service of less than a year in training assistants for

[7] C. E. Ziegler, "How can we best solve the midwifery problem," *Am. J. Pub. Health*, 1922, *12*: 409.

[8] Abraham Flexner came to much the same conclusion in his discussion of the clinical years in American medical schools. *Medical Education in the United States and Canada: A Report to the Carnegie Foundation for the Advancement of Teaching*. Bulletin no. 4. New York, 1910, p. 117.

their own staff, a level, according to Williams, at which a student is still unable to recognize, much less cope with, a serious emergency. Several of the professors admitted that they themselves were incapable of performing a Caesarean section. Williams concluded that there was only one medical school in the country properly equipped for teaching obstetrics, and he regretted that it was not Johns Hopkins. The result of this neglect of obstetrics, he saw clearly, was that poor schools with poor facilities and poor professors were turning out incompetent products who lost more patients from improper practices than midwives did from infection.[9]

But the obstetricians themselves were fighting this conception of the insignificance of their field. They argued again and again that normal pregnancy and parturition are exceptions and that to consider them to be normal physiologic conditions was a fallacy.[10] It was this view which contributed to much of the unnecessary operative interference that occurred in this period. Amused critics pointed out that women often delivered themselves while their doctors were scrubbing up for a Caesarean,[11] but other results, such as the use of high forceps previous to sufficient dilation, were less fortunate for the health of mother or child.

It was these two fundamentally different approaches to the process of childbirth, based on opposite views of its naturalness, which were responsible for many of the arguments which appeared during this period about the future of the midwife. At one extreme were those who advocated outright abolition of midwives, with legal prosecution of those who continued to practice. This was the official attitude of the state of Massachusetts and also that of most eminent obstetricians.[12] Less adamant was a second group, led by Dr. W. R. Nicholson of the Pennsylvania Bureau of Medical Education and Licensure, which favored eventual abolition, with the existing midwives closely regulated until substitutes could be furnished. A third group was pessimistic about ever abolishing the midwife and thus felt that regulation plus education would elevate the midwife to the relatively safe status she had achieved in England and on the continent. This attitude was reported from Newark, New York State generally, and New York City and Buffalo particularly. Finally, there were those, especially in the South, who felt that if, somehow, midwives could be made to wash their hands and use silver nitrate for the babies'

[9] Williams, *op. cit.*, ftn. 6 above.

[10] See for example, J. F. Moran, "The endowment of motherhood," *J.A.M.A.*, 1915, *64*: 126; J. L. Huntington, "The midwife in Massachusetts: her anomalous position," *Boston M & S. J.*, 1913, *168*: 419.

[11] "Discussion—midwife problem," *New York State J. Med.*, 1915, *15*: 300.

[12] For an impressive list, see Huntington, *op. cit.*, ftn. 10 above, p. 420.

eyes, that would, because of a host of economic and cultural reasons, be the most that could be expected.[13]

Since all but those who held the first position believed that at present there really was no substitute for the midwife, and thus she had at least temporarily to be endured, their views can be conveniently called the public health approach. Their concern was for the immediate future. The first group based its arguments on the necessity of developing obstetrics for the long-term good of American mothers, and so can be identified with the professional approach. An early analyst of this division in medical opinion described it as a conflict between the practical and the ideal,[14] but the actual arguments involved a great deal more than that.

The public health exponents did, in fact, always claim to be realistic, and they accused the professionals of "criminal negligence." [15] The aspects of the situation which they were in a position to consider were certainly important. Since midwives were registering 50% of all births, it did not seem likely that the medical profession could expand sufficiently to take care of all. Some public health officials were not even sure that such expansion was desirable. Arguments against it included the record of the medical profession as a whole, the economic problem of supporting the higher prices charged by doctors, and the attitude of the women themselves. There was also a subterranean problem of status: doctors were often considered less manageable than the more easily supervised midwife.[16]

With regard to the question whether the medical profession ever could absorb all the obstetric cases, Dr. Florence E. Kraker of the Children's Bureau in Washington felt that the midwife problem would actually grow as the preference for hospitals and laboratories among doctors increased, causing them to desert rural areas.[17] Even if sufficient expansion were possible, it would still be necessary, according to New York City Public Health official Dr. S. Josephine Baker, to keep midwives and make them safe, because immigrant women, and particularly their husbands, would allow no male attendants. They expected the simple nursing care and household help that a doctor would not provide, and for this they expected to pay the customary small fee. Providing only doctors for these groups

[13] W. A. Plecker, "The midwife problem in Virginia," *Virginia M. Semi-Monthly*, 1914-1915, *19*: 457-458; Jeidell and Fricke, "The midwives of Anne Arundel County, Maryland," *Johns Hopkins Hosp. Bull.*, 1912, *23*: 279-281.

[14] A. K. Paine, "The midwife problem," *Boston M. & S. J.*, 1915, *173*: 760.

[15] Clara D. Noyes, "The training of midwives in relation to the prevention of infant mortality," *Am. J. Obst. & Gynec.*, 1912, *66*: 1053.

[16] *Loc. cit.*, ftn. 11 above.

[17] Hardin, *op. cit.*, ftn. 2 above, p. 349.

would force them either to pay a higher fee or to use clinics with their implication of charity. Above all, they rejected hospital delivery, which would badly upset the home situation.[18]

What encouraged the proponents of the public health view most was the actual progress which had been made through legal recognition, education, and supervision of midwives. England was the chief source of inspiration, since Parliament had, as recently as 1902, established a Central Midwives Board "to secure the better training of midwives and to regulate their practice." Following this change, infant mortality, which had been 151 per 1000 in 1901, dropped to 106, in 1910, with a commensurate decrease in maternal mortality.[19] A committee of the Russell Sage Foundation, after studying the results, was entirely in favor of the change. In particular, they found that rather than replacing obstetrical practice with trained midwives, it had "increased, improved, and upheld the work of the obstetrician."[20] Germany was also much admired by those of public health persuasion, since the midwife there was a scrupulously regulated institution, trained in government clinics and working in a set district in a defined relationship with a government doctor.[21] The level of obstetric training received by German midwives was recognized as superior to that of most United States doctors.[22]

Major progress had also been made in the United States itself. Newark, after adopting a program of "conference, lectures and personal visits," reported a drop in the three years, 1914-1916, in maternal mortality from 5.3 to 2.2 per 1000 for the city as a whole, and a level of 1.7 per 1000 among mothers who "received prenatal supervision from the Child Hygiene Division and were delivered by midwives." This was aggressively compared with the rate of 6.5 for Boston, where midwives were banned. For 1916, again, Newark's infant mortality rate below one month was 8.5 for the special category, as opposed to a city rate of 36.4. The reporting of births was greatly improved, silver nitrate was in universal use, and Board of Health Officer Levy was highly pleased with his results.[23] In Philadelphia a similar program, which emphasized in addition control through registration, gave its director "hope to show statistics unequaled

[18] Josephine Baker, "The function of the midwife," *Woman's M. J.*, 1913, *23*: 197.

[19] Noyes, *op. cit.*, ftn. 15 above, p. 1054.

[20] *Ibid.*, p. 1052.

[21] A. B. Emmons and J. L. Huntington, "The midwife: her future in the United States," *Am. J. Obst. & Gynec.*, 1912, *65*: 395-396.

[22] Hardin, *op. cit.*, ftn. 2 above, p. 347; Emmons and Huntington, *op. cit.*, p. 395.

[23] Julius Levy, "The maternal and infant mortality in midwifery practice in Newark, N. J.," *Am. J. Obst. & Gynec.*, 1918, *77*: 42.

in the history of the world." [24] Midwives, more secure in their licensed status, were calling doctors earlier and oftener, neonatal ophthalmia had vanished, and all at relatively little cost.

Besides pragmatically recognizing the midwife's possibilities, many of her promoters felt a strong sympathy for her and her deficiencies. Ira S. Wile defended her on the grounds that it was " unfair to criticize the lack of an educational standard which has never been established." He felt that abolition was no more the answer than it had been for nurses of the " Sairy Gamp type," eighteenth century doctors, or present-day obstetricians, all of whom, by absolute standards, were very bad indeed.[25] Midwives also gained sympathy from their adherents because of the rudeness with which the " arrogant," " unrealistic " obstetricians treated them. Those most in favor of the midwife seemed bent on elevating her to a professional status well above that of a nurse. Recognition was to build self-respect and pride; caste and dignity would bring a more intelligent type of woman into the profession.[26]

It was with these general attitudes that the public health exponents faced the task of elevating the American midwife. The consensus which developed was that midwives should have training for at least six months to a year, including instruction on pregnancy, asepsis, care of labor, and of mother and child after confinement, and, above all, recognition of conditions that indicate when a doctor is needed. These requirements, coupled with legal proscriptions against vaginal examinations, drugs other than laxatives, douches, and the use of instruments, would, they felt, render the midwife a useful member of the community. The further elaboration of linking the midwife to a clinic and to a physician who would make examinations and be available for emergencies was advocated by some, but the problem of maintaining doctors in government employ presented such difficulties that many public health officials were forced to ignore the possibility that a doctor might not be available when needed.[27]

What is important in the plans discussed and occasionally established by public health officials is that in general these men were not simply embracing a distasteful necessity that would otherwise have been avoided. There were some, of course, who felt this way: the official who established the Philadelphia system was well aware of " the incongruity of allowing

[24] W. R. Nicholson, " The midwife situation . . . ," *Tr. Am. Gynec. Soc.*, 1917, *42*: 632.
[25] " Schools for midwives," *M. Rec.*, 1912, *81*: 517.
[26] *Ibid.*, p. 518.
[27] See, among others, Hardin, *op. cit.*, ftn. 2 above, p. 349; Plecker, *op. cit.*, ftn. 13 above, p. 457; J. A. Foote, " Legislative measures against maternal and infant mortality," *Am. J. Obst. & Gynec.*, 1919, *80*: 550; Edgar, *op. cit.*, ftn. 3 above, p. 883.

or actively sanctioning by license, the doing of distinctly medical work by non-medical persons. We cannot adduce a single argument in its favor except . . . *necessity*." [28] But the others were expressing an ideal of obstetric service whereby the ubiquitous process of childbirth could be carried on cheaply and easily, respecting modesty and the integrity of the household, and in a more natural and personal way than if rendered by doctors.

The solution offered by the obstetric profession, on the other hand, was not merely an ideal of obstetric care, but also a very realistic solution for the obstetricians' difficulties. Until this last great wave of immigration, graduating obstetricians had always found sufficient numbers of patients. J. L. Huntington, a Boston obstetrician who was partly responsible for Massachusetts' unique position and was the most vocally concerned of the professionals, observed that the midwife was not—yet—a native product of America. She comes with the immigrant, " but as soon as the immigrant is assimilated, . . . then the midwife is no longer a factor in his home." [29] It was this latest influx of immigrants from southern Europe which had given the midwife problem such dimensions, and, if left alone, her numbers would again dwindle with the slowing of immigration. But if she were given official recognition so that immigrants' sons and grandsons expected such service for their wives, the obstetric profession would, he felt, face grave difficulties. Huntington believed, therefore, that the greatest danger in recognizing the midwife lay in the effect of such recognition on the general public. If the midwife was sufficient, then calling a G. P. would be the height of caution, and there would be no need felt for obstetricians.[30] He and other obstetricians believed recognition of midwives would set the progress of obstetrics back tremendously. The 50% of all cases handled by midwives were useless for advancing obstetrical knowledge. Elevating the midwife and training her would decrease the number of cases in which the stethoscope, pelvimeter, and other newly developed or newly applied techniques could be used to increase obstetrical knowledge. The need for strengthening obstetrics courses in medical schools would diminish, and practicing doctors would think themselves so superior to the strengthened corps of midwives that they would feel no need for improvement.[31] Lowering the standard of adequacy would lower all standards.

Because they believed this situation existed, the obstetricians had very

[28] Nicholson, *op. cit.*, ftn. 24 above, p. 626.
[29] Emmons and Huntington, *op. cit.*, ftn. 21 above, p. 399.
[30] Huntington, "The midwife in Massachusetts," *op. cit.*, ftn. 10 above, p. 419.
[31] *Ibid.*

different perspectives from the public health exponents. Some physicians felt the arrangement in Germany was far from ideal, so that even if such a system could be transplanted to the United States the resulting standard of obstetrics would be inadequate. Although German midwives learned obstetrics of high quality in their six month course, that time was considered insufficient to instill an "aseptic conscience." Further, even in Germany their relationship with the physician was not one of "perfect harmony." According to Huntington's analysis, since it was profitable for a midwife to deliver each case herself, she might postpone calling a physician in time of danger; the physician, as well, might also be insufficiently cautious if he were called in, since the responsibility for complications remained with the midwife. Huntington argued further that in the United States such a plan would be impossible because (stating clearly the issue which so troubled some public health officials) the American medical profession could never be forced by law to respond to the call of the midwife in trouble.[32]

From the professional standpoint, the solution in England was also a bad one. In fact, the more midwives there were, and the more successful they were, the worse the situation would be for the community at large, according to Huntington, because this would aggravate a "double standard of obstetrics." The thirty thousand English midwives had not only taken cases that would have been better cared for by doctors but had also taken enough practice away from physicians to obtain a livelihood.[33] Dr. Charles Ziegler, who was later to become cynical about the whole debate, also complained of the estimated five million dollars collected annually in the United States by midwives "which should be paid to physicians and nurses for doing the work properly."[34] The relationship between the ideal of a "single standard" and the issue of economic competition came up clearly again when obstetricians saw the midwife to be in league with "outside" influences—optometrists, osteopaths, neuropaths, Christian Scientists, and chiropractors—who were all invading the legitimate field of medicine.[35] Massachusetts had just licensed optometrists; "if the midwives are now to be recognized we may fairly ask, where is it going to end?"[36]

The professional ideal, of course, was that all women be delivered by an obstetrician, privately, or, if they could not afford such care, in a

[32] Emmons and Huntington, *op. cit.*, ftn. 21 above, pp. 397-400.
[33] *Ibid.*, p. 394.
[34] Charles E. Ziegler, "The elimination of the midwife," *J.A.M.A.*, 1913, *60*: 34.
[35] *Op. cit.*, ftn. 11 above, p. 299.
[36] Huntington, "The midwife in Massachusetts . . . ," *op. cit.*, ftn. 10 above, p. 419.

hospital-medical school complex. Thus, at a stroke, the midwife would be eliminated and the basis established for enormous advances in obstetrics, since students would then get ample training. In suggesting such a system for New York City, Dr. J. Van D. Young felt that even if it were inaugurated at state expense, " the ultimate good to the profession and to the people would be enormous " and rapidly repaid, and, also, that it would attract serious obstetrical students to New York.[37]

The professionals saw only one way by which their goals could be reached and those of the public health approach thwarted. There had to develop a demand from the public for a higher standard of obstetrics. " We can teach the expectant mother what she deserves, and when she demands it she will get it." [38] They urged accordingly that every mother has a right to such care as shall preserve her and hers in life and health, the care which, they said, the midwife cannot provide since the necessary skills are difficult to teach. Combating the " fallacy " of normal pregnancy and delivery was necessary not only to enhance the value of obstetric skills but also to make the American mother not merely respect, but fear, possible danger and so consider no precaution excessive.

Behind both these perspectives on the midwife problem was a complicating factor with which neither side dealt adequately. The economic realities of the situation and the costs of the various programs should have been given far more consideration. Since these economic aspects were working against the obstetricians in particular, they were the most guilty in this respect. In general, the public health approach overstated the economic obstacles to the realization of the obstetricians' ideal, whereas the obstetricians tended to ignore such obstacles, with one significant exception. The problem was that the training of an obstetrician was expensive, and his practice had to be sufficiently lucrative to draw able men into the field. In addition, the expansion of hospital and laboratory facilities to train new men and for their use in practice was expensive. Public health officers, who always have many places to spend every appropriation, are not in a position to weigh these facts and their possible consequences; the chief attraction of the midwife for them was that she was cheap. Levy, who established the Newark system, considered as only rhetorical the question whether those who can only afford midwives " should be delivered in finely appointed hospitals at public expense." [39] Others presented the obstetric ideal as a sort of *reductio ad absurdum*. The

[37] J. Van D. Young, " The midwife problem in the State of New York," *New York State J. Med.*, 1915, *15*: 295.

[38] George C. Marlette, " Discussion," in Hardin, *op. cit.*, ftn. 2 above, p. 350.

[39] Levy, *op. cit.*, ftn. 23 above, p. 41.

obstetricians, on the other hand, ignored this difficulty altogether because of their hope of changing what was then a very annoying fact: the same family will pay easily for surgery but expect to pay meagerly for attendance during pregnancy and confinement.[40] All that would be needed was propaganda to solve what they felt was not really an economic problem.

Huntington felt he had another answer to the " economic necessity for the midwife." Boston Lying-in Hospital ran an Out-Patient Department to provide obstetric training for medical students, and the patients, contributing an average of $1.28 each, in 1910 paid " all the expense " of the Department, with a surplus of $807.82.[41] But his conclusion that the finest hospital care was itself inexpensive can be seriously questioned. The Boston medical school complex attracted prospective obstetricians from all over the country. Cases used for teaching amounted to nearly 20% of the total number of births in Boston in 1913.[42] Huntington thus claims an amazing percentage, and few other areas could hope to rival it, considering the scarcity of obstetricians at that time; yet it still left 80% of the births unaccounted for. It can perhaps be safely inferred that the costs of giving the rest similar treatment would rise rapidly, once deliveries had to be accomplished without the help of unpaid medical students. Yet even if the costs were indeed relatively low for caring for everyone on such a basis, the necessary expenditures on facilities to make room for all would be beyond the economic horizon of public officials forced to account closely for their use of public funds.

Only two writers proposed a solution which would make ideal obstetric care possible for all, given all the existing conditions. A. K. Paine, Huntington's only apparent critic in his home state, said that our method of government was not suited to the rigid requirements which the properly regulated midwife demands, but that the " obstetric poor " could be handled on a community basis, if the community would assume the responsibility.[43] Because of the stress Paine gave community responsibility, his argument clearly implied public institutions staffed by government employees and run with tax funds on some level or another.

Charles Ziegler, who earlier had complained of the money wasted on midwives, was a Pittsburgh obstetrician who was concerned with the midwife problem. What happened to him when he attempted to approximate ideal obstetric care for all puts an interesting light on the importance of the " ideal " elements in the original professional argument. Ziegler's

[40] Paine, *op. cit.*, ftn. 14 above, p. 761.
[41] Huntington, " The midwife in Massachusetts . . . ," *op. cit.*, ftn. 10 above, p. 421.
[42] Paine, *op. cit.*, ftn. 14 above, p. 762.
[43] *Ibid.*, pp. 763-764.

experiment also involved inexpensive delivery of the poor and, although he got his funds privately, he had even then the idea that what was essentially obstetric charity should not be borne solely by obstetricians, but should be subsidized by the community.[44] Although he had no access to public funds, he evidently could generate other sources of aid by his enthusiasm for his project. Ziegler wanted to establish a dispensary which could give the best care to those who usually did not get such care, i. e., those not in either of the extreme income categories. The aim was to demonstrate how much mortality statistics could be improved, in the hope, of course, that the result would provide encouragement for others to try to achieve the same result. Six years after opening the dispensary in 1912, $80,000 in contributions had been spent caring for 3384 confinements on both an in- and an out-patient basis. Fifty-six per cent of the cases were foreign-born and sixteen per cent were Negroes. There were two sets of results. First, maternal mortality was 17 per 10,000 as opposed to a national average of 88.5.[45] This was a remarkable result for the time and clientele. The other result was that the Alleghany County Medical Society found Ziegler guilty of breaches of professional ethics by " solicitation and attendance on cases in families able to pay for a physician [and] . . . solicitation and attendance on cases where a physician had previously been engaged." [46]

Ziegler himself was suspended from the society, and, in 1918, his hospital was commandeered for government service, finishing his experiment.[47] Ziegler concluded after all this that, given the existence of such patients, the cost of caring for them properly (about twenty times Huntington's figure of $1.28), and the strength of the enemies made in the process, the only solution would be municipal, state, and federal aid, not as charity, " but as a matter of wise public policy and of justice to those to whom we look for the perpetuation of our family and national life." [48] He saw the whole obstetric problem as an economic one in which many people could not pay for the services they deserved; an institutional redistribution of such services was therefore necessary.

He believed that his solution would bring opposition from the medical

[44] Ziegler, " The elimination of the midwife," *op. cit.*, ftn. 34 above, p. 34.

[45] Ziegler, " How can we best solve the midwifery problem," *op. cit.*, ftn. 7 above, pp. 407-408.

[46] *The Weekly Bulletin. Official Journal of the Allegheny County Medical Society*, vol. V, no. 7 (February 12, 1916), p. 5.

[47] Ziegler, " How can we best solve the midwifery problem," *op. cit.*, ftn. 7 above, pp. 412-413.

[48] *Ibid.*, p. 407.

profession, "as they are opposed to any plan which includes municipal or state aid looking toward the solution of the problem on a public-health or public-welfare basis." [49] For although Ziegler's solution ostensibly fulfills the obstetric ideal by granting every American mother her "right," by his method the natural elevation in status of obstetricians which would otherwise have occurred might be jeopardized.

Today the prospective American mother theoretically has access to high quality obstetric care. If she is from a relatively urban environment, this is available through clinics, or through a private obstetrician, for whom a group insurance plan might help pay. If she is from a rural area, a general practitioner graduated from a medical school, whose quality, both overall and in obstetrics, has greatly improved, is likely to be available. Obstetrics, both as a branch of medicine and in professional status, has advanced significantly. Can this result somehow be attributed to the developing superiority of obstetrics as performed by obstetricians, or could the forces arrayed against them have been exaggerated by the obstetricians, making the whole issue just a paper debate?

It appears that despite the potential obstetric superiority of obstetricians over midwives, the triumph of the former was probably due most to the fact that the circumstances debated in this period changed radically. It is certain that the relevant health conditions were not improving in those areas where the midwife was first being superseded. Although in Washington the percentage of births reported by midwives shrank from the 1903 high of 50% to 15% in 1912, infant mortality in the first day, the first week, and the first month of life had all increased in this period. Also, New York's dwindling corps of midwives achieved significant superiority over New York's doctors in the prevention of both stillbirths and puerperal sepsis.[50] Rather, the obstetricians triumphed because, before the public health programs became firmly established in the public mind, the obstetrician gained tremendous advantages from other sources. Immigration decreased significantly during the war and was afterwards reduced legally to a small fraction of the numbers experienced just before the war. This put time entirely on the side of the physicians, a considerable advantage in itself, while concurrently the economic problem *per se* was greatly reduced. This did not occur simply because of the "prosperity" of the 1920's, which may have had no impact at all; rather, the secular trend towards limitation of family size accelerated to include nearly the entire

[49] *Ibid.*, p. 413.
[50] Baker, *op. cit.*, ftn. 18 above, p. 196.

population. In 1919 in New York City there were 1700 midwives who were responsible for 40,000 births, or 30% of the total. In 1929, though there were still 1200 midwives, they delivered but 12,000, 12% of the total.[51] Not only did the average deliveries per midwife shrink decidedly from 23 to 10 births a year, but also total births decreased by 25%. With the limitation of births, it is possible that pregnancy and anticipated delivery seemed sufficiently rare to be generally equated with major operations and worthy of greater expense.

The other secular shift in attitudes from which the obstetricians benefited was a new, general demand for improved obstetrics, the change for which they had been most devoutly hoping. The midwife controversy itself was in some ways a reflection of this change. It was not merely the benevolent concern of public health officials about their vital statistics which was instrumental in effecting all the legislation regulating the midwife. Also responsible was a growing public demand from women, who were becoming increasingly self-conscious about their own welfare, and who were still infected with the reforming zeal of the Progressive Era which was to lead to their enfranchisement. These were, after all, the women who shortly afterward were to deluge their Congressmen and Senators with pleas for the passage of the Sheppard-Towner Bill. This bill, which Ziegler worked for, provided Federal money to the states for the " protection of maternity." With " womanhood " no longer rooted in the domestic, " natural " environment, or perhaps reflecting the struggle for release from such roots, the " natural " way of doing things was losing its appeal for the many emerging American women, and the obstetrician was increasingly there to reap the results of a growing anxiety about childbirth.

In summary, then, the professionalization process was very sensitive to external conditions and attitudes. If conditions had not changed so propitiously, if an economic problem and a conflict of attitudes had continued to exist, the obstetrician might well have found himself in the position of the present-day psychoanalyst with the public realizing that his skills solve but a small part of a complicated problem.

[51] Hattie Hemschemeyer, "Midwifery in the United States," *Am. J. Nursing*, 1939, *39*: 1182.

Forgotten Women: American Midwives at the Turn of the Twentieth Century

By

JUDY BARRETT LITOFF*

At the turn of the twentieth century, the total number of births in the United States was attended about equally by midwives and by physicians. Indeed, although statistics relating to the number of early-twentieth-century midwives are not always reliable, conservative estimates indicate that as late as 1910 at least 50 percent of all births were attended by midwives.[1] Southern black families relied heavily on midwives. In fact, in Mississippi in 1918 midwives attended 87.9 percent of all Negro births. Immigrant women, especially those newly arrived from southern and eastern Europe, also used midwives. A 1908 study revealed that 86 percent of all Italian-American births in Chicago were reported by midwives. In isolated rural areas of the United States, a friend or relative often acted as a midwife in the absence of the doctor. Moreover, there was no clear demarcation line between the woman who acted in the official capacity of a midwife once or twice a year and the neighbor who occasionally came to the aid of a friend in need.[2]

Until recently, historians have devoted little attention to this topic. The dearth of scholarly research on the turn-of-the-century

*The author is Assistant Professor of History at Bryant College. An earlier version of this article was presented at the Missouri Valley History Conference in 1976.

[1] The Bureau of the Census did not begin publishing statistical information with regard to the attendant at birth until 1937. Annual Volumes, *Vital Statistics of the United States*, 1937 - 1970 (Washington, D.C.). Most turn-of-the-century observers estimated that at least 50 percent of all births were attended by midwives. See, for example, Thomas Darlington, "The Present Status of the Midwife," *American Journal of Obstetrics and the Diseases of Women and Children* 63(1911): 870; Grace Abbott, "The Midwife in Chicago," *American Journal of Sociology* 20(1915): 684.

[2] Helen M. Dart, *Maternity and Child Care in Selected Rural Areas of Mississippi*, U.S. Department of Labor, Children's Bureau Publication No. 88 (Washington, D.C., 1921), 27; "The Midwives of Chicago," *Journal of the American Medical Association* 50(1908): 1346; Viola I. Paradise, *Maternity Care and the Welfare of Young Children in a Homesteading County in Montana*, U.S. Department of Labor, Children's Bureau Publication No. 34 (Washington, D.C., 1919), 30 - 32.

midwife is particularly striking in light of her ubiquity.[3] Certainly, an event as universal as childbirth deserves careful study by the historian. Moreover, a complete understanding of the circumstances of childbirth requires knowledge of the customs, practices, and education of those persons who have served as birth attendants.

Although the early-twentieth-century midwife was numerically significant, middle- and upper-class white Americans had little first-hand contact with her. The woman of wealthy or moderate means usually enlisted both a physician and a monthly nurse for the confinement period.[4] A growing number of well-to-do women were even choosing to have their babies in hospitals in order to employ obstetrical specialists. Hospitalization for childbirth was the exception, however, and in 1900 the vast majority of all births occurred in the home.[5]

Only the very poor, who accepted public or private charities, and the well-to-do, who could afford competent obstetricians and private rooms, went to the hospital. Families with moderate incomes could not pay the high price of hospital deliveries. Still,

[3] Recent studies of the American midwife include the following: Frances E. Kobrin, "The American Midwife Controversy: A Crisis of Professionalization," *Bulletin of the History of Medicine* 40(1966): 350 - 63; Judy Barrett Litoff, "Midwives in America, 1870 - 1930" (Ph.D. diss., University of Maine, 1975); Richard Wertz and Dorothy Wertz, "Lying-in, A History of Childbirth in America; Its Technologies and Social Relations" (unpublished manuscript, Boston, 1974). For an examination of the status of the American midwife prior to 1860, see Janet B. Donegan, "Midwifery in America, 1760-1860: A Study in Medicine and Morality" (Ph.D. diss., Syracuse University, 1972).

[4] The monthly nurse was a woman who was hired to perform medical and housewifely duties. Her employment began at the onset of labor and lasted for about one month. She did not deliver the baby, however, unless the physician was late in arriving at the home of the parturient woman.

[5] Statistics on hospital and home deliveries are sketchy for the years prior to 1940. One of the first attempts to collect information of this type occurred in 1916 when the Department of Health of New York City reported that 19.1 percent of all births in the borough of Manhattan took place in hospitals. City of New York, Department of Health, "The Supervision of Midwives in New York City," by Lee W. Thomas, *Monthly Bulletin* 9(1919): 117. A report issued by the United States Children's Bureau for the year 1921 pointed out that hospital confinements occurred more frequently in cities than in rural areas. For example, "of the births in Baltimore, 18.7 percent occurred in hospitals, as compared with only 2.6 percent of the births in Maryland outside of Baltimore." Robert M. Woodbury, *Maternal Mortality: The Risk of Death in Childbirth and From All Diseases Caused by Pregnancy and Confinement*, U.S. Department of Labor, Children's Bureau Publication No. 158 (Washington, D.C., 1926), 86. The first national statistics on hospital deliveries appeared in 1935. In that year, a study conducted by the United States Children's Bureau reported that 36.9 percent of all births occurred in hospitals. Elizabeth Tandy, *Infant and Maternal Mortality Among Negroes*, U.S. Department of Labor, Children's Bureau Publication No. 243 (Washington, D.C., 1937), 7.

prohibitive fees were not the only factor limiting the number of hospital births. Just as important was the widespread belief that the hospital was a disease-ridden institution where people went to die. Surgical operations and other types of obstetrical interference were also closely associated with hospital delivery. Thus, poor women often preferred to pay the small fee of the midwife rather than enter a charity hospital where they would allegedly be subjected to experimentation and obstetrical interference.[6]

Clearly, many immigrant and black women were attracted to midwives because of the small fees which they charged. The average fee of midwives in Waterbury, Connecticut, in 1913 was eight dollars while physicians charged between fifteen and twenty-five dollars. In rural Mississippi in 1916, the midwife's fee ranged between five and ten dollars, depending on the difficulty of the case, the distance the midwife had to travel, and the ability of the family to pay. Often, informal arrangements were made for payment in chickens, pigs, or grain or on a neighborly give-and-take basis. One black Mississippi midwife even admitted that she charged more for boys than girls because "boys are harder to handle and mothers want them more." In contrast, Mississippi physicians charged between ten and fifteen dollars for normal deliveries, plus additional fees for prenatal and postnatal visits.[7]

Midwives not only charged substantially less than did physicians but they also provided a variety of services which general practitioners did not offer. The midwife served as the birth attendant, nurse, and housekeeper. In addition to caring for the mother and newborn infant, she often cleaned the house, prepared the meals, and looked after other children in the family for three to ten days after the birth of the baby. Women who used midwives were well aware that they were receiving services not offered by physicians. A 1924 Texas midwifery survey revealed that many women preferred midwives because they were "really worth more." One woman pointed out that the midwife "did my washing and charged only $5.00." Another stated that she paid $7.50 for three and one-half days of service. Thus, the midwife combined the

[6] George W. Kosmak, "Maternity Hospital Care for the Woman of Moderate Means," *Transactions of the American Association for the Study and Prevention of Infant Mortality* 4(1913): 208; Edward P. Davis, "The Need of Hospitals for Maternity Surgical Cases," *Transactions of the American Association for the Study and Prevention of Infant Mortality* 5(1914): 196 - 97.

[7] Estelle E. Hunter, *Infant Mortality: Results of a Field Study in Waterbury, Connecticut. Based on Births in One Year,* U.S. Department of Labor, Children's Bureau Publication No. 29 (Washington, D.C., 1918), 45; Dart, *Maternity and Child Care,* 27 - 32.

duties of the physician and monthly nurse for less than one-half the fee usually charged by the physician.[8]

The preference of immigrants for midwives was reinforced by a long-established European tradition of having them serve as attendants at birth. Hence, most midwives in Europe held high positions in the community and were both well trained and well supervised. When immigrant women arrived in America, they continued to employ midwives even though very few provisions for their training and regulation existed in the United States at the turn of the twentieth century. That the midwife spoke the language of the parturient woman was also frequently important. Physicians, in contrast, were often unable to communicate in any language other than English. Most important, immigrant families employed midwives because there was a "strong sense of shame [associated] with permitting a man to attend a woman in confinement." Almost all contemporary observers agreed that the immigrants' dislike for men in the lying-in chamber had a great deal to do with the popularity of midwives.[9]

Black women also expressed a dislike for male birth attendants. The 1924 survey of the midwife situation in Texas disclosed that many black women were "ashamed to have a man at that time" and that they preferred the midwife because she "is a woman and will be more help than [the] doctor." One woman stated that "I am used to women and not strange men like doctors." The Texas women also indicated that it was traditional to use midwives. One woman remarked that she "never knew anything else but a midwife." A frequent explanation given for employing midwives was that "everybody else had them around here." Another woman commented that the midwife was "just handed down from slavery times." Black women also preferred midwives because of their easy accessibility. Southern physicians usually lived in the towns and cities and often had to travel long distances in order to reach the parturient woman. In contrast, midwives were scattered throughout the rural south. Accordingly, Texas women chose midwives because "way out in the country doctors charge too much."[10]

[8] S. Josephine Baker, "Discussion," *Transactions of the American Association for the Study and Prevention of Infant Mortality* 3(1912): 254; "Report of the Midwife Survey in Texas," mimeographed (State Board of Health of Texas, 1924), 3.

[9] Hunter, *Infant Mortality*, 45; Jessamine S. Whitney, *Infant Mortality: Results of a Field Study in New Bedford, Massachusetts. Based on Births in One Year*, U.S. Department of Labor, Children's Bureau Publication No. 68 (Washington, D.C., 1920), 31; F. Elisabeth Crowell, "The Midwives of New York," *Charities and the Commons* 17(1907): 668.

[10] "Report of the Midwife Survey in Texas," 1-3.

Any attempt to present a composite picture of turn-of-the-century midwives is complicated by the fact that no diaries, letters, autobiographies, or other manuscript materials have been uncovered. Moreover, midwifery legislation was almost nonexistent prior to 1910, and the few regulations that were enacted were usually not enforced.[11] Thus, little information with regard to the practices of midwives can be garnered from legal sources. In addition, much of the existing information about them was written by hostile observers. For example, both Northern and Southern writers frequently portrayed midwives as "dirty," "ignorant," "evil," and "inveterate quacks."[12]

Northern observers were especially concerned about the growing number of midwives who were believed to be performing illegal abortions. One early-twentieth-century study of midwives in New York City reported that 176 of 500 midwives under investigation had participated in such "criminal work." A similar study of Chicago midwives classified one-third of them as "criminal." The Chicago study also disclosed that physicians often supported the "criminal midwives" by falsifying death certificates for them.[13]

Southern reports dwelt on the superstitions and folklore of the "granny" midwives which they alleged were "so gross in many cases as to rival voodooism." Black midwives in Maryland were reported to treat hemorrhaging by placing either ice or hot

[11] As late as 1930, the health departments of ten states reported that their midwives were neither controlled nor licensed. Significantly, Massachusetts was the only state which outlawed midwives during the 1900 - 1930 period. The 1901 Medical Practice Act of Massachusetts listed midwifery as a major branch of medicine, but it did not exempt midwives from the provisions of the Act. Thus, only qualified physicians could legally serve as birth attendants. Despite the 1901 Act, many Massachusetts women continued to serve as midwives. At least one woman, Hanna Porn, a trained and practicing midwife, was convicted of violating the 1901 Act. White House Conference on Child Health and Protection, *Obstetric Education* (New York, 1932), 178 - 92, 195; Louis S. Reed, *Midwives, Chiropodists, and Optometrists: Their Place in Medical Care* (Chicago, 1932), 15 - 16; *Revised Laws of the Commonwealth of Massachusetts, 1901*, Chapter 76, Section 8; Commonwealth v. Hanna Porn, *Massachusetts Reports, 1907*, 195, 196.

[12] See, for example, J. Clifton Edgar, "The Remedy for the Midwife Problem," *American Journal of Obstetrics and the Diseases of Women and Children* 63(1916): 881; Arthur B. Emmons and James L. Huntington, "Has the Trained and Supervised Midwife Made Good?" *Transactions of the American Association for the Study and Prevention of Infant Mortality* 2(1911): 207 - 8; H. J. Garrigues, "Midwives," *Medical News* 72(1898): 235; W. C. Gewin, "Careless and Unscientific Midwifery with Special References to Some Features of the Work of Midwives," *Alabama Medical Journal* 18(1905 - 6): 629 - 35; W. A. Plecker, "The Midwife Problem in Virginia," *Virginia Medical Semi-Monthly* 18(1914): 475; W. S. Smith, "Careless and Unscientific Midwifery with Special References to Some Features of the Work of Midwives," *Maryland Medical Journal* 33(1895 - 96): 146 - 49.

[13] Crowell, "Midwives of New York," 673; "Midwives of Chicago," 1348-49.

potatoes in the hand of the parturient woman. Many "grannies" were said to believe that a difficult labor might be made easier by throwing hot coals on hen feathers and placing the ashes under the prospective mother's bed. The Southern black midwife was also characterized as an old woman who was qualified for nothing except "catching babies." A favorite quotation included in studies about Southern midwives came from an eighty-year-old "granny" who supposedly stated, "I am too old to clean, too weak to wash; too blind to sew; but, thank God! I can still put my neighbors to bed."[14]

Even studies conducted by the United States Children's Bureau, which was generally sympathetic to midwives, reported considerable ignorance and superstition among "grannies." An investigation of maternity care in rural Mississippi for the years 1916-1918 reported that two-thirds of the black midwives were illiterate. Although the white midwives were "superior" to their black counterparts, they "did not differ either in training or practice from the Negro midwives." Nine-tenths of the rural Mississippi midwives, most of whom were black, used no antiseptics. Only the "more intelligent ones" realized that puerperal fever was caused by uncleanliness, and many midwives continued to adhere to the old custom of not changing the bed coverings for at least three days after the birth. A similar study of maternity care in the north Georgia mountains for the years 1916-1918 also disclosed that midwives were "steeped in the superstitions and practices of a bygone generation." Significantly, most of the Georgia mountain midwives were white. Although the majority of the accounts of Southern midwives focused on the "ignorance" and "superstition" of the black "grannies," contemporary reports also indicated that white midwives were sorely lacking in the basic knowledge required of competent attendants at birth.[15]

Very few satisfactory training programs for midwives existed at the turn of the twentieth century. This helps to explain why contemporary observers frequently characterized them as "dirty," "ignorant," and "evil." In most instances, those midwives who wanted to learn more about pregnancy and parturition could not attain adequate training. Between 1916 and 1918, for example,

[14] Guy Steele, "The Midwife Problem and Its Legal Control," *Maryland Medical Journal* 48(1905): 2, 4; Helmina Jeidell and Willa M. Fricke, "The Midwives of Anne Arundel Country, Maryland," *Johns Hopkins Hospital Bulletin* 23(1912): 281; Marie Campbell, *Folks Do Get Born* (New York: Rinehart, 1946), 33; Carolyn C. Van Blarcom, "Midwives in America," *American Journal of Public Health* 4(1914): 198.

[15] Dart, *Maternity and Child Care*, 22 - 23; Glenn Steele, *Maternity and Infant Care in a Mountain County in Georgia*, U.S. Department of Labor, Children's Bureau Publication No. 120 (Washington, D.C., 1923), 17.

Mississippi midwives expressed an interest in having public health nurses advise them, but there were no nurses available for that purpose. Some midwives did serve apprenticeships with physicians. Usually, however, they were taught by their mothers or older midwives. Most of their training consisted of first-hand experience and observation. An important part of the educational process for many midwives was the birth of their own children. Most midwives were, in fact, married women who had borne several children.[16]

Many black women felt that proper midwifery training included a "calling by the Lord." In a recent interview, Elizabeth Singleton, a 104-year-old black midwife from Wayne County, Georgia, underscored the importance of the "calling." In recounting her experiences as a midwife, Singleton remarked,

> The good Lord taught me how to catch babies. . . . I don't know how many babies I caught; must have been more than 1000, both black and white babies. . . . When I was catching babies, I would pray for you. I would ask the Lord to help you and to help me to take care of you. I've prayed so hard, and my soul would be so full of joy. . . .[17]

A few schools for midwives existed in the northeastern and midwestern areas of the United States at the turn of the twentieth century, but the course of instruction provided at most of them was totally inadequate. Early twentieth-century midwife studies concurred in the opinion that the schools were "veritable diploma mills run for revenue only, usually by some conscienceless physician who receives lucrative returns for a minimum outlay of time and trouble." The fees charged by the physicians were, in fact, exorbitant. The average cost of a six-month course of study in Chicago in 1907 was $100-$175. This fee usually included nothing more than lectures for three to four hours each week in the physician's back office. Often, the instructor required no textbooks and provided no clinical instruction for his students. Schools for midwives in New York City provided the same type of low-quality education. A 1907 study of New York City midwives disclosed that some women who could neither read nor write held midwifery diplomas from New York schools. The quality of the education in the New York schools was so deplorable that the author of the 1907 study concluded that the "eighty-eight midwives who had no diplomas were quite as efficient and capable as

[16] Dart, *Maternity and Child Care*, 22; Glenn Steele, *Maternity and Infant Care*, 16; Hunter, *Infant Mortality*, 45 - 47; Paradise, *Maternity Care*, 31 - 33.

[17] "104 Years Old: God, Herbs Get Credit for Long Life," *Atlanta Constitution*, 16 September 1974, p. 6-a, cols. 1 - 4.

the 209 who held those worthless New York diplomas."[18]

It would be a mistake, however, to leave the impression that all turn-of-the-century midwives were poorly trained. Newly-arrived immigrant midwives were often graduates of excellent European midwifery schools. Of course, most Americans were not familiar enough with the European situation to know whether or not the foreign diplomas displayed by the midwives were from reputable schools. Moreover, the European-trained midwife often became careless in her practice once she arrived in America where few rules and regulations existed. It was also economically impossible for her to compete with the American idea of the midwife and still maintain the high standards she had been taught in Europe.[19]

There were a few American schools which provided adequate training programs for midwives. In 1883, the New York State Supreme Court granted the College of Midwifery of New York City the right to confer the diploma of Graduate in Midwifery. The College advertised that it was "the only regular institution in America incorporated for the purpose of conferring on women the diploma of Graduate in Midwifery." The faculty consisted of seven physicians. The lone woman, Sarah E. Post, M.D., served as Professor of Physiology. She was also the attending physician to the Out-door Department of the New York Infirmary for Women and Children.[20]

The course of instruction at the College included lectures, recitations, and demonstrations in English, German, French, and Spanish for a three-month period. This was followed by three months of practical work at the Metropolitan Dispensary for Women and the Woman's Infirmary and Maternity Home. The cost of the six-month course was $105. If a candidate failed to pass the final examination, she could enroll in the College a second time by paying a fee of $30. Fourteen students attended the first session, and ten satisfactorily completed the course. The faculty believed that the "interests of the institution and the community would be better served by teaching a limited number thoroughly and well, rather than send out a large class unqualified."[21]

[18] "Midwives of Chicago," 1348; Abbott, "Midwife in Chicago," 690; Crowell, "Midwives of New York," 671.

[19] Taliaferro Clark, "Training of Midwives," *Chicago Medical Recorder* 46(1924): 297 - 304; S. Josephine Baker, "Schools for Midwives," *American Journal of Obstetrics and the Diseases of Woman and Children* 54(1912): 258 - 62.

[20] *Woman's Work in the Field of Medicine* (New York: College of Midwifery, 1883), 19 - 20, 27.

[21] *Ibid.*, 7, 21 - 24.

In the original bulletin announcing the opening of the College, the Board of Trustees explained why such a school was necessary. Predictably, they pointed to the lack of training programs for midwives in the United States. They included extensive quotations from the congratulatory and commendatory notices that had appeared in some of the leading medical journals of America. These notices reiterated that the United States had "thus far . . . been destitute of any adequate provision" for the education of midwives. The Trustees defended the concept of formal training for midwives on the grounds "that it teaches, what, by experience, had been found to cover the sphere of woman's usefulness in medicine." They argued that women were especially suited for training in midwifery but that they were not, in most instances, capable of undergoing the "whole curriculum of surgery, pharmacy, materia medica, jurisprudence, etc." The failure of female medical schools to attract large numbers of students was used as proof that women did not have the ability to become regular practitioners of medicine. Moreover, the Trustees also believed that it was "not necessary to lay open the entire subject of obstetrics to the midwife. On the contrary, her practice should be strictly limited; the knowledge imparted serving mainly to indicate to her when the accoucheur is to be called in and that the office of midwife is to attend women in natural labor."[22]

The Playfair School of Midwifery in Chicago, Illinois, was another institution that provided quality education for midwives. It was established in 1896 for the purpose of interesting "such a class of women in this work that by proper opportunities we will remove the present prevailing prejudice against the midwife and finally restore her to her proper reputable position in the profession, not as a competitor to the physician but [as one] able to conduct normal labor with safety, and . . . to recognize early the nature of pathological cases and send for the timely help of the physician." The Playfair School offered diplomas in midwifery as well as certificates in obstetrical nursing to those women who did not wish to qualify fully as midwives.[23]

The 1889 annual announcement of the Playfair School listed eleven faculty members, ten of whom held the M.D. degree and six of whom were women. There were two major admission requirements. First, the prospective midwife had to present a certificate of good moral character, signed by either a physician or a minister. Second, she had to show evidence of an ability to

[22] *Ibid.*, 6-9.

[23] *The Playfair School of Midwifery: Annual Announcement, 1899* (Chicago: n.p., 1899), 6-7.

read and write in English or German. Instruction was given in both languages. The course consisted of two terms, each five months in length. Lectures, demonstrations, and recitations were scheduled daily from 9:00 A.M. to noon. Clinical work was conducted at the Playfair Lying-in Hospital Dispensary. The cost of the complete ten-month course was $110. To graduate, the student had to attend at least 80 percent of all the lectures, pass all examinations given by the various branches of the school, and show satisfactory evidence of having attended twelve cases of labor. Because of the "high grade requirements" of the Playfair School, the Illinois State Board of Health exempted its graduates from any additional state examinations required for midwives.[24]

A third school for midwives whose diplomas were of real value was the St. Louis College of Midwifery. One of its founders, Dr. A. A. Henske, was so concerned about improving the quality of midwife education that he also established a monthly journal, the *American Midwife*, which appeared from November 1895 through October 1896. The College offered a five-month course of instruction in English and German. Six of the eight faculty members were men with the M.D. and/or Ph.D. degrees. The two women on the faculty, Katherina Zratz and Annie J. Byrns, were trained midwives.[25]

Unfortunately, information about these three schools is incomplete and of uneven quality. The pioneering studies of the midwife situation in New York City and Chicago, published in 1907 and 1908 respectively, made no specific mention of either the College of Midwifery of New York City or the Playfair School of Midwifery. Possibly, the two schools were no longer in existence or else were judged to be "diploma mills." Moreover, the number of students enrolled in the three schools represented only a tiny minority of the women who acted as midwives at the turn of the century.[26]

A fourth, but more well known and longer lived, school for midwives was the municipally sponsored Bellevue School for Midwives in New York City. It was established in 1911 as a branch of the Bellevue Hospital. The original course of instruction was six months in length, but it was soon expanded to cover eight months. Both practical and theoretical instructions were given by physicians and nurses. The training program included instruction in the proper care of cases of normal labor, the necessity

[24] *Ibid.*, 7, 13 - 16.

[25] See advertisements for the St. Louis College of Midwifery appearing in each issue of the *American Midwife*, 1 - 2(1895 - 96).

[26] Crowell, "Midwives of New York," 667 - 77; "Midwives of Chicago," 1346 - 60.

of breast-feeding, the manner and methods of artificial feeding, and the essential housewifely duties to be performed by the midwife. Most of the students were of Italian, German, Polish, or Hungarian descent. There were no special admission requirements other than that the prospective midwife be able to read and write and be of good moral character. There was no charge for the course. Most reports issued by physicians and public health officials during the second decade of the twentieth century agreed that the Bellevue School for Midwives was the *only* institution in the United States that provided an adequate education for midwives. One early report, published by the New York City Department of Health, described the students as "intelligent, earnest women with sufficient education to grasp the principles of normal obstetrics, asepsis, and to recognize abnormalities. . . ." Interestingly, nurses were not allowed admission to the Bellevue School for Midwives because it did "not have accommodations suitable" for them. The School remained in existence until 1935, when a lack of students forced it to close its doors.[27]

Very few printed materials were published expressly for American midwives during the late nineteenth and early twentieth centuries. A variety of maternity and mothers' manuals appeared during this period, but they were written for the educated, middle- and upper-class woman. Significantly, most books of this type omitted any mention of the role of the midwife in the birth process. They assumed that both a physician and monthly nurse would be in attendance.[28] The growing number of obstetrical textbooks for students and practitioners that were published at this time were also unsuitable for midwives. These works were often quite lengthy and written in highly technical language that was difficult for people untrained in the medical sciences to under-

[27] Thomas, "Supervision of Midwives," 118. Information on the origins and history of the Bellevue School for Midwives is also included in the following works: Baker, *Child Hygiene* (New York, 1925), 118 - 19; Baker, "Schools for Midwives," 263 - 66; City of New York, Department of Health, "Supervision of Midwives in New York City," *Weekly Bulletin* 10(1921): 154; Hazel Wedgewood, "Midwifery in Massachusetts," *Commonhealth* 8(1921): 81 - 83.

[28] See, for example, Pye Henry Chavasse, *Woman as a Wife and Mother* (Philadelphia, 1870); John H. Dye, *Painless Childbirth: or Healthy Mothers and Healthy Children* (New York, 1884); Anna M. Fullerton, *A Handbook of Obstetrical Nursing for Nurses, Students and Mothers* (Philadelphia, 1890); Frederick Hollick, *The Origin of Life and Process of Reproduction in Plants and Animals, with the Anatomy and Physiology of the Human Generative System Male and Female, and the Causes, Prevention and Cure of the Special Diseases to Which it is Liable* (Philadelphia, 1878); George H. Napheys, *The Physical Life of Woman: Advice to the Maiden, Wife, and Mother* (Philadelphia, 1890); Prudence B. Saur, *Maternity: A Book for Every Wife and Mother* (Chicago, 1890); Alice B. Stockham, *Tokology: A Book for Every Woman* (Chicago, 1885); Tullio Suzzara Verdi, *Maternity: A Popular Treatise for Young Wives and Mothers* (Philadelphia, 1885).

stand.[29] A number of British manuals for midwives were also accessible to American women. However, midwives in the United States were discouraged from reading the British works because they were considered to be too difficult. The British manuals were deemed inappropriate for study by the "typical midwife" in the United States who was "not to be trusted with a . . . bag equipped with needles, hypodermic syringes, [and] ergot."[30]

The aforementioned *American Midwife* was probably the only turn-of-the-century journal published expressly for American midwives.[31] It was published monthly, in both English and German, from November 1895 through October 1896. Its founder, Dr. A. A. Henske, and many of the contributing authors were members of the faculty of the St. Louis College of Midwifery. Judging from the notices that appeared within its pages, the *American Midwife* was a much-needed and greatly appreciated periodical. Congratulatory letters from midwives from such diverse locations as St. Louis, Missouri, Bensenville, Illinois, and San Francisco, California, were published. Edna L. Bartells of Bensenville wrote that "the midwife ought to have something to read just as well as the doctor, so as to remind her of her duties to her calling. As a rule she does not read any journal or book but even forgets what she has learned." One early subscriber, Emma E. Peters, urged other midwives to send in their subscription fees of one dollar since "midwives are never through learning." Medical practitioners also congratulated the editors for their endeavors. In assessing the success of the periodical, the editors reported in January 1896 that "our list of subscribers increases daily; in fact, far beyond our expectations. There is no city in the country which has not added a number of names to it." They concluded that the *American Midwife* "would be the journal that will furnish the midwife with well written articles, treating on different subjects of her science, and will keep her well advised of all the

[29] See, for example, Rodney Glisan, *Textbook of Modern Midwifery* (Philadelphia, 1881); Charles Jewett, *Outlines of Obstetrics: A Syllabus of Lectures Delivered at the Long Island College Hospital* (Philadelphia, 1894); J. Whitridge Williams, *Obstetrics: A Textbook for the Use of Students and Practitioners* (New York, 1903).

[30] See, for example, Comyns Berkeley, *A Handbook for Midwives and Maternity Nurses* (New York, 1909); A. B. Calder, *Lectures on Midwifery for Midwives* (New York, 1905); Henry Fly Smith, *The Handbook for Midwives* (London, 1873); "Handbook for Midwives," *American Journal of Obstetrics and the Diseases of Women and Children* 6(1873 - 74): 700; "Reviews and Book Notes," *Public Health Nurse* 17 (1925): 220 - 21.

[31] Only three libraries in the United States possess copies of the *American Midwife*. The two most complete files of the journal are located at the Library of the College of Physicians of Philadelphia and the St. Louis Society for Medical and Scientific Education.

latest advances and of all important discoveries in the different branches of obstetrics."[32]

Most of the articles published in the *American Midwife* were written by physicians. Occasionally, however, midwives wrote about their own experiences. Lillian V. Young, a student at the St. Louis College of Midwifery, discussed the importance of clinical training. She stated that her first childbirth case was normal but that she considered it an "ordeal" because of her lack of clinical experience. Young did not hold the St. Louis College of Midwifery responsible for her predicament. She maintained that this was a problem common to midwifery colleges throughout the United States.[33]

Annie J. Byrns, a trained midwife and a faculty member of the St. Louis College of Midwifery, wrote an article in which she was highly critical of those physicians who called for the elimination of midwives on account of their alleged ignorance relating to matters of childbirth. Byrns argued that "the United States can boast of midwives who not only wash their hands with soap, but scrub them to their elbows, clean their finger nails, and then use antiseptic solution." She pointed out that thousands of concerned midwives read the *American Midwife* and that St. Louis had a Scientific Association of Midwives.[34]

The last issue of the *American Midwife* appeared in October 1896. The editors provided no explanation for its cessation. Certainly, the claim that its subscribers came from every city in the United States was an exaggeration. Nevertheless, the significance of the *American Midwife* must not be underestimated. The fact that Henske and the other faculty members at the St. Louis College of Midwifery believed that American midwives would support the journal is important. Apparently, there were conscientious midwives in St. Louis and other areas of the United States at the turn of the century who were very concerned about improving their knowledge of pregnancy and parturition and keeping abreast of developments in midwifery. For such women, the only publication to turn to was the *American Midwife*. For a brief period, American midwives had a journal in which they could relate their experiences and even reply to the criticisms of those physicians who maintained that they were "dirty and ignorant." When it ceased publication in October 1896, over two decades

[32] "Letters," *American Midwife* 1(December 1895): 6; "Editorial," *ibid.* 1(January 1896): 1.

[33] "Letters," *American Midwife* 1(February 1896): 15.

[34] Annie J. Byrns, "Midwives," *American Midwife* 1(December 1895): 4-5.

elapsed before another journal for American midwives was established.[35]

Although it is not possible to create an exact prototype of the American midwife at the turn of the twentieth century, it is possible, through the examination of a variety of sources, to envisage what she may have been like. She would, most likely, have been a married woman who had borne several children and who had received her first training from her mother or some other older woman. Whether she was an immigrant midwife living in the urban Northeast or a black "granny" living in the rual South, she would have had little, if any, formal midwifery training. Only a very small percentage of the total number of midwives were trained at quality schools such as the Bellevue School for Midwives in New York City. The smattering of education that she received focused on how to manage normal confinements and which symptoms merited calling in a physician. Her lack of formal training and her unfamiliarity with obstetric techniques meant that she usually let "nature work its course." Her practice was frequently limited to friends and relatives. Not surprisingly, therefore, the income she derived from her work was quite small. The average fee charged by the midwife was less than one-half that of the general practitioner. Moreover, arrangements were often made for payment "in kind." In addition, she also performed a variety of housewifely functions which were not required of the doctor. She had only limited contact with other midwives and, for the most part, went about her work unobtrusively. Indeed, in 1900 the American midwife appeared to be a forgotten person.

By 1910, however, physicians, public health advocates, and to a lesser extent the general public were embroiled in fierce debate over the midwife question.[36] Two unforeseen developments had brought an end to the apathy of 1900. First, physicians had become increasingly concerned about medical education reform and the related issue of "overcrowding" in the medical profession during the early years of the twentieth century.[37] Doctors maintained that "overcrowding" had resulted in a loss of their status

[35] During 1918, Ferdinand Herb, a Chicago physician, published a monthly bulletin, *Topics of Interest to Midwives.*'

[36] For additional information on the early-twentieth-century midwife debate, see Kobrin, "American Midwife Controversy," 350 - 63; Litoff, "Midwives in America," chapters 3 - 5.

[37] The most thorough examination of physicians' attitudes about "overcrowding" during the 1890 - 1910 period can be found in Gerald E. Markowitz and David Karl Rosner, "Doctors in Crisis: A Study of the Use of Medical Education Reform to Establish Modern Professional Elitism in Medicine," *American Quarterly* 25(1973): 87 - 97.

and a diminution of their income. Many physicians believed that eliminating the midwife, or at least substantially reducing her numbers, would help alleviate this problem.[38]

The second and equally significant development which was responsible for the upsurge of interest in the midwife around 1910 was the revelation that the maternal and infant mortality rates in the United States were alarmingly high. Prior to 1900, birth and death statistics were too sketchy to be meaningful. During the early years of the twentieth century, however, the United States Bureau of the Census, the United States Children's Bureau, and state and local health boards began to collect and publish birth and death statistics.[39] For example, a study conducted by the United States Children's Bureau revealed that the 1910 infant mortality rate in the United States was 124 deaths per 1,000 live births. The Bureau also reported that "childbirth caused more deaths among women fifteen to forty-four years old than any disease except tuberculosis" and that in only two of fifteen countries it had investigated had maternal mortality rates been higher than in the United States for the 1900-1910 period.[40] The publication of these birth and death statistics caused physicians and public health officials to take a closer look at the midwife's role in the birth process and to try to determine why so many American mothers and infants were dying.

The question of the midwife's status in American society was heatedly debated between 1910 and 1930. The United States Children's Bureau, the various state and city Bureaus of Child Hygiene, the American Association for the Study and Prevention of Infant Mortality, the New York Committee for the Prevention of Blindness, the Babies Milk Fund Association, and numerous physicians and public health officials examined the midwife question in detail at this time. In addition, scores of articles on the "midwife problem" appeared in most of the major American medical journals. To a lesser extent, articles on the midwife

[38] A classic example of this viewpoint can be found in J. Whitridge Williams, "The Midwife Problem and Medical Education in the United States," *Transactions of the American Association for the Study and Prevention of Infant Mortality* 2(1911): 184 - 93.

[39] U.S. Bureau of the Census, *Historical Statistics of the United States, Colonial Times to 1957* (Washington, D.C., 1960), 18.

[40] Dorothy E. Bradbury, *Five Decades of Action for Children: A History of the Children's Bureau* (Washington, D.C., 1962), 6; Grace L. Meigs, *Maternal Mortality From All Conditions Connected with Childbirth in the United States and Certain Other Countries*, U.S. Department of Labor, Children's Bureau Publication No. 19(Washington, D.C., 1917), 7, 17.

were also published in many of the popular magazines of the period.[41]

The midwife debate was lengthy and acrimonious. At one end of the spectrum were the physicians, many of whom were obstetric specialists, who were vehemently opposed to the midwife. They believed that the obstetrician would never receive due recognition in the "overcrowded" medical profession as long as women untrained in the medical sciences continued to deliver one-half of all the births in the United States.[42] At the other end of the spectrum were the public health officials who argued that the utilization of properly trained and regulated midwives would help significantly to reduce maternal and infant mortality rates in the United States.[43] There were, of course, a wide array of views that fell within these two extremes. For example, many midwife critics supported training and regulatory programs as temporary measures to be discontinued as soon as an adequate number of physicians could be properly trained to take over the clientele being served by midwives.[44] Public health officials in several states supported the regulation of the midwife with the hope that ultimately she would be regulated out of existence.[45] Finally, some anti-midwife physicians were optimistic that nurses, who had received special training in obstetrics, could be substituted for midwives.[46]

[41] Litoff, "Midwives in America," chapters 3 - 5.

[42] A leading figure in the movement to eradicate midwives was Dr. Joseph B. DeLee, founder of the Chicago Lying-In Hospital (1895). See, for example, Joseph B. DeLee, "Report of Sub-Committee for Illinois," *Transactions of the American Association for the Study and Prevention of Infant Mortality* 5(1914): 231; DeLee, "Progress Toward Ideal Obstetrics," *ibid.* 6(1915): 117.

[43] Dr. S. Josephine Baker, Director of the Bureau of Child Hygiene of the Board of Health of the City of New York for over twenty-five years, was a leading figure in the movement to establish programs for the training and regulation of midwives. See, for example, Baker, "Schools for Midwives," *Transactions of the American Association for the Study and Prevention of Infant Mortality* 2(1911): 232 - 43; Baker, "The Function of the Midwife," *Woman's Medical Journal* 23(1913): 196 - 97.

[44] A leading spokesman for this viewpoint was Dr. J. Clifton Edgar, a New York City physician. See, for example, Edgar, "The Remedy for the Midwife Problem," 881; Edgar, "Why the Midwife?" *American Journal of Obstetrics and the Diseases of Women and Children* 77(1918): 243.

[45] See, for example, S. W. Newmayer, "The Status of Midwifery in Pennsylvania and a Study of the Midwives in Philadelphia," *Monthly Cyclopedia and Medical Bulletin* 4(1911): 713, 718; Jessie L. Marriner, *Midwifery in Alabama* (Alabama State Board of Health, [1925]), 1 - 2, 10; *Report,* Board of Health of Mississippi (1919 - 1921), 198.

[46] Edgar, "The Education, Licensing and Supervision of the Midwife," *American Journal of Obstetrics and the Diseases of Women and Children* 73(1916): 391; George W. Kosmak, "Certain Aspects of the Midwife Problem in Relation to the Medical Profession and the Community," *Medical Record* 85(1914): 1015.

The midwife debate raged for two decades. When it finally subsided around 1930, the ranks of the midwives had been dissipated and their historical role appeared to be relegated to near-total obscurity.[47] The revival of the feminist movement and the increased interest in women's history over the last ten years, however, have caused historians to take a fresh look at the role of the midwife in American society.[48]

[47] Between 1900 and 1930, the percentage of midwife-attended births declined from 50 to 15 percent. White House Conference on Child Health and Protection, *Obstetric Education*, 169.

[48] In addition to the previously cited works by Donegan, Kobrin, Litoff, and the Wertzes, the question of childbirth in America has also been examined at several recent historical conferences including the 1974 Berkshire Conference on the History of Women, the 1976 Missouri Valley History Conference, and the 1976 Annual Meeting of the Organization of American Historians. In addition, feminists and women's health reformers, who are not necessarily trained historians, have also contributed to the literature on this topic. See, for example, Suzanne Arms, *Immaculate Deception: A New Look at Women and Childbirth in America* (Boston, 1975).

THE IMMIGRANT MIDWIVES OF LAWRENCE: THE CONFLICT BETWEEN LAW AND CULTURE IN EARLY TWENTIETH-CENTURY MASSACHUSETTS*

Eugene Declercq and Richard Lacroix

In 1907 the Massachusetts Supreme Court ruled that the practice of midwifery was in violation of the state's Medical Practice Act of 1894.[1] In the same year, three midwives living in Lawrence, Massachusetts—Virginia Pedrazzini, Angelina DeMarco and Laura Carpenito—attended thirty-nine of the registered births. In 1913, six years after their practice was declared officially illegal, these three women attended 442 births and registered them with the Lawrence City Clerk.[2] Overall, the proportion of all registered births in Lawrence attended by midwives increased after the court's ruling from 38 percent in 1907 to 41 percent in 1913. The campaign to abolish midwifery in Massachusetts, the influence of the practice of midwifery in Lawrence and the factors that limited the initial impact of the campaign against it are the subject of this paper.

The national campaign against midwifery in the United States has been extensively documented elsewhere.[3] The center of opposition was Massachusetts. As a Pennsylvania physician remarked in 1915, "I know of no other section of the country which has been more successful in prohibition (of midwifery) than Massachusetts."[4] The legislative restriction of midwifery in the state was accomplished in several stages during the nineteenth century culminating with the Medical Practice Act of 1894.[5] It required that physicians

* Revised version of a paper presented at the fifty-fifth annual meeting of the American Association for the History of Medicine, Bethesda, Maryland, 30 April 1982. Research was supported by a grant from the Faculty Development Committee of Merrimack College.

[1] Supreme Judicial Court of Massachusetts, *Massachusetts Reports: Cases Decided and Determined by the Supreme Judicial Court of Massachusetts* (Boston: Little, Brown, 1908), 196 (1907): 326–29 (hereafter cited as *Massachusetts Reports*).

[2] Lawrence City Clerk, Birth Registration Sheets, 1907–13, City Hall, Lawrence, Massachusetts.

[3] See Judy Barrett Litoff, *American Midwives, 1860 to the Present* (Westport, Conn.: Greenwood Press, 1978); Jane B. Donegan, *Women and Men Midwives: Medicine, Morality and Misogyny in Early America* (Westport, Conn.: Greenwood Press, 1978); Frances E. Kobrin, "The American midwife controversy: a crisis of professionalization," *Bull. Hist. Med.*, 1966, *40*: 350–63.

[4] J. M. Baldy, "Is the midwife a necessity?" *Amer. J. Obstet. Diseases Women Children*, 1916, *73*: 400.

[5] Secretary of the Commonwealth of Massachusetts, *Acts and Resolves of the Commonwealth of Massachusetts*, 1894, chap. 458, pp. 530–33 (hereafter cited as *Acts and Resolves*).

be licensed and established penalties for those practicing obstetrics without a license.[6]

Was midwifery the same as obstetrics? The physicians who controlled the Massachusetts Board of Registration in Medicine contended that it was, and in the 1907 case of Commonwealth vs. Hanna Porn, the Massachusetts Supreme Court ruled that the midwife Porn's attendance at births was "contrary to the plain intent of the statute." The judge also noted Mrs. Porn's good character and suggested that it was possible for the Massachusetts legislature to "separate by a line of statutory demarcation the work of the midwife from that of the practitioner of medicine."[7] Such a distinction was never made as neither the Board of Registration in Medicine nor the Massachusetts Medical Society showed any interest in creating a system of education and licensing of midwives, such as the one which had been successfully developed in New Jersey.[8] Instead, the Porn decision, combined with an 1897 Birth Registration Act, put midwives in a double legal bind. The registration law required midwives and doctors to report all the births that they attended to the local city clerk, under penalty of a twenty-five dollar fine.[9] Therefore, if a midwife attended a birth and reported it, she was, in fact, admitting that she was practicing obstetrics. If she did not report the birth, she was breaking the Birth Registration Law.

When faced with these legal problems, a midwife could pursue one of four options. The first was to give up her practice, as many midwives in the Boston area apparently did.[10] Second, she could continue to practice surreptitiously, hoping to avoid the attention of legal authorities. Third, she could become, in essence, an obstetrical nurse who worked under the close supervision of a physician.[11] Her final option was to join with other midwives and battle politically the medical associations opposing her. However, the midwives never developed sufficient political self awareness and organization to respond successfully to their male competitors.[12]

It has generally been believed that, given these limited options, midwifery practice in Massachusetts quickly died out.[13] This was not the case. Midwifery practice continued and, as the example of Lawrence will illustrate,

[6] Reginald Fitz, "The Legislative Control of Medical Practice," in *Medical Communications of the Massachusetts Medical Society* (Boston: Massachusetts Medical Society, 1894), pp. 277–360.

[7] *Massachusetts Reports*, 196: 328.

[8] John A. Foote, "Legislative measures against maternal and infant mortality: the midwife practice laws of the states and territories of the United States," *Amer. J. Obstet. Diseases Women Children*, 1919, *80*: 534–51. See also James L. Huntington, "The midwife in Massachusetts: her anomalous position," *Boston Med. Surg. J.*, 1913, *168*: 418–21; Julius Levy, "Maternal mortality and mortality in the first month of life in relation to attendant at birth," *Amer. J. Public Health*, 1923, *13*: 88–95.

[9] *Acts and Resolves*, 1897, chap. 444, pp. 424–29.

[10] J. Whitridge Williams, "Medical education and the midwife problem in the United States," *JAMA*, 1912, *58*: 1–7. See also Baldy, "Midwife a necessity?" p. 401.

[11] Arthur B. Emmons and James L. Huntington, "A review of the midwife situation," *Boston Med. Surg. J.*, 1911, *164*: 261.

[12] Litoff, *American Midwives*, pp. 91–121.

[13] David Stewart, *Five Standards for Safe Childbearing* (Marble Hill, Missouri: NAPSAC. 1981), p. 126.

flourished openly in some areas for almost a decade after the Porn decision. Since changes in the law did not free Massachusetts of midwives, opponents began to focus their efforts on influencing public opinion.

The most vocal opponent of midwifery in Massachusetts, Dr. James L. Huntington, argued in a 1912 article in the *Boston Medical and Surgical Journal*: "But in (trying to stop midwifery), legislation is powerless. The keynote is education. We must educate the general public to realize the necessity for good obstetrics, and place the means of obtaining it at the disposal of all, and then with or without laws against the midwife, she will disappear from our cities."[14] The public education campaign advising women to consult physicians about obstetrics and not midwives, which began in the late nineteenth century, was to continue into the 1930s.[15] One of the factors involved was a redefinition of birth as a disease rather than a natural process.[16] Physicians stressed the pain of childbirth and the value of obstetrical anesthesia such as Twilight Sleep which could be administered only by a doctor in a hospital.[17] Class and racial bias were also invoked against the midwives.[18] Finally, hospital births were portrayed as a matter of status as well as of safety.[19] The cumulative impact of this educational campaign was substantial. A woman having a midwife as a birth attendant would not only be putting herself and her baby at needless risk of death, she would also be experiencing much greater pain than necessary by trusting her fate to a woman who generally served only those too ignorant to know any better. This was the message carried directly to women by physicians in lectures and public forums and also in articles in popular women's magazines.[20] Ironically, two of many women's greatest fears, the episiotomy and the use of forceps, became symbols of the technology medicine could bring to the aid of the parturient woman.[21] Still midwives continued to practice in Massachusetts in part because of the support of the only class of medical practitioner that medical societies viewed as worse than the midwife: the "ignorant and often unscrupulous" doctors who helped them.[22]

At a meeting of the Massachusetts Medical Society on 30 December 1913, Dr. Hugh Cabot complained that some members of the society were assisting

[14] James L. Huntington,"The regulation of midwifery," *Boston Med. Surg. J.*, 1912, *167*: 86.

[15] Litoff, *American Midwives*, pp. 64–90.

[16] Joseph B. DeLee, "Progress toward ideal obstetrics," *Trans. Amer. Assoc. Study Prevention Infant Mortality*, 1915, *6*: 117.

[17] Judith Walzer Leavitt, "Birthing and anesthesia: the debate over Twilight Sleep," *Signs*, 1980, *6*: 147–64.

[18] One article described the immigrant midwife as a woman who "knows nothing of hygiene, asepsis or antisepsis and is often practically responsible for the death and invalidism of mothers as well as the death, blindness and mental and physical impairment of infants. The immigrant midwife is herself a dirty, unkempt person living in a squalid tenement." See Carolyn C. Van Blarcom, "Midwives in America," *Amer. J. Public Health*, 1914, *4*: 198.

[19] Richard Wertz and Dorothy Wertz, *Lying-In: A History of Childbirth in America* (New York: The Free Press, 1977), pp. 146–60.

[20] Litoff, *American Midwives*, pp. 81–82.

[21] Joseph B. DeLee, "The prophylactic forceps operation," *Amer. J. Obstet. Gyn.*, 1920, *1*: 34–44.

[22] Huntington, "Regulation of midwifery," p. 84.

midwives by "... handing in birth returns for cases over which they have had no supervision."[23] Cabot felt that physicians must be enjoined from this practice. One step had been taken in 1912 by a change in the Birth Registration Law which required physicians to indicate on birth returns whether or not they had personally attended. A second, more direct attempt to control physicians' activities was manifested in a 1917 amendment to the Medical Practice Act. By this a physician could lose his license for one year if he "... acted as principal or assistant in carrying on the practice of medicine by an unregistered person."[24]

With this background in mind, the status and practice of midwives in Lawrence, Massachusetts, in the early twentieth century was studied. The primary focus of the investigation was to learn how the midwives and their clients coped with this changing legislation. Did the restrictions cause midwives to stop practicing? If not, how did they avoid prosecution? Did they serve only the immigrant community as some have suggested? What kind of relationships did they have with local doctors? Finally, if legal restrictions did not diminish their practice, what did?

This study of midwives in Lawrence is based on data drawn from several distinct sources. Most important are the birth registration records filed with the Lawrence City Clerk between the years 1896 and 1915. Lawrence was chosen as the focus of the study because it fitted the description of an "immigrant city," and its birth records had been kept intact and were made available by a cooperative city clerk. The choice of the years studied was dictated by the information contained in the records of this period. Prior to 1896 birth attendants often did not sign returns and consistent records begin in Lawrence only in that year.[25] In late September 1914, midwives in Lawrence all stopped signing returns as a result of the prosecution of several of them.[26] Returns through 1915 were analyzed to get a sense of the midwives' practice after they stopped signing returns, but empirical analysis is complete only through 30 September 1914.

The number of births attended by each midwife and each doctor in every year was recorded. As a result of limited resources, complete information from all 30,000 birth returns in this period could not be coded. Only in selected years—1896, 1900, 1905, 1910, 1914—was more information gathered, and when doctors attended, only the birthplace of the parents was noted. However, in the case of midwives attending in those years, the following information was coded: child's sex and name, father's name and mother's maiden name, address of parents, birth place of each parent, oc-

[23] Walter Burrage, *A History of the Massachusetts Medical Society, 1789–1922* (Norwood, Massachusetts: Plimpton Press, 1923), p. 255.

[24] *Ibid.*

[25] Some signed records from 1892–93 were found but these were not consistently recorded.

[26] Starting in October of 1914 and continuing through May of 1915, most of the major Lawrence midwives were prosecuted for "practicing medicine without a license." All pleaded guilty and were fined $100.

cupation of the father and, in 1914, ages of each parent, occupation of mother and the ward of Lawrence in which the birth took place. Complete information was also gathered on each midwife's deliveries in her first year and, when possible, the date of each midwife's first and last recorded delivery was identified. While more complete data is desirable, overall the study is based on the examination of over 30,000 individual records and almost 3,000 coded midwife returns.

In 1913, Lawrence began to undertake a census of births in the city. In the first few weeks of a year, canvassers visited every household in the city and recorded any births in that family in the previous year. The canvasser's cards were then matched to the birth return slips. These records were valuable in two ways. First, they filled in apparent gaps in the birth returns with approximately 100–200 births recorded each year that were not covered by the returns. Second, when midwives stopped signing returns, the canvasser's card provided a clue to their continued practice. For example, a birth return would be signed by a doctor who noted that he had not personally attended the birth, while the corresponding canvasser's card would list the attendant as one of the midwives. This discrepancy was probably the result of parents, perhaps unaware of the legal situation faced by midwives, candidly responding to the canvasser's question of who attended the birth. When the census cards and birth returns were later collated, the midwife's name would frequently be crossed out or erased and the doctor's name inserted. Also, on occasion, the census card would indicate two attendants, such as "Mrs. Riehm and Dr. Birmingham." This information enabled the authors to get a sense of the relationship between various doctors and midwives. The canvasser's cards by 1918 seldom noted midwives' deliveries, although interviews suggest that some women continued to practice for two more decades. The change in 1918 may have indicated a decline in midwife activity or simply a change in data collection procedures by the canvassers. Therefore, while the canvasser's cards will be used in certain cases, primary empirical analysis will focus on the period between 1896 and 1914 when more data is available.

Since all of the midwives who attended births in Lawrence have been dead for at least twenty years, the best source of information concerning the informal side of their practice was interviews with their relatives, friends, acquaintances and clients. These people were traced through an examination of the midwives' death records, obituaries and various marriage and birth records. Those contacted were sent a questionnaire and, when possible, interviewed. The same process was used to trace the relatives of important doctors. Also, the local newspapers from 1890–1915 that were available on microfilm were examined and records of midwives' and doctors' advertising were made.[27] Finally, the data on population and immigration was drawn from United States Census records and the annual reports of state births.[28]

[27] The *Evening Tribune* was the primary newspaper studied for this period.

[28] Secretary of the Commonwealth of Massachusetts, *Annual Reports of Births, Marriages and Deaths in the Commonwealth*, Public Document No. 1 (Boston: State Printers, 1860–1930). These will be cited hereafter

Before examining the impact of the Porn decision on the midwives of Lawrence, it is important to understand why the setting of this study so aptly fitted the description of an immigrant city. Lawrence, Massachusetts, was chartered in 1847 as a six-square-mile planned mill community on the Merrimack River twenty-five miles north of Boston. Founded as a model town by Abbott Lawrence, the community soon flourished, and by 1850 the population was 6,000, most of whom were mill workers drawn from the New England states. They had the services of a library, eleven schools and a dozen doctors, all provided under the paternalistic arrangements of the mill owners.[29]

The character of the city changed as the labor supply was drawn in greater numbers from Europe. The first wave of immigrants consisted of Irish families in the 1850s and 1860s. Changes were particularly rapid in the city from 1890–1910 when Germans, Russians, Italians, Turks and Poles moved there (see Table 1). In 1890, the city population was 44,654; by 1915, it had grown to 90,259 with 45.8 percent of the population being foreign born.[30] While the birth rate changed little in this period, by 1915 the rapidly increasing population resulted in a doubling of the number of births in the city to 2,948.

By the turn of the century the city was hardly a model community as it now had a large, poor, overcrowded, generally illiterate population. Relations between laborers and mill owners were continually strained as the workers sought to organize into unions. The culmination of this tension was a strike in 1912 which drew national attention to Lawrence as a symbol of both the struggle faced by immigrants and the bitterness of union-management disputes nationally.[31] It was in this setting that the midwives worked, in many cases renewing a practice they had established in another country, and which had been interrupted when they joined their husbands who sought a better life in the mills of Lawrence.

Figure 1 illustrates the proportion of recorded births attended by midwives, male doctors and female doctors. It suggests why physicians felt so threatened by midwives that Hanna Porn was taken to court. In 1903, male doctors attended 67.6 percent of all births in Lawrence, but by 1908 the figure had dropped to 56.5 percent. Even more striking is the consistency of the gains made by midwives, who more than doubled the proportion of

---

as *Births, Marriages and Deaths*. The total births for Lawrence listed in these volumes are typically higher than the number of birth registration sheets remaining in the Lawrence Clerk's office. This is partly the result of the state totals being drawn from the summary birth registration books which have a number of entries made after the end of the calendar year. It also probably reflects a loss of some sheets—a problem largely rectified with the initiation of the birth canvass. Also an examination of ethnicity suggests that there was no systematic bias in the data.

[29] Donald Cole, *Immigrant City: Lawrence, Massachusetts, 1845–1921* (Chapel Hill: University of North Carolina Press, 1963), pp. 17–26.

[30] *Ibid.*, p. 209.

[31] *Ibid.*, pp. 1–13; 177–94. See also William Cahn, *Lawrence 1912: The Bread and Roses Strike* (New York: Pilgrim Press, 1977).

Table 1. Immigration Into Lawrence, 1890–1910

Year	Total Population	Nativity							
		Ireland	England	Canada	Germany	Russia	France	Italy	Turkey
1890	44,654	7,697	4,985	4,459	1,830	60	0	46	5
1895	52,164	7,487	5,486	5,665	2,402	426	68	263	213
1900	62,559	7,058	5,131	8,682	2,465	780	147	936	277
1905	70,050	6,557	5,153	7,597	2,388	1,297	435	2,804	1,332
1910	85,892	5,943	5,659	9,498	2,301	4,366	788	6,693	2,077
Net Change	+41,238	−1,754	+674	+5,039	+471	+4,306	+788	+6,647	+2,072

Source: Derived from Donald Cole, *Immigrant City* (Chapel Hill: University of North Carolina Press, 1963), p. 209.

births they attended between 1900 and 1908 from 19.9 percent to 41.3 percent. Female doctors played a small role in this period, except between 1898 and 1901. Their activity in those years was primarily the result of the arrival of one woman—Johanna Koehler. Dr. Koehler personally accounted for 60 percent of the 813 deliveries attended by six different female doctors in those four years. After Dr. Koehler's departure in 1902, female doctors attended, on the average, only about one in thirty births in the city. In 1914 this dropped to a low of attendance at 0.6 percent of all births.

Figure 1 also makes clear the limited immediate effect of the Porn decision of 1907. Seven years after the decision, midwives were still attending 40 percent of the deliveries in the city and *signing the birth returns* in clear violation of the law. In another sense, however, the outcome of the Porn case may well have had an effect. The steady growth in the number of midwife deliveries stopped after 1908, though other factors, discussed below, also influenced that change. Overall, however, figure 1 clearly illustrates that the legal campaign to drive out the midwives was only partially successful at the outset. As contemporary opponents of midwives noted, legislation alone was not sufficient to stop immediately midwives' practice in Lawrence or in similar communities.[32]

Another factor that probably concerned opponents was the growing number of midwives in Lawrence and the changing nature of their practice. If midwifery practice in a community was limited to one or two women, they could be singled out for special sanctions or attention.[33] However, if there were greater numbers of midwives, it was more difficult to control them and there was greater public support for their activities. In 1896, there were 327 midwife-attended deliveries in Lawrence. One woman, Louise Beck, was responsible for all of these. By 1913, there were more than a dozen active midwives attending almost 100 births a month with the busiest woman, Minnie Riehm, accounting for only 18 percent of all midwife deliveries.[34] Therefore, the opponents of midwifery could not succeed by shutting down the practice of even the most prominent midwife in the city. The fact that there were a number of midwives practicing is important to keep in mind as the reasons why the proportion of midwife-attended births remained so high are examined.

Midwifery in Lawrence continued for a number of reasons including the immigrant nature of the population, the lack of a hospital providing obstet-

[32] For example, in a 1909 study of five Massachusetts cities, Huntington found that 15 percent of all births were attended by midwives, and argued for the public education campaign described above. See Huntington, "Regulation of midwifery," p. 86.

[33] Roger W. Cobb and Charles D. Elder, *Participation in American Politics: The Dynamics of Agenda-Building* (Boston: Allyn & Bacon; paperback, Baltimore: The Johns Hopkins University Press, 1972), pp. 124–29.

[34] Lawrence City Clerk, Birth Registration Sheets, 1913. Physician obstetrical practice was also decentralized. In 1913, there were forty-one physicians, as opposed to twelve in 1896, who attended at least ten births. They averaged about 140 deliveries a month with the busiest physician, Dr. Alphonse Riopelle, attending 14 percent of all physician deliveries.

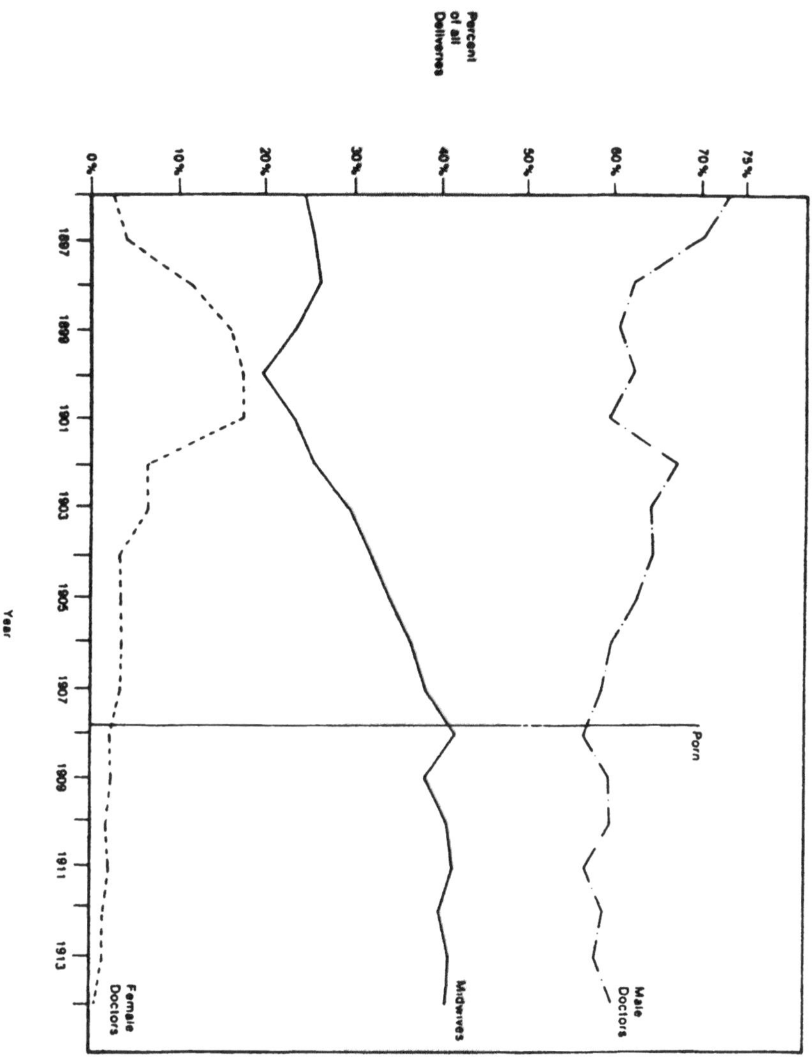

Figure 1. Percent Distribution of Recorded Deliveries in Lawrence, 1896–1914

rical care, the quality of the care provided at limited cost by the midwives, their use of advertising and finally, when the laws were more rigorously enforced, the midwives' ability to circumvent them. Of these factors, the most important was the immigrant nature of Lawrence's population. The relationship between immigration and midwifery was apparent to some midwife critics, such as Dr. Ira Wile, who noted that: "the interrelation of immigration and midwifery may not seem patent at first glance. A moment's thought, however, will show that in the problems relating to the restriction of immigration and the restriction of midwifery there are many points in common."[35] In Lawrence, between 1896 and 1914, the proportion of births to immigrants to total births was never less than 81.8 percent and was as high as 86.2 percent in 1909.[36] More important, as noted earlier (see Table 1), the immigrants in Lawrence at this time were primarily from Southern and Eastern Europe where, as Wile pointed out, "... the midwife exists as an established institution."[37] While English, Irish, and Canadian immigrants accounted for 84 percent of the total foreign-born Lawrence population in 1890, by 1910 they made up only 51 percent of all immigrants in the city.[38] Van Blarcom was prophetic when she stated:

> The desire of foreign women to employ midwives and the determination of midwives to be employed is so strong that even were midwives legislated out of existence they would still be called in by expectant mothers ... (and) among the Italians the husbands of the expectant mothers will seldom permit a physician or "man midwife" to be employed.[39]

Also, among those moving into the city were many women with formal training and established practices overseas who expected to continue their professional activities in their new home. In contrast, the ethnic groups already in the city had generally relied on doctors of their own nationality to deliver their babies. This was particularly true for Canadian mothers.[40]

Of the three active midwives in the city in 1900, two were generalists in terms of the ethnic groups they served while the third—Ann Curran—was a specialist. Almost all of the forty-two births she attended were either to women born in Ireland (thirty-one) or women born in the United States with Irish maiden names. The other two active midwives, Hedwig Himmer and Minnie Riehm, served a heterogeneous mix of women from Italy, Ireland, Poland, Germany and England. Five years later, the situation had changed considerably. In 1900, births to Canadian mothers accounted for

[35] Ira S. Wile, "Immigration and the midwife problem," *Boston Med. Surg. J.*, 1912, *167*: 113.
[36] *Births, Marriages and Deaths*, 1910, vol. 68.
[37] Wile, "Immigration and the midwife problem," p. 113.
[38] Cole, *Immigrant City*, p. 209.
[39] Van Blarcom, "Midwives in America," p. 203.
[40] For example, in 1900, 95 percent of births to Canadian mothers were attended by five doctors, primarily Omer Routhier (160), A.J. Riopelle (126) and Alphonse Petit (52). Likewise all but eighteen of the almost 400 deliveries attended by these five doctors were either to mothers born in Canada or women whose husbands were Canadian. Only nine births to Canadian mothers were attended by midwives.

almost one-third of all births in the city and those to Italian mothers one-twentieth. By 1905, the proportion of births in the city to Canadian mothers dropped to one-fourth while births to Italian mothers now numbered over 200 or one-eighth of all city births. It should also be noted that these Italian mothers relied almost exclusively on midwives, most notably, Angelina Lopiano (120 of 122 deliveries to Italian mothers), Serafina Isabella (36 of 38 deliveries) and the ubiquitous Minnie Riehm (37 of 192 deliveries). There was also a midwife who served only Syrian mothers and yet another whose clients were all Portuguese.

As these new immigrant groups moved into the city, they apparently were not deterred by, and perhaps were even unaware of, the legislative and court battles being waged in Boston. It is also noteworthy that as late as 1907 there were no Italian doctors in Lawrence attending births, and they did not become involved in more than a handful of births until 1914. An examination of city directories reveals that the two doctors who were most active in delivering babies after the midwives stopped signing returns did not appear in any directory until 1905 (Dr. Joseph Sinclitico) and 1909 (Dr. Constant Calitri).[41] Hence, when the first wave of Italian immigrants arrived in Lawrence at the turn of the century they not only brought with them a preference for midwives but they also found few Italian doctors to serve them. Therefore, a cultural preference for midwives in certain key ethnic groups and a dearth of doctors to serve these populations combined to provide a major impetus for continued midwifery practice in the city.[42]

A second factor contributing to the popularity of the midwives was the lack of opportunity to give birth in a hospital. Although much of the effort of the "reformers" of midwifery legislation was aimed at moving birth from the home to the hospital, this was not possible in Lawrence.[43] Lawrence in this period had only one major hospital. The Lawrence General Hospital had opened in 1875, but it was not until 1903 that the city records note a birth there, and it was 1911 before the hospital first recorded one hundred births in a single year. In 1913 there were 145 deliveries at Lawrence General and twenty-three more at two smaller hospitals, accounting for 6 percent of all births in the city. Four midwives and one physician had more home deliveries individually that year. The overwhelming majority of Lawrence physicians attended only home births prior to 1915. By 1920, however, obstetrical practice at the hospital had increased to 354 births or about one out of every eight in the city. The births were attended by a variety of doctors though

[41] *The Laurence Directory* (Boston: Sampson & Murdock), annual editions from 1900 to 1910.

[42] For a more complete study of the relationship between midwifery practice and ethnicity in Lawrence, see Eugene Declercq and Richard Lacroix, "The Politics and Sociology of Immigrant Midwifery Practice in Lawrence, Massachusetts," a paper presented at the annual meeting of the Organization of American Historians, Cincinnati, Ohio, April 1983.

[43] Wertz and Wertz, *Lying-In*, pp. 132–77.

certain ethnic groups, notably Italians and Canadians, still gave birth almost exclusively at home.[44]

A third factor working on behalf of the midwives was that many of them did not fit the dire images drawn of them by their adversaries. The busiest of the midwives in Lawrence were all literate, had specialized education, and were apparently concerned about hygiene. Many had been trained in Europe where, as an article in the *Journal of the American Medical Association* noted, "They are admitted to lying in asylums for poor women and are taught cleanliness and the physiology of labor theoretically as well as practically."[45] For example, Louise Beck had graduated from the "principal school of obstetrics" in Germany, Hedwig Himmer from the Royal School of Obstetrics in Dresden, Serafina Isabella from the Clinica Obstetrica in Naples and Virginia Pedrazzini from the University of Milan. Some of the midwives received their training in the United States with Minnie Riehm (New York School of Midwifery) the most prominent example.[46] In addition, the midwives were often members of various social and religious groups in the city and, in serveral cases, their spouses were also prominent men in the community.

A fourth incentive for the use of midwives was financial. The standard cost for midwifery services was five dollars for which a mother often received, "... attendance at confinement, simple nursing care, help in the household duties and general nursing and oversight of the home until such time as she is able to resume her work."[47] Daily checkups from midwives for eight to ten days were common, while physicians would usually limit themselves to one or two postpartum visits. Of equal importance to some of those interviewed was the fact that most midwives would accept payment in kind such as food and services, while doctors usually wanted to be paid their ten dollar fee in cash. Flexible payments of this type were important since the average mill worker in Lawrence in 1912 made eight dollars and seventy-six cents for working a fifty-four hour week.[48]

Another reason why midwives retained their prominence was advertising. At almost no time between 1896 and 1911 did a daily edition of the *Lawrence Evening Tribune* appear without an advertisement for at least one midwife in it. Louise Beck, Minnie Riehm, and Hedwig Himmer advertised most frequently. With the exception of Serafina Isabella, the Italian midwives never advertised in the *Tribune*, perhaps either relying on informal communication networks or a more specialized Italian newspaper. The *Tribune*

[44] Thomas Leavitt, *Mill Owners and Missionaries: A History of the Lawrence General Hospital* (Lawrence: Lawrence General Hospital, 1975), pp. 1–28. See also City of Lawrence, Birth Registration Summary Volumes, 1900–1930, City Hall, Lawrence, Massachusetts.

[45] "Supervision of midwives," *JAMA*, 1907, *48*: 712.

[46] This information was drawn from the midwives' obituaries, their advertisements, and interviews with their descendants.

[47] S. Josephine Baker, "The function of the midwife," *Women's Med. J.*, 1913, *23*: 197.

[48] U.S., Congress, Senate, *Report on Strike of Textile Workers in Lawrence, Massachusetts, 1912*. Prepared under Charles P. Neill, Commissioner of Labor. 62nd Cong., 2nd Sess., 1912, Document #870, p. 72.

advertisements were generally straightforward and were quite similar to those used by physicians at the time. In fact, several of the midwives, including Hedwig Himmer, referred to themselves as doctors.[49] Minnie Riehm, for most of her eight years of advertising, also stated that she was a "successor to Louise Beck," which she was, quite literally. The last advertisement for Louise Beck appeared on 8 May 1899 (her last recorded delivery in Lawrence was on 11 May before she moved to Paterson, New Jersey), followed the next day by a "successor" advertisement for Mrs. Riehm who even lived at the same address that Mrs. Beck had. This use of advertising continued after the Porn decision but only by Mrs. Himmer. Minnie Riehm's final advertisement appeared on 7 May 1907 and a month later Serafina Isabella's last advertisement was published. Mrs. Himmer continued running advertisements until 3 June 1911, but under the category of doctors.

Finally, when pressure from some physicians forced the midwives to be less conspicuous, they adopted several tactics which allowed them to continue their practice. As noted earlier, in 1911 and 1912 a change on birth registration forms was gradually implemented. A line was added which read, "I did (doctor's name) personally attend this birth." This was a means used to identify those doctors who might be aiding midwives and, indeed, in some cases most of a doctor's birth returns would involve deliveries he did not attend. The fact that midwives attended the mothers involved in these cases is based on evidence drawn from the canvasser's census cards attached to the birth returns. There were references to virtually all midwives on the canvasser's cards even after they had stopped signing birth returns in 1914. In many cases, a midwife appears in conjunction with a doctor. However, from examining the records, the exact nature of the relationship between the midwives and the physicians is unclear.

There were apparently two strategies used by midwives in these cases. In some instances, midwives working with a cooperative physician would deliver the baby and the doctor would later check on the mother and complete the birth return. According to the descendants of several of the midwives, several doctors agreed to these informal cooperative relationships. In other cases, involving less friendly doctors, the midwives would attend the birth, clean up and leave, and have the parents get in touch with a doctor. According to one physician from that era, it was this practice that led him to contact state authorities in an unsuccessful attempt to have several midwives arrested in the early 1920s.[50]

[49] The first "doctor" advertisement for Hedwig Himmer appeared on 4 June 1902 in the *Evening Tribune*, p. 7 and similar ads ran until 3 June 1911. The text of Himmer's advertisement was as follows: "Dr. H. Himmer, Midwife, 190 Park St., Lawrence. Graduate from the Royal School of Obstetrics at Dresden, Germany. I am prepared to respond to all calls made upon me. Telephone 740-11," *Laurence Evening Tribune*, 5 January 1905. Serafina Isabella's advertisement referred to her as a "Lady Physician and Midwife" and noted that she was bilingual and responded to calls at all hours while charging five dollars for eight to ten days' attendance, *Laurence Evening Tribune*, 4 January 1904.

[50] Interviews with Dr. N. F. Decesare and descendants of midwives Angelina Lopiano, Elena Stella, Concetta Leonardi, Virginia Pedrazzani, Angelina DeMarco and Paola Leone.

A careful examination of birth records revealed another strategy adopted by certain midwives: having fathers complete birth returns and sign as attendants. Prior to 30 September 1914, the proportion of birth returns signed by fathers was never greater than 1 percent. In the final three months of 1914, it was almost 5 percent. However, the assumption of midwives' involvement was based on more than inference. Canvasser's cards attached to birth returns signed by fathers frequently listed midwives as the attendant. The midwife most commonly cited in this regard was Minnie Riehm.

It might appear from the above discussion that the midwives were organized in some formal or informal relationship. Interviews with their descendants and analysis of the dates of births attended by midwives indicate that relations between the midwives were cordial at best. There was no formal organization of midwives and no evidence to suggest that, for example, one midwife might cover for another on vacation. It appears that some of the busiest midwives never took a vacation since no clear break in the dates of their deliveries occurs. Even within ethnic groups, the relationships between midwives appear complex with factors such as birthplace within a country, neighborhood and training all playing a role. For example, most of the Italian midwives were divided into Sicilians and Neapolitans, which in turn influenced the area of the city in which they lived and, therefore, practiced.[51]

Eventually, the combination of legal restrictions, physicians' opposition, the greater influx of foreign-born doctors, the rise in hospital births, the passage of restrictions on immigration in the 1920s, and the assimilation of immigrants resulted in the diminution of midwifery practice. By the late 1920s midwives were the attendants at only a small fraction of the births in the city. Interviews with their descendants, however, indicate that several of the midwives continued to practice into the 1930s. Also, in the *Lawrence Directory*, in the listing of nurses, Angelina DeMarco (1933), Concetta Leonardi (1938) and Angelina Lopiano (1938) continued to have the word midwife added after their name well into the 1930s.[52] By this time, their practice was limited primarily to family and friends.

Overall, this research has shown that changes in the legal restrictions regulating midwifery practice had little immediate impact on the activities of midwives in Lawrence, Massachusetts. For at least seven years after supposedly being legislated out of existence, midwives continued to practice openly in the city and, for some time after, practiced surreptitiously. The factors that enabled them to continue practicing despite the legal changes were primarily the immigrant nature of the population, the midwife's own skill and standing in the community, their minimal fees in a working-class community, and their ability to circumvent the statutes, often with the help of cooperative

[51] *Ibid.*

[52] *The Lawrence Directory*, annual editions from 1933 to 1938.

physicians. As conditions changed, most notably with the arrival of doctors who were also immigrants and who did not cooperate with midwives, the law became a larger barrier for the midwives. In essence, the first thrust of the campaign against midwifery—legal changes—served as a necessary, but clearly not a sufficient, condition to eliminate midwifery practice. Eventually, by 1940, as limits on immigration cut down the flow of newcomers who supported the midwives, midwifery practice in Lawrence largely disappeared.

"Science" Enters the Birthing Room: Obstetrics in America since the Eighteenth Century

Judith Walzer Leavitt

At the end of the eighteenth century, Dr. William Shippen, Jr., of Philadelphia attended all the childbearing women in the well-established Drinker family. The family members chose Shippen instead of a woman midwife, in spite of their ambivalence about having a man in the traditionally all-female birthing room, because they believed the physician offered the best hope for a successful outcome. The Drinkers, and many others like them, considered themselves fortunate to be living at a time when male physicians began replacing female midwives in the birthing rooms of the American urban elite. The families expected—and believed that they received—better care at the hands of physicians than they thought possible with traditional female attendants. This article examines the promises of the new physician-directed obstetrics—beginning in the 1760s, when physicians entered obstetrics, and ending in the 1940s, after they dominated the field—and evaluates the extent to which those promises were kept.[1]

Before 1760 birth was a women's affair in the British colonies of North America. When a woman went into labor, she "called her women together" and left her husband and other male family members outside. "I went to bed about 10 o'clock," wrote William Byrd of Virginia, "and left the women full of expectation with my wife." Only in cases where women were not available did men participate in labor and delivery, and only in cases where labor did not

Judith Walzer Leavitt is associate professor of the history of medicine and women's studies at the University of Wisconsin, Madison. This paper was written for and first delivered at the Seventh International Symposium on the Comparative History of Medicine—East and West, Susono-Shi, Japan, Sept. 19-26, 1982. This symposium is held by the Division of Medical History, the Taniguchi Foundation.

[1] Cecil K. Drinker, *Not So Long Ago: A Chronicle of Medicine and Doctors in Colonial Philadelphia* (New York, 1937), 50-62; Jane B. Donegan, *Women and Men Midwives: Medicine, Morality, and Misogyny in Early America* (Westport, Conn., 1978); and Catherine M. Scholten, "'On the Importance of the Obstetrick Art': Changing Customs of Childbirth in America, 1760 to 1825," *William and Mary Quarterly*, 34 (July 1977), 426-45. The scope of the subject of changing obstetric practices necessitates a synthetic analysis and does not permit full documentation here of all the points raised.

progress normally did physicians intervene and perhaps extricate a dead fetus. The midwife orchestrated the events of labor and delivery, and the women neighbors and relatives comforted and shared advice with the parturient.[2] Women suffered through the agonies and dangers of birth together, sought each other's support, and shared the relief of successful deliveries and the grief of unsuccessful ones. This "social childbirth" experience united women and provided, as Carroll Smith-Rosenberg has argued, one of the functional bonds that formed the basis of women's domestic culture.[3]

Within their own homes, birthing women controlled much of the experience of childbirth. They determined the physical setting for their births, the people to attend them during labor and delivery, and the aids or comforts employed. Midwives traditionally played a noninterventionist, supportive role in the home birthing rooms. As much as possible they let nature take its course: they examined the cervix or encouraged women to walk around; they caught the child, tied the umbilical cord, and if necessary fetched the placenta. In complicated cases, midwives might have turned the fetus—podalic version—or fortified women with hard liquor or mulled wine. They may have manually stretched the cervix or, rarely, administered ergot. Midwives spent most of their time, as the written record reveals, comforting the parturient and waiting. The other women attendants supported the midwife and the birthing woman, and the atmosphere in the birthing rooms—if everything proceeded normally—was congenial and cooperative. Parturient women, who felt vulnerable at the time of their confinements, armed themselves with the strength of other women who had passed through the event successfully.[4]

Despite the very positive aspects of social childbirth, a romantic image of childbirth in this period would be misleading. Women garnered support from their networks of companions, but they continued to fear their births because of the possibilities of death or debility that could and frequently did result from childbirth. Although statistics do not exist to measure these dangers precisely, women's fears were not unfounded. By all accounts maternal and infant mortality rates were high. Furthermore, postpartum gynecological problems

[2] Louis B. Wright and Marion Tinling, eds., *The Secret Diary of William Byrd of Westover, 1709-1792* (Richmond, 1941), 79. The phrase "called her women together" is common in early childbirth accounts. See, for example, the diary of midwife Martha Moore Ballard of Augusta, Maine, November 21, 1785—"Mrs. Cowen called her women together this evening; was safely delivered of a daughter about the middle of the night and is comfortable"—and February 18, 1786—"Mrs. Fletcher called her women again this morn, and was safely delivered of a daughter." Charles Elventon Nash, *The History of Augusta: First Settlements and Early Days as a Town, including the Diary of Mrs. Martha Moore Ballard (1785 to 1812)* (Augusta, Maine, 1904), 243, 246.

[3] Carroll Smith-Rosenberg, "The Female World of Love and Ritual: Relations between Women in Nineteenth-Century America," *Signs*, 1 (Autumn 1975), 1-29. For a discussion of social childbirth, see Richard W. Wertz and Dorothy C. Wertz, *Lying-In: A History of Childbirth in America* (New York, 1977), 1-26.

[4] On midwives' practices, see Donegan, *Women and Men Midwives*, 9-11, 25, 127; Scholten, "'On the Importance of the Obstetrick Art,'" 429-31, 432-34; Claire E. Fox, "Pregnancy, Childbirth and Early Infancy in Anglo-American Culture: 1675-1830" (Ph.D. diss., University of Pennsylvania, 1966), 122-27; and Janet Bogdan, "Care or Cure? Childbirth Practices in Nineteenth Century America," *Feminist Studies*, 4 (June 1978), 94.

resulting from unsutured perineal tears, prolapsed uteri, or vesico-vaginal and recto-vaginal fistulas caused some women extreme discomfort and disability throughout the rest of their lives. Women's fears of death and physical debility led them away from traditional birthing patterns to a long search for safer and less painful childbirths. Thus some women, especially those who were economically advantaged, tried to modify traditional births by incorporating new possibilities as they became available. Like the Drinkers, these eighteenth-century women readily invited physicians to attend them, despite their worries about the propriety of having men participate in intimate female events, in hopes that the "man-midwives" could provide easier and safer births.[5]

The entrance of physician-accoucheurs into the practice of obstetrics in America during the second half of the eighteenth century marked the first significant break with tradition. The story of this new midwifery, familiar to historians of American medicine, centers on Shippen, who in 1762 returned from his studies in London and Edinburgh and established the first systematic series of lectures on midwifery in America. Shippen initially trained both female midwives and male physicians in anatomy (including the gravid uterus), but he soon limited his lectures to male students. He established a private practice of midwifery and became a favorite of Philadelphia's established families. The Drinkers found him "very kind and attentive" during labor and delivery and noted that he remained with his patients even during protracted labors and "sleep't very little."[6]

Shippen was the most famous of late-eighteenth-century physicians who practiced midwifery, but he was not alone. Numerous doctors expanded their practice of medicine and began to attend laboring women. The transition to male attendants occurred so easily among advantaged urban women that it can only be explained by understanding the women's impression that physicians knew more than midwives about the birth process and about what to do if things went wrong. Women overturned millennia of all-female tradition and invited men into their birthing rooms because they believed that men offered additional security against the potential dangers of childbirth. By their acknowledgement of physician superiority, women changed the fashions of childbearing and made it desirable to be attended by physicians.[7]

Women had good reason to believe that physicians could provide services that midwives could not. Many of the physicians who practiced obstetrics at

[5] For more on women's perceptions of childbirth as a time of danger, see Judith Walzer Leavitt and Whitney Walton, "Down to Death's Door: Women's Perceptions of Childbirth in America," in *Proceedings of the Second Motherhood Symposium: Childbirth: The Beginning of Motherhood*, ed. Sophie Colleau (Madison, 1982), 113-36. On efforts to compute maternal mortality, see B. M. Willmott Dobbie, "An Attempt to Estimate the True Rate of Maternal Mortality, Sixteenth to Eighteenth Centuries," *Medical History*, 26 (Jan. 1982), 79-90; and Louis I. Dublin, "Mortality among Women from Causes Incidental to Childbearing," *American Journal of Obstetrics and Diseases of Women and Children*, 78 (July 1918), 20-37.

[6] Drinker, *Not So Long Ago*, 60-61; Lewis C. Scheffey, "The Earlier History and the Transition Period of Obstetrics and Gynecology in Philadelphia," *Annals of Medical History*, 2 (May 1940), 215-16.

[7] Scholten, "'On the Importance of the Obstetrick Art,'" 434-36.

the turn of the nineteenth century had trained in Great Britain, where a tradition of male accoucheurs had already developed. The men had access to education then denied to women, which provided theoretical understanding of female anatomy and the process of parturition. Whereas women midwives relied on practical experience and an appeal to female traditions—attributes to some extent taken for granted and unappreciated—men physicians had the extra advantage and prestige associated with formal learning. Even though most American practitioners had not attended medical school and were themselves apprentice trained, physicians carried with them the status advantages of their gender and of the popular image of superior education. Furthermore, birthing women perceived that the male presence had already contributed opium and forceps to obstetrics and promised even greater benefits in the future. The appeal to overturn tradition was strong.[8]

When Shippen attended Sally Drinker Downing's 1795 birth, which was complicated by a footling presentation, he administered opium to relieve her suffering. Two years later, faced with another of Downing's difficult labors, Shippen "was oblig'd to force her mouth open to give some thing with a view of reviving her." In 1799 Downing again suffered a protracted labor, and Shippen took fourteen ounces of blood and then gave her eighty to ninety drops of liquid laudanum. According to Downing's mother, when labor still did not progress, Shippen gave "an Opium pill three grains he said, in order to ease her pain, or to bring it on more violently." When this still did not produce the desired result, Shippen threatened to use his instruments, but finally Downing delivered without them.[9]

Shippen's practice of allaying painful and lengthy labors by bleeding, giving opium, and occasionally using forceps illustrates why women wanted physicians to attend them. The prospect of a difficult birth, which all women fearfully anticipated, and the knowledge that physicians' remedies could provide relief and successful outcomes led women to seek out practitioners whose obstetric armamentarium included drugs and instruments.[10]

The promise of the new obstetrics developed in part through formal physician education in midwifery. Shippen's first lectures covered pelvic anatomy, the gravid uterus, the placenta, fetal circulation and nutrition, natural and unnatural labor, and the use of obstetrical instruments. He demonstrated on manikins and on patients—poor women for whom he provided accommodation—and used drawings and textbooks. Other physicians followed his example, and courses in midwifery became available in Boston and New York as well as in Philadelphia.[11]

During the first half of the nineteenth century medical education in obstet-

[8] Bogdan, "Care or Cure?" 96–97; Donegan, *Women and Men Midwives*, 141–57.

[9] Drinker, *Not So Long Ago*, 51–53, 58–61.

[10] Jane B. Donegan argues that William Shippen practiced conservative obstetrics when compared to the "meddlesome midwifery" of others. Donegan, *Women and Men Midwives*, 118–19. For more on Shippen, see Betsy Copping Corner, *William Shippen, Jr.: Pioneer in American Medical Education: A Biographical Essay* (Philadelphia, 1951).

[11] Lawrence D. Longo, "Obstetrics and Gynecology," in *The Education of American Physicians: Historical Essays*, ed. Ronald L. Numbers (Berkeley, 1980), 205–08.

rics expanded. To many professors and students, the subject was embarrassing, and students generally did not observe women in labor but received only a theoretical education. Samuel D. Gross, a student who observed Thomas Chalkley James teaching obstetrics at the University of Pennsylvania early in the nineteenth century, noticed that "it was seldom that he . . . looked squarely at his audience. His cheeks would be mantled with blushes while engaging in demonstrating some pelvic viscus, or discussing topics not mentionable in ordinary conversation. It was often painful to witness his embarrassment."[12]

Although the embarrassment of physicians about their role in obstetrics soon disappeared, the question of a man's proper behavior in a woman's birthing room continued to influence the teaching and the practice of obstetrics. Of William Potts Dewees, who succeeded James at the University of Pennsylvania, Gross observed, "he did not hesitate to call things by their proper names. No blush suffused his cheek in the lecture-room." But Dewees, whose *A Compendious System of Midwifery* went through an influential twelve editions, remained as horrified by the idea of ocular inspection as his most modest patients. Using manikins, he taught his students how to perform unsighted digital explorations of parturient women. Even when applying forceps, Dewees taught, "every attention should be paid to delicacy . . . the patient should not be exposed . . . even for the drawing off of the urine. . . . The operator must become familiar with the introduction of the instruments without the aid of sight."[13]

Students graduating from such didactic obstetrics courses were forced to enter the birthing rooms of their first patients in relative ignorance. Never having witnessed actual births, and armed with only theoretical knowledge, they must have been somewhat apprehensive. Yet doctors knew that they had to be confident to gain confidence, and they forged ahead and delivered babies. One medical graduate wrote that when he delivered his first baby he examined the laboring woman, "but whether it was head or breech, hand or foot, man or monkey, that was defended from my uninstructed finger by the distended membranes, I was as uncomfortably ignorant, with all my learning, as the foetus itself that was making all this fuss."[14] Rejecting the practical experience of the midwives' training, those physicians who had formal medical education tried to raise the practice of obstetrics to a higher level by emphasizing anatomy and physiology.

Through their theoretical training, this physician elite had the potential to expand the practice of obstetrics beyond individual experience. Apprentice-trained midwives and physicians could develop expertise only insofar as their

[12] *Autobiography of Samuel D. Gross, M.D., with Sketches of His Contemporaries*, ed. [Samuel Weissel Gross and Albert Haller Gross] (2 vols., Philadelphia, 1887), II, 240.

[13] *Ibid.*, 247; William P. Dewees, *A Compendious System of Midwifery, Chiefly Designed to Facilitate the Inquiries of Those Who May Be Pursuing This Branch of Study* (Philadelphia, 1843), 289. See also Irving S. Cutter and Henry R. Viets, *A Short History of Midwifery* (Philadelphia, 1964), 156–57.

[14] Wertz and Wertz, *Lying-In*, 50.

mentors' or their own experiences took them, and wider perspectives remained elusive. But when some doctors took it upon themselves to study anatomy of the female pelvis and activity of the gravid uterus, they removed knowledge from its anchor in individual human experience and brought it to a more abstract level. Learning what was possible and probable in labor and delivery, what was normal and abnormal, provided these birth attendants with knowledge to make judgments on the individual cases they examined.

While the potential for this increased enlightenment may have existed, the question remains whether or not individual medical graduates related their theoretical knowledge to the actual cases they faced in their practices. Did male physicians enhance or improve childbirth, as women believed they would? Did "science," the symbol of the promises of physician-directed obstetrics, come to the aid of birthing women?

Either because of their training or because of families' expectations, male physicians, the apprentice trained and medical school graduates alike, intervened in the birth process more than midwives. Walter Channing, professor of obstetrics at Harvard, advised that a doctor, when called to attend laboring women, "must do something. He cannot remain a spectator merely, where there are many witnesses, and where interest in what is going on is too deep to allow of his inaction. Let him be collected and calm, and he will probably do little he will afterwards look upon with regret."[15]

Physicians' favorite interventions during the first half of the nineteenth century were bloodletting, drugs, and forceps, frequently all used together. Dewees advocated substantial bloodletting. In one of his difficult cases, for example, with the woman standing on her feet, he took "upwards of two quarts" until she fainted. Dewees remarked that "every thing appeared better . . . I introduced the forceps, and delivered a living and healthy child." Physicians believed that venesection could relieve pain, accelerate labor, soften a rigid cervix, ease podalic version, and reduce inflammation. They even bled patients who were hemorrhaging, using the logic that further reducing circulation would produce blood clotting and stop the hemorrhage. They also relieved puerperal convulsions by bloodletting. In fact, as one historian has concluded, "bloodletting . . . was uncritically accepted as the fashion in early American obstetric practice."[16]

The use of opium or laudanum (tincture of opium) seems to have been equally popular among physician-accoucheurs in the nineteenth century. In cases of protracted labor, as in the Shippen-Downing cases cited above, physicians tried opium to accelerate cervical dilation and ease suffering. They also employed cathartics to open the bowels, ergot to stimulate contractions, tobacco infusions to encourage the cervix to dilate, and manually breaking the waters to accelerate labor. In cases of extreme need physicians could surgically separate the pubic bones to facilitate passage of the fetus's head or they could

[15] Walter Channing, *A Treatise on Etherization in Childbirth. Illustrated by Five Hundred and Eighty-One Cases* (Boston, 1848), 229.

[16] Dewees, *Compendious System*, 354, 356–57; A. Clair Siddall, "Bloodletting in American Obstetric Practice, 1800–1945," *Bulletin of the History of Medicine*, 54 (Spring 1980), 101–10.

introduce the crochet, the instrument used for fetal dismemberment and extraction.[17]

The forceps constituted the favorite instrument of physician intervention, and women both feared and respected the "hands of iron." When Shippen referred obliquely to forceps in front of Sally Downing's mother, she "was afraid to ask him, least he should answer in the affermative" that he needed to use it. Her confidence in its benefits, however, remained intact. Women were grateful for the tool that could extricate a fetus in compacted labors.[18]

In 1812 a medical graduate of the University of Pennsylvania entered practice in a town where two aging physicians already practiced. These physicians "had never used forceps, and were in the habit of resorting to Smellie's scissors and the crotchet in all cases where the foetal head became obstructed in the pelvis." The young doctor soon established himself among the women in the community by successfully using forceps to deliver healthy babies who might have otherwise been destroyed. This sort of success story achieved a legendary quality in the nineteenth century as physicians expanded the use of forceps at the same time as they developed their practices.[19]

When well used, forceps could save lives; when misused, they could increase women's perineal lacerations and cause head injuries to the fetus. Dewees called attention to the "mischief" that forceps could cause and believed that their dangers were enhanced because physicians used them too often and unnecessarily. He cautioned: "The greatest care must be taken, before we begin our traction, that no portion of the mother is included in the locking of the blades—this must be done by passing a finger entirely round the place of union. . . . I was once called to a poor woman who had had a considerable portion of the internal face of the right labium removed, by having been included in the joint of the short forceps."[20] Physicians who had been trained to use forceps only on manikins and who were required by custom to perform the forceps operation without the benefit of sight ran considerable risk of creating new problems for the women whose obstructed labors they tried to ameliorate.

Countless stories testify to the severe lacerations nineteenth-century women suffered in childbirth, and they suggest an increase in the problem over what women had previously experienced. The accusation of "meddlesome midwifery" followed physician-accoucheurs, and textbooks cautioned against forceps misuse often enough to suggest that a significant problem existed. The midwifery professors repeatedly warned against unnecessary use of forceps. But their students or apprentice-trained physicians in practice in America's communities found forceps a very valuable tool, and because of their eagerness or their limited practical experience, they may have overused and misused

[17] Bogdan, "Care or Cure?" 96–98; Scholten, "'On the Importance of the Obstetrick Art,'" 437–39. The crochet was the classic instrument to destory the fetus in utero and permit extraction.

[18] Drinker, *Not So Long Ago*, 60–61.

[19] Robert P. Harris, "History of a Pair of Obstetrical Forceps Sixty Years Old," *American Journal of Obstetrics and Diseases of Women and Children*, 4 (May 1871), 55–59.

[20] Dewees, *Compendious System*, 290.

them. Dewees observed so many cases of misused forceps that he concluded, "The forceps . . . are nearly as fatal as the crochet itself."[21]

If forceps were at fault in the "meddlesome midwifery" of the early nineteenth century, they were not the only problem. Almost any intervention by the physician created a potential for harm. If a birth could not proceed without help, the physician provided a service not available elsewhere and necessary to saving lives. If, however, as was statistically more probable, labor was proceeding normally and physicians intervened anyway, their actions introduced dangers not otherwise present. Dewees's caution about careful use of forceps inadvertently informs us about the concurrent dangers of infection. He taught his students to check that no part of the mother was caught in the blades of the forceps by "passing a finger entirely round the place of union." An unwashed and ungloved finger could have carried a higher risk to women's lives than a perineal laceration.

H. B. Willard, a medical graduate who practiced obstetrics in Wisconsin beginning in 1849, rarely used forceps because "the idea of instruments is *horrible* to *friends* & *patient* beside there is much liability to injure the parts." But Willard had no reservations about using opium and ergot, internally manipulating the fetus to change its presenting part, and routinely rupturing the waters with his fingernails. Willard chose his therapeutic activities by weighing the effects they would have on his reputation in the community. He tried not to use emetics, for example, because he knew "the idea of being vomited at such a time is exceedingly repugnant to the patient & to friends." By the same reasoning, Willard, when called to attend a laboring woman, followed Channing's dictum to do something. He knew his patients expected action. The only cases in which Willard did not interfere were those in which the baby had been born before his arrival. In those cases he might still have had opportunity to extract the placenta manually.[22]

Physicians' obstetrics courses taught them the theoretical basis of their craft, their apprenticeships gave them tools with which to effect a successful birth, but nowhere did they receive clear guidelines for the practical application of their knowledge. Doctors had numerous techniques at their command and complete leeway in their use. If physicians used forceps too often, or if they intervened in the birth process too eagerly, it was because they were more persuaded by the faces of women in agony than by the cautions of their elders. Their decisions about intervention were made on the spot and in relative isolation. Even the professors at the medical schools and the leading textbooks taught by anecdotal example, making generalizations hard if not impossible to construct. Physicians could convince themselves easily and in good conscience that their judgment to intervene in labor was in the best interests of the patient. The majority of successful outcomes in each

[21] *Ibid.*, 286.

[22] H. B. Willard Obstetrical Journal, June 29, 1854, p. 23, H. B. Willard Papers (State Historical Society of Wisconsin, Madison); *ibid.*, Feb. 4, 1856, p. 29. For a woman's perceptions of physicians' interventions, see Harriet Connor Brown, *Grandmother Brown's Hundred Years, 1827–1927* (Boston, 1929), 93.

individual's practice underlined the truthfulness of these conclusions. Early obstetric "science" provided knowledge and wherewithal, but the principles of the practical application remained at the bedside in the hands of individual, isolated doctors such as Willard.[23]

The decision of whether or not to employ the skills of the physician remained with women, where it had traditionally been. The parturient, her midwife, and her assistants frequently decided to call a doctor after labor had begun and then gave or withheld permission for each procedure suggested. Dewees, for example, after one successful forceps operation, was called to other cases because "the influence of this case upon many of the midwives of this city, procured me many opportunities of applying the forceps." Similarly the young Pennsylvania doctor's success in delivering babies using forceps led women to refuse to let other doctors use the crochet. Although physicians had broken the gender barrier and birth was no longer exclusively a woman's event, women continued to hold the power to shape events in the birthing room.[24]

Despite the strength of tradition, however, birth had changed for the women who invited physicians to attend them in their homes. These women formed a minority of all birthing women, and they probably were limited geographically to the major cities and economically to the advantaged classes. Most Americans still could not afford doctors and employed midwives and delivered their babies in the same ways as their mothers and grandmothers had. But for those women who chose physicians instead of or in addition to midwives, birth became less a natural process and more an event that could be altered and influenced by a wide selection of interventions. Women and physicians realized that fate no longer held women in such a tight grip and that decisions could be made and actions could be taken that would determine what kind of a birth a woman would have and perhaps whether she and her baby lived or died. This mental perception of the ability to shape the birth experience became even more important in the second half of the nineteenth century when anesthesia emerged as the paramount birthing panacea.

Fanny Longfellow's exuberant description of her childbirth under ether in 1847 (the first in the United States) indicates just how ready women were to change their childbirth experiences. "I never was better or got through a confinement so comfortably," she wrote her sister-in-law. "I feel proud to be the pioneer to less suffering for poor, weak womankind. This is certainly the greatest blessing of this age, and I am glad to have lived at the time of its coming and in the country which gives it to the world."[25] By the middle of the century middle-class women had become accustomed to male birth attendants, although a large segment of the population—probably growing as immigration soared in the latter part of the century—remained faithful to female

[23] See, for example, Willard Obstetrical Journal, Oct. 27, 1849, p. 3; *ibid.*, Dec. 25, 1849, p. 2; *ibid.*, May 7, 1850, p. 4.

[24] Dewees, *Compendious System*, 281; Harris, "History of a Pair of Obstetrical Forceps," 57.

[25] Edward Wagenknecht, ed., *Mrs. Longfellow: Selected Letters and Journals of Fanny Appleton Longfellow (1817-1861)* (New York, 1956), 129-30.

midwives and traditional birth procedures. Advantaged urban women sought every obstetric improvement that male physicians could offer because they continued to fear childbirth and its attendant discomforts. As one woman wrote about her fourth birth in 1885, "Between the oceans of pain, there stretched continents of fear; fear of death and dread of suffering beyond bearing."[26]

Women who experienced their childbirths as the hour in which they "touched the hand of death" eagerly sought relief from the frightful event. Ether and chloroform promised such relief, and women like Longfellow embraced anesthesia enthusiastically. One of Channing's patients told him after her etherized birth "how wonderful it was that she should have got through without the least suffering, and how grateful she was."[27]

Women, in fact, were initially more eager than physicians to use anesthesia. Among physicians, there was some uncertainty about the safety of the new drugs for midwifery practice. Charles D. Meigs of Philadelphia rejected chloroform and ether and carried on a well-publicized campaign against their use, claiming that he had "not yielded to several solicitations as to its exhibition addressed to me by my patients in labour." Meigs relied upon women's painful contractions to help him determine labor's progress and believed that their inhibition would make him a less effective birth attendant.[28]

Walter Channing, one of ether's most ardent supporters, in 1848 surveyed forty-six Boston-area physicians' use of anesthesia in labor and found that they held back on using the drugs except in cases when "patients have demanded it with an emphasis which could not be resisted . . . in many cases, and in the practice of some physicians, it has only been used when such demand has been made."[29] A. R. Thompson of Charlestown, Massachusetts, wrote Channing the following account, which was not unusual. "This lady had informed herself fully as to the use of ether, and had made up her mind to take it. . . . When called to her, I frankly told her that I had never used the ether, nor had I ever seen it used in any case, but that I had no prejudice against it, and would consent to its administration in her case. . . . she was resolute, and demanded the ether. . . . I poured an ounce of ether into the sponge, and the lady held it to her mouth and nose." A successful outcome and a happy patient convinced this doctor to use the drug in subsequent cases. After his second trial of ether Thompson concluded confidently, "My conviction at the time was strong, that the ether had greatly diminished the sufferings of the mother, and shortened the term of her travail for many hours."[30]

[26] Elizabeth H. Emerson, *Glimpses of a Life* (Burlington, N.C., 1960), 4–5.

[27] Mrs. Hal Russell, "Memoirs of Marian Russell," *Colorado Magazine*, 21 (Jan. 1944), 35–36; Channing, *Treatise on Etherization*, 165. For more on women's fears of death and debility, see Leavitt and Walton, "Down to Death's Door."

[28] "Dr. Meigs' Reply to Professor Simpson's Letter," *Medical Examiner and Record of Medical Science*, 11 (March 1848), 148–51. See also John Duffy, "Anglo-American Reaction to Obstetrical Anesthesia," *Bulletin of the History of Medicine*, 38 (Jan.-Feb. 1964), 32–44.

[29] Channing, *Treatise on Etherization*, 300. Walter Channing did not report what proportion of these physician-attended births used anesthesia.

[30] *Ibid.*, 334–35. The woman who insisted on using ether was forty-three years old and had had five children.

Perceptions of safety and patterns of anesthesia use varied enormously among physicians in the second half of the nineteenth century. The medical journals reported both safe and hazardous results of ether and chloroform in midwifery. A Massachusetts physician, for example, wrote in the *Boston Medical and Surgical Journal* that chloroform was "a dangerous and often deadly agent," and a Detroit physician concluded in the *Journal of the American Medical Association*, "I have yet to see my first case of the least evil result to mother or child." With such variation in the literature, individual physicians relied heavily on their own experiences and on the desires of their patients. A rural Iowa doctor wrote about his five hundred obstetric cases: "I do not use an anaesthetic of any kind, especially in forceps cases. I want the patient to know what is going on." Another physician came to the opposite conclusion and recommended anesthesia "not only in troublesome instrumental labor, but in all cases where the pains of travail fall upon women."[31]

Many physicians felt pressed, if their time was limited and other patients were waiting, to use forceps, anesthesia, or both to direct labor into patterns under their control. This inclination was reinforced by women eagerly seeking relief from their suffering. A Colorado physician related that after several hours of hard labor one of his patients "implored me to do something, and, with many misgivings, at last I decided to use instruments [and] chloroform."[32]

Physicians came to adopt anesthesia so generally that one physician in 1895 observed that "the profession has come to regard the use of chloroform in parturition as almost utterly devoid of danger," so that "chloroform is given in labor often recklessly, carelessly, and copiously." As physicians delivered the babies, other attendants—"ignorant nurses, husbands, bystanders, and even . . . the patients themselves"—dripped chloroform or ether onto a sponge or cloth and held it to the woman's nose. No standard procedures guarded physicians' drug dosages.[33]

Physicians' reports of their obstetric practices in the second half of the nineteenth century indicate that use of anesthesia did not necessarily lead to increased forceps use. While doctors did come to use anesthesia routinely in forceps deliveries, the reverse was not true. Physicians did not use forceps routinely on patients to whom they gave ether and chloroform. Physicians employed forceps in approximately 8 percent of their births, whereas some used anesthesia at almost every birth they attended, and on the average about 50 percent of all physician-attended births utilized chloroform or ether.[34]

[31] B. E. Cotting, "Anesthetics in Midwifery," *Boston Medical and Surgical Journal*, 59 (Dec. 9, 1858), 369; Bedford Brown, "The Therapeutic Action of Chloroform in Parturition," *Journal of the American Medical Association*, 25 (Aug. 31, 1895), 355; A. D. Bundy, "Obstetrics in the Country," *Medical and Surgical Reporter*, 56 (Feb. 12, 1887), 201; D. M. Barr, "Anaesthesia in Labor," *ibid.*, 42 (March 13, 1880), 221.

[32] Charles Fox Gardiner, *Doctor at Timberline* (Caldwell, Idaho, 1938), 211. See also Barr, "Anaesthesia in Labor," 227.

[33] Brown, "Therapeutic Action," 354; Duffy, "Anglo-American Reaction," 38. See also J. F. Ford, "Use of Drugs in Labor," *Wisconsin Medical Journal*, 3 (Oct. 1904), 257–65.

[34] Ford, "Use of Drugs," 257–58; Bundy, "Obstetrics in the Country," 200–01. In 91,000 births in Iowa physicians used forceps in 7 percent of cases. E. D. Plass and H. J. Alvis, "A Statistical

Thus, despite the haphazard use of open-drop ether or chloroform and the consequent potential for overdosing, actual anesthesia use must have remained light. Profound anesthesia would have caused labor to decelerate and would have made forceps necessary to lift the baby that the woman was unable to push out. But with light analgesia physicians did not require forceps, and in the nineteenth century forceps abuse did not increase as a result of increased use of anesthetics. Physicians aimed at pain relief, not total unconsciousness. If a woman administered her own drugs on a handkerchief she held up to her nose, her arm would periodically drop away, decreasing the drug dose. One physician advised maintaining what he called a "dreamy sleep, in which the patient follows in her imagination the direction of the physician." While labor progressed, he conversed with his patients about scenes from their childhood or the Sunday school picnic. One of his patients "almost immediately after the first inhalation burst out in a beautiful song, and continued singing one after another until her babe, a large boy, first child, was born."[35]

Most physicians continued to intervene in the birth process in the second half of the nineteenth century as they had earlier. Their safety record when measured by mortality matched the record of midwives, who continued to follow a basically noninterventionist birth policy. Dorothy Reed Mendenhall studied births in Wisconsin at the beginning of the twentieth century and concluded that for both physicians and midwives maternal mortality was higher than it needed to be but that "we must admit that the midwife is, on the whole, probably less culpable in regard to the deaths of parturient women than physicians in the state."[36] Similar maternal mortality rates for midwife- and physician-attended births indicate that physicians, with all their expertise and intervention techniques, did not, as they had promised, enhance the safety of the birth experience for women. Medicine may have improved comfort levels and may have rescued some women from complicated labors, but it did not, on the whole, increase women's chances of survival.

There are other indications that physicians' techniques created new problems for birthing women and actually increased the dangers of childbirth. Inappropriate forceps use and the careless administration of ether and chloroform introduced serious lacerations and breathing disorders that otherwise might not have developed. Most significant, physicians carried puerperal fever, which was potentially disastrous, to birthing women. Because their medical practices included attending patients with communicable diseases, doctors were more likely than midwives to bring with them on their hands and on their clothing the agents of infection. Epidemics of puerperal fever developed

Study of 129,539 Births in Iowa, with Special Reference to the Method of Delivery and the Stillbirth Rate," *American Journal of Obstetrics and Gynecology*, 28 (Aug. 1934), 297.

[35] Barr, "Anaesthesia in Labor," 226–27. In the twentieth century, obstetricians appear to have used anesthesia with the intent to produce unconsciousness, and forceps use consequently increased.

[36] Dorothy Reed Mendenhall, "Prenatal and Natal Conditions in Wisconsin," *Wisconsin Medical Journal*, 15 (March 1917), 353. See also the comments of Dorothy Reed Mendenhall and Florence Sherbon, in American Association for Study and Prevention of Infant Mortality, *Transactions of the Seventh Annual Meeting, Milwaukee, October 19–21, 1916* (Baltimore, 1917), 67–68, 63–64.

even in the practices of physicians like H. H. Whitcomb of Norristown, Pennsylvania, who did "as little meddling as possible" in normal labor and delivery. In 1886 one of Whitcomb's parturient patients developed fever because Whitcomb brought the infection from a previous patient who had scarlet fever. That winter and spring Whitcomb transmitted the fever to thirty-two more birthing women.[37]

Physicians offered some women relief from suffering and aided others through compacted labors, but because of the variations in ability and practices of their birth attendants, most women continued to experience discomfort and to fear childbirth. One woman described her physician-attended delivery as "hell. . . . It bursts your brain, and tears out your heart, and crushes your nerves to bits. It's just hell."[38] Despite their continued suffering, those middle-class women who had chosen physicians to attend them did not want to return to midwives. They believed that if birth were to be eased, improvements would come from progress in medicine. Instead of turning to tradition, these women demanded more of their physicians and continued to hope that safe and comfortable deliveries would come to them from the medical world.

As the symbol of what science had to offer, anesthesia enhanced the place and role of physicians in birthing rooms across America. Women who could afford physicians and their new panacea demanded the advantages of painlessness. Despite the presence of men and modern technology in the birthing rooms, however, the birth experience of nineteenth-century middle- and upper-class women retained many important elements from traditional births. Anita McCormick Blaine's first childbirth in 1890 illustrates this. During her pregnancy Blaine corresponded with her mother, who was in Europe seeking a cure for a hearing loss, and sought the traditional female support network to help her through the impending crisis. "If you could but be with me now, what wouldn't I give," wrote Blaine to her mother, Nettie Fowler McCormick. Despite all of Blaine's preparations and the doctor and nurse who would attend her, McCormick yearned to be with her daughter. She wrote detailed instructions about her care, advising, for example, rubbing olive oil over the abdomen and perineal area to ease delivery. She worried that only a mother could rightfully do such an intimate job. "I don't know if you have a person you could let do it," she wrote, "but I wish I were there to do it." Blaine sequestered herself in her childhood Chicago home, where "every chair and table speaks to me of dear familiar times . . . nothing is so sweet as to feel the presence of all it reminds me of." She surrounded herself with helpers, including her old friend Harriot ("Missy") Hammond, who traveled from Virginia to be with her. Strengthened by these traditional comforts, Anita delivered her baby while under the influence of chloroform, supported by her nurse and by Hammond

[37] H. H. Whitcomb, "A Report of 616 Cases of Labor in Private Practice," *Medical and Surgical Reporter*, 56 (Feb. 12, 1887), 201. Puerperal sepsis caused the largest proportion of maternal deaths at the beginning of the twentieth century. See American Association for Study and Prevention of Infant Mortality, *Transactions of the Seventh Annual Meeting*, 67.

[38] Russell Kelso Carter, *The Sleeping Car "Twilight"; or, Motherhood without Pain* (Boston, 1915), 10–11.

and attended by a male physician. Her husband waited outside. She united the old and the new in obstetric experiences and planned the whole event to meet her expectations. The doctor managed the birth in the context that the woman created.[39]

The decision-making process in the turn-of-the-century birthing rooms reveals how the old and the new intermingled. Doctors, who may have had only minimal practical experience, were invited to attend women in their own homes in the presence of other women, many of whom had had considerable birth experience and had developed strong opinions about birth procedures. Within the birthing rooms, these attendants negotiated. There were desires and expectations on both sides. Women retained a lot of power in their own homes, and physicians bowed to it or risked damaging their reputations among a whole community of women and losing patients. As the new obstetrical techniques—from forceps to anesthetics—became available, they worked to the advantage of physicians, who held the monopoly over their use, while centuries of female traditions and the domestic environment in which they operated worked to the advantage of women.

Inexperienced physicians sometimes welcomed the knowledge of other attendants. Morris Fishbein admitted that he learned more from a laboring woman whose eighth birth he attended than from all his classroom experience. Other physicians found attending a birth in the presence of well-informed women intimidating. One physician recalled, "A young doctor, fresh from medical college, can pass many embarrassing moments in the presence of the neighborhood midwife." Another recalled that a mother's instructions to him "rattled me so that I hardly knew what I was doing."[40]

Women invited physicians to attend them in order to benefit from their expertise and technology, yet doctors could not obtain patients' compliance with all procedures. An Oklahoma physician explained why he could never try to shave a patient's pubic hair even though he thought it would help prevent infection. "In about three seconds after the doctor has made the first rake with his safety [razor], he will find himself on his back out in the yard with the imprint of a woman's bare foot emblazoned on his manly chest, the window sash round his neck and a revolving vision of all the stars in the firmament presented to him. Tell him not to try to shave 'em."[41] Another practitioner realized that a doctor "has his living to make and cannot be too insistent with his patient over whom, usually, he has no control." Yet physicians could not

[39] Anita McCormick Blaine to Nettie Fowler McCormick, Aug. 24, 1890, folder 2B, box 46, Nancy Fowler McCormick Papers (State Historical Society of Wisconsin); McCormick to Blaine, Aug. 1890, folder 1E, box 459, *ibid.*

[40] Morris Fishbein, *An Autobiography* (Garden City, N.Y., 1969), 25; Helen MacKnight Doyle, *A Child Went Forth: The Autobiography of Dr. Helen MacKnight Doyle* (New York, 1934), 322; Gardiner, *Doctor at Timberline*, 211-12. See also Leon Herman, *A Surgeon Thinks It Over* (Philadelphia, 1962), 60.

[41] S. H. Landrum to editor, *Journal of the American Medical Association*, 58 (Feb. 24, 1912), 576. See also George S. King, *Doctor on a Bicycle* (New York, 1958), 61-63; Marcus Bossard, *Eighty-One Years of Living* (Minneapolis, 1946), 39-40; and Mary Bennett Ritter, *More than Gold in California, 1849-1933* (Berkeley, 1933), 219.

come into the birthing room and do nothing. One Kansas doctor admitted, "Perhaps the best way to manage normal labor is to let it alone, but you cannot hold down a job and do that." Women and physicians negotiated the procedures that would be used, and the result represented a compromise between the two worlds of women's tradition and men's medicine. The compromises held until the twentieth century, when physician-directed obstetrics finally became master of the birthing room.[42]

At the turn of the twentieth century physicians delivered approximately half of the nation's babies. Most of these births took place in the woman's home and combined aspects of traditional and modern techniques. Although most of the medical profession accepted the need for aseptic conditions—sterile gloves, shaved perineum, antiseptic infusions, sterile instruments—they could not always achieve them. Whether because of their own abilities or their patients' demands, physicians intermingled modern surgical techniques with wide individual variations and traditional practices. One physician writing in 1912 about the management of normal labor observed that only when the fetal head was resting on the perineum was it necessary "to expose the perineum so that its condition may be constantly watched." The inference, harking back to William Dewees, was that before this stage ocular examination should remain limited. Another doctor refused to shave his patients because the attempt "would cause such a violent attack of hysteria that the physician would cease to be of any further use to that family."[43] Physician practice—susceptible to the physical environment, to the opinions of other attendants, and to the physician's own training and inclination—varied from individual to individual. Physicians acted when they were called to women in labor, but the nature of their interventions followed particular circumstances more than any predetermined science of obstetrics.

The lack of a systematic approach to the practice of obstetrics in the early twentieth century can be directly traced to the quality and emphasis of obstetric education, which had not changed substantially during the nineteenth century. After the middle of the nineteenth century, "demonstrative midwifery," or teaching students by having them observe actual laboring women, became available, but many medical schools ignored this innovation and

[42] J. H. Mackay to editor, *Journal of the American Medical Association*, 58 (March 9, 1912), 720; J. H. Guinn to editor, *ibid.* (March 23, 1912), 880. Women physicians, although small in number, provided a bridge between the two worlds of domesticity and medicine, and many women who wanted the benefits of medicine within the comforting female sphere chose women doctors as birth attendants. More research is needed in this area, beginning with women's hospitals such as the New England Hospital for Women and Children, which, one could argue, tried to provide a milieu in which traditional women's supports could be maintained. See, for example, Virginia G. Drachman, "Female Solidarity and Professional Success: The Dilemma of Women Doctors in Late Nineteenth-Century America," *Journal of Social History*, 15 (Summer 1982), 607–19; and Regina Markell Morantz and Sue Zschoche, "Professionalism, Feminism, and Gender Roles: A Comparative Study of Nineteenth-Century Medical Therapeutics," *Journal of American History*, 67 (Dec. 1980), 568–88.

[43] "Management of Normal Labor," *Journal of the American Medical Association*, 58 (Jan. 27, 1912), 274; William M. Gregory to editor, *ibid.* (Feb. 24, 1912), 577. See also F. W. MacManus to editor, *ibid.* (March 9, 1912), 720; and Landrum to editor, ibid. (Feb. 24, 1912), 576.

continued their didactic teaching from textbooks and manikins. In 1910, although most practitioners now received a formal medical education, many still graduated having witnessed few or no live deliveries. Such training at best prepared students to understand birth pathology and perhaps how to intervene to rescue a woman in trouble, but it did not prepare physicians to attend women in normal labor.[44]

J. Whitridge Williams, professor of obstetrics at the Johns Hopkins Medical School, surveyed obstetrics education in 1912 and concluded that the "average practitioner, through his lack of preparation for the practice of obstetrics, may do his patients as much harm as the much-maligned midwife." Williams found that most medical students had the opportunity during their training to watch only one woman deliver, and one-quarter of the medical schools admitted that their graduates were not competent to practice obstetrics. Yet most physicians did deliver babies as part of their medical practices, spending on the average approximately 30 percent of their time attending childbirth.[45] In the era when scientific investigations began to permeate the medical world, when medical schools increasingly built laboratories and trained their students in research methods and findings, and when specialization and hospital expansion transformed medical practice, physicians' obstetrical practices were characterized by individual variation and unsystematic application of general principles.

Williams believed that only the developing specialty of obstetrics practiced in the hospital setting could improve the marginal situation. Even as a significant portion of American women continued to be attended by midwives in their own homes, and most others continued to invite general practitioners to attend them at home, increasing numbers of women from the middle and upper classes became convinced that childbirth in the hospital offered them the safest experience. Many factors converged to encourage women to move to the hospital in the early years of the twentieth century, including the new anesthetic agent scopolamine (best monitored in the hospital), the preference of the specialists, the growth of the hospitals themselves, and the increasing technology and ease of management in the well-equipped and well-staffed hospital setting.[46] Still seeking more comfortable births and safer deliveries

[44] Longo, "Obstetrics and Gynecology," 211-14; Virginia G. Drachman, "The Loomis Trial: Social Mores and Obstetrics in the Mid-Nineteenth Century," in *Health Care in America: Essays in Social History*, ed. Susan Reverby and David Rosner (Philadelphia, 1979), 67-83; American Association for Study and Prevention of Infant Mortality, *Transactions of the Seventh Annual Meeting*, 63-64; Francis A. Long, *A Prairie Doctor of the Eighties: Some Personal Recollections and Some Early Medical and Social History of a Prairie State* (Norfolk, Nebr., 1937), 29.

[45] J. Whitridge Williams, "Medical Education and the Midwife Problem in the United States," *Journal of the American Medical Association*, 58 (Jan. 6, 1912), 1, 2, 5; R. H. Riley, "The Public Health Aspect of the Teaching of Obstetrics in Undergraduate Medical Schools," *ibid.*, 106 (April 25, 1936), 1438. See also Lawrence D. Longo, "John Whitridge Williams and Academic Obstetrics in America," *Transactions and Studies of the College of Physicians of Philadelphia*, 3 (Dec. 1981), 221-54.

[46] I have explored some of these points elsewhere; see Judith Walzer Leavitt, "Birthing and Anesthesia: The Debate over Twilight Sleep," *Signs*, 6 (Autumn 1980), 147-64. See also Morris J. Vogel, *The Invention of the Modern Hospital: Boston, 1870-1930* (Chicago, 1980); and Judy

with minimal negative aftereffects, many women decided to try the newest that obstetrics had to offer and go to the hospital to be attended by specialists. "I have placed myself in the hands of. . . . a specialist in obstetrics," wrote Lella Secor to her mother in 1918. "I have every confidence in him, and it is a great relief."[47]

In hospital deliveries women left their family and friends at the door of the labor room and faced their birthings alone, as one account of birth in the 1930s indicated:

> Arriving [at the hospital], she is immediately given the benefit of one of the modern analgesics or pain-killers. Soon she is in a dreamy, half-conscious state. . . .
>
> She knows nothing about being taken to a spotlessly clean delivery room, placed on a sterile table, draped with sterile sheets; neither does she see her attendants, the doctor and nurses, garbed for her protection in sterile white gowns and gloves; nor the shiny boiled instruments and antiseptic solutions. She does not hear the cry of her baby when first he feels the chill of this cold world, or see the care with which the doctor repairs such lacerations as may have occurred. . . . Finally she awakes in smiles, a mother with no recollection of having become one.[48]

This woman was separated from the people she loved, she was in an unfamiliar environment controlled by others, and she was unconscious during her childbirth. Women did not view the stay in the hospital as a time when they lost important parts of the traditional birth experiences, but rather as a time when they gained protection for life and health, aspects of birth that had been elusive and uncertain in the past. Women gave up some kinds of control for others because on balance the new benefits seemed more important. In seeking life and health, women relinquished consciousness and self-determination.

The hospital appealed to women because it was modern, well equipped, and staffed by experts: it represented the newest medical advance. Also, it physically separated women from their domestic chores and allowed them to relax. One wrote, "My stay in that hospital was like a lovely vacation." "I can't tell you the relief I feel as I walk out my door headed for the hospital to have a baby," wrote another. "I have nothing to worry about . . . and have only to concentrate on giving birth. All this peace of mind, plus expert medical attention, makes me wonder why anybody would consider it a 'privilege' to

Barrett Litoff, *American Midwives: 1860 to the Present* (Westport, Conn., 1978). The declining number of midwives in this period contributed to the trend toward hospital deliveries and was affected by many of the same factors. See Frances E. Kobrin, "The American Midwife Controversy: A Crisis of Professionalization," *Bulletin of the History of Medicine*, 40 (July-Aug. 1966), 350-63; Neal Devitt, "The Statistical Case for Elimination of the Midwife: Fact versus Prejudice, 1890-1935," *Women and Health*, 4 (Spring 1979), 81-96; *ibid.* (Summer 1979), 169-86. The midwife was the major victim of advancing obstetrics. Physicians took almost two centuries to replace midwives in America's birthing rooms, but by the 1940s medicine successfully superseded female midwifery. Since few women were obstetricians, when midwives "disappeared," women lost the occupation for their sex; they also lost with midwifery centuries of female tradition, ritual, and unity, which today they are seeking to reclaim.

[47] Barbara Moench Florence, ed., *Lella Secor: A Diary in Letters, 1915-1922* (New York, 1978), 170.

[48] Roy P. Finney, *The Story of Motherhood* (New York, 1937), 6-7. See also Alan Frank Guttmacher, *Into This Universe: The Story of Human Birth* (New York, 1937), 192-267.

have her baby at home." Home did not hold for mid-twentieth-century women the same comforts and sustenance that Blaine had found so reassuring. The "hospital is equipped with every modern device for the safe delivery of babies," wrote one mother. "Nursing and medical attention is available at any hour of the day or night. How much simpler—and more restful—to be in a hospital where babies are an accepted business."[49]

The move to the hospital was hastened by specialists' attempts to wrest birth away from general practitioners and to systematize birth procedures within the hospital setting. One very influential move in this direction was made in 1920 by Joseph B. DeLee of Chicago in the first volume of the new journal for specialists, the *American Journal of Obstetrics and Gynecology*. DeLee argued that birth was a "pathologic process" and that "only a small minority of women escape damage during labor." He continued, "So frequent are these bad effects, that I have often wondered whether Nature did not deliberately intend women should be used up in the process of reproduction, in a manner analogous to that of salmon, which dies after spawning?" Because of its dangers, DeLee believed birth needed careful monitoring in skilled hands. He recommended reducing birth to predictable patterns by using outlet forceps and episiotomy routinely and prophylactically in normal deliveries. DeLee sedated the parturient with scopolamine, allowed the cervix to dilate, gave ether during the second stage, performed an episiotomy, and lifted the fetus with forceps. He then extracted the placenta, gave ergot to help the uterus contract, and stitched the perineal cut.[50]

DeLee's operation achieved wide acceptance. It represented the new move in the 1920s and 1930s to make obstetrics scientific, systematic, and predictable by putting it under the control of the specialist. Not all specialists wanted to use prophylactic forceps, but hospital-based obstetricians did develop routines for managing childbirth that incorporated systematic use of pain-relieving drugs, labor inducers, and technological intervention. Mothers-to-be learned they could plan when and how they would have a baby, and doctors could predict the course of labor because they controlled it. "The old way [of having a baby] was no fun," wrote one father about the 1916 birth of his first daughter. In 1938 his second daughter "was born the new way—the easy, painless, streamlined way." His wife, in consultation with her doctor, decided which day to deliver, and after a matinee and dinner went into the hospital. Pituitrin induced her labor, Nembutal and scopolamine deadened her perceptions of it, and the doctor delivered her baby. "Why, I wouldn't mind

[49] Gladys Denny Shultz, "Journal Mothers Report on Cruelty in Maternity Wards," *Ladies' Home Journal*, 75 (May 1958), 44; M. F. Ashley Montagu, "Babies Should Be Born at Home!" *ibid.*, 72 (Aug. 1955), 52. See also Betty MacDonald, *The Egg and I* (Philadelphia, 1945), 108, 163. Betty MacDonald found the hospital a place of luxury, wonderful food, and good care—almost, she said, enough to keep her pregnant the rest of her life. Hospital stays may have looked attractive because women's own networks of home helpers were diminishing in this period. This hypothesis needs further research.

[50] Joseph B. DeLee, "The Prophylactic Forceps Operation," *American Journal of Obstetrics and Gynecology*, 1 (Oct. 1920), 40–41, 34–35.

having another baby next week," she said, "if that's all there is to it."[51] Increasing numbers of middle-class women turned to the hospital and the specialist for their childbirths, believing, as one of them put it, "the vexation of hospital routine shrinks to infinitesimal importance beside the safety of the delivery room."[52]

But was streamlined childbirth safe? Had medicine at last provided safer and more comfortable childbirth for women, as it had promised since the 1760s? Observers in the 1930s realized that while the practice of obstetrics now could relieve women of much of their discomfort, childbirth remained unsafe. Maternal mortality in the 1930s remained "unnecessarily high," according to a group of concerned physicians in New York. The physicians claimed hospital deliveries contributed to the high mortality with a "high incidence of operative interference during labor . . . undertaken when there was no indication or a plain contra-indication." Birth in the hospital encouraged interference because the equipment and staff were readily accessible, and this interference increased the number of maternal deaths. Rather than making childbirth safer, physicians in the 1920s and 1930s, according to their own evaluation, were responsible for maintaining high rates of maternal mortality.[53]

In home deliveries of the nineteenth century, increased anesthetic use had not caused an increase in forceps deliveries, but in hospital deliveries of the early twentieth century, a direct relationship existed between anesthesia and forceps. The New York doctors noted, "The frequent use of instrumentation is based upon the easy accessibility of anaesthesia. . . . the increase in the use of anaesthesia is a factor in keeping the maternal mortality rate stationary." According to the New York study, use of anesthetic agents led directly to increased instrumentation because drugged women were less effective in pushing the baby out. Approximately 25 percent of hospital deliveries were operative. "The increase in the use of instrumentation brings with it an increased hazard," the doctors found. "Clearly a reduction of the mortality rate can be achieved through a reduction in operative interference."[54]

During the early 1930s the medical profession publicly confessed the shortcomings of its obstetric practices. Rudolph Wieser Holmes declared at a crowded American Medical Association meeting, "I have seen hundreds of

[51] J. P. McEvoy, "Our Streamlined Baby," *Reader's Digest*, 32 (May 1938), 15-16. For reaction to prophylactic forceps, see J. Whitridge Williams, "A Criticism of Certain Tendencies in American Obstetrics," *New York State Journal of Medicine*, 22 (Nov. 1922), 493-99.

[52] "I Had a Baby, Too: A Symposium," *Atlantic Monthly*, 163 (June 1939), 768. See also Lenore Pelham Friedrich, "I Had a Baby," *ibid.* (April 1939), 461-65. Clara Rust delivered five babies at home before going to the hospital to have her sixth in 1926. She was apprehensive about leaving home but went to the hospital on the doctor's advice. Jo Anne Wold, *This Old House: The Story of Clara Rust* (Anchorage, 1976), 207-08.

[53] New York Academy of Medicine Committee on Public Health Relations, *Maternal Mortality in New York City: A Study of All Puerperal Deaths, 1930-1932* (New York, 1933), 213-15, 125-27.

[54] *Ibid.*, 113-17, 126-27. An Iowa study found that 11.8 percent of all births and 23 percent of hospital births were operative statewide. Plass and Alvis, "Statistical Study," 293-305.

FIGURE 1
Maternal Mortality Rates.
Birth Registration States or United States, 1915–1964.

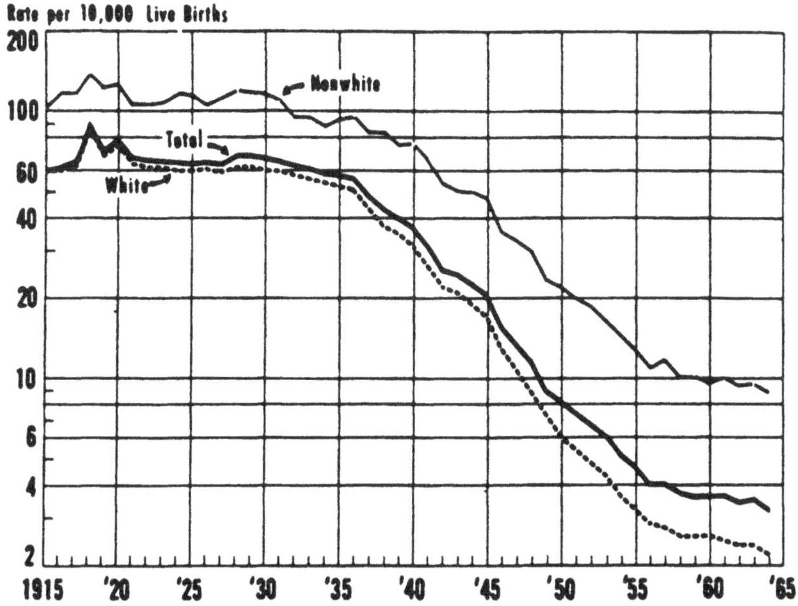

Source: Sam Shapiro, Edward R. Schlesinger, Robert E. L. Nesbitt, Jr., *Infant, Perinatal, Maternal, and Childhood Mortality in the United States* (Cambridge, Mass.: Harvard University Press, 1968), 145. Reprinted by permission.

women die on the delivery table because of the wrongful use of drugs." Holmes blamed his own role in accelerating scopolamine use for many of these deaths. The public health commissioner for the state of New York calculated that maternal deaths were actually increasing in the twentieth century and concluded that "they represent the results of meddlesome and unskillful obstetrical practice."[55] Philadelphia doctors agreed that 56 percent of preventable maternal deaths could be blamed on physician errors of judgment and technique.[56] A national study concluded similarly that "artificial delivery is becoming increasingly frequent, especially in hospital practice," and "that interference with normal labor is accompanied by some added risk to both mother and child." Although the indictment was not universally accepted by

[55] "Childbirth: Nature v. Drugs," *Time*, May 25, 1936, p. 36; Matthias Nicoll, Jr., "Maternity as a Public Health Problem," *American Journal of Public Health*, 19 (Sept. 1929), 967. See also R. W. Holmes, R. D. Mussey, and F. L. Adair, "Factors and Causes of Maternal Mortality," *Journal of the American Medical Association*, 93 (Nov. 9, 1929), 1440–47.

[56] Philadelphia County Medical Society, Committee on Maternal Welfare, *Maternal Mortality in Philadelphia, 1931–1933* (Philadelphia, 1934), 130. See also New York Academy of Medicine, *Maternal Mortality*, 32–38.

physicians in the 1930s, the statistics indicated that going to a hospital to have a baby managed by a physician and under the influence of twentieth-century drugs and instruments did not necessarily give a mother an advantage and may have put her in greater jeopardy than her neighbor who stayed home.[57]

Obstetrics by the 1930s had not achieved a record of safety commensurate with its abilities. Aided by the New York Academy of Medicine's 1933 revelations about preventable maternal and infant deaths, however, physicians moved toward regulation and standardization of hospital obstetrics practice in their attempts to decrease the overuse and misuse of drugs and operative procedures. Their success in establishing minimum standards for delivery procedures is evident in the fact that hospital births increased from 35 percent of all births in 1933 to 72 percent ten years later and "for the first time was not associated with higher rates of puerperal death." Other factors converged with hospital regulations to cause the decrease in maternal mortality after 1935. The prenatal-care movement spearheaded by middle-class women succeeded in gaining adherents and in educating the public about the importance of care during pregnancy. Probably most important in the decelerating death rates was the wide adoption of sulfonamides, blood transfusions, and, after World War II, antibiotics, which were successful in combating infection and hemorrhaging, two of the major causes of maternal deaths. After 1935 maternal mortality fell dramatically.[58] (See Figure 1.)

Even though birth became safer in the 1940s and 1950s, women who went to the hospital to deliver their babies—95 percent of American women by 1955—missed some of the features of traditional social childbirth and found hospital births sterile both in the antiseptic sense and in the human dimension. Continuing to appreciate the safety factors they acknowledged to exist for hospital births, women as early as the 1950s attacked the "cruelty in maternity wards." One woman from Elkhart, Indiana, wrote to the *Ladies' Home Journal*, which exposed these conditions: "So many women, especially first mothers, who are frightened to start out with, receive such brutal inconsiderate treatment that the whole thing is a horrible nightmare. They

[57] White House Conference on Child Health and Protection, *Fetal, Newborn, and Maternal Morbidity and Mortality: Report of the Subcommittee on Factors and Causes of Fetal, Newborn, and Maternal Morbidity and Mortality* (New York, 1933), 14, 220. For information about the effects of instrumental deliveries on the children, see Charles Edwin Galloway, "Prevention of Birth Injury and Its Resulting Mortality from the Standpoint of the Obstetrician," *Journal of the American Medical Association*, 106 (Feb. 15, 1936), 505–07.

[58] Joyce Antler and Daniel M. Fox, "The Movement toward a Safe Maternity: Physician Accountability in New York City, 1915-1940," in *Sickness and Health in America: Readings in the History of Medicine and Public Health*, ed. Judith Walzer Leavitt and Ronald L. Numbers (Madison, 1978), 386; Lawrence D. Longo and Christina M. Thomsen, "The Evolution of Prenatal Care in America," in *Proceedings of the Second Motherhood Symposium*, ed. Colleau, 29-70. During the 1920s and 1930s, when increasing numbers of women moved to the hospital to have their babies, maternal mortality rates remained as high as they had been earlier in the century, approximately 60 deaths per 10,000 live births (over 100 per 10,000 for nonwhite women). See Sam Shapiro, Edward R. Schlesinger, and Robert E. L. Nesbitt, Jr., *Infant, Perinatal, Maternal, and Childhood Mortality in the United States* (Cambridge, Mass., 1968), 144–45. When maternal mortality rates started falling after 1935, the decrease was not due to the hospital per se but to measures such as antibiotics that could have been used at home.

give you drugs, whether you want them or not, strap you down like an animal." A woman from Columbus, Ohio, concurred that a new mother was "foiled in every attempt to follow her own wishes."[59] These women noticed that the physical removal of childbirth from the woman's home to the physician's institution shifted the balance of power. Birth was no longer part of the woman's domain, as it had been during all the years it remained in the home. It had become instead a medical affair run by medical professionals. Women were no longer the main actors, but instead physicians acted upon women's bodies. Women who were attended by physicians in their own homes could still determine what would happen—could refuse to be shaved or could demand ether. They still controlled much of their own births. But women who entered the birthing rooms of medicine were captured by the routine and by the expertise surrounding them. They could not decide what kind of births they would have.

Some hospitals and some doctors did not depersonalize birth with institutional routine and were able to provide satisfying birth experiences. But many women agreed with the Bozeman, Montana, mother who wrote, "The cruelest part of [hospital] childbirth is being alone among strangers." She found nothing familiar to comfort her through the difficult hours, only the routine of hospital life that she and others described as an assembly line.[60] Physician-directed hospital obstetrics had not met the expectations of American women by protecting a woman's dignity and integrity at the same time as it insured safety. Women wanted the psychologically comforting practices of their traditional birthing rooms to be incorporated into the modern practices of the birthing rooms of science.

The two images of birthing women in America—one "brought to bed" in her own home by the women she had called together and the other drugged and "alone among strangers" in an impersonal hospital—frame the American obstetric experience. The eighteenth-century woman felt vulnerable to death and debility despite the strength she derived from her friends; the twentieth-century woman felt vulnerable to the institutional routine despite the strength she derived from encouraging maternal-mortality statistics. Neither woman had what she knew she needed at the time of her birth: the certainty of a healthy outcome with the freedom to make choices about how to conduct the important event.

For most of American history women controlled the events in their own birthing rooms. They negotiated with their birth attendants and decided, as much as their bodies and available technology allowed, how the birth would proceed. But the physical forces of birth did not always cooperate, and women felt at the mercy of fate. When physicians entered the women's birthing rooms with the promises of increased safety, women shared their traditional jurisdiction. Forceps, therapeutic aids, and especially anesthesia seemed to offer some insurance against the uncontrollable terrors of birth. Women found that

[59] Shultz, "Journal Mothers Report on Cruelty," 44–45.
[60] *Ibid.*, 44.

they could, if they wanted to, give their bodies up to labor and to the physician and return to consciousness after the event. Birthing women and their physicians, in the company of other women or family members, negotiated the particulars of birth procedures behind the closed doors of the birthing room and achieved a compromise that recognized the needs, wishes, and abilities of all participants.

But physicians could not achieve the safety that they had promised. While some women were relieved or saved by medical intervention, on balance women's experiences of birth were not significantly enhanced by the entrance of medicine. Physicians remained unable to control their own use of obstetric technology for the first 170 years they were engaged in delivering America's babies, and they frequently added to women's problems by increasing the danger of infection, overdosing with anesthesia, and mutilating with forceps.

In the twentieth century the hospital offered an alternative that appealed to women and to doctors because it promised at last the safety that both had sought. Removing birth from women's homes seemed just another step in the progression of changing practices. But women soon discovered that the birthing rooms of medicine differed fundamentally from their own birthing rooms. In hospitals women lost the ability to make choices for themselves and surrendered to the medical community the power to determine what would be done to their bodies. The early years of hospital-based obstetrics did not even provide additional safety for women. As the doctors themselves eventually realized, the hospital made interventions so easy that doctors resorted to operations and drugs in excess of what was indicated and by their own action kept the rates of maternal mortality high. Only after 1940 did medicine begin to achieve a record of safety commensurate with the promises it had held out to women centuries earlier.

Each major transition in American childbirth history—from midwives to physicians, from home to hospital, from "hands of flesh" intervention to "hands of iron" interference—represents in a different form the lure of science and its promise to improve the childbirth experience.[61] As women and their attendants came to perceive birth as an event that could be shaped and manipulated, their *mentalité* of pathology and impending emergencies led each generation to seek its own kind of ideal childbirth. Ultimately it was the promise of continual advances that pushed birth into new patterns throughout American history. Women and their birth attendants believed that medicine could solve their birthing problems and make procreation safe, and they put their faith in scientific advances years before science had significant impact on obstetric practices. Systematic application of tested principles did not characterize obstetrics until the twentieth century, yet medical activities in the birth room were valued much earlier because physicians carried an image of expertise and knowledge along with the instruments and drugs in their medical bags.

[61] The dichotomy between hands of flesh and hands of iron is used particularly effectively by Adrienne Rich, *Of Woman Born: Motherhood as Experience and Institution* (New York, 1976), 128–55.

Despite the lack of a systematic practice of obstetrics, women did not want to turn back to traditional practices. Only in very recent years has any sizable group of American women tried to change direction. Today some women are trying to alter the patterns of childbirth by seeking practices that were common in the past. These women, still a minority and predominantly middle-class, search out midwives or demand that doctors turn back the clock to a time when decision making involved all the birth participants. Women in America today who are seeking to control their own births are fighting the legacy of childbirth as structured by the medical profession and are demanding that choice be reintroduced to the childbirth agenda. They are not trying to overturn science but rather to control it within the traditional female context.[62]

The two themes of social childbirth and scientific childbirth have persisted throughout American history. In the seventeenth and eighteenth centuries, social childbirth practices prevailed. The two vied for supremacy during the nineteenth century, and not until the middle of the twentieth century did the medical model succeed in dominating American childbirth. Yet physician-directed childbirth has not met all the needs of birthing women. The pendulum swing between the two traditions has not yet found its resting place.

[62] As an example of contemporary interests, see Barbara Katz Rothman, *In Labor: Women and Power in the Birthplace* (New York, 1982).

feminine hygiene, fashion and the emancipation of american women

fred e. h. schroeder

In an essay in *Modern Methods in the History of Medicine,* Charles E. Rosenberg distinguishes between the disciplines of history of science and history of medicine by pointing out that "Medicine, like science, is a body of knowledge and a community of men. But unlike science, it is an organic social function."[1] Further, he writes that "Until comparatively recent times, most medical practice has been in the hands of informal, rural, semi-educated practitioners and such men and women leave few tracks in the archival sands." As a consequence, most sources derive from "a self-conscious and comparatively articulate urban elite," thus making the history of medicine a high-culture success story.[2] It might equally well be stated that the concerns of his elite have emphasized illness, trauma and abnormality rather than normal and popular health care. Thus the documentary tracks of the everyday aspects of the organic social function are covert, elusive, scattered and implicit.

A case in point is normal feminine hygiene. Although this has become more openly and explicitly discussed during the past half-century, the historical development of today's menstrual care practices is almost completely hidden, and even contemporary practices of normal care are rarely topics for professional or academic literature. They do surface in commercial advertising literature, yet even there, they tend to reflect the age-old covert folk tradition. For example, in the fall television season of 1975, advertisements for sanitary napkins and tampons were for the first time scheduled during evening "family-viewing" network programs, thus implying almost total liberation from traditional attitudes, but the content of the commercials remained traditional. Most of these commercials showed two or more attractive young women engaged in private conversations—in a car-pool going to work, in an afternoon coffee-hour, in a quiet walk on the beach—sharing with one another their experiences with the advertised products. This, of course, is a depiction of traditional oral transmission of knowledge among a cultural sub-group, regardless of how much it has been modernized, commercialized and glamourized.

The glamour implied by contemporary advertising for menstrual care products is indicated by the use of two techniques. One of these glamourizing techniques appears in the freedom of movement in sophisticated environments—at beaches, tennis courts, elegant living-rooms, among career women; the other is indicated by fashionable garments—form-fitting pants and straight skirts, tennis shorts, gauzy beach-jackets and bikini bathing suits. These are emblems of "New Freedom," which, significantly, is the name of a menstrual absorbent that was introduced for sale in the early seventies, at the cresting of the women's liberation movement. These examples are clear indicators that there is a new freedom among American women, and that it relates somehow to feminine hygiene, but it should be equally apparent that there is a complexity of interrelationships impinging upon these organic social functions that eludes easy analysis.

With such a web of factors—social-political movements, fashion, folklore, commerce, advertising and medical practice—the problem of unravelling influential and causative factors from unrelated parallel threads cannot be ignored. Dr. Owsei Temkin, in an article on "Historiography of Ideas in Medicine" in the volume named above, notes the "broader issue of how far ideas are linked logically, and how far irrational factors, be they psychological or social, account for their origin, their spread, their modification and their decline."[3] In the present essay, the *idea* (in the sense of history of ideas) is contained in such semantic variants as "emancipation of women," "equal rights," "women's liberation" and "new freedom." The particular *concern* of this essay is with certain presumably "irrational factors" relating to the idea of New Freedom. The *thesis* of this essay is that technological and commercial advances in normal menstrual hygiene have had a causal influence on this idea, and that there has been a concomitant influence on women's fashions, which, in turn, are reciprical indicators of the idea of liberation.

Fashions in women's clothing as they relate to women's liberation are at least symbolic of the degree of emancipation in a given time and place, but it is probable that fashions are more than emblems and metaphors. The fact that until about 1920 almost the entire history of civilized and agricultural human society in both the orient and the western world is marked by the wearing of ankle-length garments by women[4] suggests that the long skirts are not merely frivolous fashions, nor senseless traditions, nor sexist hobbles imposed by males, nor simply graceful expressions of femininity. To a degree, long skirts have been all of these, but in addition they have operated as social defense mechanisms equal in importance to the traditional behavior stereotypes of "feminine" weakness, irrationality and unpredictability. Long skirts have been functional garments for unembarrassed movement in a civilized society. Indeed, the recent history of women's emancipation can be paralleled by the history of fashion, not simply as an outward manifestation of liberation, but as a contributory factor in freeing women for opportunities equal to those of men. To understand this, we might examine menstruation as a social phenomenon.

Menstruation, unlike pregnancy, cannot be controlled by independent non-participation by the woman, and, again unlike pregnancy, menstruation has never been surrounded by a masculine cult aura of madonnahood and protective chivalry. Quite the contrary. Menstruation has been regarded as a curse, as punishment, as tabooed uncleanliness, and as shameful in non-civilized cultures; while in civilized cultures it has been masked by silence, by euphemism, by mystery and by long dresses. The primitive and tribal behavior patterns surrounding the menstrual period are varied, but the usual social scheme is some kind of ostracism, designed, it would seem, to impress upon the woman's ego, with cosmic regularity, that she is regarded as unequal, unpopular, unwanted and unclean.

In European and American urban and industrial culture the behavior patterns surrounding menstruation have been analogous to the primitive practices of ostracism, but until 1921 in the United States, they were almost exclusively made part of the feminine underground, to be practiced and perpetuated individually, without even the dubious social security afforded primitive women by ritualized practices. Modern women will find it difficult to sympathize with the latter viewpoint, but it should be recognized that in tribal structures it was quite unnecessary for a woman to expend energies on developing ruses and disguises to keep her menstrual period a secret from husband, family or society. Menstruation may have been regarded by primitive societies as signal of the fall from grace, a curse inflicted upon women from some primal transgression, but it was still an inescapable natural fact, no more *personal* a punishment than mortality is for all humankind. For the tribal woman, ready-to-wear psychological attitudes were provided, and her monthly state was openly related to the cosmos and her culture. No such open provisions are part of non-tribal societies, for the whole affair has been totally covered by silence. It was not merely a pattern of taboos; the subject itself was taboo. Even such sex-objects as the heroines of the classic erotic literatures do not menstruate. The point of this is that if the *sub rosa* erotic literature tradition (a largely male *genre,* significantly) has had its taboos against menstruation, it goes without saying that *supra rosa* there would be few references to the menses.[5] This is in fact true, for while nineteenth-century novels abound in cases of "sick headaches," "slight indispositions," "the vapours," "green-sickness" and "the blues," these terms are oblique and ambiguous diagnoses. They are equally applicable to hypochondria, melancholia, malnutrition, malaise and menstruation, and thus, it was possible then and remains possible today for a woman to disguise her menstrual period in a sea of vague ailments. Instead, it seems fair to suggest that much of the "weakness" of many women in the recent past resulted from the social necessity of inventing enough irregular ailments to hide their regular "sickness."

An early twentieth-century medical adviser to college women at Stanford, Dr. Clelia Duel Mosher, was well aware of this debilitating feedback: "... the traditional treatment of rest in bed, directing the attention solely to the sex zone of the body, and the accepted theory that it is an inevitable 'illness' while at the same time the mind is without wholesome occupation produce a morbid attitude and favor the development and exaggeration of whatever symptoms there may be."[6] This attitude was turned to personal advantage by many women, Dr. Mosher noted: one of her college advisees simply told her, "My mother has always stayed in bed every month and I mean to too."

How far back in American history these defensive hypochondriac practices were common is difficult to determine—one can hardly feature such a self-indulgent expenditure of a woman's time on the frontier—but in 1855, Dr. Edward H. Dixon included among his *Scenes in the Practice of a New York Surgeon* a chapter entitled "Woman. What are the Causes of the Early Decay in American Women?" His answer was surprisingly modern, because he assumes that while boys and girls start in equal health, at school age the demands of highly restrictive ladylike behavior initiate the decay of healthful breathing and active blood circulation among girls, and that at puberty, this is augmented by the "fee-seeking" members of the medical profession who further weaken girls with "confinement and physic."[7] But even Dixon is not exempt from the penchant for augmenting hypochondriac disturbances. Although Dixon does ascribe the "weakness" of women to social causes rather than to inherent inequality, like almost all writers on gynecology and feminine hygiene of the nineteenth and early twentieth centuries, he is incapable of divorcing female problems from fashionable pursuits.[8] Thus novel-reading is debilitating in Dixon's view.[9] In a similar vein, Dr. Edward John Tilt, in *On Diseases of Menstruation and Ovarian Inflammation* (1851), condemns the overexcitement to the organs of reproduction caused by the "prurient incitement of passion-stirring pictures, statues, music, novels and theatres."[10] As recently as 1926, one popular treatise on *The Sexual Life of Woman in its Physiological, Pathological and Hygienic Aspects* warned women to discontinue singing during menstruation.[11] In 1891, Horatio R. Bigelow's *Social Physiology; or, Familiar Talks on the Mysteries of Life* ascribed premature menstrual flow to (among other causes), "a long visit to cities [and] a diet of exciting food."[12] Bathing during menstruation was alternately condemned or advocated by different authorities, and among the advocates, hot and cold water were alternately condemned and advocated. For married women, "excessive marital indulgence" was related to "profuse menstruation,"[13] and as recently as 1916 sexual *pleasure* is tied to female problems, for "the best mothers, wives and managers of households know little or nothing of the sexual pleasure. Love of home, children and domestic duties are the only passions they feel."[14]

All these pronouncements seem designed to produce anxiety and hypochondriac responses rather than reassurance, and at times the most knowledgeable authorities seem to be guilty of the same designs. In 1890, Dr. Alice B. Stockham referred to "certain physiologists" who "claim that *all* sanguineous flow is abnormal, that there should be *no* show of blood in a perfectly healthy woman."[15] Dr. Stockham does not share this exaggerated position, but her own views are precursors of the twentieth-century manuals that discount the inconvenience, the discomfort and the occasional pain of menstrual and pre-menstrual periods. For several decades now, in an effort toward creating an attitude of positive thinking in young women, the booklets prepared by the sanitary products industry for distribution in women's physical hygiene programs tend to dismiss dysmenorrhea—painful menstruation—as an abnormality caused by poor diet and inadequate rest and exercise, and to dismiss discomfort and anxiety as being largely psychological. As the feminist Germaine Greer suggests in *The Female Eunuch,* these ideas, when coupled with the secrecy surrounding the onset of the menses, can produce in a young woman the feeling that "the pain attending this horror is in some way her *fault,* the result of improper adaptation to her female role. . . ." Probably Dr. Greer strikes a reasonable balance in the closing sentence to her chapter on "The Wicked Womb": "Menstruation does not turn us into raving maniacs or complete invalids; it is just that we would rather do without it."[16]

Throughout the history of feminist and women's liberation movements the menstrual period has served as the unspoken but undeniable basis for discrimination. It is possible that the final drive for equal rights has resulted as much from the mass production and distribution of feminine hygiene products as from development of the birth control pill. "The pill" has been the apparent cause for the intensified liberation movement, but this is because it provided a dramatic counter-argument to the overt sexist argument that pregnancy is the sole rationale for job discrimination, when in reality it is more likely that the discriminatory rationale is to be found in male (and even some female) ideas about menstruation, its attendant discomforts, and the consequent psychological tensions to which many women are subject. Thus Dr. Mosher, writing at about the time that women attained suffrage in the United States, states that in her debates with college professors, even the most liberal-minded men who denied any intellectual differences between the sexes invariably "assume a periodic handicap."[17] It was not only the men who believed this: the militant pioneer in the movement to liberate women through birth control, Margaret H. Sanger, wrote in *What Every Girl Should*

Know (1916) that "out of 1,000 girls questioned, only 16 per cent were entirely free from pain, which proves that the time has come for women to cease being ashamed of this function, and insisting upon at least one day's rest at the expense of her employer."[18] Mrs. Sanger's statistics are not to be regarded as absolute, however. Dr. Mosher had found a remarkable change in the percentage of college women who were *free* of menstrual pain from 19% in 1894 to 68% in 1915-1916.[19]

The startling advance in the space of two decades is not easily accounted for. Sexual education had done little to dispel the superstitions of "the curse" and bed-ridden disability.[20] Dr. Mosher gives credit for the physiological improvement not to education, but to fashion, and she makes a remarkably strong case for it. "In 1893-96," she wrote, "the average width of skirts worn by 98 young women was 13.5 feet—the widest 15 and the narrowest 9 feet. The weight of the *outside* skirt alone was often nearly as much as the weight of the entire clothing worn by a modern girl (circa 1923). At that period, too, every woman must have a wasp-like waist while several petticoats were also carried from the waist," and, "as the skirt grew short and narrower and the waist grew larger, the functional health of women improved." Thus, Dr. Mosher concluded, "An extraordinary close correlation was found between the fashion of dress and the menstrual disability of women."[21]

There is undoubtedly considerable validity to this analysis. Relieving the stress on the water-logged premenstrual tissues, particularly around the waist and lower abdomen, in addition to reducing the discomfort resulting from the heat that must have been doubly oppressive in unairconditioned summers would be markedly helpful to the overall health of women. But one other clothing-related change at this time in history would have done more than relieved *stress*; it would have relieved *distress* as well. In the two-decade span of time of which Dr. Mosher speaks, a silent revolution in feminine hygiene garments was taking place, but of this revolution, the only evidence to survive is in the mail-order catalogs of Montgomery Ward, of Sears, Roebuck and Company and of Harrod's of London.

The techniques for the absorption of menstrual discharge are almost entirely hidden throughout the history of womankind, this information being passed on among women solely by the spoken word. Every woman's knowledge of regular menstrual treatment seems to have been presumed by physicians. Thus, in one of the first medical descriptions of internal tampons (in 1856) the careful instructions for preparing the tampon ends by stating briefly that "They should be kept there by a napkin, worn as for the menstrua. . . ."[22] The tampon prescribed here is for post-parturitient bleeding, as are the sanitary pads in the earliest published reference that could be uncovered in the library of the "Kinsey" Institute for Sex Research at the University of Indiana, this being in *The Eugenic Marriage; The Knowledge guide to the new science of better living and better babies* (*circa* 1913).[23] To judge from all accounts, up to this time all napkins were homemade affairs of clean cloths pinned as a diaper or folded into pads to be pinned to underclothing. The assumption is that these cloths were not regarded as disposable, but were washed out much as cloth baby diapers are today, although there is no direct description of laundering. In 1908, one popular work described a disposable, but homemade pad for parturition to be made of purchased cotton and cheesecloth,[24] and in 1905, Mary Wood-Allen in *What a Young Woman Ought to Know*[25] provides a recipe for making a reusable cloth envelope for holding napkins, this being supported by shoulder straps.

These, then, appear to be the only popular published descriptions of absorbent pads until the marketing of Kotex in 1921. They hardly suggest a liberation in underclothing adequate to account for the "new woman." For this, we must turn to the mail-order catalog. Not only did these catalogs display manufactured pads and elastic belts in the mid 1890's, but they described their use in the practical and forthright style that still marks the catalogs, more than a century after Aaron Montgomery Ward issued his first catalog in 1872. This easy availability has never before been documented, and it has been included in no medical, educational or popular literature other than the mail-order catalogs.[26] From Montgomery Ward's 1895 catalog, these two descriptions:

> Ladies Faultless Serviette Supporter, made of soft sateen with a rubber band across hips. Meets with universal approval. Sizes are every inch from 22 to 36. $0.25 each.
>
> The Faultless Serviette or Absorbent Health Napkin; economical, comfortable, healthful. Recommended by physicians and fast superseding birdseye linen, more absorbent, antiseptic, no washing, burned after using, invaluable while traveling, cheaper than laundering. Medium size $0.50/dozen.

The 1897 Sears, Roebuck catalog lists belts and pads in two "departments" one stating, "This belt . . . is worn by ladies during their menstrual period. . . ." And in the Harrod's of London 1895 Catalogue, one can find a somewhat more oblique offering of "Hartmann's Hygienic Towelettes for Ladies . . . for Ladies Travelling . . . they are invaluable and indispensable. They are supplied at the actual cost of washing. *After Use they are Simply Burnt.*" In these easily procured commercial products, therefore, may be found the liberation of Dr. Mosher's college women from unpleasant drudgery, from possible vaginitis, from embarrassing inconvenience when away from home, and from long heavy skirts that could protect a woman from anxiety-producing accidents from seepage and overflow.

Women's fashions are not so frivolous as are popularly supposed, and the rapid changes in women's clothing in twentieth-century America are not simply the results of campaigns for suffrage, equality and liberation. They are the outward expressions of inner confidence, something that was surely augmented by the development of cheap, absorbent and disposable menstrual products. To many men and to some modern women this may seem to be overstated, but even today, the menstrual period for many women has some awkward moments caused by premature or profuse flow, by running out of napkins, or by the demanding time-schedules of work, play or travel. But if we were to eliminate the availability of all commercial sanitary products it takes little imagination to find good reasons for long skirts, for staying close to home and for maintaining a mystical pose of fragile unpredictability. Unfortunately, we have little direct historical evidence of this concern because it was expressed in the silent underground of women only. Conceivably it might yet be documented by feminist historians today.[27]

But if this quiet mail-order revolution took place in the period from 1890-1910 (and if, indeed, it served to liberate women from long skirts), it may be wondered why there was a lag in fashion, for we usually ascribe the rise in the hem-line to the 1920's. Actually, the hem-line rise began around 1914, but it did not reach knee level until the later 1920s. There are several reasons that help to account for this. For one thing, fashions came from continental Europe where mass distribution of personal products such as America's mail-order houses developed did not exist. Secondly, the inertia of tradition and superstition related to all sex-related practices is a powerfully conservative force. But the third reason is a complexly interrelated story of technological, marketing, and advertising history, involving both liberated women and men.

During World War I, the shortage of surgical cotton for bandages spurred the development of synthetic substitutes. Among these was a cellulose substance developed by Ernest Mahler, a chemist working with the Kimberly-Clark paper company of Wisconsin. Mahler's product, later named Kotex, was found by Red Cross nurses to be an effective sanitary napkin, and at the close of the war, Kimberly-Clark decided to market it. For the first two years, it was something of a one-woman battle to get the product into retail stores, for marketing was given over to Miss Nesta Edwards, who was an industrial relations consultant.[28] But in 1921, Kimberly-Clark persuaded Albert D. Lasker,[29] a Chicago advertising genius, to take on their account. Lasker responded by preparing straightforward advertising copy and by using his influence to bully magazines into printing it, beginning in 1921 with an advertisement picturing a Red Cross nurse. Eight years later, in 1929, Kotex had become a $19 million business, and women's fashions were fully emancipated. The complicated nature of emancipation is further compounded by the fact that both magazines and women were sufficiently liberated in 1920 to accept this advertising. Shortly after, in 1936, Dr. Earle Haas' invention of an internally worn tampon for normal flow was marketed as Tampax, and once again nurses were pictured in advertising copy to provide "medical" validation of the new technique, which nonetheless won acceptance slowly at first because of unwarranted concerns about virginity and morality. Today the revolution is complete.

To summarize: over the passage of three-fourths of a century, three social phenomena relating to women have coincided: the liberalizing of legal and social status, the liberalizing of outer dress styles and the development of reliable widely distributed feminine hygiene products. Traditionally the coinciding of the former two phenomena has been regarded as *merely* coincidental, but research into the last phenomenon suggests that these are all interrelated, and that convenient menstrual care products were needed before women's claims to social and occupational equality could be backed up by equally free personal behavior patterns.[30] Adjunct to these hygienic products are biochemical products for symptomatic relief of certain aspects of dysmenorrhea, but these are refinements that follow the effective causes of liberation, and while they do serve to broaden the social impact of the established mechanical devices, they are not as yet free of questionable physiological side effects for some women. Finally, the traditional view of female inequality and the stereotyped "protective discrimination" against women have until recent years probably constituted a convenient way of humanizing primitive practices of ostracizing menstruating women. But the times have changed, and thanks to technology, mass production, mass distribution, education and advertising, women need no longer accept elaborate nineteenth-century behavior patterns along with puberty, and like today's infants, who are given the option of being invested with universal disposable diapers and sexually ambiguous green hair ribbons, the liberalized conventions of dress for women permit absolute freedom of choice in image and activity.

University of Minnesota, Duluth

footnotes

1. Charles E. Rosenberg, "The Medical Profession, Medical Practice and the History of Medicine," in Edwin Clarke, ed., *Modern Methods in the History of Medicine* (London: The Athlone Press, 1971), 22.

2. *Ibid.*, 24.

3. Owsei Temkin, "The Historiography of Ideas in Medicine," in Clarke, 8.

4. Even Amelia Bloomer's dress reforms of the mid-nineteenth century are not exempt. The pyjama trousers were very loose and covered by a knee-length overskirt. The exceptions to long garments were generally for exotic professionals, such as dancers (but the *tu-tu* does not appear until the latter part of the nineteenth century), and acrobats (and they may have excused themselves from work during their menstrual periods, as prostitutes do today); or for peasant laborers in certain areas of Europe and the orient who needed freer movement in wet fields and paddies.

Men's costumes such as robes, caftans, burnooses and togas are similar to women's dress, but may be regarded as irrelevant to this thesis because of the equally frequently encountered kilts, hose, tights, knee-breeches and trousers. Undoubtedly some civilized cultures and subcultures have been equally modest in dress for women and for men, but then the women were further covered by the restrictions of cloister, purdah, or periodic ostracism (see *Leviticus* 12).

5. See Mary Jane Lupton and Emily Toth, "Out, Damned Spot!," *MS* (January, 1974), 97-99, for an authoritative and wide-ranging overview of oblique and direct references to the menses in literature.

6. Dr. Clelia Duel Mosher, *Woman's Physical Freedom* (New York: The Women's Press, 1923), 25.

7. Dr. Edward H. Dixon, *Scenes in the Practice of a New York Surgeon* (New York: DeWitt and Davenport, 1855), 111-114.

8. A great deal of research into nineteenth-century sex-manuals, Victorian stereotypes, and the opinions of male-dominated medical and scientific establishments has been done in the past few years. See, for example, Elaine and English Showalter, "Victorian Women and Menstrua-

tion," *Victorian Studies*, Vol. 14 (September, 1970) and Janice Law Trecker, "Sex, Science and Education," *American Quarterly*, Vol. 26 (October, 1974). The wealth of material on these subjects is reflected in the lack of significant duplication among the primary sources employed by these scholars and by this article. See also Vern Bullough and Martha Voight, "Women, Menstruation, and Nineteenth-Century Medicine," *Bulletin of the History of Medicine*, XLVII:1 (January-February, 1973).

9. Dixon, 114-118.

10. Dr. Edmund John Tilt, *On Diseases of Menstruation and Ovarian Inflammation* (New York: Samuel S. and William Wood, 1851), XXVI.

11. Heinrich F. Kirsch, *The Sexual Life of Women in its Physiological, Pathological and Hygienic Aspects* (New York: Allied Book Co., 1926), 126.

12. Horatio R. Bigelow, *Social Physiology; or, Familiar Talks on the Mysteries of Life* (New York: Union Publishing House, 1891), 64.

13. Florence Dressler, *Feminology*, 3rd edition (Chicago: C. L. Dressler & Co., 1903), 433.

14. T. W. Shannon and W. J. Truitt, M.D., *Nature's Secrets Revealed, Scientific Knowledge of the Laws of Sex Life and Heredity of Eugenia* (Marietta, Ohio: S. A. Mullikin, 1916), 162.

15. Dr. Alice B. Stockham, *Tokology: A Book for Every Woman* (Chicago: Alice B. Stockham & Co., 1890), 253. The italics are mine.

16. Germaine Greer, *The Female Eunuch* (New York, 1970), 42-43.

17. Mosher, 12. See also Trecker, note 4 above.

18. Margaret H. Sanger, *What Every Girl Should Know* (Reading, Pa.: Sentinal Printing Co., 1916), 32.

19. Mosher, 30

20. Frank A. Manny, "Bibliography of Sex Hygiene," *Educational Review*, Vol. 46 (Sept. 1913), 168-176. Many of the materials listed refer to prostitution and venereal disease, and the more "normal" materials come from the period after 1910, clearly reflecting radically progressive views.

21. Mosher, 20-30. The fact that social pressures can produce menstrual discomfort was demonstrated as early as 1876 in a brilliant statistical study by Mary Putnam Jacobi, M.D., in her prizewinning *The Question of Rest for Women During Menstruation* (New York, 1877). Dr. Jacobi found that 84% of unmarried women were prone to monthly pain, as opposed to 11% for married women, and she ascribed this primarily to depression because in our society "celibacy implies social failure" (209).

22. Charles D. Meigs, M.D., *Obstetrics: The Science and The Art*, 3rd edition (Philadelphia: Blanchard & Lea, 1856), 254.

23. W. Grant Hague, *The Eugenic Marriage: The knowledge guide to the new science of better living and better babies* (New York: Reviews of Reviews Co., *circa* 1913), Vol. 1, 62-66.

24. Emma Frances Angell Drake, *What a Young Wife Ought to Know*, new revised edition (Philadelphia: The Vir Publishing Co., 1908), 194-195.

25. Mary Wood-Allen, *What a Young Woman Ought to Know* (Philadelphia: The Vir Publishing Co., 1905), 149.

26. It would be impossible to demonstrate how wide-spread was the use of manufactured pads and belts. Both obstetricians and the educational divisions of the major manufacturers of feminine hygiene products are apparently unaware of any mass-distributed products prior to 1921, when Kotex was first marketed widely, but on the other hand, the design of Kotex duplicated the mail-order products, and obviously derived from them, only substituting cellulose materials for cotton-wool. It is also quite probable that the earlier products were available in dry-goods stores.

27. Oral histories of the "*Foxfire*" type would be valuable. I have for instance, been told by a staff-member of Tampax that her grandmother, who was a one-room schoolteacher, said that many times she was "saved" only by her long skirts during the long, unprivate schooldays (in the mid-nineteenth century many rural schools had no privies at all). Interviews in nations that have recently undergone technological revolution might be even more productive of evidence both as to older informal practices and as to the social-psychological impact of cheap, reliable and disposable menstrual care products.

28. "50 Years of Confidence," *Cooperation* [marketing publication of Kimberly-Clark] (Fall, 1969), 1-3. Both Miss Edwards and Dr. Mosher are excellent counter-evidence to the fallacious stereotypes of vocational inequality.

29. John Gunther, *Taken at the Flood! The Story of Albert D. Lasker* (New York, 1960), 150-154.

30. Advertising copy continues to respond to some women's anxieties about wearing certain fashions. In the September, 1976 issue of *Woman's Day*, for example, an advertisement depicting a group of young adults playing volleyball has one woman stating: "It was also the first time I'd dared to wear my low-cut pants with a full-size napkin" (131). Viewed in the context of this article, the advertisement can serve as an icon of the interrelationships among the factors of fashion, feminine hygiene, liberation of women's behavior patterns and commercial advertising.

Using Oral History to Chart the Course of Illegal Abortions in Montana

Diane Sands

Well, in 1969 I was sixteen and I found out that I was pregnant. And, of course, the first thing that I thought of was that I didn't want to be pregnant, and started asking around. Abortion was extremely illegal then. I first went to Dr. — here in town, who was my gynecologist, and he said absolutely not, that he saw no medical or psychiatric indications for an abortion. And I said, "Oh, come on, there's something, there must be something you can do." And he just said, "Absolutely not." And so then I went to Dr. — and I had sort of rumors that, had heard that somebody in town was doing them, and I couldn't find who it was. So I told my parents that I was pregnant, and they agreed with me that an abortion would have been the best procedure for me, and they talked to Dr. —. And he referred us to a doctor in Kalispell. And then, I'm pretty sure that that was Dr. — and we went up there, and he was real, real nervous and sort of said out of the corner of his mouth, "I'm not doing them right now, but there's a doctor in Shelby who will do it." So we went from Kalispell over to Shelby and located this guy's office. And that was Dr. — and he was over the, had an office over the Rexall drug store on the main street in Shelby, Montana.

It seems to me it was $400 in cash, up front. And we went up there and it was just really, really a strange office, you know. There was no receptionist. There was this little old guy, and he just—ancient, way in his eighties—sort of came doddering out of the office. And he looked, I mean at the time I wasn't, I was really young, but I'm pretty sure now he was an alcoholic. You know, he had that sort of, the red nose and the bloodshot eyes, and his hands shook. And he was just filthy. He had food stains dripped down, he was wearing this really old suit and had food stains dripped down the front of this suit. You know, gravy on his tie and all that. And he told us to come back at—several hours later—it seems to me probably after

Diane Sands is a native Montanan whose interests range from teaching women's studies to establishing a dialogue between Indian and non-Indian women in Montana. Sands currently directs the Montana Women's History Project and is active in the Montana Oral History Association. She is also the director of a women's employment project, Gearing Up: Women in Higher Wage Occupations.

hours, five o'clock or so, and to bring the money. And he was real concerned that, he wanted to make sure that, he didn't examine me, but he was very concerned about when my last period was. He wanted to make sure that I wasn't over whatever specified time limitations he had. He told me to bring a box of sanitary pads and some aspirin and come back. And so I, we, left and we sort of drove around Shelby for a while and came back.

And he took me into his back office, and it was . . . really strange. I'd never seen anything like that, even since. It was not, not any sort of a table. It was a chair where you sat upright, and it had stirrups on it, and you were supposed to be sitting upright. And he told me to take off my panty hose and my underpants and my shoes and sit up in this chair and put my feet up in the stirrups. And I did, and I looked around and, God, it was just, a stainless steel basin right by, right next to the chair with these instruments in it, with this sort of . . . the water was bloody and there was a sort of film of crud over the instruments, and the floor was dirty, and it had, there was blood on the floor, and there was another bowl that had these sort of bloody looking sponges in it, and I was thinking, God, you know, I've heard terrible stories, you know, my mother had told me about, oh, women she knew in the thirties and forties who had abortions, and one woman who had tried to, or had aborted herself with a, with a crochet hook, and how these women just, you know, died. They got infections and they hemorrhaged and they died. And I sat there and I realized, God, this is going to happen to you. I mean, this is just, this is not good. And he sat down and he took out a speculum and inserted that, and then took out what I realize now was probably a uterine catheter, and I looked at it, and, God, his hand was shaking, and I just said, "I've got to leave." So he just took the, oh, he told me, he told me that it was going to be very painful, and, but that if I screamed, that he would immediately stop the procedure, and throw me out. You know, he said, "If you want this, you know, you'd better be quiet." And I said, "Well, what are you going to do?" And he said he was going to dilate my cervix and then pack my uterus with gauze soaked in some sort of chemical, and that when I got back to Missoula, I was supposed to go right to the emergency room at the hospital and tell them what had been done, and that they would take care of it from there, but that this chemical, whatever it was, was going to start the abortion process. . . .

The realities of reproduction, or at least potential reproduction, and the desire to control it are shared by all women. But, in proportion to the importance of these issues to women present and past, relatively little historical examination has occurred. The above quote is from the project entitled, "An Oral History of Illegal Abortion in Montana, 1880-1973,"[1] which, as an outgrowth of the Montana Women's History Project, began to examine women's reproductive history. In 1975, the MWHP interviewed elderly women about their lives and contributions to Montana history. As part of those interviews, questions were asked about sexuality and reproduction. In 1980, the Montana Committee for the Humanities funded our project[2] to conduct research into illegal abortion using oral history as the primary methodology. Twenty interviews were conducted: ten explored the private experience and values of the women—of various ages and backgrounds—who had sought illegal abortions; the other ten interviews concentrated on persons in the public sphere who had knowledge of abortions, and the function of abortion in the community.[3]

The project also incorporated traditional research methodology into the history of illegal abortion. We assumed that such sources would be very limited, but this assumption proved incorrect. We knew in advance that material existed from trials of two abortionists, but we expected to find little else. The material we found within legal records, however, was considerable, though more illuminating by its volume than by its depth.

There are many reasons for the lack of historical research into the topic of female reproduction and its control. A primary one is that reproduction has not always been viewed as being within the historical process. Women have babies, have babies, have babies. This is seen as an ahistorical act, relatively unaffected by the events historians traditionally examine. Further, until the rise of the new social history, historians primarily examined events in the public sphere. Generally, reproduction has been viewed as existing totally within the private sphere, within the confines of the family. This study suggests that illegal abortion is to a large degree a "public sphere," or normal, community phenomenon. Finally, perhaps the most basic reason for the lack of historical examination is that female sexuality and reproduction exist within the realm of women's total life experience under patriarchy. In a society that continues to devalue women in all economic, social, and political arenas, it is not surprising to find that few resources have been invested in examining these areas of women's lives. Fortunately, recent emphasis by the women's movement on family and women's history has included the study of reproduction.[4]

Women have often been defined in terms of reproductive capacities. Women's contribution in the bearing of children has been extolled as women's primary role. The other side, the underside, of women's contribution is the control of, or limiting of, reproduction. In the interest of a better quality of life for themselves, their children, and their families, women have spent considerable time and energy *not* having children. The overwhelming evidence from the Montana project, as well as from cross-cultural studies conducted by Norman Himes and George Devereux, for example, is that women wanted children when they planned for and were able to provide for them, and sought to limit reproduction when conditions were less than desirable. Women have spent hours talking to husbands and sexual partners about birth control, pregnancy, childbearing, and ideal family size. They have passed endless days waiting and worrying for the late or missing menstrual period. They have read and consulted friends, doctors, and pharmacists about family planning techniques and "female problems." Unplanned and unwanted pregnancies were discussed in cloaked language, and if abortion was opted for, then more energy was required to find an abortionist and obtain the procedure. All this and more occurred within the context of repressive laws and social mores discouraging public discussion and dissemination of information on these topics.

Women's Experience of Abortion

Who were the women who had abortions in Montana before 1973? Adding together the women interviewed and the women represented by death certificates and coroners' records, we found over seventy women. Just over half were married, just under one-third were single. The rest were divorced, widowed, or of unknown marital status. Except for three black women from the early part of this century, all were white. The economic status of most is unknown. Several informants have stated that in one town "one abortionist worked on coloreds and immigrants" while another worked "on the respectable women." The relationship of economic and ethnic status to access to competent medical care has been explored in other research and needs to be applied to this topic in future studies.

A case study will serve to illustrate some of the information gained in the interviews:

E.M., the oldest informant, had three abortions in the early 1930's during her first years of married life. The beginning of the Depression and a strong moral sensibility as to the obligations parents owed offspring led her and her husband to delay child rearing for ten years. Attempts at birth control ranged from cold water or turpentine douches to condoms and diaphragms. With the aid of a male family pharmacist, E.M. obtained two abortions from a woman in a neighboring city for the sum of $100 each. The informant guessed from several clues that the abortionist was a prostitute. These successful abortions were done with catheterization, followed by sterile packing of the uterus. Her husband accompanied her to the first abortion, but for economic reasons she went alone for the second. A third abortion was obtained with the assistance of a friend, a neighboring ranch woman. This was done with a length of peeled, sharpened slippery elm, sold in most drug stores, which was inserted into the uterus and left for several hours. The slippery elm worked by puncturing the amniotic sac and also by slowly swelling and thereby dilating the mouth of the uterus. All abortions were done without pain killers and were quite painful. Stressing that she had never regretted the abortions, E.M. emphasized that she and her husband had felt it "unethical" to have children for whom they could not provide. In the 1940's, after ten years of marriage, they had two children. She stressed her daughters' successful careers and families, implying a relationship to their upbringing as "planned" children at a time when the family farm was economically strong. Other than her husband, her mother, and the persons directly involved in the abortions, the interviewer was the only person with whom she had ever discussed her abortion experiences.

Most of the women interviewed had tried various birth control techniques, but then as now, most methods were unreliable even when used correctly and regularly. Those who found themselves pregnant and decided on abortion did so primarily for socio-economic or "quality of life" reasons. For single, divorced, or widowed women, lack of economic resources, as well as the scorn of the community for the unwed mother and her illegitimate child influenced their decisions. Married women hoped to provide more economic and social resources for their children by having fewer children. Also, many women were aware of the health cost to the mothers of large families. Interestingly, health and safety concerns were seldom mentioned as a major concern in most women's attempts to find an abortionist.

Women who attempted self-induced abortions were likely to use a female network to obtain information about techniques. Crochet hooks, knitting needles, heavy lifting, coat hangers, turpentine drinks, throwing oneself down stairs, lysol or phisophex douches were among techniques reported. From the interviews and the over fifty death certificates showing illegal or self-induced abortion as the cause of death, it is hard to get a clear picture of the relative dangers of self-induced versus professionally induced abortions, but we assumed that professional abortionists had a lower complication rate.

In contrast to what we had expected, most women who sought abortions from "professionals" went through male networks to obtain this information. One could speculate that this is related to the access males have to "public" information on sexuality in our society. Male doctors, pharmacists, boyfriends, and men "who knew about these things" gave women the addresses of abortionists and, in some cases, even made the appointments. Although a community may have had a known abortionist, women tended to go to other towns to insure privacy.

How did the women feel about the abortion? "Relieved" was the word women used repeatedly. None of the ten expressed excessive guilt over the abortion. Several women commented on the pressure they felt from family and friends to "feel guilty" when instead they either "felt numb" or "relieved." One woman even tried to respond to the cues to feel guilty, being quite conscious that she did not feel that way. For these women there were few people around them who were supportive of their choice or who were even good listeners.

It is very important to remember than ten women is not a large sample and is self-selected in many ways. Those women who had physical complications or emotional distress did not elect to talk to the project. This is, of course, a major methodological problem with oral history. We speak to the survivors and to willing survivors at that.

The abortion experience did have a marked, though varied, effect on the relationships of the women with their families. In cases where the women were married and the abortion was a mutual decision, as in the case study above, the women commented about how the experience brought husband and wife together. In another case, a marriage already in serious trouble was pushed closer to the edge by the experience: "On my first night home, he didn't pick me up at the airport and he had invited two friends to stay overnight in our one-room apartment. . . . It did contribute to our ultimate divorce." In yet another case, a young single woman told her parents she was pregnant. The father said, "You're going to have an abortion. Arrange it and send me the bill," and walked out of the house. He later told her that because of the abortion "no one will ever want to marry you." To prove to her father that this was not so, she married within six months of the abortion.

Men rarely accompanied women to the abortionist. More often a mother, sister, or close female friend went along. In these cases the women spoke very warmly of their feelings. "I wouldn't have gone with anyone else. My mother was the daughter of a physician and I knew if anything was a little peculiar, mother would pick it up."

Finally, I cite a few examples of the effect of the "illegality" of the procedure on the women as they saw it. Most importantly, illegality made circuitous behavior necessary in obtaining an abortion. Many women felt the need for deception. The trick was to find a competent abortion before the end of the first trimester of the pregnancy had passed. Secondly, the need for secrecy and deception took its toll; as one interviewee said, "Now I'm aware how demeaning that was, that the whole thing was so shameful. You had to go away, you had to keep it a secret, you had to pretend it never happened. It's just denying such a part of yourself. I tried to do that for years and years and years, and I couldn't do it." Lastly, two of the women were politicized by the experience, becoming feminists in the late 1960's. One started a referral service to assist women in obtaining legal abortions out of Montana; the other assisted a doctor in performing illegal abortions. "I saw myself in that situation as victimized and trapped. When it was over, I just said, 'God, that is never going to happen to me again, ever. If I have anything to do about it, it's never going to happen to anybody that I know ever again.' That's the essence of feminism, it's taking control of your own life and being responsible for your own life instead of being a victim."

Abortion in the Community

According to Malcolm Potts, Peter Diggory, and John Peel, "While abortion is an unexpected and irregular event in the life of an individual woman it can be a relatively predictable aspect of fertility control in a community."[5] Using this premise, we looked at illegal abortion as a *normal* part of the community; we presumed its presence and started looking for the documentation that would validate this assumption.

At the beginning of the project we knew of six abortionists and two cases of legal action. Searching the records of eight Montana communities we now suspect over thirty persons of being "professional" abortionists in the period from 1882 to 1973, at which time abortion was legalized as a result of *Roe v. Wade.* Only seven abortionists came into the legal arena through a coroner's inquest or trial. Of these, two were convicted of abortion-related crimes. In contrast to our stereotypes of "back alley quacks" this study shows most, but not all, Montana abortionists to be medically trained and reasonably competent, often prominent persons around town, practicing on "Main Street" and retaining full privileges in the major hospitals (Catholic and non-Catholic) of their communities. Every major town in Montana had at least one abortionist. Some towns, such as Missoula, have a traceable series of abortionists from the 1880's straight through to 1973 when abortion became legal.

In the community part of this project, ten persons were interviewed who could shed light on this area of public policy and community life. Among those interviewed were two abortionists, several physicians who did not perform abortions and whose reactions ranged from sympathetic to antagonistic toward the topic, social workers, attorneys on both sides of cases that came to trial, and law enforcement personnel. Much more research needs to be done in this area, and questions can be only tentatively answered—often only with more questions.

Who were the "alleged" or suspected abortionists? The term "alleged" is used because absolute confirmation can only come from the abortionist or a client. If reliable people who worked with the alleged abortionist related the information, we generally assumed it to be the truth. Substantiation often consisted of noting the suspected abortionist's name appearing over and over on death certificates of women who were listed as having died from abortions. A further indication comes from the suspected person's involvement in a coroner's inquest or from having been tried for an abortion-related crime, even if never convicted. We feel strongly that our use of the label "abortionist" is correct about 90 percent of the time, but we acknowledge that in some cases there is a significant margin for error.

For the purposes of this study, the "professional" abortionist is a person who spent a significant percentage of his or her time performing abortions and who was generally known as an illegal abortionist. There are also numerous references to family doctors in the data. These doctors performed abortions for a few regular patients or for another doctor's family members. Often these were done under the guise of cleaning out an incomplete miscarriage or some other medical reason. Though these physicians performed abortions, they were neither labeled nor self-identified as illegal abortionists. While several people interviewed mentioned the family doctor abortionist, none of these doctors was interviewed, and it remains a subject for future research. How many abortions these family physicians are actually responsible for is unknown, and this creates another factor in the difficult assessment of the true number of abortions. It is an educated guess that any deaths resulting from these procedures probably were registered as deaths from some other cause.

Surprisingly, the deaths resulting from procedures of professional abortionists tend not to be disguised. At least there are a sufficient number of death certificates listing abortion as cause of death and the name of the attending physician/abortionist to allow the surmise that in many cases disguise was not necessary. We located nearly sixty death certificates between 1883 and 1973 that we identified as being abortion-related deaths.

Most professional abortionists had some medical training. Many were regular physicians, but there were also large numbers of homeopaths, osteopaths, and chiropractors. There were two with some nursing training. There was even a "magnetic" physician. Some, such as one prostitute, are assumed to have no professional medical training. Only six of the professional abortionists were women. One was an M.D., one a chiropractor, three had nursing backgrounds of a questionable nature, and one was a prostitute.

The relative acceptance of the abortionist in the community by other medical persons and public officials may be one reason it was unnecessary to disguise the cause of abortion-related deaths. Only seven abortionists are known to have had encounters with law enforcement officials. Five were actually tried in abortion-related cases, and two were convicted. The "magnetic" physician, Dr. Elijah Hoyt, was sentenced to two years in the state prison in 1882, after he had been convicted of malpractice, even though his patient had recovered from her abortion. Rose Husted, in 1939, was sentenced to one year in prison for manslaughter. Three of the six women abortionists were involved in legal proceedings (two trials, one conviction), resulting in the termination of their practices.

Remarks from medical people and public officials I interviewed fit into an "abortion as a necessary evil" framework. More than one doctor commented on his own shock as a young doctor entering a community where an abortionist practiced, often sharing privileges in the same hospitals. Two doctors commented that they came to see the medically trained abortionist as preferable to either self-induced abortion practices or nonmedically trained abortionists. Health and safety were the primary issues in these cases.

> There were abortions being performed, and I'm being very honest this time when I say I can't remember the names of a couple that were doing them. And the only cases that I would run into were those that had been botched up, maybe come in with infection, hemorrhage, what-not. That's when I first learned, in that way, that illegal abortions were going on. What did I do about it? First of all, I got all hot and bothered, because this was not the way I was trained, the way I was brought up, and then I found out that the, in a reasonable period of time, that the individual who had been well trained was doing abortions, without any complications, no infections, no deaths, no hemorrhages at all, whereas these others were really being botched up. And, finally as a, oh, you might even call it a growing up process, I recognized that abortion, an abortionist, even though it was an illegal sort of thing, fulfilled a social need, that was going to be met by a person who was capable of doing it, or a person who was not. And the efforts were made, as best one could, to at least dry up the abortion process by people who were not well trained. Who were doing it in a septic fashion and all.

Doctors said they never spoke directly to the abortionist about his/her practice though they may have practiced in the same town for twenty years.

> Yeah, and I'd be at the same parties with him, you know, everything like that. Socially, a very fine person, nice individual. Well, I wasn't going to attack him at a party or anything like that, and I guess this is the sort of attitude that developed.

The few cases where abortionists were prosecuted are suggestive of the way public policy on abortion does not totally prevent but regulates abortion. In four of the seven cases that came under the scrutiny of the law, the abortionist had very questionable medical skills, or little or no training. In one case, a Mrs. Gertrude Pitkanen assumed the abortion practice of her husband, Dr. Gustavus Pitkanen, upon his death in 1936. She often called herself "doctor" and was in the abortion business for over twenty years in Butte. Also, in the cases of Rose Husted and Dr. Elijah Hoyt, medical competency was doubtful.

Another intriguing case is that of the practice of Dr. Edwin Kellogg, 1893-1915, in Helena. In four separate cases he appeared before coroner's juries, and each jury called for his indictment in an abortion-related death. Although Kellogg was tried once, he was not convicted, and questions of jury tampering and other suspicious dealings played a part in all of his legal encounters.

Some abortionists were highly respected members of their communities and their profession. For example, one abortionist was a prominent doctor who served on the Montana Board of Medical Examiners, according to a fellow board member. Another example is Dr. Sadie Linderberg of Miles City, who was a widely known abortionist and who also delivered over 8,000 babies. In 1953 she was named "Woman of the Year" by the Business and Professional Women of Miles City and was later honored by the Montana Medical Association for her long years of service. One client recounted her perception of Dr. Sadie's practice:

> Dr. Sadie was like a little old lady doctor and I found it quite remarkable that she was doing what she was doing with such fervor. She described everything that was going to happen, what could happen, and what could not happen. She was very fair about the whole thing. . . . Actually, the person I remember more than Sadie is one of her nurses. She ran the nursing home, and when there were empty beds she brought the abortees in. She was extraordinarily kind and patient, really a lovely, lovely lady. The experience itself was not horrible; if you're going to

> have an abortion it is probably one of the best ways to do it, with people like that. They were really dedicated to what they were doing. They believed in it. That's why they were doing it.

Most of these cases, and others, are illustrative of the "turn the other way" attitude of most public officials. The law was selectively enforced when they felt that health and safety standards were not being met, or when it suited the purposes of these officials, such as when the state attorney general, in order to "clean up the town" made a statewide sweep against prostitution, gambling, and abortion in 1959. One woman was interviewed who told of being hired by a group of doctors seeking a witness to shut down an abortionist in another town. She pretended to be pregnant, made an appointment, and when the abortion procedure began she claimed to have changed her mind and left. The case was never pressed. Finally, the glaring fact is not the prosecution of cases but the absence of prosecution. Abortion was an unpleasant but necessary community service.

Several interesting questions emerged from the project that will need further research. First, the relationship of abortion to prostitution is intriguing. Several abortionists regularly served prostitutes, especially in Bozeman and Miles City. In fact, in Bozeman a hotel contained both an abortionist and prostitutes, each working separate floors. Further, a Bozeman social worker claimed that one of the Bozeman abortionists owned a hotel noted for prostitution. In what ways are these related occupations? Is there a tendency to "clean up" a town of prostitution and abortion in the same sweep? Do payoffs to officials occur with abortion as with prostitution, as was suggested by several informants? What questions are raised by being both a part of the "underworld" and the "culture of deviance" as the sociologists understand it?

Also, the process of "criminalization" of the abortionists themselves raises some interesting concerns. In some cases, other community professionals seemed to have had a strained relationship with abortionists. What effect did stigmatization have on the abortionists and their families? What effect did being outside of the sanctioning/peer review process have on the quality of work? Were illegal abortionists part of a "subculture of deviance" in the eyes of the community? How did abortionists see themselves? More work needs to be done on the public functioning of abortion within the community setting. Most questions remain unanswered and further work in this area will shed light on these questions.

A final word on methodology. As regards written sources—documents and records—death certificates did, in fact, often list the cause of death as abortion or self-induced abortion. Death certificates also contain the name of the attending physician, and certain names turn up over and over again. The length of time attending the deceased and time of any procedure performed are clues as to whether the attending physician performed an abortion or whether the physician was attending a woman who was already aborting from natural or self-induced causes. The argument that the woman was already aborting was used frequently by those few abortionists who found themselves facing a coroner's jury. At least one abortionist routinely required clients to sign a document stating that they were miscarrying before she would touch them.

In the course of the project, other records turned up that included inquests into the deaths of a dozen women, and a coroner's inquest into the disposal of a fetus in the sensational Masonic Temple Furnace Case in 1893 in Helena. Missoula's city sanitation records of fetuses in the sewage system, and their subsequent burial in an unmarked area of the cemetery, were also found. There are prison records of those abortionists who served time, and a file in the Catholic diocesan headquarters under the title "abortion" containing letters from parish priests who had absolved women parishioners of sins related to abortion. We were told of the last source by the historian for the diocese, but did not examine them because of confidentiality.

As regards the impact of the oral interviews, I believe I was able to achieve a more balanced perspective about the abortion experience because I had been able to talk with women who had survived abortions and in most cases felt positively about them, and I was also able to talk with other public figures involved. My judgment of the abortionist became much more sophisticated as the project developed. For example, as I gained information on each abortionist, I found myself placing them along a continuum of competent to incompetent, based on factors such as perceived sympathy toward patients, "acceptable" death and complication rates, and evidence of alcoholism. Conversely, my research assistant, Sarah McHugh, developed a strongly negative view of illegal abortionists, based on the records and documents that she found. I would like to suggest that the oral histories we conducted as part of the project gave perspective to the whole history of illegal abortion in Montana. Furthermore, information from the interviews often sent us back to sources we had not thought of, for confirmation or for additional information.

Many oral history projects avoid asking sexuality and reproduction questions of women. Perhaps because these issues are considered to be private, we do not feel we can ask about them. Often, as interviewers, we are ourselves uncomfortable in discussing these issues. To interview successfully on these topics or establish the necessary rapport on "sensitive" issues it is imperative that the interviewer be absolutely comfortable with the issues herself. When I first started asking these question in the context of life review interviews with older women, I found that adding in questions about early sex education and menstruation provided clues about women's willingness to talk about these topics.[6] Body language, laughter, and other verbal and nonverbal clues give fairly clear messages to a sensitive interviewer.

The conceptualization of reproduction and sexuality as functioning primarily in the private sphere has contributed to the invisibility of these important issues. Further examination outside of the paradigm of public/private spheres may prove more fruitful for understanding reproductive choice within a community context. Given the centrality of reproduction and sexuality to contemporary women and to our foremothers, these issues need to be a priority for women's history.

NOTES

1. Tapes, transcripts, and research materials resulting from this project are deposited in the University of Montana Oral History Archives of the Mike Mansfield Library and at the Montana Historical Society. As the Montana Women's History Project is committed to public education, it plans to convert the research into a traveling Chautauqua program for Montana audiences.

2. Research was conducted jointly by myself and Sarah McHugh. I conducted the twenty oral interviews with one exception.

Enormous support and assistance in helping me "see the forest for the trees" came from other women historians of the Northwest, especially Sue Armitage of Washington State University and Corky Bush of the University of Idaho.

3. Finding people to interview was not as difficult as I had anticipated: through the use of women's networks and through the presentation of numerous "in progress" reports, we found almost all of the ten women who had had abortions. Referrals and personal contact produced better results than newspaper and newsletter articles in finding informants. We also quickly learned that we should never assume that people will automatically be shocked or dismayed by a "sensitive" research topic; sources of information may be found where you least expect them. For example, I lunched with a sixty-five-year-old mother of a friend—a devoted Catholic and, for the most part, a conservative. When she asked about the topic of my current research, I told her what I was doing. She brightened and said, "Did I ever tell you about 'Abortion Mary'?"

The study did not include any Native American women; none appeared in the death records or other documents surveyed, and we did not include any in the oral interviews. This does not mean that Native American women did not seek abortions; it probably reflects the fact that they did not enter the white culture's system for handling unwanted pregnancies—they had their own system. There is also good reason to believe that for many Native Americans, the principal reproductive issue of the time period covered by this study has been forced sterilization rather than access to abortion.

4. The work of Linda Gordon (*Woman's Body, Woman's Right: Birth Control in America* [New York: Penguin Books, 1977]) and Carl Degler (*At Odds: Women and the Family from the Revolution to the Present* [London: Oxford Univ. Press, 1981]) were especially helpful in formulating a framework for this study. Other sources consulted were: George Devereux, "A Typological Study of Abortion in 350 Primitive, Ancient, and Pre-Industrial Societies," in *Abortion in America*, ed. H. Rosen (Boston: Beacon, 1967); Norman Himes, *Medical History of Contraception* (1936; rpt. New York: Schocken Books, 1970); James Mohr, *Abortion in America* (London: Oxford Univ. Press, 1978); Malcolm Potts, Peter Diggory, and John Peel, *Abortion* (London: Cambridge Univ. Press, 1977).

5. Potts, Diggory, and Peel, p. 30.

6. An oral history interviewing technique that worked especially well on this project involved starting the interview with the general statement, "Please go through and tell me your experience with illegal abortion. When you are done, we can go back through your story with any questions I might have." This open-ended question brought responses from ten to thirty-five minutes in length, while I listened, took notes, and did not interrupt. This practice worked especially well for the ten women interviewed who had experienced illegal abortions, but less well in the interviews with the ten public figures, because their experiences were not all of a piece, as were those of the abortees.

Copyright Information

Scholten, Catherine M. "'On the Importance of the Obstetrick Art': Changing Customs of Childbirth in America, 1760 to 1825." *William and Mary Quarterly* 34 (1977): 426-445. ©Dr. Paul Scholten, M.D., San Francisco, California, USA.

Bullough, Vern, and Martha Voght. "Women, Menstruation, and Nineteenth-Century Medicine." *Bulletin of the History of Medicine* 47:1 (1973): 66-82. ©The Johns Hopkins University Press, Baltimore, Maryland, USA.

Smith-Rosenberg, Carroll, and Charles Rosenberg. "The Female Animal: Medical and Biological Views of Woman and Her Role in Nineteenth-Century America." *The Journal of American History* 60:2 (September 1973): 332-356. ©Organization of American Historians, Indiana University, Bloomington, Indiana, USA.

Wood, Ann Douglas. "'The Fashionable Diseases': Women's Complaints and Their Treatment in Nineteenth-Century America." *The Journal of Interdisciplinary History* 4:1 (Summer 1973): 25-52. "Reprinted from *The Journal of Interdisciplinary History*, IV) (1973), 25-52, with permission of the editors of *The Journal of Interdisciplinary History* and the MIT Press, Cambridge, Massachusetts, USA. ©1973 by the Massachusetts Institute of Technology and the editors of *The Journal of Interdisciplinary History*."

Axelsen, Diana E. "Women as Victims of Medical Experimentation: J. Marion Sims' Surgery on Slave Women, 1845-1850." *Sage* 2:2 (Fall 1985): 10-13. ©*Sage: A Scholarly Journal on Black Women*, Women's Educational Press, Inc., Atlanta, Georgia, USA.

Smith-Rosenberg, Carroll. "The Hysterical Woman: Sex Roles and Role Conflict in 19th-Century America." *Social Research* 39 (1972): 652-678. ©*Social Research* (An International Quarterly of the Social Sciences), Graduate Faculty of Political and Social Science, New School for Social Research, New York, New York, USA. Reprinted with permission of the Quarterly and the author.

Johnson, Michael P. "Smothered Slave Infants: Were Slave Mothers at Fault?" *The Journal of Southern History* 47:4 (November 1981): 493-520. ©Southern Historical Association, Athens, Georgia, USA.

Morantz, Regina Markell. "Making Women Modern: Middle Class Women and Health Reform in 19th Century America." *Journal of Social History* 10 (1977): 490-507. ©Carnegie-Mellon University Press, Pittsburgh, Pennsylvania, USA.

Haller, John S., Jr. "From Maidenhood to Menopause: Sex Education for Women in Victorian America." *Journal of American Culture* 6:1 (Summer 1972): 49-71. ©Journal of American Culture, Bowling Green Popular Press, Bowling Green State University, Bowling Green, Ohio, USA.

Leavitt, Judith Walzer. "Birthing and Anesthesia: The Debate over Twilight Sleep." *Signs: Journal of Women in Culture and Society* 6:1 (Autumn 1980): 147-164. "©1980 by The University of Chicago. All rights reserved." Chicago, Illinois, USA.

Gordon, Linda. "Voluntary Motherhood: The Beginnings of Feminist Birth Control Ideas in the United States." *Feminist Studies* 1 (1973): 5-22. ©Professor Linda Gordon, Madison, Wisconsin, USA.

Brumberg, Joan Jacobs. "Chlorotic Girls, 1870-1920: A Historical Perspective on Female Adolescence." *Child Development* 53 (1982): 1468-1477. ©1882 by the Society for Research in Child Development, Inc., at The University of Chicago Press, Chicago, Illinois, USA. All rights reserved.

Leavitt, Judith Walzer. "Under the Shadow of Maternity: American Women's Responses to Death and Debility Fears in Nineteenth-Century Childbirth." *Feminist Studies* 12:1 (Spring 1986): 129-154. ©by Feminist Studies, Inc., Women's Studies Program, University of Maryland, College Park, Maryland, USA.

Kobrin, Frances E. "The American Midwife Controversy: A Crisis of Professionalization." *Bulletin of the History of Medicine* 59 (Summer 1985): 232-246. ©The Johns Hopkins University Press, Baltimore, Maryland, USA.

Litoff, Judy Barrett. "Forgotten Women: American Midwives at the Turn of the Twentieth Century." *The Historian* 40:2 (1978): 235-251. ©Phi Alpha Theta International Honor Society in History, Allentown, Pennsylvania, USA.

Declercq, Eugene, and Richard Lacroix. "The Immigrant Midwives of Lawrence: The Conflict between Law and Culture in Early Twentieth-Century Massachusetts." *Bulletin of the History of Medicine* 59 (Summer 1985): 232-246. ©The Johns Hopkins University Press, Baltimore, Maryland, USA.

Index

Bei Fragen zur Produktsicherheit wenden Sie sich bitte an:
If you have any questions regarding product safety,
please contact:

Walter de Gruyter GmbH
Genthiner Straße 13
10785 Berlin
productsafety@degruyterbrill.com